D1036763

Moscow's Third World Strategy

ALVIN Z. RUBINSTEIN

Moscow's Third World Strategy

Princeton University Press
Princeton, New Jersey

Copyright © 1988 by Princeton University Press
Epilogue © 1990 by Princeton University Press
Published by Princeton University Press, 41 William Street,
Princeton, New Jersey 08540
In the United Kingdom: Princeton University Press,
Oxford

All Rights Reserved

Library of Congress Cataloging-in-Publication Data:

Rubinstein, Alvin Z.
Moscow's Third World strategy.
Bibliography: p.
Includes index.
1. Developing countries—Foreign relations—Soviet Union.
2. Soviet Union—Foreign relations—Developing countries.
3. Soviet Union—Foreign relations—
1975– . I. Title.
D888.S65R83 1988   327.4701724   88–15097
ISBN 0–691–07790–8
ISBN 0–691–02332–8, pbk.

First Princeton Paperback printing, with Epilogue

This book has been composed in Linotron Bulmer and Baskerville

Clothbound editions of Princeton University Press books are printed
on acid-free paper, and binding materials are chosen for strength and
durability. Paperbacks, although satisfactory for personal collections,
are not usually suitable for library rebinding

Printed in the United States of America
by Princeton University Press,
Princeton, New Jersey

10 9 8 7 6 5 4 3 2

Always
Frankie

Contents

Preface

Remember . . . what is written on paper affects history. But not life. Life is a different history.
—Mario Puzo, The Sicilian

THIS is a study of what the Soviet Union has done in the Third World since the mid-1950s. My assumptions are that Moscow's actions are the truest measure of its aims, and that the patterns of its behavior in the Third World can help us understand the significance of that involvement for the USSR's broader foreign policy. What is done can be observed; why, can only be adduced.

Despite the increasingly extensive record of Soviet involvement, agreement on interpretation of motives, objectives, and even accomplishments eludes us. Soviet writings do little to explicate the well-springs and aims of Soviet foreign policy—that has never been their purpose. We must direct our focus elsewhere—to the Third World itself—if we are to understand why Soviet leaders are in the Third World; what it is they seek; what means they have used; what have been their achievements and setbacks; what has been their impact; and what are the main considerations in their thinking as they look to the future.

A century ago the British statesman-scholar George Curzon wrote a landmark book on Russia's expansion in Central Asia and its implications for British policy and Anglo-Russian relations. If one substitutes "Third World" for "India" and "United States" for "Great Britain," his questions assume a contemporary relevance:

> Upon no question is there greater conflict of opinion in England than Russia's alleged designs upon India. Are we to believe . . . that "no practical Russian general believes in the possibility of an invasion of India," and that "the millennium will take place before Russia invades India?" Or are we to hold . . . that "the Russian invasion of India is perfectly possible, though not easy?" Or, rejecting the mean and the extreme opinion on the one side, shall we fly to the other, and confess ourselves of those who trace from the apocryphal will of Peter [the Great] down to the present time a steadfast and sinister purpose informing Russian policy, dem-

onstrated by every successive act of advance, lit up by a holocaust of broken promises, and if for a moment it appears to halt in its realisation, merely *reculant pour mieux sauter* [drawing back to take a better leap], the prize of its ambition being not on the Oxus or even at the Hindu Kush, but at the delta of the Ganges and the Indian Ocean? Or, if territorial aggrandisement appear too mean a motive, shall we find an adequate explanation in commercial cupidity, and detect in Muscovite statesmanship a pardonable desire to usurp the hegemony of Great Britain in the markets of the East? Or, again, joining a wider school of opinion, shall we admit the act, but minimise the offensive character of the motive, believing that Russia intentionally keeps open the Indian question not with any idea of supplanting Great Britain in the judgment-seat or at the receipt of custom, but in order that she may have her rival at a permanent disadvantage, and may paralyse the trunk in Europe by galling the limb in Asia? Or, lastly, shall we affect the sentimental style, and expatiate on the great mission of Russia, and the centripal philanthropic force that draws her like a loadstone into the heart of the Asian continent?[1]

Western responses to these and similar attitudes toward Soviet policy in the Third World will have a profound effect on the future of Soviet-American relations and the conduct of the Cold War into the twenty-first century. The Cold War, that troubled peace that followed the end of the Second World War, has acquired a stability and predictability in Europe and the Far East. But not in the Third World. There, superpower relations are unpredictable, hence dangerous. There, in the years ahead, inadvertent and unwanted escalations of tension arising out of irresistible strategic temptations for Soviet leaders are apt to frustrate the plodding efforts at improving U.S.-Soviet relations. And there, in the Third World, Moscow pursues a dexterous diplomacy that upholds "peace" and "progressive" movements and regimes even as it carries the rivalry with the United States into arenas that are remote from the Soviet homeland. Since Stalin died, nothing has happened to suggest that the Kremlin would have it any other way.

This work owes much to the efforts of scholars in the West and the Third World who have written on various aspects of the USSR's far-ranging policies and activities in key countries and regions. Their contributions are cited in individual chapters and in the Bibliography.

---

[1] The Hon. George N. Curzon, M.P., *Russia in Central Asia in 1889 and the Anglo-Russian Question* (London: Longmans, Green, 1889), 11–12.

Given the profusion of information (often contradictory and incomplete), the scope of Soviet involvement, and the need continually to assess and reassess the dynamic nature of Soviet relationships with major and minor Third World actors, the interdependency of interested scholars is inevitable—and should be recognized and more systematic ways of exchanging views established. I owe much to many and acknowledge their assistance with appreciation: to Roger E. Kanet, Stephen S. Kaplan, Mark N. Katz, Frederic L. Pryor, Ann Reid, and Peter H. Vigor for the care with which they read parts or all of the manuscript—their thoughtful comments helped shape the final draft; to the Earhart Foundation for its support at a preliminary stage in the research; to Harry Shukman, Director of Soviet Studies, St. Antony's College, Oxford University, for arranging affiliation for a term; to the Library staff at the Royal Institute of International Affairs in London; to Thelma Prosser of the Foreign Policy Research Institute and Kay Gadsby and Jennifer Gibbons of the University of Pennsylvania's Department of Political Science for typing several drafts with unfailing good humor and despatch; to Graham Eyre for copy-editing the typescript; and to Gail Ullman, Jenna Dolan, Wendy Wong, and the staff of Princeton University Press.

Moscow's Third World Strategy

CHAPTER ONE

Moscow's Imperial Strategy

The greatest danger of conflict between the Soviet Union and the United States inheres in their rivalry in the Third World. It is there that they find themselves face-to-face in a number of explosive and unpredictable situations not always of their own making. The issues are often far from clear and the stakes not vital to the territorial defense or basic security of either superpower. Yet their growing commitments of men, matériel and prestige to the Third World bespeak a pervasive rivalry of an intensity that is disproportionate to the indeterminate strategic advantages involved. The risk of confrontation is magnified by the unsettling extent to which the interaction between the U.S. and the USSR—and indeed their overall relationship—is complicated, even significantly determined, by the behavior of their Third World clients. These states, of which there are far more in the international arena than at any other time in history, today enjoy a greater autonomy of action than ever before. Their capacity for maneuver is augmented by the acquisition of vast quantities of modern weaponry that lower the threshold of local wars and increase the probability of superpower involvement. And, where one superpower goes, the other is not far away.

The USSR's global outreach has juxtaposed Soviet power, commitment, and interest to American, leaving little room for political indifference or random probing. The ambiguity as to the areas and issues for which each is prepared to use its armed forces—the uncertainty as to how far the other is prepared to go on behalf of its client—creates situations in which modest risk-taking becomes a spur to escalation. In such settings, the recklessness or ambitions of clients can negate the calculations of patrons, and the unpredictable behavior of both clients and patrons can trigger confrontations that neither superpower expected or desired.

Even on occasions when no security interest was involved, when the benefits to be derived were dubious at best and far from cost-effective, and when the action was especially ill-timed for its impact on Soviet-American relations, Moscow has manifested its determination to project power into regions far removed from the Soviet Union. This was demonstrated in November 1984. On the eve of presidential elections

3

in the United States and at the very moment the Soviet leadership had accorded top priority to the campaign of pressuring President Ronald Reagan to cancel scheduled tests of an antisatellite (ASAT) weapon and accept a ban on its development, a number of Soviet ships were heading for Nicaragua loaded with weapons. Moscow knew Washington would protest sharply, but, far from downplaying the episode or mollifying the United States, it intensified criticisms of Reagan's "aggressive" Central American policy. The furor lasted only a few days—until U.S. intelligence was satisfied that no MiG aircraft (a weapons system Washington had said it would not tolerate being introduced into Nicaragua) had been offloaded. Tensions eased, and arrangements for a meeting between Secretary of State George Schultz and Foreign Minister Andrei Gromyko (held on January 7–8, 1985) proceeded as if nothing had happened. But in the process Moscow strengthened Nicaragua's military capability; conveyed its intention of continuing to probe the limits of possible Soviet involvement in America's backyard; and demonstrated, as it had so often in the past, that its policy in the Third World would not be shaped to conform to Washington's standards of suitability for improved relations with the United States.

The willingness of the Soviet leadership to bear the costs and take the risks it does in the Third World in the face of limited and often ephemeral gains is a puzzle to many in the West. They reason that the Soviet Union, like the United States, is deeply troubled by the unresolved nuclear issues that grow more complex and ominous, is interested in ameliorating tensions, and is eager for expanded trade and technical exchanges, if only to improve the quality of life for the average Soviet citizen. The general sense of this position is that the quest for advantage in the Third World, being by its very nature capricious and indecisive, should not be allowed to disrupt the process of superpower accommodation; that the Soviet leadership basically shares this view; and therefore with greater effort and understanding on both sides contentious issues can be resolved.

The record of Soviet policy since the mid-1950s, however, suggests that the Third World is more than a distracting sideshow to the Kremlin; that Moscow's distinctive historical experience has inspired a strategic vision of how to deal with an adversary—in the present era, preeminently the United States—at the heart of which are very different assumptions, perceptions, and priorities. To Moscow, the superpower rivalry in the Third World, which includes involvement in liberation struggles and the use of force in certain kinds of situations, is continuation of the Cold War by other means. This paraphrase of Clausewitz's dictum that "war is simply the continuation of politics by other means" is consonant with Lenin's view that Clausewitz's "other means" implied "violent" means, and with the general Soviet perspective which regards the concept of war as encompassing "a political aspect; armed struggle, that is, military operations on a varying scale; other kinds of activity carried on to ensure the achievement of the political aims of the war directly or through measures promoting the armed struggle—economic, ideological, and also non-military forms of political activity (diplomacy, the activities of parties, voluntary organizations, etc)."[1] Viewed in this light, the line between "war" and "Cold War" becomes tenuous indeed.

The Kremlin's strategy in the Third World derives from three major sources: the czarist experience of imperialist expansion at the expense of Muslim peoples; Lenin's legacy in foreign policy; and post-Stalin Soviet perceptions of the evolving international system. As in any alloy, the components are no longer discreet, each having merged with and been transformed by the others. The czarist experience provides historical roots and a source of continuity of advance; Lenin contributed an outlook and doctrinal framework for approaching the non-Western world; Stalin's successors fashioned a consensus that built on the legacies of the past and added a globalism suitable to their military power and to the epoch they operated in. Since the mid-1950s, each leadership in the Kremlin has proceeded in ways that reflected shrewd adaptation to systemic and regional developments as well as coherence of outlook. Possessing more power than any previous rulers of Russia, today's Soviet leaders, steeped in their history and doctrine, are ambitious and determined. To understand the origins and evolution of the USSR's policy toward the Third World and to distinguish what is new from what is inherited, a look at the czarist experience is in order.

THE IMPERIAL IMPERATIVE: THE CZARIST EXPERIENCE

Russia has had long experience with an imperial tradition. Emerging at the end of the fifteenth century from more than 250 years of Mongol domination, it expanded in all directions over the next two centuries, variously defeating Swedes, Poles, Lithuanians, Ottoman Turks, and Tartars, and spreading eastward rapidly across Siberia to the Pacific and the outer reaches of China. Russia's imperial age may be considered to have begun in earnest during the reign of Peter the Great (1682–1725) when "the state came to include more and more peoples

---

[1] *Marxism-Leninism on War and Army* (Moscow: Progress Publishers, 1972), 16, 22.

other than the Great Russians."[2] It was Peter who dropped the word *russkii* (meaning ethnically Russian) and introduced the adjective *rossiiskii* (meaning Russian in the administrative, not ethnic, sense), which was to emphasize the multi-ethnic character of the state, described as the "Russian" Empire.[3] It was also Peter who moved Russia's capital to St. Petersburg (Leningrad)—the city he built on the Baltic Sea in a style befitting the center of an empire—where it remained until necessity forced the Bolsheviks to move the capital back to Moscow in early 1918. During the eighteenth and nineteenth centuries, the state acquired its contemporary form, as successive czars added vast territories and diverse peoples, ruling over a land mass that encompassed one-sixth of the earth's surface.

By the nineteenth century, Russia's empire was solidly established. Like the Mongol, the Moghul, the Persian, the Ottoman—to mention but a few early empires that enjoyed a lengthy stint on the historical stage before being superseded by stronger actors—the Russian Empire rested on the principle of caesarism. A system of rule was developed in which centralized, absolute power was exercised through a series of bureaucratic institutions that controlled much of society. When czarism collapsed in 1917, the Bolsheviks succeeded in establishing a new, far more effective system of absolutism, with the result that among the great metropolises of the modern age, only the capital of the USSR remains what it has been for more than 400 years, the hub of an extensive imperial system. Although it encompassed both European and non-European peoples, Russia's expansion at the expense of the latter is the subject of the general comments that follow, because it is the experience with the Muslim peoples and regions that bears more directly on the evolution of Soviet policy toward the Third World.

The Russian Empire was special even in the heyday of the European empires; and its various distinctive characteristics contributed to its longevity. First, it was unusually homogenous. Not only were the Great Russians the largest ethnic group, but they represented a solid bloc in all the central regions of the empire; "and if we add to the Great Russians the Ukrainians and the White Russians, the numerical preponderance of the Russian stock over the non-Russian nationalities

[2] Nicholas V. Riasanovsky, *A History of Russia*, 3d ed. (New York: Oxford University Press, 1977), 235.

[3] Marc Raeff, "Patterns of Russian Imperial Policy toward the Nationalities," in Edward Allworth, ed., *Soviet Nationality Problems* (New York: Columbia University Press, 1971), 22.

becomes even more decisive."[4] The domination of the Slavs was a crucial factor in the preservation of the polyglot empire and in its expansion eastward, which fed the Slavs' hunger for land.

Second, the empire grew gradually, giving the impression of inevitability not rapaciousness. After Russia's defeat of Sweden at Poltava in 1709 and its acquisition of the eastern shore of the Baltic by the Treaty of Nystadt in 1721, none of its subsequent expansion resulted from war with any major power but only from defeats of weak, often anachronistic, regimes. Also, because it spread by land, peasant settlement by peasant settlement, advancing with the elemental, spasmodic movement of a giant amoeba, over relatively empty lands or politically marginal polities, it did not come into conflict with the maritime expansion of Britain and France until well into the nineteenth century and did not arouse fears among the other major European powers. For the most part, Russia's easterly and southerly expansion met with indifference in the chancelleries of Europe: what it acquired counted for little. This made for an unhurried pace that, in turn, bred deliberateness and patience. Not until the 1830s was Russia's imperial advance perceived by European powers as a threat to leading constellations of power among the major international actors.

Third, there arose an unquestioned belief in the necessity of territorial expansion for strategic defense. The Great Russians associated territorial depth with security, a conception of defense that emerged during the struggle against the Mongol occupation and was reinforced during the time of Ivan IV and his conquests of the khanates of Kazan (1552) and Astrakhan (1556), giving Moscow control of the entire length of the Volga River. While this or that khanate in Central Asia may have been seized by a swashbuckler in the field without express sanction from the center, the ruling circles were wholeheartedly disposed toward acquiring territory. It could never be said of the empire—as was said of the British Empire—that it had been "conquered and peopled . . . in a fit of absence of mind."[5]

Lacking any defensible border, Russia expanded in a restless search for security. From Moscow east to the Ural Mountains and south to the Black Sea and the Caucasus the land is flat, a tempting terrain for invaders and unruly nomadic peoples. Protection of Russian settlers and Russian interests became inextricably linked to the absorption of new lands. At times the movement of peasants to the open steppe

---

[4] Michael Karpovich, *Imperial Russia, 1801–1917* (New York: Henry Holt, 1944), 5–6.

[5] Sir John Seeley, *The Expansion of England* (1883), as quoted in William L. Langer, *The Diplomacy of Imperialism 1890–1902*, 2d ed. (New York: Knopf, 1960), 69.

frontier prompted government support to protect them; at other times it was the government's military moves extending the frontier that attracted waves of new settlers, who in turn needed protection.

Both at the beginning of this process in the sixteenth century and at its end in the second half of the nineteenth, territorial consolidation for the sake of security was hardly to be distinguished from outright expansion and seizure of sparsely settled lands held by nomadic people on a lower (from the Russian point of view, of course) level of cultural and economic development.[6]

By the nineteenth century, with increasing numbers of non-Russian Muslim peoples coming under Russia's control, it had become imperial policy to incorporate whatever contiguous territory was ripe for the taking and to think later about the problems in assimilating alien peoples. Like the movement of unchanneled waters, Russian power flowed in all directions, sometimes diverted, sometimes slowed, until finally stopped by a substantial obstacle.

Fourth, the ruling Russian elite was never forced to question the wisdom of expansion, never faced with fierce opposition to empire at home, as were their British and French counterparts:[7] there was no pressure from political parties, colonial peoples, economic lobbies, or intellectual gadflies. The absence in the Russian tradition of any need to justify one territorial acquisition after another can be explained by the autocratic character of the political system and the predisposition toward acquiring territory that had prevailed in ruling circles since at least the seventeenth century.

For the most part, Russian rulers did not use religion as incitement or justification for expansion, though one does find scattered instances of court philosophers who spoke of Moscow as the center of an ecumenical empire, as the Third (and presumably the last) Rome, a notion attributed to Ivan III at his marriage in 1472 to a niece of the last Byzantine emperor to rule in Constantinople before it was conquered by Ottoman Turks in 1453. They had no need to cloak expansionism in universalistic or pious cant. Russia did not spawn a Rudyard Kipling to give romantic embodiment to empire and "The White Man's Burden." Not until after Russia's defeat in the Crimean War did the Slavophiles, who exalted czarism, Orthodoxy, and Russian culture as the

---

[6] Raeff, "Patterns of Russian Imperial Policy," 28–29, 39.

[7] There is a considerable literature on British and French experience. See A. P. Thornton, *The Imperial Idea and Its Enemies: A Study in British Power* (New York: Doubleday, 1959); and Miles Kahler, *Decolonization in Britain and France: The Domestic Consequences of International Relations* (Princeton: Princeton University Press, 1984), for the post-1945 period.

highest form of civilization, urge expansion into Central Asia. Prince A. M. Gorchakov's oft-cited 1864 memorandum to the Czar on the responsibility that impels "the more civilized state to exercise a certain ascendancy over neighbors whose turbulence and nomad instincts" make them troublesome and a threat to "all security and all progress" is a rare instance of hypocritical rationalization of aggressive actions.[8] But even it did not play a central role in the leadership's thinking imperially about the utility of additional territory.

Finally, Russia's empire was so enduring because it consisted of one geographic entity that had grown like a gigantic snowball, accreting more and more mass unto itself, and because there was no power strong enough to conquer it (though on occasion some defeated it in a limited war fought for limited objectives).

None of Russia's adversaries, not even Napoleon, sought to reverse its eighteenth- and nineteenth-century expansion into Muslim areas. Russia's rivalry with Britain, which developed early in the nineteenth century and continued until shortly before the outbreak of World War I, was an unanticipated consequence of the conquests that brought the two expanding empires into contact with each other, resulting in sharp friction. Though each viewed the other as the principal threat to imperial ambitions, the rivalry was not ideological or economic or a direct challenge to the vital security of either. Nevertheless, it was bitter and widespread, extending along the entire southern perimeter of Russia's southern border from the Balkans to China and affecting fundamental alliance arrangements in Europe.

The initial issue was Moscow's drive to wrest control of the Bosporus and Dardenelles—the gateway to the Mediterranean—away from the tottering Ottoman Empire, dubbed the "sick man of Europe" by Czar Nicholas I. For its part, Britain wanted the Straits left in Turkish hands and sought throughout the century "to prevent the Russian fleet from gaining access to the Mediterranean" so as to forestall any possible threat to its line of communication to India.[9] Preventing Russia from becoming a Mediterranean power was a key objective (as it was to be for the United States after 1945). Moscow's ambitions—and Turkish weakness—led Russia to war in 1853, in 1876, and in 1914, and to Cold War in 1945, each time with far-reaching and adverse consequences.

From the 1840s on, tensions mounted, and with them Britain's Rus-

---

[8] A copy of the memorandum is contained in W. K. Fraser-Tytler, *Afghanistan*, 3d ed. (London: Oxford University Press, 1967), 333–37.

[9] Royal Institute of International Affairs, *Political and Strategic Interests of the United Kingdom: An Outline* (London: Oxford University Press, 1939), 102–3.

sophobia.[10] Russia's growing influence in northern Persia and conquest of Central Asia heightened British edginess. With the absorption of Tashkent (1865), Samarkand (1868), Khiva (1873), Bokhara (1876), and Merv (1884), Russian power reached the northern border of Afghanistan and was in a position to control Afghanistan and threaten India—or so reasoned British leaders, who wondered where Russia would stop. Geography, Russophobia at home, and a muddled strategic outlook led to exaggeration of Russia's capabilities and aims and to a series of costly and inconclusive British military expeditions into Afghanistan. But neither Britain nor Russia wanted war, and a number of border commissions worked out arrangements that eased the situation. In 1887 the two powers reached agreement on the Russo-Afghan border, and eight years later they fixed Afghanistan's northeast boundary in the Wakhan area of the Pamirs, Afghanistan receiving a sliver of land that insulated British India from direct contact with Russia. In 1907, Russia's deteriorating strategic position in the Far East and Europe, where Japan and Germany, respectively, emerged as its main adversaries, prompted an Anglo-Russian accommodation, which included agreement that Afghanistan lay in the British sphere of influence and that Persia would be divided into Russian and British spheres of influence.

By the turn of the twentieth century, czarist expansion had come to an end. A number of generalizations having relevance for Soviet–Third World policy can be hazarded about the determinants, priorities, and style of Russia's expansion toward the Muslim regions to the south and east, without contravening the arguments of scholars who have convincingly demonstrated that under czarism foreign policy was the exclusive preserve of the ruler; that his actions were matters of mood as well as material calculation; that his confidantes seldom had a broader conception than he of what is today called "the national interest"; that public opinion was nonexistent; and that foreign policy was largely divorced from the pressures of domestic politics.[11]

Still, when viewed historically, czarist foreign policy behavior, idiosyncratic and improvisational as it may have been at times, proves no less rational than that of other imperialist powers of the time. Indeed, Russia's vulnerability to invasion and attention to territorial defense elevated geographic determinism to the status of a perennial consid-

---

[10] John H. Gleason, *The Genesis of Russophobia in Great Britain: A Study of the Interaction of Policy and Opinion* (Cambridge, Mass.: Harvard University Press, 1950), admirably analyzes the key factors.

[11] For example Richard E. Pipes, "Domestic Politics and Foreign Policy," in Ivo J. Lederer, ed., *Russian Foreign Policy* (New Haven, Conn.: Yale University Press, 1962), 145–70.

eration of foreign policy. Given the inhospitable terrain on which the Muscovite state took root in the fifteenth, sixteenth, and seventeenth centuries, the policy options available to Russia's czars were few and obvious.

Without question, the chief characteristic of czarist foreign policy was the preeminence of strategic considerations. It was not necessary that Russian rulers have a broad conceptual vision in order to cope with threats to Russia's security. Nor did they need much wisdom to know that Russia lacked natural defensible borders, to realize the easy penetrability of the frontiers on the steppe, and to see how easily they could obtain the additional territory that would enhance the state's ability to absorb and counter invasion. Even Czar Paul I (1796–1801), "who tried to substitute inducement and accommodation for the widely preferred techniques of bluster and aggression" of his mother (Czarina Catherine the Great) realized that "a foothold in the Caucasus and favorable relations with Iran were considered strategically valuable because they would enable Russia to apply pressure to the eastern provinces of the Ottoman Empire."[12]

During the eighteenth and nineteenth centuries, Russia went to war for territory and was, for the most part, the aggressor and not the victim. All the wars enlarged the empire. From the time of Peter the Great, Russia enjoyed a basic military superiority over the Ottomans, Persians, and khanates of Central Asia. Though backward compared to the advanced powers of Europe, it possessed weapons and skills that gave it an edge over its Muslim adversaries. It also had a sophisticated military doctrine that "offered a way of compensating for technical weakness by exploiting their numerical strength and the tenacity and excellent fieldcraft of the Russian soldier."[13]

Though differing on tactics, Russian rulers were wedded to a policy of expansion, which sometimes included such bizarre and ill-conceived ventures as Paul's campaign in 1801 to undermine Britain by invading India.[14] Their underlying rationale was described by Edward Luttwak:

imperial territory is found to be in peril, or at least is disturbed by enemies based in lands that are beyond the limits of the empire, the security of the empire therefore requires that the frontier be moved outward, to encompass and suppress the danger at its

[12] Muriel Atkin, "The Pragmatic Diplomacy of Paul I: Russia's Relations with Asia, 1796–1801," *Slavic Review* 38, no. 1 (March 1979), 60–61.

[13] Edward N. Luttwak, *The Grand Strategy of the Soviet Union* (New York: St. Martin's Press, 1983), 14–15.

[14] Atkin, "Pragmatic Diplomacy," 68–69.

source. When that slice of expansion is duly achieved, by outright annexation or else by the creation of subservient client-states, it is soon discovered that the new frontier of the empire is also troubled from without—and thus the stage is set for more expansion which again may be explained away as defensive in intent.[15]

Soviet historians stress the economic motivations that underlay czarist expansion and minimize the strategic. Regarding Central Asia, they argue that, with cotton in short supply on the international market because of the American civil war, the region "now assumed significance as the source of an important raw material."[16] Non-Marxist historians, on the other hand, believe that official policy was determined by other considerations. While not denying that Russian merchants and manufacturers were interested in expanding into Central Asia, they add that, under the autocratic, hierarchical czarist system, the ruling Great Russian bureaucratic-military elites had little truck with commerce, and the economic interest groups were for the most part remote from the makers of foreign policy. According to Seymour Becker, "the history of the discussions leading up to the conquest [of Central Asia] and of the conquest itself indicates that neither in the capital nor among the military commanders in the field were economic considerations of much importance."[17] The subsequent process of absorbing the khanates of Bokhara and Khiva also demonstrated the paramountcy of strategic consideration. The government did "the inescapable minimum" to protect and promote the Russian private sector: "Concern for her own strategic position was more important to official Russia than were the economic interests of her subjects."[18] An impressive study on the social and political implications of the attitudes of Great Russian mercantile groups toward economic growth and modernization notes that well into the middle of nineteenth century these businessmen tended to be backward and rarely kept pace with the advance of empire: "In Russia trade and industry followed the flag only grudgingly."[19]

A second characteristic of czarist expansion was its undeviating persistence. The boundaries of the empire were moved forward with gla-

[15] Luttwak, *Grand Strategy*, 74–75.

[16] N. A. Khalfin, as translated and condensed by Hubert Evans, *Russia's Policy in Central Asia 1857–1868* (Oxford: St. Antony's College, Soviet Affairs Study Group, 1964), 50.

[17] Seymour Becker, *Russia's Protectorates in Central Asia: Bukhara and Khiva, 1865–1924* (Cambridge, Mass.: Harvard University Press, 1968), 23.

[18] Ibid., 191. See also Dietrich Geyer, *Russian Imperialism: The Interaction of Domestic and Foreign Policy 1860–1914* (New Haven, Conn.: Yale University Press, 1987), 86–100.

[19] Alfred J. Rieber, *Merchants and Entrepreneurs in Imperial Russia* (Chapel Hill: University of North Carolina Press, 1982), 73.

cial inexorability. The tenacity that had surmounted Mongol domination, rebuffed repeated invaders, and consolidated the autocratic
system of rule later created a mindset that was ever alert to opportunities and quick to exploit an adversary's weakness. With the accretion
of power came a growing readiness to use it to gain strategic advantage. Moreover, in an environment of fluid frontiers instead of natural
lines of division, the relative backwardness of neighbors to the south
and east was a magnet for the restless, tough soldiers and settlers
whose step-by-step advance carried forward the czarist domain. Occasional defeats were seldom suffered for long.[20] Russian drive and
power proved too overwhelming.

Third, Russia was prepared to sacrifice accommodation with Britain, its primary adversary in the Near East and Central Asia, on the
altar of imperial ambitions. During periods of growing military power,
it was indifferent to repeated British warnings of the danger of war.
After the crushing defeat of Persia in 1828 and the concessions under
the Treaty of Turkomanchay, Russia's new dominant position in Persia magnified British fears of impending threat to India. Tensions
over the future of the Ottoman Empire, Persia, and Afghanistan triggered innumerable border clashes and intrigues, as well as several
lurches to the brink of war. In the case of the Crimean War (1853–
1855), Russia badly miscalculated, as Britain went to war to prevent it
from gaining control of the Straits. By the 1890s, however, developments in Europe led both countries to a rapprochement. The unification and rise of Germany, the drastic realignment of European alliances prompted by the Kaiser's reversal of Bismarck's policy of
friendship with Russia, plus Germany's growing influence in the Ottoman Empire and efforts to acquire a foothold on the Persian Gulf
persuaded Russia and Britain to rein in their rivalry and agree in 1907
to an apportionment of spheres of influence.[21]

Fourth, despite the vastness of the empire, poor communications,
and the zest of local commanders for new annexations, czarist policy
managed to strike a balance between ambition and prudence. When
faced with formidable opponents or internal troubles, it generally

[20] The costs of conquest in Central Asia were modest. A. I. Makshevev, a czarist histo-
rian, estimated that Russian losses in all the Central Asian campaigns during the 1847–
1873 period numbered fewer than 400 dead and about 1,600 wounded. Cited in Richard
A. Pierce, *Russian Central Asia 1867–1917: A Study in Colonial Rule* (Berkeley: University
of California Press, 1960), 42, 44.

[21] There is a significant literature on the end of the "Great Game," a term the British
used to describe their rivalry with Russia in Central Asia. See David Gillard, *The Struggle
for Asia 1828–1914: A Study in British and Russian Imperialism* (London: Methuen, 1977),
chapter 8; for an excellent bibliography, see 186–97.

showed restraint, settling for what it could get. Thus, in 1830 and 1877, though well-positioned for a major drive against the Turks, Russia had to pull back to avoid war with Britain, whose interests could not tolerate czarist control of the Straits. And after the Crimean War, during a period of economic weakness and social unrest, when another confrontation with Britain was looming, the Czar sold Alaska and the Aleutian Islands to the United States (1867) in order to reduce the risk of a British attack in the North Pacific.[22] Perhaps he also calculated that the United States, having acquired a major stake in the North Pacific, would side with Russia against Britain, or that even the possibility would act as a restraint on Britain and thereby strengthen Russia's security in the Pacific. Prior to World War I, Russian expansion toward the Straits and the Persian Gulf was stymied on a number of occasions by the superior naval power of Great Britain (a lack of naval power also helps explain the later failure of Stalin to exploit his position vis-à-vis Turkey and Iran after 1945, the countervailing naval power then being the United States); and its expansion toward the Gulf was also hampered by the absence of a suitable infrastructure of railroads and bases in the Indo-Persian land corridor.[23]

Finally, though the end of the czarist period saw the emergence of important differences of opinion over foreign policy, particularly over whether to court Britain or Germany, still there was an apparent consensus favoring continued activity in the Near East and Central Asia within the limits of what was possible without jeopardizing alliance politics in Europe. Thus, the Anglo-Russian agreement of 1907 sharply curbed but did not completely stop Russian intrigues; only the coming of world war in August 1914 effectively ended Russia's probes in Persia and Afghanistan.

LENIN'S LEGACY

The revolution that brought the Bolsheviks to power in November 1917 began a new era for Russia—and the world as well. After surviv-

[22] Mairin Mitchell, *The Maritime History of Russia, 848–1948* (London: Sidgwick & Jackson, 1949), 245.

[23] For Moscow, "the essential logistical prerequisites for a successful penetration to the Persian Gulf did not exist until the completion of Russia's three strategic railheads at the entrance to the Indo-Persian Corridor. These were: (1) in Azerbaijan, the Julfa railhead at the Iranian border (1907) and an extension of this line to Tabriz (1916); (2) the Transcaspian Railway (1880–88), with its branch line to Kushka (1900) opposite Herat; and (3) the second railhead on the Afghan border at Termez (1916), connected with the Transcaspian as well as with the Orenburg–Tashkent line (1905)." Milan Hauner, "Soviet Eurasian Empire and the Indo-Persian Corridor," *Problems of Communism*, 36, no. 1 (January–February 1987), 28.

ing a foreign intervention and civil war—during the period the Soviets call "war communism"—Lenin concentrated on consolidating Communist Party rule and encouraging domestic recovery. He also broke out of the diplomatic isolation that Britain and France tried to impose on the new Soviet state and, among other moves, established close contacts with the revolutionary Kuomintang party of Dr. Sun Yat-sen in Canton, China, using the Comintern as an instrument of diplomacy, a tool Stalin honed to his personal requirements in the 1930s.

In foreign affairs, Lenin's most enduring legacy may be the view that permeates his writings on the "East": namely, that the advanced capitalist world of the West could be undermined through revolution in the Third World (in pre-1945 parlance known as the colonial and semi-colonial areas). This belief goes well beyond the ideological formulations and long-term projections set forth in his theory of imperialism which extends Karl Marx's concept of the class struggle from the domestic to the international arena and seeks to demonstrate thereby that World War I has stemmed from the struggle of newcomer capitalist countries such as Germany and Japan to compel the older capitalist countries such as Britain and France to relinquish their choice colonies and markets. According to Lenin, in a maturing capitalist economy there is a fundamental disequilibrium between production and consumption that makes profitable employment of capital increasingly difficult. To overcome the declining rate of profit, the capitalists compel their compliant governments to seek relief for them abroad in the form of colonies and spheres of influence. These acquisitions are exploited as sources of cheap labor and raw materials, as well as markets for surplus capital and for surpluses of manufactured goods. During the decades prior to the outbreak of global war in 1914, capitalism was temporarily able to postpone catastrophic depressions and revolutions through its expansion in Asia, Africa, and the Middle East. However, once the choice colonial areas were absorbed, the persistent pressure for profit, a matter of compulsion under capitalism, drove the dissatisfied capitalist states into mortal competition over the redistribution of the spoils. This inevitable rivalry could only be settled by war, the ultimate "contradiction of capitalism."

Lenin believed that the inter-capitalist world war would weaken capitalism as a system and loosen its hold on colonial areas. He sensed the political potential in the quest for independence of the nascent national revolutionary movements in the East and made them an integral concern of Soviet thinking about world affairs. Though his active interest in this issue waned under the impact of the struggle to consolidate Bolshevik power and forestall another attack from a coalition of capitalist powers, his appreciation of its potential did not.

By early 1920 the situation in Russia had stablilized: the Bolsheviks emerged triumphant from the civil war and the foreign interventions petered out. In June, Lenin focused on the revolutionary potential of the "East." In preparation for the second congress of the Communist International (Comintern), which convened in late July, he submitted for discussion his "Preliminary Draft Theses on the National and Colonial Questions."[24] These became the guiding principles for the mobilization under the leadership of the Soviet Union of a joint struggle by the proletariat of the advanced countries and the subjugated peoples of the colonial areas. Acknowledging that liberation movements would usually have a bourgeois-nationalist character initially, Lenin nevertheless endorsed temporary cooperation with them, provided that the proletarian movement, however rudimentary, maintain its sense of identity and independence of action.

To underscore the revolutionary potential of the colonial areas, at Lenin's instigation a Congress of the Peoples of the East was convened by the Comintern in Baku in September.[25] It called for world revolution and tried to attract the support of Muslims of the East for an all-out struggle against the West. At the time this meant opposition to British and French power in the Middle East; association of Soviet Russia and the Bolshevik Revolution with the aspirations of indigenous peoples seeking independence; and penetration of bourgeois-nationalist freedom movements by pro-Moscow communists. The Baku Conference never fulfilled Lenin's hopes. But its theme became a permanent part of the Soviet foreign policy outlook. Though Lenin did not live to see Russia reap the benefits of decolonization, he anticipated the demise of colonial empires:

> The movement in the colonies is still regarded as an insignificant national and completely peaceful movement. However, that is not the case. For great changes have taken place in this respect since the beginning of the twentieth century, namely, millions and hundreds of millions—actually the overwhelming majority of the world's population—are now coming out as an independent and active revolutionary factor. And it should be perfectly clear that

[24] V. I. Lenin, *Sochineniya*, vol. 25: *1920* (Moscow: Partizdat, 1937), 285–90. For elaboration of the discussion on the colonial and national question at the Comintern congress, see Edward Hallett Carr, *The Bolshevik Revolution 1917–1923*, vol. 3 (New York: Macmillan, 1953), 251–70. For a useful overview, see Roger E. Kanet, "The Soviet Union and the Colonial Question, 1917–1953," in Roger E. Kanet, ed., *The Soviet Union and the Developing Nations* (Baltimore: Johns Hopkins University Press, 1974), 1–50.

[25] Stephen White, "Communism and the East: The Baku Congress, 1920," *Slavic Review* 33, no. 3 (September 1974), 492–514.

in the coming decisive battles of the world revolution, this movement of the majority of the world's population, originally aimed at national liberation, will turn against capitalism and imperialism and will, perhaps, play a much more revolutionary role than we have been led to expect.[26]

The essential correctness of his general thesis was to lead the successors to his successor on to a path that would have great significance for the Soviet Union, the West, and the Third World. But all this lay in the future.

After Lenin's death in January 1924, Stalin made the colonial question part of his own program in the maneuvering to possess Lenin's mantle of legitimacy. In a series of lectures entitled *The Foundations of Leninism*, which he gave three months later, he directed attention to the movement of national self-determination of peoples struggling against colonialism and imperialism (that is, Western rule). Stalin lauded Lenin for illumining the interrelationships that exist and affect the future of national liberation movements and their struggle, the prospects of the proletarian revolution in Europe, and the strengthening of socialism in the Soviet Union. He reiterated Lenin's thesis that the bastions of capitalism could be toppled by depriving them of the raw materials and markets of the colonies, declaring that "the road to victory of the [proletarian] revolution in the West lies through the revolutionary alliance with the liberation movement of the colonies and dependent countries against imperialism."[27]

By 1925–1926, however, the Colonial Question was subordinated in the Comintern to other issues, as Stalin's attention was drawn elsewhere. At home, he was absorbed for more than a decade with the institutionalization of his tyrannical system of rule and the transformation of Soviet society, as well as with the reimposition of control over Turkic-speaking areas of Central Asia, parts of which tried unsuccessfully in the decade or so after the Bolshevik Revolution to avoid

[26] V. I. Lenin, *The National-Liberation Movement in the East* (Moscow: Foreign Languages Publishing House, 1957), 289–90. Indeed, in his last article, written on March 2, 1923 and devoted primarily to the need for improving the efficiency of the state bureaucracy, Lenin expressed optimism over the outcome of the struggle of the Soviet Union to defend itself against the imperialists by virtue of the fact that Russia, India, China, and others "account for the overwhelming majority of the world's population," and they have been drawn into the struggle for liberation, thus assuring the final outcome of the complete victory of socialism. V. I. Lenin, "Luchshe men'she, da luchshe" [Better fewer, but Better], *Sochineniya*, vol. 27: *1921–1923* (Moscow: Partizdat, 1937), 416–17.

[27] Joseph Stalin, *Works*, vol. 6 (Moscow: Foreign Languages Publishing House, 1953), 144–45.

the Soviet yoke.[28] Abroad, by the mid-1930s, Stalin was confronted with major threats to the security of the Soviet state from Germany and Japan, and in June 1941 with the supreme struggle to survive the Nazi onslaught. In view of all this, he chose not to incite communist agitation in the colonies for fear of provoking the already deeply ingrained suspicions of Britain and France, the principal colonial powers and his prospective allies against Hitler. Nor in any event was he in a position to do much: the ruling colonial powers were firmly in control; the national liberation movements were still in their formative stages; the communists were weak; and the Soviet Union lacked the capability for direct involvement.

The end of World War II brought no major change in Soviet policy toward the colonial world. Stalin's priorities were elsewhere, his resources limited. His absorption was with reconstruction and recovery, the Stalinization of Eastern Europe, the struggle for Germany, the Titoist challenge, and the coming to power of the communists on the mainland of China. Though not completely ignored—witness Stalin's attempts to cow Turkey and Iran into quasi-dependency, his half-hearted efforts to acquire a trusteeship over the former Italian colony of Libya, the USSR's involvement in the Palestine question at the United Nations, and the failures of the Moscow-inspired communist uprisings in Burma, India, Indonesia, and the Philippines—the Third World was not important to him. Stalin's foreign policy was riveted to historic axes of advance along the Eurasian land mass.

After Stalin's death in March 1953, a number of systemic changes in the international system ushered in an new era in Soviet foreign policy. First, decolonization brought an end to the European empires and a concomitant increase in the number of new nations operating in the world arena. Notwithstanding their weakness and dependence on foreign assistance, these offspring of the defunct empires showed themselves fully capable of pursuing independent foreign policies that went contrary to the preferences of their former rulers. Second, the polarization of regional politics in the Third World—a consequence of Washington's globalization of its policy of containment—had the effect of opening the way for Soviet penetration. Third, many Third World elites, having rejected "capitalism" as the Godfather of colonialism, looked to "socialism"—and for a time the Soviet Union—for an alter-

[28] Sir Olaf Caroe, *Soviet Empire: The Turks of Central Asia and Stalinism* (London: Macmillan, 1953), passim. See also Alexandre Bennigsen and Chantal Lemercier-Quelquejay, *Islam in the Soviet Union* (New York: Praeger, 1967); and Alexandre Bennigsen and S. Enders Wimbush, *Muslim National Communism in the Soviet Union* (Chicago: University of Chicago Press, 1979).

native model of development and nation-building. And, finally, there was the new look in Moscow, where Stalin's successors rejected his hostility toward bourgeois-nationalist elites in the Third World and offered them an alternative to alignment with the United States. In the process they moved Soviet foreign policy along lines very different from anything in the past.

THE KHRUSHCHEVIAN WATERSHED

Nikita Sergeyevitch Khrushchev was the greatest innovator to rule Russia since Czar Alexander II in the 1860s. His reforms and tinkering left no institution of Soviet society untouched.[29] They included restoration of the role of the Communist Party of the Soviet Union (CPSU) as the key center of political power; a diminished power for the secret police; reorganization of governmental bureaucracies in the search for ways of increasing production and productivity; educational reform; and cultural relaxation which reawakened the intelligentsia. There is continuing disagreement among Western analysts over what Khrushchev meant for Soviet society, whether his rule was an interesting interregnum between conservative eras or a major watershed. In the field of foreign affairs, however, there is no such doubt: Khrushchev had a profound effect on the course and character of Soviet foreign policy and nowhere more than in relation to the Third World.

Khrushchev forged a strategy inspired by Lenin's ideas: he modernized Leninist formulations on the colonial and national questions and operationalized them, in the process moving the Soviet Union into the mainstream of Third World developments. At the CPSU's twentieth congress, in February 1956 (whose place in Soviet history was assured by his denunciation of Stalin's crimes against the party and country), Khrushchev spoke of the momentous changes, such as the emergence to independence of many former colonies, that were occurring in the international system. He declared that as a result of "the disintegration of the imperialist colonial system now taking place," a vast "Zone of Peace," which included the overwhelming majority of the population of our planet, had emerged:

> The new period in world history which Lenin predicted has arrived, and the peoples of the East are playing an active part in

[29] See for example, R. F. Miller and F. Feher, eds., *Khrushchev and the Communist World* (Totowa, N.J.: Barnes & Noble, 1984); Martin McCauley, ed., *Khrushchev and Khrushchevism* (Bloomington: Indiana University Press, 1987).

deciding the destinies of the whole world, are becoming a new mighty factor in international relations. In contrast to the pre-war period, most Asian countries now act in the world arena as sovereign states or states which are resolutely upholding their right to an independent foreign policy. International relations have spread beyond the bounds of relations between the countries inhabited chiefly by peoples of the white race and are beginning to acquire the character of genuinely world-wide relations.[30]

Doubtless having in mind the dramatic improvement the USSR achieved within less than two years in its relations with Afghanistan, India, Indonesia, and Egypt, Khrushchev called on the new nations to draw on the accomplishments of the Soviet Union "to build up an independent national economy and to raise the living standards of their peoples": "Today they need not go begging for up-to-date equipment to their former oppressors. They can get it in the socialist countries, without assuming any political or military commitments."[31]

With a verve not generally associated with Soviet diplomacy, he offered Third World nations a Soviet option. The range of initiatives, the commitment of extensive resources, the restless tinkering with ideological criteria in order to find some convincing categories (possibly to win over the skeptics in the Kremlin) for grouping countries according to their pro-Soviet affinities and potential, all reflected his innate optimism about Moscow's future and stake in the Third World.

Khrushchev embarked the Soviet Union on a new course, momentous in its long-term foreign policy implications. He introduced new dimensions of risk-taking, as the Soviet leadership searched for ways of assessing trends and adapting to events in a turbulent part of the world, of responding to what Shakespeare called "unacquainted change." In contrast to Stalin, whose attention to the colonial question from the very beginning of the postwar period had been centered in the United Nations and used to embarrass the West, Khrushchev in the mid-1950s approached Third World countries as a free-hunting ground where the Soviet Union might be able to improve its overall political-strategic position relative to the West or, as a Yugoslav journalist wrote, "as a potential strategical reserve which may be helpful in achieving ascendancy over a rival or attaining world dominance."[32]

[30] N. S. Khrushchev, *Report of the Central Committee of the Communist Party of the Soviet Union to the 20th Party Congress, February 14, 1956* (Moscow: Foreign Languages Publishing House, 1956), 23, 26.

[31] Ibid., 27.

[32] Dj. Jerković, "Comments on the Change," *Review of International Affairs*, 12, no. 260 (February 5, 1961), 9.

Foreign policy was one of the issues that Khrushchev used to defeat his opposition in the post-Stalin struggle for control in the Kremlin in the 1953–1955 period. Though not a key issue—foreign policy differences seldom determine the outcome of domestic political rivalries—it may have been more than usually salient at this time because of the leadership's recognition that Stalin's legacy was damaging to long-term Soviet interests in Eastern Europe, Western Europe, the Near East (Turkey and Iran), and the underdeveloped world.

On some aspects of policy, apparently all factions in the Kremlin agreed. There was, for example, a general recognition of the need to improve relations with Turkey and Iran: therefore the Soviet note of May 30, 1953, publicly acknowledging that Stalin's policy of pressure had been a mistake and unequivocally renouncing all Soviet territorial claims against Turkey; and the invitation of talks with Iran to settle a number of their border problems and mutual financial claims. Also, in July the Soviet delegate at the U.N. Economic and Social Council announced that the Soviet Union was prepared to participate in programs designed to assist developing countries. Individually, none of these initiatives had immediate consequences, but together they foreshadowed a new adaptability and realism in Soviet foreign policy.

In outmaneuvering his rivals, Khrushchev shifted his position on foreign policy issues several times: in early 1954, he supported Foreign Minister V. M. Molotov's hardline position toward the West against Premier Georgii Malenkov's more conciliatory approach; a year later, he overrode Molotov and persuaded the party leadership to end the Soviet occupation of eastern Austria and accept a peace treaty calling for that country's neutralization and to normalize relations with Tito's Yugoslavia.[33] By the time of the CPSU's Central Committee plenum in July 1955, the debate in the Kremlin on foreign policy was over. Khrushchev had defeated Molotov and convinced his fellow oligarchs to underwrite his forward policy in the Middle East and Southern Asia. Two months later, Nasser's announcement of a major Egyptian-Czech arms deal (in which Prague served as Moscow's surrogate) stunned the West and revolutionized Arab world politics.

Khrushchev's diplomatic offensive was noteworthy for two reasons. First, convinced that the situation in the Third World was ripe for "socialism," that "progressive forces" capable of weakening the camp of capitalism were emerging and that they could significantly improve

[33] David J. Dallin, *Soviet Foreign Policy after Stalin* (Philadelphia: Lippincott, 1961), 135, 220–21, 229: and C. Grant Pendill, Jr., " 'Bipartisanship' in Soviet Foreign Policy-Making," in Erik P. Hoffmann and Frederick J. Fleron, Jr., eds., *The Conduct of Soviet Foreign Policy*, expanded 2d. ed. (Hawthorne, N.Y.: Aldine, 1980), 68–69.

the USSR's position in the world, Khrushchev persuaded the party that this was the opportune time for bold actions. He enabled the new nations to adopt policies whose effect was to alienate them from the West, thus carrying forward Lenin's injunction to attack the industrial heartland of capitalism by undermining its relationship with the non-Western world. At the twentieth party congress, Khrushchev provided the doctrinal justification for the "forward policy" in the Third World. As always in Soviet foreign policy, practice precedes ideology. Khrushchev used ideological innovations, as had Lenin and Stalin, to justify major policy shifts that were adopted over the stern opposition of his opponents and to isolate his rivals in the party.

Second, Khrushchev's diplomacy, a foreshadowing of selective détente, was alternately conciliatory and contentious, an often bewildering contrast to Stalin's, with its uniform hostility to the West and pervasive bipolarity. For example, at the very time that Khrushchev was meeting with the leaders of the United States, Britain, and France in Geneva in July 1955 to discuss arms control and ways of improving East-West relations (and a week after his foreign policy initiatives for undermining the West in the Third World had been approved by the CPSU's Central Committee), he was concluding his arms deal with Egypt and preparing for greater involvement in the Middle East and Southern Asia—all part of a strategy to establish the Soviet Union as a new force in the Third World. The possibility that challenges in the Third World, still regarded by Western leaders as theirs to dominate though perhaps not to rule openly, would undercut his efforts to reach agreement in Europe or to improve bilateral relationships seems not to have been considered seriously by Khrushchev. Very possibly, his concerns in this regard were minimal because Western responses to Soviet moves were indecisive, even forbearing. Khrushchev saw nothing in Western behavior that suggested the inherent contradiction between "peace" campaigns in the West and multifaceted offensives against Western positions or clients in the Third World. He discerned the "divergence of imperialist interests" and exploited it, in the spirit of Lenin's words: "We must make systematic use of the discord between them to hamper their struggle against us."[34] As a Leninist, he believed the economic self-interest of the ever-competing individual capitalist powers would prevent their sustained cooperation or resistance to Soviet initiatives.

Khrushchev saw unlimited possibilities for the Soviet Union in the

---

[34] V. I. Lenin, *On the Foreign Policy of the Soviet State* (Moscow: Progress Publishers, n.d.), 297.

Third World. The particular direction that he set for Soviet policy was no more foreshadowed by Stalin's intimations at the CPSU's nineteenth congress, in late 1952, of a new responsiveness toward the newly independent bourgeois-nationalist countries—what Marshall Shulman called "the quasi-Right strategy—the use of detente, of diverse action, nationalism, the peace sentiment, and anti-imperialism, an indirect policy of maneuver to strengthen the Soviet bloc and weaken the Western bloc, in place of a direct advance toward social revolution"[35]— than were the policies of John F. Kennedy and Lyndon B. Johnson that led to deeper and deeper involvement in Vietnam simply a continuation of the containment policy developed by Truman and adapted by Eisenhower. A new dimension was added in both cases.

Perhaps the Khrushchevian revolution in foreign policy was the inevitable consequence of the USSR's emergence as a superpower and the fragmentation of the international system. Yet leaders can make a difference; and Khrushchev's diplomatic strategy—with its mixture of activism, risk-taking, ideologically engendered optimism—launched the Soviet Union on a course of expanding involvement in Third World affairs. It was an open challenge to the West, one it has yet to meet successfully.

Khrushchev's chosen strategy was by no means the only one possible at the time: a less flamboyant, more low-key approach might have brought comparable benefits and far fewer tensions with the West. When he launched his "forward policy," the USSR was in a position of considerable nuclear inferiority vis-à-vis the United States: it possessed only a modest nuclear capability, and even that could not threaten U.S. targets; it lacked a power projection capability (PPC) for intervening on behalf of prospective clients in the Third World; it had a navy suitable only for coastal defense; and its economy was far from equipped to handle extensive assistance to developing countries. Not until the late 1960s would the Soviet Union be in a position to sustain Khrushchev's initiatives and implicit commitments. All the more remarkable, then, was the policy he chose.

First, Khrushchev changed the traditional Russian preoccupation with the Eurasian land mass by shifting from a continental-based strategy to a global strategy. In the past, the military-political thinking at the center was directed toward securing and expanding the periphery of the empire. The result, whether intended to counter adversaries or enhance influence, was a coherent strategic outlook that was shaped

[35] Marshall D. Shulman, *Stalin's Foreign Policy Reappraised* (Cambridge, Mass.: Harvard University Press, 1963), 264.

by an interest in adjacent lands. Notwithstanding the episodic and fleeting attention various czars paid to Africa, especially Ethiopia at the end of the nineteenth century,[36] there was no quest for colonies or overseas bases. Neither Russian conceptions of security nor Russian leaders' images of themselves or of their role in the world required any.

When Khrushchev leapfrogged over Turkey and Iran into the thick of Arab politics, his political-military interest in *noncontiguous* regions was something very new in Russian and Soviet diplomacy. It signified the advent of the globalization of the Kremlin's outlook. Khrushchev exposed the weaknesses of the U.S. policy of containment in the Middle East and demonstrated to Arab (and other Third World) regimes who had little first-hand experience with the Soviet Union that Moscow was prepared to help those who opposed the West's efforts to retain a major influence in the region through its network of interlocking military alliances.

His reaction to the U.S. efforts at encirclement was to counter with offers of assistance to regimes opposed to U.S.-sponsored military pacts, in this way stiffening their resolve to resist American policy. The Truman administration had tried, but failed, to elicit interest in the Arab world in containing the Soviet Union. In June 1953, shortly after Eisenhower had taken office, Secretary of State Dulles visited Egypt in an unsuccessful attempt to convince the new regime of Gamal Abdel Nasser of the urgency of combining in a military alliance to protect the Middle East against the enemy. Nasser is supposed to have asked, "Who is the enemy?" Whereas to Dulles it was international communism, to Nasser it was Britain, which still occupied Egyptian territory, the Suez Canal zone. Dulles found alliance-building difficult to generate because no Arab regime had reason to fear a Soviet attack or subversion by pro-Moscow communist parties. He did bring Turkey and Iraq together in a Pact of Mutual Cooperation, commonly known as the Baghdad Pact, which was signed in Baghdad on February 24, 1955. Iran joined in October, after the Soviet Union had started to arm Egypt, Syria, and Afghanistan: "Iran was already quite uncomfortable with the development of the Soviet position in Afghanistan" and saw the USSR's thrust into the Arab world as a threatening flanking maneuver.[37] In addition, Moscow's ties to Iran's Tudeh (Communist) Party exacerbated the Shah's uneasiness over traditional Russian

[36] Sergius Yakobson, "Russia and Africa," in Lederer, ed., *Russian Foreign Policy*, 453–87.

[37] Rouhollah K. Ramazani, *Iran's Foreign Policy 1941–1973: A Study of Foreign Policy in Modernizing Nations* (Charlottesville: University Press of Virginia, 1975), 277.

imperialism and hastened his accession to the Pact. But the net effect of Dulles's effort proved detrimental to the West and beneficial to the USSR, as in the cases of Egypt, Syria, and Iraq (after the revolution of July 1958 toppled the pro-Western Hashemite monarchy).

Of longer-term significance was Khrushchev's quest for overseas military facilities, which surfaced in Yemen in 1955, in Egypt in 1961, and in Cuba in 1962, suggesting that global considerations were implicit in his forward policy from the very beginning. His aim went beyond strategic denial—to prevent a *Pax Americana*; it sought also to acquire influence and play an active role in the Third World. Opportunities in the 1950s, however, were few, due to the USSR's limited military capability, its unwillingness to push hard for fear of provoking a forceful U.S. response (which explains why Moscow used Czechoslovakia to conclude the arms deal with Egypt), and its lingering reputation as a source of communist-fomented revolutions.

By globalizing its foreign policy, Moscow has expanded the areas of unpredictability in Soviet-American relations without seeming to have improved its overall security. It has not only increased the probability of confrontation over Third World clients and issues but also complicated the process of stabilizing the overall superpower relationship.

A second characteristic of the Khrushchevian transformation of traditional Russian imperial and early Soviet policy was the willingness to run risks for clients and in pursuit of interests that were not directly related to the security of the homeland. Risk-taking is easier to identify than account for, since we know very little about the decisional influences—perceptions, intentions, expectations, and domestic context—that prompt Soviet leaders to run risks in order to change the status quo.[38] In his taped reminiscences Khrushchev says that the idea for implanting missiles with nuclear warheads in Cuba was his and that the aim was to deter a U.S. invasion to topple Castro, but he tells us nothing about the deliberations in the Kremlin, the calculations of risk, the perceptions of probable American responses, or the contingency planning.[39]

What we can say is that under Khrushchev the tentativeness of Moscow's Third World policy in the late 1950s and the early 1960s gave

[38] Robert Jervis, *Perception and Misperception in International Politics* (Princeton: Princeton University Press, 1976), 50–57 and passim. For a detailed study of the elements of risk-taking in specific Soviet decisions on Germany in the late 1950s and early 1960s see Hannes Adomeit, *Soviet Risk-Taking and Crisis Behavior: A Theoretical and Empirical Analysis* (Boston: Allen & Unwin, 1982).

[39] *Khrushchev Remembers*, trans. and ed. Strobe Talbott (Boston: Little, Brown, 1970), 546–55.

way to high-powered, high-risk assertiveness, of which the 1962 missile crisis was the most dramatic and dangerous example. However, the rearming of Egypt and Syria after their defeat in June 1967 and the intervention in Ethiopia in 1977–1978 were typical examples of the cast of the Kremlin's new strategic outlook—its shift from inhibiting and undermining Western options and activities to forcefully advancing its own diverse interests and ambitions.

Soviet risk-taking has introduced a new dimension into the uneasy relationship with the United States. When it is added to the nuclear arms competition, the face-off of sizable numbers of combat ready forces in the center of Europe, the difficulty both sides have had in sustaining serious negotiations on any issue for very long, and the base insinuations each makes about the other's motives and outlook, the globe becomes a very dangerous place—a bundle of incendiary packages with shortened fuses.

Third, Khrushchev accelerated the construction of an all-oceans navy.[40] By the 1960s this naval buildup was further confirmation of Moscow's determination to extend czarist and Soviet Eurasian strategy and provide the force structure needed for a forward policy. The mid-1950s was apparently a critical time of decision. According to Admiral of the Fleet Sergei G. Gorshkov, Commander-in-Chief of the Soviet Navy from 1956 to 1985 and creator of the USSR's "blue water" fleet, the CPSU Central Committee decided "roughly" at that time "to build a powerful oceanic nuclear fleet."[41] He castigates those who question the USSR's need for a modern ocean fleet able "to ensure its state interests." They—presumably Western critics—purport to see this development as a threat, only to justify their own "constantly inflated expenditures on armaments"; and they ascribe aggressive purposes to Soviet intentions in order "to hide the improper activities of their own fleets, performing gendarme functions in suppressing national liberation movements and acting as the main strike force of imperialism in the World Ocean."[42] As a skilled lobbyist eager for a bigger piece of

[40] See Bradford Dismukes and James M. McConnell, eds., *Soviet Naval Diplomacy* (New York: Pergamon Press, 1979), chapter 1; Michael MccGwire, *Military Objectives in Soviet Foreign Policy* (Washington, D.C.: Brookings Institution, 1987); Michael MccGwire, ed., *Soviet Naval Developments: Capability and Context* (New York: Praeger, 1973); Michael MccGwire and John McDonnell, eds., *Soviet Naval Influence: Domestic and Foreign Dimensions* (New York: Praeger, 1977); and Norman Polmar, *Guide to the Soviet Navy* (Annapolis: Naval Institute Press, 1983); and *Soviet Oceans Development*, U.S. Senate report, 94th Congress, 2d session (Washington, D.C.: U.S. Government Printing Office, 1976).

[41] S. G. Gorshkov, *The Sea Power of the State* (Annapolis: Naval Institute Press, 1979), 179.

[42] Ibid., 180.

defense pie, Gorshkov stressed the significance of naval power for the implementation of the forward policy, an essential component of which is defense of pro-Soviet national liberation movements.

There are, of course, cogent reasons for the Soviet Union to build a balanced and multipurpose all-oceans fleet: to deny the United States "command of the sea"; to counter U.S. nuclear threats from carrier-based aircraft and *Polaris* and *Trident* submarines with its own SLBMs (submarine-launched ballistic missiles tipped with nuclear warheads) and impressive ASW (antisubmarine warfare) capability; and to limit U.S. foreign policy options in the Third World. Looked at functionally, in wartime a navy can provide strategic offensive, strategic defense, and support for ground operations; in peacetime, its aims are a combination of deterrence, prestige-building, and promotion of state interests by supplying additional foreign policy options and forcing an adversary to proceed with caution in the use of power.[43] Moreover, as a major maritime power (the Soviet Union's merchant fleet is the most modern in the world), the USSR has reason to make its presence felt in upholding open sea lines of communication and its rights—for example, fishing and oceanographic surveying—on the high seas.

It is inevitable that comparisons are made between the role of Soviet naval power in aggravating the already tense Soviet-American relationship and the sweeping "challenge delivered by Wilhelmine Germany to Britain's naval supremacy" in the period prior to World War I:

> In both cases, the dominant land power discards its traditional naval strategies of coastal defense and guerre de course and, by embarking upon the construction of an oceangoing "great navy," creates a threat to the dominant sea power. In both cases, the land power is led to present this challenge only after a protracted internal debate, in which the expansion of naval power is championed by an outstanding and dedicated naval leader, who is fascinated by the history of Anglo-Saxon sea power, determined to awake his country to a sense of its naval destiny, and fired with the doctrines of Alfred Thayer Mahan—in the earlier case, Admiral Alfred von Tirpitz; in the more recent one, Admiral S. G. Gorshkov.

[43] These are the same functions as Soviet analysts attribute to the U.S. Navy: see for example N. Shaskolskii, *Krasnaya zvezda*, June 4, 1983, 5. However, in the event of large-scale war the Soviet Navy would not have to maintain open sea lines of communication with allies, the Warsaw Pact members all being part of the Soviet bloc's continental land mass.

In both cases, the challenger is gravely handicapped by the burden of maintaining its position of dominance in land power, and
especially by the fact that it faces potential enemies on two fronts.
The challenger is also handicapped by its inexperience, by its lack
of a strong naval tradition, by the inferiority of its navy to its army
in terms of political and bureaucratic influence, and by the facts
of geography, which give it only limited access to the open sea. In
both cases, however, these handicaps, while they rule out the possibility that the challenger will ever achieve naval dominance of
the kind the Anglo-Saxon opponent possesses, are not so great
that they cannot bring the opponent's dominance to an end. For
von Tirpitz, whose "risk strategy" was intended not to ensure that
Germany would rule the waves in place of Britain but only to limit
Britain's freedom of maneuver, and perhaps also for Gorshkov,
this is as much as naval expansion is meant to accomplish.

In both cases, too, the dominant sea power reacts to the challenge in a spirit of righteous indignation. For Britain, it was said
then as it is said of America now, sea power is a necessity because
of its dependence on trade and its position as the center of an
imperial system or coalition of states divided by sea. For a continental land power, it was said then as it is now, sea power is a
luxury.[44]

Nevertheless, continues Hedley Bull, there are three important differences between the two cases. "First, naval power is not as decisive an
instrument of foreign policy as it was at the time of the Anglo-German
naval rivalry . . . it does not have the geopolitical significance it had
when air communications did not exist and land communications were
what they were three quarters of a century ago. Nor does control of
'the great highway' of the sea lay coastal states and peoples open to
domination as readily as it did in the era of imperial expansion." Second, the United States is in a far stronger economic and technological
position vis-à-vis the Soviet Union than Britain was vis-à-vis Germany,
which was in the process of emerging, if it had not indeed already
done so, as the world's leading industrial power. Finally, the spectre of
nuclear war disciplines the Soviet-American naval rivalry.[45]

Hedley Bull's conclusion is persuasive: the threat from the Soviet
Navy should not be exaggerated. Compared to the other branches of
the Soviet armed forces, the Navy has had a minor role in advancing

[44] Hedley Bull, "The Rise of Soviet Naval Power," *Problems of Communism* 30, no. 2
(March–April 1981), 60.
[45] Ibid., 61.

Soviet objectives and protecting clients in the Third World.[46] Moreover, by the late 1970s there were signs that naval deployments and shipbuilding were being downgraded, as the Soviet General Staff under Marshal Nikolai Ogarkov trimmed the Navy's appropriations, focused on the modernization and upgrading of conventional forces in Europe and the Far East, and edged away from commitment to a liberating mission in the Third World.[47] Indicative, too, of this lessening interest in the navy as a major instrument of power projection in the Third World is the apparent decision to alter the design of the largest Soviet aircraft carrier under construction so that it will be "capable of accommodating only 'jump jets' and helicopters rather than high-performance aircraft such as those that fly from U.S. carriers."[48] The reasons are doctrinal and budgetary, influenced by both the commanding global reach of the U.S. Navy and the realization that the Soviet Union could not soon hope to develop "a capability to land combat forces against armed opposition, even of the limited sort that would come into play in most Third World crises."[49]

Yet the Khrushchevian revolution has left a gnawing concern that the Soviet Navy is designed to do more than just protect the homeland, hunt American nuclear submarines, enhance deterrence (with ballistic-missile firing Typhoon-class nuclear submarines), and keep open its sea lines of communication and commerce; that it is intended also to show the flag and through strategic denial to limit U.S. options and operations in Third World areas. The USSR's strategy does not call for fighting the United States over clients. Nor does its power projection capability aspire to troop landings on hostile territory. Rather, it assumes that any prospective client will be able to provide secure land bases to facilitate the power projection that Moscow does best:

[46] A number of studies document this point: see for example Stephen S. Kaplan, ed., *Diplomacy of Power: Soviet Armed Forces as a Political Instrument* (Washington, D.C.: Brookings Institution, 1981). On the other hand, Dismukes and McConnell (*Soviet Naval Diplomacy*, chapter 8) see naval power as having been more useful in promoting Soviet objectives.

[47] Francis Fukuyama, *Soviet Civil-Military Relations and the Power Projection Mission*, R-3504-AF (Santa Monica, Calif.: Rand Corporation, April 1987), 30–49. Fukuyama's well-developed argument is shared by Rajan Menon: "The lack of doctrinal emphasis on power projection, and the absence of any indication that strategic amphibious assaults outside the umbrella of shore-based aircraft are being prepared for, suggests that the Soviet naval infantry is not intended for distant intervention." *Soviet Power and the Third World* (New Haven, Conn.: Yale University Press, 1986), 111. For a valuable analysis of the evolution of Ogarkov's thinking, see Mary C. Fitzgerald, *Marshal Ogarkov on Modern War: 1977–1985* (Alexandria, Va.: Center for Naval Analyses, March 1986).

[48] Robert C. Toth, *Los Angeles Times*, October 22, 1987.

[49] Fukuyama, *Soviet Civil-Military Relations*, 47.

massive resupply of arms, air defense, and combat forces to assist in protecting a client during a period of heightened jeopardy. It is in this context that the Soviet Navy makes possible—perhaps even feasible—Moscow's boldness and willingness to probe the parameters of the possible in its rivalry with the United States in the Third World.

In his historical perspective on naval power going back to Peter the Great, Admiral Gorshkov noted that "Any potentate with a land army has one hand but he who also has a fleet has two hands."[50] Since 1968, when the Soviet Navy started to maintain a flotilla on permanent station in the Mediterranean, Soviet assertiveness in regional conflicts has increased. Sometimes dangerous, as in the October 1973 Arab-Israeli War, it also has less serious manifestations, such as interference with U.S. naval exercises and periodic games of "chicken" on the high seas. The Soviet naval presence in Third World seas and Moscow's capacity to increase its operational deployments in any of these areas certainly very quickly affect U.S. options, as was evident in the Persian Gulf in the spring of 1987 when Moscow's indication of a willingness to protect Kuwaiti ships from possible Iranian attack was quickly followed by the Reagan administration's decision to reflag eleven Kuwaiti oil tankers, provide them with a U.S. naval escort, and increase the number of combat ships on station in the area.

It may well be that comparisons between Soviet-American naval rivalry and the Anglo-German case are invidious and would best be eschewed. Yet, the USSR's powerful navy, coming on line in a tense period of escalating U.S.-Soviet military-technological rivalry, is affecting U.S. (and Soviet) military-political perceptions. Some fear that, as the Soviets expand their navy and with it their seaborne options, they may find the "opportunities to nickel and dime the West by selective and carefully tailored applications of violence" irresistible.[51] Writing of Anglo-German relations in the period prior to the First World War, Paul Kennedy observed that "the question of German *intentions*" turned out to be far "less significant than the impact of German actions" (italics added).[52] So too, what really matters now is not Soviet intentions but the impact of what Moscow is doing: and the USSR's naval expansion is perceived by the U.S. leadership as threatening not only its ability to supply Western Europe and Japan in the event of war but, with the development of SLBMs and long-range cruise missiles

[50] Gorshkov, *The Sea Power of the State*, xi.

[51] George H. Quester, "Assessing the Balance of Naval Power," *Jerusalem Journal of International Relations* 2, no. 2 (Winter 1976–1977), 32.

[52] Paul M. Kennedy, *The Rise of the Anglo-German Antagonism 1860–1914* (London: Allen & Unwin, 1980), 457.

"deployed on civilian as well as military carriers," also the United States itself.[53] Furthermore, since this expansion is proceeding in a political atmosphere of recurring American Russophobia, there are enough disturbing similarities to the role that the naval factor played in generating the Anglo-German antagonism for the issue to be considered seriously.[54]

Finally, Khrushchev bequeathed an outlook that assumes developments in the Third World can be exploited to the Soviet Union's advantage in the ongoing rivalry with the United States. Its quintessentially Leninist perspective sees the United States without illusions, as the main threat to Soviet security and ambitions, as an undeniable force with which Moscow must deal on a wide range of issues, but not at the sacrifice of existing positions or prospects. Inherent in this outlook are perceptions, priorities, and policies that presage an indefinite period of tensions. One need only read well-crafted Soviet critiques of U.S. policy in the Third World and its role in aggravating Soviet-American tensions, intended to show how reasonable and much-maligned the Soviet Union is, to appreciate how wide is the gap between Moscow and Washington.

Genrikh Trofimenko, one of the USSR's able and accessible "Americanists," argues that the United States has overreacted to Soviet military activities in the Third World; that it seeks "stabilization," but only on its own terms and in disregard of the natural course of events in developing areas, which desire radical economic and social change and liberation from the neocolonialist exploitation of Western multinational corporations; that it aspires to superiority through military means, including threatening naval deployments; and that it shows no signs of realizing "that elaboration of certain more specific rules of conduct stands little practical chance of success in view of the objective factors leading to revolutionary changes in the Third World, and in light of the conflicting evaluations given to these phenomena by the capitalist and socialist countries, by the United States and the Soviet Union in this particular case."[55]

This assessment by a Soviet "moderate" affords little ground for optimism, given the evident continuity of the Khrushchevian outlook in the early Gorbachevian period.[56]

[53] C. G. Jacobsen, "Soviet Strategy: The Naval Dimension," *Naval War College Review*, 40, no. 2 (Spring 1987), 27.

[54] Kennedy, *Rise of Anglo-German Antagonism*, 416.

[55] Henry Trofimenko, "The Third World and the U.S.-Soviet Competition: A Soviet View," *Foreign Affairs* 59, no. 5 (Summer 1981), 1021–40, 1037.

[56] For example, Ye. Primakov, "Leninskii analiz imperializma u sovremennost" [A Len-

A New Imperial Policy

Over the years since the mid-1950s, the objectives of the Soviet Union in the Third World have been to undermine the ability of the United States to threaten the Soviet Union, to divert U.S. resources and attention away from Europe, and to keep the United States on the defensive, constantly concerned over shifting vulnerable areas and thus unable to mount a stiff or sustained challenge anywhere. Moscow regards the rivalry as protracted in nature; it accepts the inevitability of setbacks, but persists.

The New Imperial Policy (NIP) is the approach adopted by the Kremlin to realize these objectives.[57] The impulses that drive it differ significantly from czarist and pre-1953 Soviet antecedents. Though old Russian imperialist ambitions remain very much alive toward contiguous Turkey, Iran, and Afghanistan, the impetus underlying the Kremlin's activism in the Third World is political, not territorial. Intrusiveness not expansionism epitomizes the strategy; that is to say, there is no reason to believe the Soviet Union's security needs and political ambitions will impel it toward additional territorial acquisitions. Afghanistan has given new impetus to the description of Soviet Union as an expansionist power, and it is probably true that Moscow would not pass up an opportunity to gain control of parts of Iran or Pakistan should they disintegrate and ethnic separatism pave the way for the establishment of "people's republics" under Soviet control. Still, my argument is that present Soviet policy in Afghanistan is not indicative of Kremlin aims elsewhere in the Third World; if anything, the USSR's experience in Afghanistan may bring home to the Kremlin the

---

inist Analysis of Imperialism and the Contemporary Era], *Kommunist*, no. 9 (June 1986), 102–13; N. S. Beglova, "Politika Vashingtona v zona Indiiskogo Okeana" [Washington's Policy in the Indian Ocean Zone], *S.Sh.A.*, no. 3 (March 1986), 39–48.

[57] My term describing Soviet strategy in the Third World differs from Richard Lowenthal's "counterimperialism" in a number of ways: it assumes the primacy of military and strategic considerations, particularly in the context of Moscow's view that the United States is the USSR's primary adversary; it holds that neither the quest for markets nor the quest for raw materials has determined Soviet policy toward any Third World country, even those adjacent to the Soviet Union; it does not see "strengthening the Soviet bloc's economic basis and . . . reducing the West's economic superiority" as a central motive of Soviet strategy; and it does not discern in Soviet policy an effort to establish "a 'stable division of labor' with a group of developing countries, and of an alliance with their raw material producers against the Western imperialist monopolies": the Soviet Union just does not possess the economic clout to attract enough Third World countries to make this credible, though at the time that Lowenthal put forward his thesis there were possible grounds for such a hypothesis. Richard Lowenthal, "Soviet 'Counterimperialism,' " *Problems of Communism* 25, no. 6 (November–December 1976), 52, 57.

exorbitant costs of new conquests and lead it, in the future, to move far more cautiously in comparable circumstances of great geostrategic temptation.

The aim of Moscow's intrusiveness is influence to shape events. It is this overriding strategic objective that lends coherence to all that the Soviet Union has done in the Third World since the mid-1950s.

NIP is a shrewd response and adaptation to a changed international system that is inhospitable to imperialism, meaning the wresting of territory from sovereign entities or independent peoples, the imposition of alien rule on unwilling peoples and their incorporation into a foreign empire. The last instance of such imperialism succeeding in the twentieth century was Moscow's absorption of Latvia, Lithuania, and Estonia in 1940. Since the end of World War II, no nation state, however much it may be dominated by a great power, as Afghanistan has been since 1979, has lost its existence as a sovereign, formally independent, country. Except for the Soviet Union and Ethiopia, empires have gone out of style.

The NIP's search for advantages in distant regions of marginal utility to the security of the Soviet homeland has repeatedly dissipated prospects for a U.S.-Soviet accommodation. By way of illustration, in the summer of 1979 when the SALT (Strategic Arms Limitation Talks) II treaty, which Moscow wanted, was up for consideration by the U.S. Senate, the USSR abruptly dismissed the Carter administration's allegation that the USSR's "brigade" in Cuba violated the 1962 informal Kennedy-Khrushchev understanding about the kinds of forces the Soviet Union could maintain there. It was "obviously puzzled" but "could not believe that the United States, with its sophisticated intelligence, could not have known of the presence of the unit"; nor was it willing to pay "the price demanded—the withdrawal of the unit—" for the ratification of the nuclear arms treaty "in which Brezhnev had invested so much effort."[58] Again, several months later, Moscow's propaganda egged on the Iranians during the incarceration of the fifty-two American diplomatic personnel in the seized embassy compound in Tehran. In both instances, Moscow's rejection of Washington's request

[58] David Newson, who was Under Secretary of State for Political Affairs at the time of the "combat" brigade affair, contributes an insightful assessment that stresses the casual (mis)use of intelligence data, the domestic political motives of key Congressional actors, "the unrealistic expectations of diplomacy," and the reluctance of President Carter "to rein in the expressions of separate views and separate nuances by close members of their circles." *The Soviet Brigade in Cuba* (Bloomington: Indiana University Press, 1987), 51–52, 58–59.

for restraint suggests that Soviet leaders have very different ways of perceiving and reacting to developments.

Much has been written about the effects of Marxism-Leninism on Soviet foreign policy behavior. George Kennan, for example, describes the USSR's pattern of policy as "not foreign to the normal practice of great powers," yet says that one requirement of its policy is "the protection of the image of the Soviet Union as the central bastion of revolutionary socialism throughout the world, and of the Soviet Party leadership as . . . an indispensable source of guidance for Communist and national-liberation forces everywhere. This, obviously, is the ideal, not the complete present-day reality. . . . [but] It is the pretense, if not the reality, and it must, in the eyes of the men in the Kremlin be defended at all costs" or the result would be isolation from the communist, as well as, capitalist, world, and insecurity, because the legitimacy of the regime would be thrown into question.[59] This attempt to reconcile realpolitik and ideology does not advance us far toward understanding actual Soviet policy: the first half leads to underestimation of what is distinctive in post-Stalinist policy toward the Third World, and the second to a millenarian vision of the USSR's aims.

Hopefully, as a working construct, the New Imperial Policy will provide a closer mesh between the nonideological explanations of Soviet actions in the Third World. In its reliance on maneuver, manipulation, and multiple instruments of statecraft to exploit opportunities and pursue the limited accretion of adjacent territory and influence, NIP resembles traditional Russian policy: it is not driven by any crusade to spread communism or support communist parties; no communist ecumenicism impels Soviet diplomacy in the Third World. But NIP also involves actions that go well beyond mere opportunism in quest of advantages for security or wealth—hallmarks of traditional great powers—because it is impelled by a preeminent strategic goal: the derangement of a particular adversary, the United States. NIP is very much crafted for an epoch in which all-out war between nuclear powers is unthinkable. But its long-term perspective enables the Soviet leadership to see NIP as a way of working toward the weakening of the United States in one area of the world, even while trying to work out accommodations with it on advantageous terms in other areas. The operational aspects of NIP embrace the following:

[59] George F. Kennan, *The Cloud of Danger* (Boston: Little, Brown, 1977). See also Harry Gelman, *The Brezhnev Politburo and the Decline of Detente* (Ithaca, N.Y.: Cornell University Press, 1984), 218.

- incrementalism,
- influence-building,
- flexibility,
- subordinacy of ideology,
- limited linkage.

Incrementalism assumes that marginal gains over time can bring about a qualitative change in the "correlation of forces" (*sootnosheniye sil'*), a term the Soviets use instead of the Western concept, balance of power.[60] Whereas, to the Soviets, balance of power connotes assessment of a static, essentially military relationship, correlation of forces requires a more all-encompassing framework of analysis in which political, economic, ideological, and cultural, as well as military, considerations are included; it accords more attention to the changing character and interrelationship of different elements of power and to the psycho-political dimension of strategic assessments.[61] In its expectation that small changes can cause major realignments, incrementalism is consonant with Marxist-Leninist philosophy and methodology.

Influence-building seeks to improve the strategic context within which Soviet diplomacy operates by enabling Third World leaderships to pursue preferred policy options of which the Kremlin does not always approve but which it is nonetheless prepared to support. The premium is on improving the USSR's position in key countries.

Flexibility requires a capacity for adaptation to local conditions and a consistency of purpose that can tolerate setbacks while keeping basic aims clearly in mind.[62] It entails a readiness to enter into agreement

[60] See Raymond L. Garthoff, "The Concept of the Balance of Power in Soviet Policymaking," *World Politics* 4, no. 1 (October 1951), 85–111.

[61] For example Michael J. Deane, "The Soviet Assessment of the 'Correlation of World Forces': Implications for American Foreign Policy," *Orbis* 20, no. 3 (Fall 1976), 625–36; R. Judson Mitchell, *Ideology of a Superpower: Contemporary Soviet Doctrine on International Relations* (Stanford: Hoover Institution Press, 1982), passim.

[62] The distinction, slight as it may be, between flexibility and opportunism is important: the former entails an adaptation within the framework of an overall strategy; the latter, an exploitation of developments without a consistent set of principles in mind. Thus, what Lord Curzon wrote about Russian policy in Central Asia in the late nineteenth century would not be sufficient for an understanding of Soviet policy a century later: "I am not one of those who hold that Russian policy has, either for a century or for half a century, or for a less period, been animated by an unswerving and Machiavellian purpose, the object of which is the overthrow of British rule in India, and to which every forward movement is strictly subordinated. . . . So far from regarding the foreign policy

with any regime. Ideological antipathy is no bar. Moscow is not ham-
strung by moral considerations or by a need for accountability; it has
a basic cynicism about the motives and outlook of those with whom it
deals.

Subordinacy of ideology implies the paramountcy of strategic-military
considerations in decision-making circles. It would be pointless to repeat here the endless and unresolved arguments over importance or
unimportance of Marxism-Leninism in the shaping of Soviet foreign
policy decisions, propositions that are in any event beyond proof. But
my own approach, affecting the analysis developed in subsequent
chapters, requires comment.

I believe that the record of Soviet policy in the Third World demonstrates that practice precedes ideological revision. The "creative"
reinterpretations in the 1960s of the tenets of Marxism-Leninism—
that is, the role of the national bourgeoisie, the national democratic
state, the revolutionary democratic state, the military as a progressive
substratum of the bourgeoisie, and so on—all trailed in the wake of
changed Soviet policies. These new formulations ideologically sanctioned the targets and commitments of Khrushchev's forward policy.
Soviet scholars kept recategorizing regimes, searching for typologies
that could fit into doctrinally devised boxes. But none of this had the
slightest discernible effect on the nature of the bilateral relationship
between the Soviet Union and particular Third World governments
or on the diverse activities of Soviet diplomacy. Khrushchev adapted
to vexing situations as long as the courted regime was anti-American
in orientation (anti-imperialist, in the Soviet parlance). He was concerned with strategic context, with the extension of Soviet influence,
and with the acquisition of privileges. The prospects of local communist parties and congenial ideological outlooks were expendables.

It is difficult to take seriously the professions of ideological affinity
that are the staples of meetings and diplomatic exchanges between Soviet and Third World leaders. The Russians in the Kremlin are intensely suspicious, treating even East European communists with
whom they share longstanding political beliefs and experience in the
world communist movement with reserve, often distrust. A deep-
rooted Russian paranoia toward the non-Russian world can make
Moscow an inhospitable environment even to the party faithful. If this

of Russia as consistent, or remorseless, or profound, I believe it to be a hand-to-mouth
policy, a policy of waiting upon events, of profiting by the blunders of others as often of
committing like herself." The Hon. George N. Curzon, *Russia in Central Asia in 1889 and
the Anglo-Russian Question* (London: Longmans, Green, 1889), 314–15.

is the case—and we have an extensive émigré and defector literature on the subject—then how much less confidence must the Kremlin have in self-proclaimed "progressives" and "communists" in Africa, the Middle East, and Latin America. Third World elites learn quickly that friendly relations is not the same thing as friendship.

Whatever legitimizing function ideology plays within the Soviet communist hierarchy and whatever its usefulness as a medium for communication and conflict within the world communist movement, it is not central to Soviet policy formulation toward the Third World, in which context it is more a figleaf of Western imagination than a determinant of Soviet decision-making.

Limited linkage refers specifically to Moscow's rejection of U.S. efforts to predicate an improvement in Soviet-American relations on changes in Soviet policy in the Third World. In 1972–1973, the Nixon-Kissinger strategy of détente sought to entice Moscow into "a web of economic ties that would deepen the USSR's material stake in continued détente with the United States. The price for such continuation would be ever-greater Soviet restraint" in the Third World.[63] Moscow quickly rejected this concept of cooperation, insisting that agreements within a particular policy realm might be coupled, but that agreement in one realm should not depend on progress in a totally different one. The attempt to link "different situations in order to pressure the Soviet Union," wrote an important scholar and spokesman, "virtually blocks any solution of major problems."[64] Another scholar blamed U.S. insistence on linkage for the end of détente:

Under the influence of a propaganda campaign unleashed by Washington itself, the government of the United States considered it possible to introduce into the process of the entire spectrum of international problems in Soviet-American negotiations the method of "linkage" of questions on the limitation of strategic

[63] George W. Breslauer, "Why Detente Failed: An Interpretation," in Alexander L. George, ed., *Managing U.S.-Soviet Rivalry: Problems of Crisis Prevention* (Boulder, Colo.: Westview, 1983), 326.

[64] Evgeni [Yevgeny] M. Primakov, "The USSR and the Developing Countries," *Journal of International Affairs* 34, no. 2 (Fall 1980–Winter 1981), 272. Moscow's own readiness to utilize linkage was displayed in March 1985 when diplomatic talks led to resumption of arms-control negotiations, which had been broken off by the Soviet Union in November 1983 in the wake of the U.S. deployment of Pershing-II and cruise missiles in Western Europe. Foreign Minister Andrei Gromyko said, "the question of either strategic weapons or intermediate-range nuclear weapons cannot be examined without the question of space, or to be more precise, without the question of preventing the arms race in space." *New York Times*, January 14, 1985, 5.

offensive arms with perfectly groundless and far-fetched demands that the USSR terminate assistance to national-liberation
movements, that it "not intervene" in the affairs of independent
countries. The American side arbitrarily "linked" progress in SALT
negotiations with the situation in Angola, Ethiopia, Indochina
and sought unlimited freedom of action for itself and its partners
to smother the national-liberation movement. This "method" of
American diplomacy significantly complicated negotiations between the USSR and the USA on SALT. . . .[65]

In NIP, the Soviet leaders have inherited from Khrushchev an approach and a policy that has a keen appreciation of regional opportunities and constraints and has proved its fitness for the continuation
of an imperial tradition. What began in tentative fashion in the weeks
and months after Stalin's death has matured and taken on policy dimensions that were unthinkable at the time.

[65] V. A. Kremenyuk, *S.Sh.A.: Bor'ba protiv natsional'no-osvoboditel'-nogo dvizheniya* [USA:
The Struggle against the National Liberation Movement] (Moscow: Mysl, 1983), 56. See
also V. A. Kremenyuk, V. P. Lukin, and V. S. Rudnev, *S.Sh.A. i razvivayuschiesya strany 70-
gody* [The USA and the Developing Countries in the 1970s] (Moscow: Nauka, 1981), 66.

CHAPTER TWO

Involvement

At the time of Stalin's death, the Soviet Union's foreign policy, like its economy, was in need of extensive overhaul, and Soviet leaders embarked on a course of sweeping changes at home and abroad. Eastern Europe was militarily and politically secure as a result of the transformation of the socio-political structures wrought by Stalinization and Sovietization; but, despite its exploitation economically, it was on the threshold of becoming more a liability than an asset. The interests of imperial consolidation required a new relationship that would foster cooperation among the countries of the bloc—a relationship and a process Khrushchev was to term a "socialist division of labor." In the Far East, the negotiations that had dragged on through 1951 and 1952 had to be concluded and the fighting on the Korean peninsula ended. For Moscow, the adventure that Kim Il-Sung had persuaded Stalin to support had borne little fruit;[1] instead it had accelerated NATO's military buildup and a return of U.S. military power to the Pacific for the first time since the end of World War II. The relationship with Mao Tse-tung's People's Republic of China (PRC) seemed stable: Stalin had learned from his experience with Tito that independent communist leaderships would resist any efforts to subvert their national prerogative, and the newly established PRC recognized its vulnerability to U.S. power and need of Soviet support. But continued fighting in Korea was not in the USSR's long-term interest, especially since China's influence in North Korea had, with the dispatch of "volunteers" to fight the Americans, grown at Moscow's expense.

Relations with the United States could hardly have been worse. Tensions existed in every sector and their net effect was to spark an American remilitarization that threatened Soviet security and raised the costs of controlling Eastern Europe.

Looking at the Third World, the Kremlin viewed with concern the extension of containment—the effort of the United States to enlist the nations located to the south of the Soviet Union in a network of military pacts that would enable nuclear-armed U.S. long-range bombers

---

[1] Edward Crankshaw, commentary to *Khrushchev Remembers*, trans. and ed. Strobe Talbott (New York: Bantam, 1970), 400–2.

to refuel en route to targets in the southern and central parts of the country. Stalin's alienation and neglect of the neighboring nations of the Middle East and South Asia had played into the hands of the West. The application of a strategy originally intended to isolate Eastern Europe from Western Europe (the so-called Zhdanov line that divided the world into two camps and was formulated by the Cominform at its founding session in September 1947) had in the process isolated the Soviet Union from the Third World.

The political environment in the Third World was conducive to a reversal of Soviet policy. Decolonization gave birth to new nations, jealous of their independence, averse to alignment with either the U.S. or the Soviet bloc, and eager to modernize, to find their own path toward a vaguely defined kind of socialism. Their elites made the transition from revolutionaries to rulers quickly, pragmatically distinguishing between two very different kinds of threat: that posed by Soviet power and that posed by local communists. They showed considerable acumen in accommodating to the former and in coping with the latter, and in exploiting both in their relations with the West. Though newcomers to power, they grasped the fundamentals of how to strengthen security and foster foreign policy goals; and, to the surprise of their former rulers, whose patronizing attitudes persisted well into the post-colonial period, they needed no guidance in adapting to regional variants of the classical balance-of-power game.

Moscow recognized the differentiation in the Third World sooner than Washington. The Korean War had matured its perspective. During the 1951–1953 period, Soviet officials in the United Nations came to realize the fallacy in uncritically treating all the newly independent former colonial countries as part of the "capitalist camp." For example, the role played by Indian and Burmese diplomats in the behind-the-scenes discussions that eventually led to negotiations for ending the Korean conflict demonstrated the potential usefulness of former colonies who had important political differences with their former rulers.

1953 was a key year. Whereas in Moscow a change in leadership brought with it a readiness to explore new approaches to a changing Third World, in Washington, by contrast, the election of Dwight D. Eisenhower ushered in an administration determined to globalize containment and to foist it on countries who neither felt threatened by Soviet attack nor saw anything emanating from the Soviet Union that necessitated alliance with the West. The driving force behind this policy was Secretary of State John Foster Dulles, who sorely misread the mood in the new nations. By uncritically extending to the Third

World a strategy designed for Europe and the Far East, he was guilty, much like Stalin, of a rigid and parochial application of a policy perfectly good for one place to an environment for which it was ill-suited. His "success" in creating military pacts in the Middle East and South Asia proved a boon to Moscow: it did more to assure an eager welcome for Soviet wares and accelerate the decline of Western influence in these regions than any other single development of the period. Khrushchev could not have accomplished as much so quickly in the mid-1950s without the inadvertent assistance of Dulles.

INITIATIVES

The first objective of the Kremlin's new policy was to improve diplomatic relations with the countries situated along its southern border: Turkey, Iran, and Afghanistan. By far the biggest problem was with Turkey, which had joined NATO in 1952 out of fear that Moscow might at any time renew its pressure for concessions regarding the Straits. The Soviet Note of May 30, 1953, sought to undo the harm done by Stalin, to reestablish the good diplomatic relationship that had prevailed in the 1920s, and to negotiate outstanding differences. It openly declared that the Soviet Union did not have "any kind of territorial claims on Turkey," and was a rare instance of public acknowledgment by the Kremlin that a previous policy had been a mistake. This apology gratified the Turks but hardly ended their deep-rooted suspicions of Muscovite ambitions. Nonetheless Moscow persisted, changing its ambassador, offering credits and expanded trade, and settling a lingering dispute over Turkey's share of the cost and benefits of the Serdarabat Dam, situated on the frontier in northeastern Turkey, and the use of the Arak River waters. Not until 1963, however, did Turkey respond to Soviet blandishments, and then primarily in reaction to strains in the U.S.-Turkish relationship arising out of signs of a U.S.-Soviet détente.

Iran, too, reacted with caution to Soviet overtures. Moscow offered trade, but settled for some minor agreements on old border and financial questions. Relations were slow to normalize, hampered by a combination of the Shah's residual suspicions of the Soviet Union and Moscow's unhappiness at Iran's accession to the Baghdad Pact in October 1955. However, the national interests of both countries militated for improvement, and in June 1956 the Shah visited Moscow, where he was received with pomp and ceremony.

Afghanistan, a target of Russian imperial ambitions, had kept distant from the Soviets all through the 1930s and 1940s. This policy was

reversed by Prime Minister Mohammed Daoud Khan, who wanted Soviet weapons to build up the army as an effective match for Pakistan
and hoped to enlist Soviet support on the Paktoon issue—his attempt
to detach the Pashto-speaking areas of Pakistan's North West Frontier
Province and incorporate them into an enlarged Afghanistan. Moscow
was happy to oblige. (A generation later, Daoud's irredentist ambitions
turned out to have undermined the monarchy and set the stage for
the end of Afghanistan's independence.)

The USSR's foreign economic assistance program made its debut in
Afghanistan: on January 27, 1954, Kabul and Moscow signed an
agreement arranging for the construction of two large grain elevators,
a bread-baking plant, and a flour mill, and a Soviet credit for $3.5
million. Very quickly, there followed a succession of Soviet assistance
for a variety of projects, including an irrigation and hydroelectric system, development of the port of Quizil Qala on the Oxus, oil storage
tanks, a technological institute in Kabul, and extensive road-building
and modernization of airports (both of which proved very useful to
the Soviet Union when it invaded the country in December 1979). By
the end of the decade Afghanistan was one of the Soviet Union's major recipients of economic credits, a close third behind India and
Egypt.

That Moscow was looking beyond its southern-tier neighbors to
other Third World countries as well was evident from the reversal of
its previous stand to oppose all U.N. programs for helping less-developed countries (LDCs) on the grounds that they were dominated by
Western nations and designed to perpetuate Western investments. By
participating in U.N.-sponsored aid programs and demonstrating the
professionalism of Soviet technicians, Moscow hoped to publicize the
benefits of Soviet aid and convince the LDCs that Soviet aid would not
be used to subvert existing governments or promote communist activities within the recipient countries. Never important to the Soviet
Union as a conduit for Soviet economic and technical assistance, the
United Nations and its Specialized Agencies were used to dispel suspicion of the USSR and lend respectability to its bilateral aid programs.

The second—and far more momentous—step was the exploitation
of regional conflicts. The aims were not only diplomatic normalization
and establishment of a presence but also tangible advantages in areas
hitherto outside Moscow's purview. The policy bore Khrushchev's imprint. Audacious and provocative, it was a gauntlet flung into the
American camp. Over the years, the policy was extended, refined, and

reinforced; none of Khrushchev's successors ever reversed or significantly modified it or the rationale on which it is predicated.

Khrushchev sought clients in the regional conflicts that broke out in the Middle East and Southern Asia in the wake of decolonization and Dulles's pactomania. Inevitably, he looked to India and Egypt—the two regional powers most adversely and directly affected by the U.S.-inspired alliance systems, the Baghdad Pact (renamed the Central Treaty Organization, CENTO, in 1959) and the Southeast Asia Treaty Organization (SEATO). That these two countries were also the most prominent powers in their respective regions greatly enhanced their attractiveness to Khrushchev and encouraged him to venture far beyond the USSR's immediate security sphere.

Russia's interest in India dates from its nineteenth-century rivalry with Britain in the Near East and Afghanistan. In 1920, as part of his strategy of intensifying pressure against British imperialism and thereby diverting attention away from the new Bolshevik state, Lenin helped establish the Communist Party of India (CPI) with membership in the Communist International (Comintern). However, in the 1930s Stalin, eager for closer diplomatic cooperation with the colonialist powers against Germany and Japan, ordered the Comintern to proceed more circumspectly in the colonies. One consequence was the CPI's loss of political ground when, in World War II, it sided with the British against the Congress Party of Gandhi and Nehru, who agitated for immediate independence; and when, in 1948, it turned to armed rebellion against the newly independent government of India. This brought about the alienation of the CPI from the nationalist movement and severely damaged the prestige of the Soviet Union. In the early 1950s, Moscow made a few, fleeting gestures of reconciliation. For example, in January 1952 a Soviet official at the International Industries Fair in Bombay talked of an exchange of Soviet manufactures for Indian raw materials, but nothing came of the overture, which was not followed up by Moscow.

Although a new Soviet ambassador in September 1953 signalled Moscow's desire for improved Soviet-Indian relations and a five-year trade agreement was signed in December, it was U.S. policy that triggered New Delhi's volte-face toward Moscow and gave the Soviets their golden opportunity to influence developments in the subcontinent. Washington's decision in early 1954 to provide military assistance to Pakistan—India's arch-enemy—and make Pakistan a member of SEATO, a hastily contrived smorgasbord of countries (the United States, Great Britain, France, Australia, New Zealand, Thailand, the Philippines, and Pakistan) seeking in some undefined way to preserve the status quo of South Vietnam and counter China, infuriated Prime Minister Nehru and pushed him along the road to nonalignment. More important, it made him receptive to Soviet offers of aid, not only for economic reasons but also as an opening move calculated to give him increased leverage in dealing with and maneuvering between the two superpowers.

On February 2, 1955, after months of discussions and surveys, the two governments signed an agreement calling for the construction in the public sector of a giant steel complex in the Bhilai region of central India. With a projected capacity of one million tons of steel ingots and 750,000 tons of rolled products, the Bhilai plant was designed to provide about 20 percent of India's steel capacity by 1961. Even more significantly, it heralded the beginning of the USSR's extensive involvement in India's economic (and in time military) development. In June 1955 Nehru visited the Soviet Union; and in November–December Khrushchev and his premier, Nikolai Bulganin, went to India, thus ending a productive year of what was to prove over the following decades the most enduring and stable of the Soviet Union's relationships with a Third World country.

Soviet scholars took their cue from Soviet leaders and revised their previous interpretations of Indian history and politics. The first major revision appeared in a book review (an important outlet and testing ground for sophisticated assessments of current developments) of the Russian translation of Nehru's *Discovery of India*, which was published in the June 1955 issue of *Kommunist*, the cpsu's authoritative organ, to coincide with Nehru's visit to the Soviet Union. A. M. Diakov and V. Balabushevich, the doyens of Soviet Indology, acknowledged the failure of Soviet scholars to appreciate the importance of Gandhi's role in the national liberation struggle of India against Britain.[2] Thus, whereas in 1949 Diakov had denounced the Indian Government as "the main agent of Anglo-American imperialism in Southeast Asia," in his 1955 book review he lauded India's fight for peace, citing as evi-

---

[2] This analysis was elaborated in two important articles: A. M. Diakov and I. M. Reisner, "Rol Gandi v natsionalno-osvoboditel'-noi borbe narodov Indii" [The Role of Gandhi in the National Liberation Struggle of the Peoples of India], *Sovetskoe vostokovedenie*, no. 5 (1956), 21–34; and A. Guber, "Letter to the Editor," *International Affairs*, no. 3 (March 1956). However, in some party circles there was continued resistance to reinterpreting Gandhi's role. For example, Gandhi was not discussed in the first volume of the revised second edition (1960) of *Diplomaticheskii slovar'*, an encyclopedia setting out the official party position on key issues and personalities of contemporary history and international relations; and Yu. P. Nasenko, *Respublika Indiia* [The Republic of India] (1960), ignored Gandhi in his discussion of Indian political development in 1946 and 1947 and stressed Nehru's role.

dence India's opposition to the Korean War and efforts to end the war in Vietnam, its support for the PRC's application for admission to the United Nations, and its policy of strengthening ties with the Soviet Union. By setting in motion the Soviet Union's discovery of India, Khrushchev transformed the international politics of South Asia.

For the Soviet Union, this friendship meant a link with the region's leading unaligned country and a safeguard against its joining a Western military alliance. India also offered a huge showcase for Soviet aid—a demonstration to others of the benefits to be derived from a Soviet connection; it brought the Soviet Union respectability at a crucial phase of Moscow's courtship of Afro-Asian nations; and it served as a studied contrast to the bipolar view of the world then dominant in Washington.

In 1955 Khrushchev made an even more dramatic breakthrough— the arms deal with Egypt; in time, this would profoundly affect U.S.-Soviet relations. The Soviet move into the mainstream of Arab-world politics took less than a year to effect. In 1954 the Soviet delegate on the U.N. Security Council had vetoed a Western resolution calling for free navigation through the Suez Canal for all nations, reversing Moscow's previous aloofness on the issue and throwing support behind Egypt in its conflict with Israel. Moscow also backed Syria's position in U.N. discussions of Israel's plans to divert water from the Jordan River for irrigation purposes. On April 16, 1955, the USSR Ministry of Foreign Affairs issued a major policy statement. After months of criticizing Iraq for aiding Western designs on the Arab world, the Ministry denounced the Baghdad Pact (of which Iraq was the only Arab member) and offered to cooperate with countries opposed to Western intrusions in the area, stating that the USSR "cannot be indifferent to the situation which is developing in the area of the Near and Middle East, because it is directly connected with the security of the Soviet Union, situated, in contrast to certain other powers, in the immediate vicinity of this area." At the Bandung Conference of Afro-Asian nations, which was held in Indonesia later in the month, Nasser raised with China's Premier Zhou En-lai the question of purchasing arms from the Soviet bloc, and a month later the Soviet ambassador in Cairo, Daniel Solod, began discussions with Nasser. An agreement was concluded in August, and on September 27, at a photography exhibition in Cairo, Nasser made his first public reference to purchase of Czech arms.

By providing arms to regional actors opposed to Western policy (another, much smaller sale of Soviet weapons to Syria in late 1954 often gets overlooked because of the understandable attention paid the arms deal with Egypt), Moscow established the basis for a permanent presence in the Arab world. When it vaulted over the ragtag network of U.S.-cajoled alliances in the Middle East, taking advantage of existing regional rivalries to align itself with countries opposed to U.S. policy and interests, its policy was determined by realpolitik. It was Moscow not Washington that seemed in accord with the anticolonial and anti-imperialist sentiments sweeping the Arab world.

Nor did Khrushchev neglect the lesser actors—Burma, Cambodia, Indonesia, Yemen, Sudan, Argentina. Like a seasoned gambler he wagered on all kinds of possibilities, his aim being a Soviet presence wherever he could establish one. The rapidity and scope of his activities were impressive. By the time of the twentieth congress of the CPSU, in February 1956, most of the instruments of Soviet diplomacy that we see in the Third World today had been introduced: economic aid, expanded trade, technical assistance, military aid, high-level political-military exchange visits, diplomatic support on a bilateral basis and in international forums, and cultural exchanges. Only two weapons remained to be added to this armory: direct Soviet military intervention on behalf of endangered clients and the use of surrogates.

The USSR had the advantages of being a new major power on the Third World scene. It came with "clean hands," unburdened by a colonialist past in the Arab world, Southern Asia, Africa, and Latin America; its imperialist record toward Turkey, Iran, and Afghanistan was ignored or deemed irrelevant by most LDCs. As is often the case in diplomacy, timing was all-important: the Soviet Union arrived at the right moment. Its offers of assistance enabled nationalist leaderships to explore alternatives to reliance on the West; its commitment to "socialism" accorded nicely with the generally positive attitude toward "socialism" held by most of the founding fathers of the newly independent bourgeois-nationalist regimes; and its immediate aims did not conflict with those of the prospective recipients of its aid.

By the early 1960s the Soviet Union had established aid relationships with twenty-five Third World countries. More than $4 billion of the approximately $6 billion in credits was allocated for economic assistance and the rest for military purchases. Its foreign assistance program got off to a fast start. A concatenation of circumstances contributed to the auspicious beginning: the difficulties encountered by the LDCs in obtaining large-scale credits from the West for public-sector projects or arms purchases; the LDCs' disenchantment with the limited funds for development available from U.N. organizations; the readiness of the USSR to accept proposals with minimal preconditions or examination; the USSR's favorable terms of repayment; and the LDCs' desire to avoid heavy dependence on the West. The Third World countries very quickly sensed the extent to which acceptance of Soviet credits improved their bargaining position with the West. They were now courted competitively by powerful political antagonists, both of whom initially held exaggerated expectations of what could be achieved with aid packages. Whenever possible, developing countries took assistance from both East and West, using help from one as a lever to pry more from the other.

When Khrushchev was deposed in October 1964 the Kremlin could look back on a decade of accomplishment in the Third World: better relations than ever before with all-important tier countries (Turkey, Iran, and Afghanistan), including their recognition that economic assistance and political normalization depended on prohibiting the implacement of U.S. missiles on their territory; diplomatic ties with all nonaligned countries; insinuation of a presence in the regional politics of key areas; expanded economic ties; high-visibility development projects in countries such as India, Egypt, and Afghanistan, which stimulated the interest of other countries; deference of the LDCs to Soviet policy positions on issues, such as disarmament, European security, and Eastern Europe, that were not of central concern to them; and a narrowing of U.S. options. An impressive list for so short a period and so limited an involvement.

PATTERNS: FROM KHRUSHCHEV TO GORBACHEV

Reassessments of Soviet economic involvement in the Third World began to appear often in Soviet journals soon after Khrushchev was overthrown.[3] Marked by a growing sophistication, they grappled with a number of interrelated, knotty issues, such as the difficulties involved in the transition to socialism; the complexities subsumed under the ideological rubric of "the noncapitalist path of development"; the need to temper optimism about "progressive" trends; and the continual underestimation of "the political backwardness of the bulk of the peasantry," the tenacity of feudal influence in the countryside, the use of "religious superstitions and anti-communist falsifications" to spread distrust between the urban proletariat and the peasantry, the preva-

[3] A number of Western scholars have traced the emergence and evolution of this direction in Soviet scholarship. See L. Sirc, "Changes in Communist Advice to Developing Countries," *The World Today* 22, no. 8 (August 1966), 326–35; Roger E. Kanet, "The Recent Soviet Reassessment of Developments in the Third World," *Russian Review* 27, no. 1 (January 1968), 27–41; and Elizabeth Kridl Valkenier, "New Trends in Soviet Economic Relations with the Third World," *World Politics* 22, no. 3 (April 1970), 415–32.

lence of clashes among different social groups with a consequent re-inforcement of social backwardness and political divisiveness, and "the growing complexity of the problem of Afro-Asian nationalism," which "continues to combine within itself, frequently in highly whimsical forms, progressive and reactionary aspects," with the latter often pre-dominating.[4]

Some analyses suggested that political considerations had been given too much weight, to the neglect of economic factors, and that an LDC's "progressive" political orientation was no suitable indicator of its "ability either to absorb aid effectively or even to prevent a general decline in its economy; and that, unless economic factors were taken into account together with political ones, Soviet aid would tend to be misdirected, so that its ineffectiveness would minimize both its poten-tial economic benefit to the recipient country and the political credit gained by the USSR in originally offering its assistance."[5] There was growing recognition that Soviet aid could supplement and stimulate economic development, but not substitute for Western capital and markets, and that therefore anti-imperialism could not be carried to the extreme of severing connections between the Third World and the West, because, as A. A. Lavrishchev conceded, "for the developing countries in general the developed capitalist countries still remain their main partner in foreign trade and principal source of credits and industrial equipment."[6] Others cautioned against the pitfalls of exces-sive nationalization and expansion of the state sector and suggested that Third World countries needed to moderate rather than intensify radical land reform, to accept a slower rate of industrialization, and to encourage small businesses in the private sector.[7]

Implicit in these and related reappraisals was the realization that Soviet resources were limited and that the USSR could not assume the principal burden for the development of Third World clients, even favored, ideologically promising regimes. By the end of the Khru-shchev period, there was greater Soviet appreciation of the enormity and long-term character of the barriers to the socio-economic trans-formation of states committed to the noncapitalist path of develop-

[4] K. N. Brutents, *National Liberation Revolutions Today*, vol. 1 (Moscow: Progress Publish-ers, 1977), 224, 226, 252, 273.

[5] R. A. Yellon, "Shifts in Soviet Policy towards Developing Areas 1964–1968," in W. Raymond Duncan, ed., *Soviet Policy in Developing Countries* (Waltham, Mass.: Ginn-Blaisdell, 1970), 242.

[6] Quoted in David Morison, "USSR and Third World II: Questions of Foreign Policy," *Mizan* 12, no. 2 (November 1970), 70.

[7] Valkenier, "New Trends," 426–31.

ment and of the complexities and "contradictions" inherent in undue efforts to force the pace of modernization. Moreover, there were Soviet officials whose concern over the lagging domestic economic growth and problems at home and in the Comecon community apparently led them to question the wisdom of allocating scarce resources to Third World countries.[8] The result of these signs of Soviet discontent with the state of economic involvement in the Third World was a heightened expectation in Western circles of inevitable Soviet retrenchment and concentration on internal problems.

In regarding these Soviet writings as "evidence" that Moscow intended to rationalize its economic assistance and cut back on its general involvement in the Third World, the U.S. administration's assessments in the mid-1960s seriously misjudged the Kremlin's determination to preserve the stake it had acquired. In 1966, President Lyndon Johnson's hope for Soviet restraint was confounded when Moscow stepped up its military and economic assistance to North Vietnam.[9] A year later the June War was another stunner. Many top U.S. officials were surprised by Moscow's decision to resupply the defeated Egyptian and Syrian armies and undertake their reconstitution as effective fighting forces; they had assumed that the Soviet Union "was finished in the Middle East," that it would not pour in enormous amounts of new resources to bail out its Arab clients, and that it would opt for démarches, not direct military involvement, and seek to dampen regional tensions, if only to strengthen its policy of détente in Europe and quest for Western technology and credits.

The basic flaw in this line of approach has manifested itself again and again—in 1973 (the Arab-Israeli War), in 1975 (Angola), in 1977 (Ethiopia), in the 1980s (Nicaragua). It stems from the tenaciously held belief that policy intentions can be gleaned from Soviet writings and the uncritical alacrity with which Soviet writings are marshaled as "evidence" to advance a preferred policy assessment. Over the years this has resulted in a number of deceptively gratifying notions: that the growing "realism" of Soviet academic writings on the Third World indicates the Kremlin's greater readiness to be more accommodating in areas where its aims clash with Washington's; that the inability or unwillingness to subsidize inefficient LDCs will bring a levelling-off of

---

[8] Milton Kovner, "Trade and Aid," *Survey*, no. 43 (August 1962), 48–50.

[9] Reporting at the time from Washington, D.C., Max Frankel wrote, "there remains great hope here that Moscow will help to end the conflict. Some officials contend that Moscow could have imposed a more moderate line on Hanoi if it had wanted to do so. Others argue that Soviet influence is still too feeble to expect quick results." *New York Times*, January 14, 1966.

Soviet economic assistance; that Moscow is disappointed with its gains and is looking to curtail its commitments; and so on. None of these suppositions has proved to be correct, yet they have been embedded in U.S. assessments. Washington continues to impute to Moscow the same disillusionment that it feels over its own meager political returns from economic assistance and to hope that Moscow's involvement in the Third World will diminish owing to the disruptive effect of developments there on what are regarded as the really vital areas of policy, such as arms control, European security, and trade.

One instance of wishful thinking occurred in the Levant in the summer of 1982. Moscow's initial reaction to Israel's invasion of Lebanon in June 1982 and its run of military victories over the Palestine Liberation Organization (PLO) in southern Lebanon and the Syrian Air Force in the Bekaa Valley in the eastern part of the country was an unusual restraint, followed by a relatively tame arraignment of "Israel's blatant brigandage." Many U.S. officials deduced from this that the infirm and aging Brezhnev leadership was experiencing a crisis over what to do or, indeed, whether to do anything. They failed to credit the Kremlin with keeping its perspective and priorities clear, despite its long record of doing so. As Syria, Moscow's main client in the Arab world, was in no immediate danger, the Soviet leadership proceeded with unhurried calculation. Its delayed and low-key response did not signify any wavering in commitment to the Assad regime or basic reappraisal of the centrality of the Syrian connection in its Arab world policy. Given the steady arms flow that started soon after the fighting began—first replenishment, then a vastly expanded buildup—it is not easy to understand why Western analysts were discerning crisis (or passivity, for that matter) in Soviet policy. Even such a consistently perceptive observer of Soviet foreign policy as William Hyland thought Brezhnev's "passivity" remarkable and as possibly portending a "fundamental change" in policy.[10] But there was neither passivity nor change, only consistency. Within a little more than a year, the Soviet Union "provided some $2.5 billion worth of equipment, roughly double what had been lost during the 1982 war, and including advanced fighter aircraft and tanks in numbers exceeding what had been destroyed by the Israelis. It also provided Syria with sophisticated surface-to-air missiles [SAM-5s]"; and thousands of Soviet personnel to man air defense installations and train Syria's army.[11]

[10] William G. Hyland, "What's the Soviets' Role in the Mideast?" *Washington Post*, October 3, 1982.

[11] Larry L. Fabian, "The Middle East: War Dangers and Receding Peace Prospects,"

Because the late 1980s show signs of misassessments like those in the past, close attention should be paid to the exact nature of Soviet policy in the Third World and to the changes that have occurred since the 1960s. Twenty years later the tableau is much the same: Soviet "debates" on the Third World and serious problems at home are seen by many in the West as likely to bring significantly lower levels of Soviet support for Third World countries.[12] Soviet commentaries convey some of the frustrations and disappointments of operating in developing countries and lament that economic ties are as narrow and tenuous as ever. That "the new types of relations form yet a very small part of the overall pattern of economic dealings with the developing countries" is as true now as when it was said by one Western scholar in 1970; and today little remains of the expectations then entertained of the USSR's "willingness and ability to extend long-term aid, to correlate aid with trade, to intermesh planning, as well as to import manufactured goods, respond to the needs of new nations for long-range program aid on a continuing basis and for expanded markets for their new industries," none of which has come to pass.[13] Yet, notwithstanding these shortcomings, when Mikhail Gorbachev became General-Secretary of the CPSU in March 1985 Moscow's programs were more extensive than ever before and far more costly; however, the amount for development was less, the terms were tougher, and the purposes were tied more tightly to political-strategic goals.

For evidence of the degree and nature of the involvement we turn, not to Soviet writings, but to the USSR's reactions to regional developments and its relationships with specific countries. The Third World elites themselves are for the most part uninterested in, even ignorant of, Soviet writings on their problems. Few of their scholars study the Soviet Union, and their officials who deal with the Soviets are absorbed with the concrete issues and programs that shape the bilateral relationship and do not concern themselves with Soviet attempts to conceptualize and classify Third World developments.

The pattern of the USSR's involvement in the Third World since the mid-1960s reveals a deepening commitment, in which a number of features can be recognized. First, contrary to Western expectations, economic assistance has continued to grow, albeit slowly. Soviet eco-

---

Foreign Affairs: America and the World 1983, special issue of *Journal of Foreign Affairs*, 1983, 634–35.

[12] See Elizabeth Kridl Valkenier, *The Soviet Union and the Third World: An Economic Bind* (New York: Praeger, 1983); and Jerry Hough, *The Struggle for the Third World: Soviet Debates and American Options* (Washington, D.C.: Brookings Institution, 1986).

[13] Valkenier, "New Trends," 431–32.

nomic commitments—the total of subsidies provided and credits offered—remain an integral part of the USSR's overall Third World
policy. Whereas during the Khrushchev period (1954–1964) the
USSR offered about $3.4 billion in economic assistance, in the follow-
ing decade the totals more than tripled to about $11 billion: "Erratic
year to year patterns have not affected the distinctly upward movement of commitments."[14] Actual Soviet economic outlays rose
throughout the 1970s, and by 1984 they approximated $7 to $9 billion
annually, of which about $4 billion went to Cuba in the form of var-
ious subsidies, about $1 billion to Vietnam, and a somewhat lesser
amount to sustain the puppet regime in Afghanistan. In 1984 almost
seventy LDCs received some kind of Soviet economic assistance, though
the bulk went to the favored few: Cuba, Vietnam, Afghanistan, Turkey, India, Ethiopia.[15]

Viewed either as a percentage of the USSR's gross national product
(GNP) or in comparison with the West's transfers, Soviet economic assistance to LDCs is not impressive. According to one study, the Organization of Economic Cooperation and Development (OECD) calculates
that the Soviet Union's aid "shows a 0.15 ratio to GNP, equal to that of
the lowest performing OECD member."[16] Not so, argues Moscow, dis-

[14] Orah Cooper, "Soviet Economic Aid to the Third World," in *Soviet Economy in a New Perspective: A Compendium of Papers*, U.S. Congress, Joint Economic Committee, 94th Congress, 2d session (Washington, D.C.: U.S. Government Printing Office, 1976), 190. As with all statistics dealing with Soviet assistance, the figures do not make much sense unless some estimate of "real value" is calculated—for example, deflating by the world trade price index. I am grateful to Fred Pryor for this observation.

[15] The information on Soviet economic commitments and credits is drawn from a number of sources: the periodic reports on "Communist States and Developing Countries: Aid and Trade" that were issued by the Bureau of Intelligence and Research of the Department of State until the early 1980s; occasional papers made available by the CIA; publications of the Congressional Research Service of the Library of Congress; reports of Congressional committees; the Organization of Economic Cooperation and Development (OECD), Paris; and the Foreign and Commonwealth Office, London.

Apart from barter agreements, Soviet economic relations with developing countries generally fall into four main categories: concessional disbursements for communist clients ("which had a net value of $7.6 billion in 1985, and were mostly directed to Cuba, Vietnam, and Mongolia"); arms for communist clients; arms sales to noncommunist regimes ("at least one third in convertible currency . . . which included sales worth about $3 billion in 1985 to Iraq, Syria, and Libya"); and comparatively small amounts of economic assistance to noncommunist countries. "The global pattern of Soviet economic activities in the Third World is unlikely to alter in the short term, with the communist developing countries continuing to absorb the vast majority of concessional disbursements, and the noncommunist developing countries remaining the main recipients of Soviet arms." Emilio Gasparini, "East-South Economic Relations: Growing Burden of Communist Client States," *NATO Review* 35, no. 4 (August 1987), 25.

[16] Iqbal Haji, "Finance, Money, Developing Countries and UNCTAD," in Michael Zammit

puting such assessments and comparisons: at a 1982 conference of the U.N. Industrial Development Organization (UNIDO), the Soviet representative insisted that the USSR's Official Development Assistance (ODA) ratio (the amount of concessional flows or "aid" as a percentage of GNP) was 1.3 percent for the 1976–1980 period, far surpassing that of the highest performing Western country. One British scholar's attempt to reconcile Soviet claims with available Soviet and other information resulted in the calculation that the net cost of Soviet economic aid for that period might have amounted "to 0.29 percent of Soviet GNP," which is somewhat higher than the OECD's figures, but far less than Moscow asserts.[17] Other Western scholars also have difficulty, in the absence of detailed data, in taking the Soviet claims seriously.[18]

But comparative percentages are somewhat beside the point. What is noteworthy is the continued, modest but steady increase in absolute terms of Soviet economic assistance to communist and Marxist regimes and in some cases, noncommunist ones as well (India, Algeria, Argentina, among others). While the small group of Marxist-Leninist regimes receives a disproportionately large amount of the assistance, throughout the 1970s and into the early 1980s, "the scale of Soviet economic aid to the non-communist LDCs" also grew, "although at a reduced pace in recent years, especially when deflated for price change."[19] Soviet writings certainly convey the impression that economically the USSR remains active in the Third World.[20] And at the

---

Cutajar, ed., *UNCTAD and the South-North Dialogue: The First Twenty Years* (Oxford: Pergamon Press, 1985), 152–53.

Among the statistical estimates of the economic costs of Soviet support for the eleven Marxist-Leninist regimes outside of Eastern Europe (namely, Cuba, Mongolia, Vietnam, Kampuchea, Laos, North Korea, Angola, Ethiopia, Mozambique, Afghanistan, and the PDRY), one NATO study gives a figure of 0.4 percent of GNP—*New York Times*, January 23, 1983; a Rand study places the costs somewhat higher but "well within the bounds that have been acceptable to imperial powers in the past"—Charles Wolf, Jr., K. C. Yeh, Edmund Brunner, Jr., Aaron Gurwitz, Marilee Lawrence, *The Costs of the Soviet Empire* (Santa Monica, Calif.: Rand Corporation, September 1983), 50.

[17] Quintin V. S. Bach, "A Note on Soviet Statistics on Their Economic Aid," *Soviet Studies* 37, no. 2 (April 1985), 274.

[18] Abraham S. Becker, "Soviet Union and the Third World: The Economic Dimension," *Soviet Economy* 2, no. 3 (July–September 1986), 246–47.

[19] Ibid., 247.

[20] For a Soviet view of economic cooperation with Third World countries see G. Kim, "Sovetskii Soyuz v natsionalno-osvoboditelnoe dvizheniye" [The Soviet Union in the National Liberation Movement], *Mirovaia ekonomika i mezhdunarodnye otnosheniye*, no. 9 (1982), 25–28. According to Kim in 1981, the USSR signed economic cooperation agreements with sixty-five LDCs and promoted closer ties between them and the Comecon countries. For a usual Soviet commentary, long on generalizations and short on system-

seventh quadriennial session of the U.N. Conference on Trade and Development (UNCTAD), the Soviet Minister of Foreign Trade, Boris Aristov, stated that the Soviet Union provided $23 billion in economic assistance to developing countries in 1986, but gave no particulars.[21] The Soviet stake becomes more pronounced when military assistance and transfers are examined.

A second indication of deepening Soviet involvement is the shift in overall commitments from economic to military assistance. During the Khrushchev years economic assistance slightly exceeded military aid, although the latter showed higher rates of delivery.[22] By the late 1960s, in part as a consequence of stepped-up arms deliveries to North Vietnam, Egypt, and Syria, military assistance came to predominate; and by the end of the 1970s, it did so by a factor of 3 or 4. Overall, from 1954 to 1970, the USSR committed about $18 billion in economic credits "to developing, nonaligned countries," of which approximately $8.2 billion or 45 percent of the total was utilized; by contrast, during this same period, military credits for an estimated $47.3 billion were extended, of which $35.3 billion or 75 percent were utilized.[23] Like all statistics for Soviet assistance, these figures are estimates, but they do give some idea of the growing disparity in Soviet commitments between military and economic assistance.[24] Though ad-

---

atic, detailed data, see A. Kaufman, "The Soviet Union and Developing Countries," *International Affairs*, no. 3 (1985), 39–44.

[21] Paul Lewis, *New York Times*, July 14, 1987.

[22] Stephen T. Hosmer and Thomas W. Wolfe, *Soviet Policy and Practice toward Third World Conflicts* (Lexington, Mass.: Lexington Books, 1983), 18, 24.

[23] Roger F. Pajak, "Soviet Arms Transfers as an Instrument of Influence," *Survival* 23, no. 4 (July–August 1981), 166. A more recent source, published under the auspices of the Stockholm International Peace Research Institute, estimates that, "between 1971 and 1985, major conventional weapons valued at $286 billion in constant (1985) US dollars were imported" by Third World countries (an amount "that is almost four times the value recorded" for the 1951–1970 period); of the total, the USSR accounted for 36.6 percent of total deliveries, or about $105 billion (these estimates include both arms sold for hard currency and on credit). Michael Brzosha and Thomas Ohlson, *Arms Transfer to the Third World, 1971–85* (New York: Oxford University Press, 1987), 1.

[24] Differences in the estimates of ACDA, the CIA, and the State Department have long existed. See for example Gur Ofer, "Soviet Military Aid to the Middle East—an Economic Balance Sheet," in *Soviet Economy in a New Perspective*, U.S. Congress, Joint Economic Committee, 94th Congress, 2d session, 216–39. When the Reagan administration took office, William Casey, the Director of the CIA, discontinued publication of *Communist Aid Activities in Non-Communist Less Developed Countries* (as well as other valuable compilations of basic data about the Soviet Union), making it far more difficult to trace Soviet economic and military aid flows and activities in the Third World. The reasons for closing the data tap may have to do with Casey's conviction that the U.S. government should not tell the Soviets what it knows about them. Some CIA analysts have (off the record) indi-

equate for tracing a pattern, Western estimates of Soviet military assistance may, in fact, grossly underestimate the actual value of Soviet arms transfers.[25] For example, given the high cost of modern weaponry and the massive quantities being transferred, the ACDA (U.S. Arms Control and Disarmament Agency) figure of $2.36 billion for the cost of Soviet arms deliveries to Egypt during the 1967–1976 period seems quite low.[26] Indeed, in early 1972, at a conference in Cairo, Egyptian officials placed a $5 billion price tag on Soviet military assistance—more than double the ACDA estimate.[27]

Military assistance has become a major manifestation of Moscow's continuing consensus on the utility of a high level of involvement in the Third World. The Soviet Union provides more than forty LDCs with arms: since the mid-1970s, more than 90 percent has gone to Libya, Syria, Vietnam, Cuba, Algeria, Iraq, India, Ethiopia, and the two Yemens. It has emerged as the world's leading exporter to the Third World of combat aircraft, tanks, self-propelled guns, air defense weapons, and armored personnel carriers.[28]

There are political and military as well as economic advantages to military assistance, and Moscow has seized them all. Thus, arms diplomacy brought the USSR entrée into countries (Libya, Algeria, Nigeria, Iran under the Shah, Afghanistan under Daoud) where the general outlook had previously been antithetical to the establishment of close ties. By providing some countries (for example, Syria, Iraq, Libya) with sophisticated weapons that can be maintained and operated only with Soviet technicians and expertise, Moscow reinforced depen-

---

cated that "the reporting on Soviet defense may have been eliminated because it disclosed serious analytic problems and uncertainties in the CIA effort in this area." See Anthony H. Cordesman and Benjamin F. Schemmer, "The Failure to Defend Defense: Weinberger and Casey Fail to Strike the Proper Military Balance," *Armed Forces Journal International*, March 1983.

[25] A study that reassesses how we calculate the cost of Soviet arms is Moshe Efrat, "The Economics of Soviet Arms Transfers to the Third World—a Case Study: Egypt," *Soviet Studies* 35, no. 4 (October 1983), 437–56. According to Efrat, "American official estimates of the value of Soviet military aid to the Third World are grossly mistaken; its value is at least two, and more probably, three times as high as their assessments" (454).

[26] U.S. Arms Control and Disarmament Agency, *World Military Expenditures and Arms Transfers 1967–1976* (Washington, D.C.: U.S. Government Printing Office, 1978), 158. Efrat believes the amount is at least two, possibly three, times more ("The Economics of Soviet Arms Transfers," 452–53).

[27] Raymond H. Anderson, "Soviet Arms Aid $5-Billion, Cairo Says," *New York Times*, March 31, 1972.

[28] For data on the 1981–1985 period, see U.S. Arms Control and Disarmament Agency, *World Military Expenditures and Arms Transfers 1986* (Washington, D.C.: U.S. Government Printing Office, April 1987), 151–53.

dency, with a resulting "large number of Soviet military advisers and technicians in these countries."[29] It has offered alternatives to reliance on Western suppliers and frustrated U.S. attempts to forge regional alignments and determine the outcome of regional conflicts. And through arms sales it earns, especially from oil-rich Middle Eastern states, a major portion of its hard currency.

Moscow has also found that the shift to primarily military packages accords with what most Third World leaderships covet above all else. Arms are a highly prized commodity—and Moscow is delighted to oblige: "Neither the ideology of the recipient, nor its policies toward indigenous communist movements, seems to have significantly affected Russian military aid decisions."[30] In pursuing their political objectives, Soviet leaders do not cavil at the uses to which arms are to be put—they sold to Idi Amin at the height of his brutal rule in Uganda,[31] and to the Argentinean military junta in the early 1980s; nor do they object to selling weapons that are obviously inappropriate to the nation's security needs—in the early 1970s they sold Peru's (then) military dictatorship high-performance supersonic combat aircraft, saddling that poor country with a military debt of upwards of $1 billion, which in the austere economic conditions of the mid-1980s it cannot possibly repay.[32]

Moscow recognizes that military assistance is its strong suit in the Third World game. Arms are economical to dispense, because of the Soviet military establishment's penchant for maintaining large stockpiles of all kinds of weapons as part of its propensity to build redundancy into operational requirements; arms can be committed quickly, because of the centralized decision-making structure; for the most part, they are relatively uncomplicated, making them easy to learn to operate;[33] and, of all types of foreign assistance, they are the least likely to result in socio-economic disruption, so are valuable in entrenching in power the rulers Moscow seeks to help. There are, inev-

[29] Rajan Menon, "The Soviet Union, the Arms Trade and the Third World," *Soviet Studies* 34, no. 3 (July 1982), 383.

[30] Joshua Wynfred and Stephen P. Gibert, *Arms for the Third World: Soviet Military Aid Diplomacy* (Baltimore: Johns Hopkins University Press, 1969), 152. This observation is as true in the 1980s as it was in the 1960s.

[31] *The Times* (London), April 28, 1975.

[32] In September 1983, Peru reached an agreement with Moscow for rescheduling $409 million of its debt. FBIS/USSR International Affairs, September 21, 1983, K2.

[33] However, in transferring arms, the Soviet Union has been known to be "laggard in the training, logistical, and other support services that it offers to contractual partners." William H. Lewis and Stephen C. Moss, "The Soviet Arms Transfer Program," *Journal of Northeast Asian Studies* 3, no. 3 (Fall 1984), 5.

itably, policy problems. Among those that loom large at present are requests from prime customers for the most advanced technology or co-production of certain weapons systems, some of which are not even available to Warsaw Pact members; Moscow's insistence on "higher prices and Western currencies" and shorter repayment periods; and its reluctance to provide a full range of "spare parts and other replacement items" in large quantities, in part because the Soviets themselves "normally make little effort at first or second-echelon repair or maintenance for front-line forces."[34]

A third characteristic of the USSR's policy is the emphasis on cementing existing relationships through cultivating multiple ties. Perhaps the most important innovation symbolizing this Soviet aim was the treaty of friendship and cooperation.[35] First concluded with Egypt in May 1971, in order to reassure Anwar Sadat (who had just consolidated his position as Nasser's successor by purging a group of Nasser's close aides whom Moscow had regarded as pro-Soviet) that the Soviet Union had no intention of interfering in Egypt's domestic politics, the treaty served to formalize the special military and political relationship that developed between the two countries after the June War. Like most friendship treaties, it contained provisions calling for both sides to coordinate their positions in the event of threats to the peace and security of either; and for them to enhance their defense potentials. The treaty was not needed for these purposes in this instance, since Moscow had already demonstrated in the War of Attrition between Egypt and Israel in late 1969 and early 1970 the great lengths to which it was prepared to go to defend Egypt. But the importance of the treaty provisions was evident in the treaties to come. The defense provisions were, for example, crucial considerations for Prime Minister Indira Gandhi, who in August 1971 made India the second nation to conclude such a treaty with the USSR. Her aim was insurance against China in the event of an Indo-Pakistani war.

By 1987 Moscow had concluded friendship treaties with thirteen countries; eleven of these treaties are still operative (see Table 1). The existing differences in them reflect the specific regional conditions and the degree of the client's need to be reassured of the USSR's readiness

34 William H. Lewis, "Emerging Choices for the Soviets in Third World Arms Transfer Policy," *World Military Expenditures and Arms Transfers 1985* (Washington, D.C.: U.S. Government Printing Office, August 1985), 32–33.

35 The friendship treaties signed with Third World countries in the 1970s and 1980s differ significantly in purpose, obligation, and scope from those that the Soviet Union signed in the 1920s with Iran and Turkey; accordingly, they are considered a new instrument of Soviet foreign policy.

TABLE 1
USSR Relationships with the Third World in 1986–1987

Country	Economic assistance	Military assistance or relationship	Legality of Communist Party	Marxist-Leninist regime	Friendship treaty signed	Status of friendship treaty	Military facilities or privileges	Anti-American orientation
Afghanistan	Yes	Yes	Yes	Yes	Dec. 5, 1978	Operative	Yes	Yes
Algeria	Yes	Yes	No	No	None	—	No	No
Angola	Yes	Yes	Yes	Yes	Oct. 9, 1976	Operative	Yes	No
Congo (Brazzaville)	No	Yes	Yes	Yes	May 13, 1981	Operative	No	Yes
Cuba	Yes	Yes	Yes	Yes	None	—	Yes	Yes
Egypt	No	No	No	No	May 27, 1971	Abrogated by Egypt Mar. 15, 1976	No	No
Ethiopia	Yes	Yes	Yes	Yes	Nov. 20, 1978	Operative	Yes	Yes
India	Yes	Yes	Yes	No	Aug. 9, 1971	Operative	No	No
Iran	No	No	No	No	None	—	No	Yes
Iraq	Yes	Yes	No	No	Apr. 9, 1972	Operative	No	Yes
Kampuchea	Yes	Yes	Yes	Yes	None	—	No	Yes
Laos	Yes	Yes	No	No	None	—	No	Yes
Libya	No	Yes	Yes	Yes	None	—	No	Yes
Madagascar	Negligible	Negligible	Yes	Yes	None	—	No	No
Mozambique	Yes	Yes	Yes	Yes	Mar. 31, 1977	Operative	No	No
Nicaragua	Yes	Yes	Yes	No	None	—	No	No
Nigeria	Yes	Yes	No	No	None	—	No	Yes
PDRY	Yes	Yes	Yes	Yes	Oct. 25, 1979	Operative	Yes	Yes
Somalia	No	No	No	No	July 11, 1974	Abrogated by Somalia Nov. 13, 1977	No	No
Syria	Yes	Yes	Yes	No	Oct. 8, 1980	Operative	Yes	Yes
Turkey	Yes	No	No	No	None	—	No	No
Vietnam	Yes	Yes	Yes	Yes	Nov. 3, 1978	Operative	Yes	Yes
Yemen Arab Republic	Yes	Yes	No	No	Oct. 9, 1984	Operative	No	No

to support it in the event of trouble.[36] Thus, whereas the treaty with Afghanistan, concluded in December 1978, states merely that the two parties "will consult each other and by agreement take appropriate measures to ensure the security, independence and territorial integrity" of each (Article 4), the one with Syria, signed in October 1980, conveys a sense of greater urgency in providing that, "In cases of the emergence of situations jeopardizing peace or security of one of the parties or posing a threat to peace or violating peace and security in the whole world," the two parties "shall enter without delay into contact with each other with a view toward coordinating their positions and to cooperation in order to remove the threat that has arisen and to restore the peace" (Article 6).

The Soviet Union, as "a signatory to more than ten thousand known and live conventions, treaties, agreements and protocols," has long favored extensive use of international legal instruments as adjuncts of its diplomacy and overall foreign policy, and believes friendship treaties to be useful in a number of ways. First, they improve the strategic context within which the USSR conducts its diplomacy, since they oblige the signatories not to enter "into any alliance or join any grouping of states, provide any facility, or undertake any obligation, military or otherwise, directed against either of them, or incompatible with the treaties." Second, they predispose Third World signatories to be sensitive to Moscow's preferences on issues that are not important to them in order to ensure Soviet support in situations that do bear on their security and survival. Third, by calling for expanding military cooperation, they deepen a Third World regime's military dependency on the Soviet Union.[37]

Moscow knows the friendship treaty is no stronger than the bonds between the signatories: India, Iraq, and Mozambique have never extended the military privileges the Soviets had expected. Like any other treaty, it can be overturned at will by partners whose outlook suddenly changes: in Egypt (1976) and Somalia (1977), leaders who had been major beneficiaries of Soviet military and economic assistance nonetheless unilaterally abrogated the treaties when it suited their purposes. One is reminded of the quip attributed to Charles de Gaulle: "A treaty is like a rose and a young girl—nice as long as it lasts." Despite this, Moscow considers treaties a useful way of reassuring vulner-

[36] Daniel S. Papp, *Soviet Policies towards the Developing World During the 1980s* (Maxwell Air Force Base, Ala.: Air University Press, 1986), 70–71.

[37] Zafar Imam, "Soviet Treaties with Third World Countries," *Soviet Studies* 35, no. 1 (January 1983), 53, 60–61.

able clients—and, incidentally, as demonstrating to skeptics in the Kremlin the wisdom of the forward policy.

Of the eleven operative friendship treaties, seven are with countries ruled by a communist party (Vietnam) or Marxist-Leninist-oriented vanguard party (Afghanistan, Angola, Congo-Brazzaville, Ethiopia, Mozambique, and the People's Democratic Republic of Yemen, PDRY). Such political elites are considered more reliable long-term associates than bourgeois-nationalist elites.[38] But the Soviet leadership knows that the "Marxism-Leninism" is in many cases papier-mâché, a political cloak and easily discarded (Somalia is a case in point). Moreover, even if a regime is genuinely Marxist-Leninist, its own nationalism and conception of national interest can lead to hostility toward the Soviet Union. China, Yugoslavia, and Albania are ever-present reminders of the acentrism prevailing among adherents of Marxism-Leninism. Accordingly, Moscow approaches the task of creating a network of interrelated and reinforcing political relationships pragmatically, adapting to each situation and each elite on its own terms. It may prefer a Marxist-Leninist regime—after all, Cuba and Vietnam do provide the most extensive military facilities and privileges—but non-Marxist Syria and India are politically even more valuable.

Finally, Moscow persists in trying to expand economic ties—that is, the aggregate of project assistance, trade, and subsidies—even though they have not lived up to its expectations. Initially, Soviet economic assistance did bring handsome political benefits, but by the mid-1960s the honeymoon period was over. LDCs discovered the aid was costly and often inefficient. There were too many "red elephants": cement that caked in tropical rain on the docks of Burma and Guinea; a pharmaceutical plant in India that produced obsolete antibiotics and had

---

[38] The conviction that "only a vanguard party adhering to a genuinely socialist ideology can foster the transformation" of society and move it successfully along a noncapitalist path of development was expressed by leading Soviet scholars. See especially the writings of G. I. Mirskii: for example, "Politicheskaya rol' armii v stranakh Azii i Afriki" [The Political Role of the Army in the Countries of Asia and Africa], *Narody Azii i Afriki*, no. 6 (1968), 14; and *Armiya i politika v stranakh Azii i Afriki* [Army and Politics in the Countries of Asia and Africa] (Moscow: Nauka, 1970), 317. In "Rol' armii v sotsialnom razvitii stran Azii i Afriki" [The Role of the Army in the Social Development of Asian and African Countries], *Voprosy filosofii*, no. 3 (1979), 108, Mirskii writes: "The only condition that can guarantee the truly progressive development of the developing countries is the organization of the masses and the creation of a vanguard party based on a platform of scientific socialism. This kind of party can guide the leadership of the army and assist in transforming it into a people's armed force that is free from 'elitist' and caste biases." See also R. Ulyanovsky [Ulianovskii], *Socialism and the Newly Independent Nations* (Moscow: Progress Publishers, 1974), 171.

no research and development capability; heavy machinery that arrived months before the plant had actually been constructed; and factories that were too complicated to operate efficiently. As a result, though in dire need of capital investment and industrial projects of the type the USSR can furnish, LDCs have utilized less than half of the credits extended them, preferring to shop in the West.

Nor did trade, the historic criterion of improving relations, take Moscow very far, once the early rapid growth from an insignificant base was over. Moreover, despite the growth in the 1970s and early 1980s, "Soviet bloc trade probably does not account for more than 8 percent of LDCs' turnover"; and in this total "at least 40 percent of Soviet exports consist of arms."[39] Apart from arms, the Soviet Union relies on industrial machinery and oil to penetrate LDC markets. Its prospects for expanding in Third World markets are not promising, "unless Soviet machinery becomes substantially more competitive, or Moscow finds that more of its import needs can be satisfied from LDC sources—e.g., the newly industrialized countries (NICs), who may be able to meet some of the requirements stemming from Gorbachev's modernization program."[40]

Once the Kremlin realized the difficulties of making significant economic inroads—certainly, by the late 1960s—it turned disappointment to advantage: it shifted commitments strongly to the military sector and encouraged LDCs, even those with whom it was closely aligned politically, to look to the West for their economic needs. The elaborate and self-serving rationale for this approach emerged in the Soviet literature in the form of advice to aid recipients to "take various practical steps to put their economic house in order and use Soviet credits more efficiently"[41] and to adopt more pluralistic policies, including even the "preservation of some elements of capitalism" essential for economic and political development.[42] Increasingly, Moscow was reluctant to finance high visibility, noneconomic projects, as it had done in the late 1950s and early 1960s for megalomaniacs such as Nkrumah of Ghana and Sukarno of Indonesia. Nonetheless, when expediency requires, the Soviet leadership continues to extend economic assistance for politically motivated projects, as in 1984, when, at a time of mass starva-

[39] Emilio Gasparini, "East-South Economic Relations: Warsaw Pact Shifts to Military Deals with Developing World," NATO Review, no. 2 (April 1985), 27.

[40] Becker, "Soviet Union and the Third World," 253.

[41] Elizabeth Valkenier, "New Soviet Views on Economic Aid," Survey, no. 76 (Summer 1970), 22.

[42] Thomas J. Zamostny, "Moscow and the Third World: Recent Trends in Soviet Thinking," Soviet Studies 36, no. 2 (April 1984), 227.

tion in parts of Ethiopia, Moscow gave Mengistu $50 million for prettifying showpiece party buildings in Addis Ababa, not for food relief. What Soviet discussions on the economic aspects of Third World developments indicate is that the day of the blank check and optimism over the future of socialism there is over. And the men in the Kremlin have ample reason for being skeptical of the utility of economic instruments to affect political outcomes. As one American economist observed in criticizing the shortcomings of Western theoretical models of economic development in the Third World, "economic logic must always be subjected to the test of what happens in the real world."[43] In that real world, the Soviets encountered "facts" that contravened expectations based on theory and that led them to adapt accordingly. Moscow learned what any businessman knows—namely, that the debtor is not without influence over the creditor, a point Nasser made in discussions with Western journalists.[44] Realizing, too, that LDCs often exploit the superpower rivalry for their own advantage,[45] and that they seldom place economic development at the top of their list of priorities,[46] Moscow saw little need to make sacrifices in order to

---

[43] Nicholas W. Balabkins, "Collecting Information in a Developing Country," *Harvard Library Bulletin* 32, no. 1 (Winter 1984), 65.

[44] Q. "Are you not afraid of being swallowed up by the Soviet bloc economy?" A. "The matter is not as complicated as you think it is. If you are indebted to someone, then you are in a strong position. Those indebted are always stronger than their creditors." *Newsweek*, February 3, 1969.
Q. "Are you not facing a massive debt . . . to the Soviet Union. Does this not give the Soviet Union a firm hold on your economy?" A. "I think that an indebted person is always in a stronger position than the creditor. What applies to individuals also applies to peoples. An indebted person has only to refuse to pay if he feels that unjust pressure is being put on him. We were indebted to the USA when relations between us became tense. We stopped paying those debts." BBC, Summary of World Broadcasts, ME/3380/A/5 (May 16, 1970).

[45] In the spring and summer of 1979 the Yemen Arab Republic (YAR) adroitly manipulated a number of would-be patrons. Though regarded as pro-Western, the YAR concluded a major arms deal with the Soviet Union in the late summer of 1979, only months after the United States had arranged for an airlift of weapons to help the YAR in its conflict with the PDRY. "The YAR's sudden turn to the Soviet Union for new arms constituted a Yemeni assertion of partial independence from Saudi Arabia and was the direct result of the Saudis' insensitive handling of both the transfer of United States arms and the diplomatic situation after the border fight and the unification agreement [with the PDRY]. The $300 million triangular USA-Saudi-YAR arms deal, accelerated with great show by the Carter administration during the border fight, did not result in the political gains that arms transfers are supposed to yield." Robert D. Burrowes, "The Yemen Arab Republic and the Ali Abdallah Salih Regime: 1978–1984," *Middle East Journal* 39, no. 3 (Summer 1985), 297.

[46] One example may suffice. At the opening of the twenty-first meeting of the Organization of African Unity (OAU) in Addis Ababa in July 1985, a number of Western officials

provide costly assistance, which was not essential for the promotion of Soviet political objectives. In dealing with ruling elites, it does not care much about winning the hearts and minds of the people. It gives to acquire influence, not make converts. And it accepts the limits to its ability to affect elites and events.

All of this contributes to Moscow's discontent with economic assistance and to its encouragement of LDCs to look to the West for their economic needs. It helps explain Moscow's reluctance to grant them freer access to the Soviet market and increase purchases of their semi-manufactured and manufactured goods, and (at least until the advent of the Gorbachev period) its unwillingness "to participate meaningfully in multilateral endeavors such as North-South negotiations."[47] There are some indications that Gorbachev plans to change past policy, but the results will not be assessable for some years. The Soviet Union is not prevented by "ideology" from joining in cooperative economic endeavors with the West to help LDCs. Nor, as some argue, are "the Soviet Union's economic performance and capacities the Achilles' heel of Moscow's operations in the Third World."[48] On the contrary, after more than three decades of involvement in the Third World, Moscow fully realizes that neither directly assisting economic development nor participating in programs to foster that development is essential for the advancement of Soviet objectives.[49]

The Soviet leadership recognizes the validity of what a number of its leading scholars have been arguing: namely, that economic and social transformation will not take place as quickly or easily as had originally been expected. Disappointment with unanticipated hurdles in the 1960s had sparked debates among Soviet scholars. These revealed deep underlying disagreements over appropriate developmental strategies, the extent to which capitalist forms are compatible with a social-

---

were quoted as saying that African leaders recognize their worsening economic situation, "but whether they are really willing to take the hard steps necessary to change that is very much in question." *New York Times*, July 19, 1985. At the end of the meeting, at which a number of recommendations for economic development were adopted, one East African official said that "some countries have already begun to initiate reforms," but that most "quite frankly, seem to have different priorities." *New York Times*, July 21, 1985. The paltry contributions of oil-rich members, such as Algeria, Nigeria, and Libya, to drought and starvation relief, mock the notion that the amply endowed members have an underlying sense of concern for the less fortunate ones.

[47] Padma Desai, "The Soviet Union and the Third World: A Faltering Partnership?" in Jagdish N. Bhagwati and John Gerard Ruggie, eds., *Power, Passions, and Purpose: Prospects for North-South Negotiations* (Cambridge, Mass.: MIT Press, 1984), 281.

[48] Elizabeth K. Valkenier, "A New Soviet Mood," *New York Times*, September 13, 1981.

[49] See below, Chapter Seven.

ist orientation, the need for and role of a vanguard party, and so on.[50] They heighten our awareness, as Elizabeth Valkenier has thoughtfully noted, that "some circles" in the leadership "are coming to grips with the demonstrable fact that there are limits to Soviet power in the Third World, as well as to the advantages to be derived from close identification with post-colonial grievances."[51] They also tell us that Moscow knows full well that reality is more complex than doctrinal attempts to explain it, that heed must be given to the differentiated character of the Third World environment, and that policy must be flexible and adaptive.

The foremost exponent of a materialist philosophy that places economic determinants at the heart of individual and systemic behavior, the Soviet leadership nonetheless accords minimal importance to economics in its foreign policy toward those whose plight and aspirations should, but actually do not, lead them to place special emphasis on economic and economically related instruments of change. But, to paraphrase what Stalin customarily answered on occasions when he was compelled to explain away glaring "contradictions" between what doctrine postulated and what reality illustrated: "Is there a contradiction? Yes, of course, there is. Some Comrades seem to forget that it is only through contradictions that change occurs."

VARIABLES IN POLICY DETERMINATION

Analyzing Soviet policy in the Third World is like palm-reading: the lines are there, but their meaning is a matter for speculation. Much depends on the importance the interpreter attaches to one or another variable, and the assumptions of foreign policy analysts are rarely made explicit. Three factors that are sometimes heavily weighted—

---

[50] The essentials of these academic debates have been carefully studied by Western scholars: see for example Hough, *The Struggle for the Third World*; Roger E. Kanet, ed., *The Soviet Union and the Developing Nations* (Baltimore: Johns Hopkins University Press, 1974); Valkenier, *The Soviet Union and the Third World*; and Zamostny, "Moscow and the Third World." See also Uri Ra'anan, "Moscow and the 'Third World,'" *Problems of Communism* 14, no. 1 (January–February 1965), 22–31; Oles Smolansky, "Moscow and the Problem of National Socialism: An Ideological Approach," *Canadian Slavic Studies* 1, no. 2 (Summer 1967), 172–95, and "The Soviet Union and the Underdeveloped World (1955–1963): An Ideological Interpretation," *Il Politico*, no. 4 (December 1965), 796–815; and Edward Taborsky, "The Class Struggle, the Proletariat, and the Developing Nations," *Review of Politics* 29, no. 3 (July 1967), 370–86. Among the Soviet scholars prominent in these debates are Karen Brutents, Sergo Mikoyan, Yevgeny Primakov, Viktor Sheinis, Nodari Simoniya, and Rostislav Ulianovskii.

[51] Valkenier, *The Soviet Union and the Third World*, 150.

ideology, China, and the central strategic balance—turn out, in my judgment, to have been overrated as determinants of the Kremlin's policies: whatever significance they may have had at a few particular times in the past was short-lived, and they fail to take us very far toward a more accurate understanding of the impetus underlying the Soviet Union's involvement. But, since the role of these three factors is downplayed in my analysis of the substantive and thematic aspects of the USSR's New Imperial Policy that follows in subsequent chapters, a few comments are in order on the reasoning that has guided my thinking and my weighting of the evidence on Soviet behavior.

Ideology

That Marxism-Leninism, like all ideologies, is infinitely malleable and offered successive Soviet leaders alternative justifications for preferred courses of policy was explored in our analysis of the changes Khrushchev brought about in the USSR's policy toward the Third World.[52] In justifying his changes in the ideology—and by implication the new policies he set in motion—he would berate the quote-gatherers who repeated what Lenin had said decades ago about the inevitability of war, class struggle, and revolution but failed to take account of the changed conditions in the world. He said it was necessary to observe and understand the specifics of concrete situations and apply doctrine creatively in the light of contemporary conditions, not in accordance with a predetermined formula:

> One must not only know how to read, but must also understand correctly what one reads, and know how to apply it to the concrete situations of our time, to take account of the existing situation, of the actual balance of forces. A political leader who does so shows that he is not only able to read, but also to creatively apply revolutionary theory. If he does not, he is like the man of whom the people say that "he reads with his eyes shut."[53]

Khrushchev did more to revise doctrine than any Soviet leader since Stalin. In February 1956, at the CPSU's twentieth congress, his revision of Stalin's "two camp" thesis and enunciation of the concept of a "zone of peace" justified the policy of supporting newly independent Third World countries who did not join Western-sponsored military pacts. In November 1960, at the Moscow Conference of 81 Communist and Workers' Parties, he introduced the concept of the "national demo-

[52] See above, Chapter One (section entitled "The Khrushchevian Watershed").

[53] N. S. Khrushchev, *On Peaceful Coexistence* (Moscow: Foreign Languages Publishing House, 1961), 247.

cratic state" to describe Third World countries that met the following criteria:

1. a foreign policy of nonparticipation in Western alliances and a pro-Soviet complexion;
2. resistance to Western economic penetration and "neo-colonialism";
3. a commitment to expansion of the public sector and adoption of a "noncapitalist path of development"; and
4. a readiness to guarantee the masses "broad democratic rights and freedoms," and especially to end persecution of local communists.

In 1963, he added the formulation, the "revolutionary democratic state," to single out for praise regimes that looked favorably on local communists.

But Khrushchev's ideological revisions bore little relationship to the levels of economic and military assistance that he extended. Nor did they have any bearing on the risks he was prepared to run in defense of a particular regime. Instead he played ward politics on an international scale and ignored the typologies he had foisted on compliant scribes. He did not allow tensions in relationships to deflect Soviet policy from seeking the advantages that had motivated the courtship in the first place. Disagreements and quarrels were part of the rough and tumble of politics. In Egypt Nasser cracked down on the communists, in Algeria (in late 1962, soon after Algeria gained its independence) Ben Bella banned the Communist Party, and in Iraq (in the late 1950s and early 1960s) Qasim slaughtered communists, but Khrushchev did not alter Soviet policy or renege on an economic or military agreement during the period of tension.[54] In the interest of opposing "imperialism," he was prepared—as have been his successors—to tolerate a great deal in relations with an anti-American Third World regime. As he told the twenty-first congress of the CPSU,

> We do not deny that we and some of the leaders of the United
> Arab Republic [Egypt] have divergent views in the ideological

[54] On occasion, as in an interview with Algerian, Ghanaian, and Burmese journalists, published on December 21, 1963, Khrushchev vented his anger at the persecution of communists: "Socialism cannot be built on positions of anti-communism, by opposing the countries in which socialism is victorious, by persecuting communists, these valiant fighters for the national liberation of their countries from the imperialist yoke, ardent patriots and fighters for the new social system, for social progress." *Soviet News*, no. 4934 (December 23, 1963), 155.

sphere. But in the matter of fighting against imperialism, of consolidating the political and economic independence of the countries which have freed themselves from colonialism, of combating the war danger, our attitude coincides with theirs. Differences in ideological views should not impede the development of friendly relations between our countries or our joint struggle against imperialism.[55]

Khrushchev's successors have shown little interest in new ideological categories for the types of regimes in the Third World; and the occasional abstruse academic study on the subject has become the exception rather than the rule.[56] Instead, Soviet policies have proceeded along the lines laid down by Khrushchev:

- programs of assistance are initiated in response to an LDC's request;
- assistance is rendered, irrespective of a regime's political outlook, even if it is anticommunist or represses local communists;
- programs or defense commitments are never terminated out of ideological antipathy, but only when the Third World regime itself decides to end them.

Such behavior warrants the conclusion that ideological considerations do not loom large in the Kremlin's formulation of its Third World policy.

China

Like ideology, the China factor has been greatly overrated as a cause of the USSR's deepening involvement in the Third World.[57] No one

[55] Khrushchev, *On Peaceful Coexistence*, 54.

[56] For example V. E. Chirkin, *Revolutsionno-demokraticheskoe gosudarstvo sovremennosti* [Contemporary Revolutionary Democratic Governments] (Moscow: Nauka, 1984); and L. I. Reisner and N. A. Simoniya, eds., *Evolyutsiya vostochnykh obshchestv: sintez traditsionnogo i sovremennogo* [The Evolution of Oriental Societies: A Synthesis of Traditional and Modern] (Moscow: Orientalist Literature Publication, 1984).

[57] In this study I do not consider China to be part of the Third World. By its very size and population, and status as a nuclear power, China warrants special attention. It and the two Koreas (also excluded) are located in a strategic quadrant of the globe that merits separate assessment, quite apart from socio-economic criteria. Although China seeks to associate itself with the less-developed countries, their positions and institutions, it ranks, according to Lillian Craig Harris and Robert L. Worden, "well above other developing nations in per capita GNP, GNP growth rate, physical quality of life, life expectancy, literacy and public education, and military expenditures. China is also well below Third World averages for birth and death rates, does not share the direct colonial occupation experience of many Third World states, and unlike most developing countries, is an ex-

would deny that Moscow has a serious China problem, though few in the West would go so far as Edward Luttwak in his contention that the Soviet Union regards China, not the United States, as the main enemy.[58] The Sino-Soviet rift, which developed in the late 1950s and widened in the following decade, proved unbridgeable in the 1970s; and in 1980 China allowed the 1950 treaty of alliance to lapse.[59] The ruptured alliance was the Soviet Union's most damaging diplomatic setback since the end of World War II. It meant an increased security burden, mandated greater permissiveness in Eastern Europe, split the world communist movement, and brought the United States an unexpected strategic windfall.

Nevertheless, from the mid-1950s the unfolding of the USSR's policy in the Third World was influenced only minimally by any calculation of China's potential long-term military-political challenge. Khrushchev's courtship of Afghanistan, Turkey, India, Iran, Syria, and Egypt antedated Moscow's troubles with Beijing—and Beijing's tensions with New Delhi, which were to have adverse consequences for Sino-Soviet relations. Indeed, in those early years the Kremlin had reason to be pleased with the patrimony Stalin had bequeathed them in the Far East: alliance with China and a minimal need for military presence along that border and in Mongolia. The focus of Khrushchev's policy—prompted by fear of the U.S. containment policy—was on areas remote from China's core security interests.

---

tremely large country blessed with a variety of development resources." Lillian Craig Harris and Robert L. Worden, eds., *China and the Third World: Champion or Challenger?* (Dover, Mass.: Auburn House, 1986), 1.

[58] Edward H. Luttwak, *The Grand Strategy of the Soviet Union* (New York: St. Martin's Press, 1983), 90–101. He argues that, since the United States has not shown itself "implacable in opposing Soviet aims," the Soviets regard the United States as "a manageable diplomatic adversary." By contrast, they see China as so threatening that a preemptive nuclear strike to partition it cannot be ruled out. In the meantime, Moscow seeks to surround China, presumably in preparation for an attack sometime in the future.

[59] The causes of the rift have been extensively studied. Suffice it to note here that a number of discrete but interconnected factors were at work. For his part, Mao Tse-tung perceived Khrushchev's quest for improved relations with the United States and courtship of bourgeois-nationalist regimes as a downgrading of the Soviet Union's commitment to help China regain Taiwan and contribute to its economic development; understood Khrushchev's de-Stalinization speech as a personal rebuke; resented his support for India at a time of Sino-Indian tensions and war; and believed he was entitled to higher status in the world communist movement. Of particular interest in analyzing the roots of the rift are the following: George Ginsburgs and Carl F. Pinkele, *The Sino-Soviet Territorial Dispute 1949–64* (New York: Praeger, 1978); William E. Griffith, *The Sino-Soviet Rift* (Cambridge, Mass.: MIT Press, 1964); Richard Lowenthal, *World Communism: The Disintegration of a Secular Faith* (New York: Oxford University Press, 1964); Donald S. Zagoria, *The Sino-Soviet Conflict, 1956–1961* (Princeton: Princeton University Press, 1962).

China may have a nuclear capability (and must therefore be seen as a threat by Moscow) but it is not yet a great power. Nor is it likely to develop a credible military posture vis-à-vis the Soviet Union before the early decades of the twenty-first century. The limits of its conventional capability were glaringly evident in early 1979, when it set out to "teach the Vietnamese a lesson" for daring to invade Kampuchea and depose the pro-Beijing Pol Pot regime. Instead, China received an embarrassing drubbing: its aircraft, tanks, artillery, and tactics were no match for Vietnam's, prompting Premier Deng Tsaio-ping to revamp the military establishment and accelerate the pace of modernization.

Those in the West who think that fear of China is an important factor motivating Moscow's Third World policy rely too heavily on Soviet writings, which convey the image of a militarily aggressive and dangerous China and which are not averse to exacerbating atavistic fears of the "yellow peril." But this is not likely to affect the assessments of Soviet military planners who know China's weaknesses.

Lacking a power projection capability, China can not outbid the USSR in the competition for strategically useful clients. The thesis that "the more China dedicates itself to compromising Soviet positions in the Third World, the more impetuous the Soviet Union will be in areas of instability,"[60] may give a plausible reason for Soviet moves in Southern Africa in the mid-1970s, but it does nothing to illumine the whats and whys of Soviet policy in the Arab-Israeli sector, the Caribbean, the Horn of Africa, or Afghanistan; nor does it ring true in Southeast Asia, where proximity and overseas Chinese minorities might be expected to give Beijing some advantages, but instead elicit suspicion of China by the ruling Thai, Malay, Burmese, Indonesian, and Vietnamese elites.

Economically, when it came to providing assistance the Soviet Union dwarfed anything China could do. China had one showpiece project, completed in the early 1970s, the Tanzam (Tanzania-Zambia) railroad, which enabled landlocked Zambia to bypass the then white-dominated transit route through Rhodesia (Zimbabwe) and export its copper ore via Tanzania. The thousands of Chinese laborers brought in to lay track through jungle and swamp enhanced China's prestige, but they also incurred some resentment as well. In the matter of arms shipments, China's inability to match the Soviet Union is telling, inevitably exposing China for what it is—an Asian power, unable to affect

[60] Robert Legvold, "The Super Rivals: Conflict in the Third World," *Foreign Affairs* 57, no. 4 (Spring 1979), 769–70.

developments in areas distant from its home base in any meaningful way.

On the ideological front, there was a brief period in the 1960s when the Sino-Soviet rift was at a dangerous stage (with intense border clashes in 1969) and Moscow felt hard-pressed by the ideological challenge mounted by Mao in the Third World. But his ideological appeal soon faded. Mao's Calvinistic brand of communism, with its aura of revolutionary zeal and success, at first attracted African leaders such as Julius Nyerere of Tanzania and Sékou Touré of Guinea, who were impressed by the discipline, drive, and dedication they saw in China and who thought to emulate Mao's "mass line" of mobilizing the populace for internal transformation and for the struggle against "imperialism." But the Maoist model proved inappropriate for the African scene. Also, the more remote China was from an area, the more revolutionary it seemed; but countries closer to home—the bourgeois-nationalist regimes of Burma, Nepal, Laos, Thailand, and Cambodia—realized that, in seeking better relations with them, Mao was no more ideological than Khrushchev had been.[61]

Nor was China's suffering at the hands of imperialism and its underdeveloped status ever translated into psychological advantage in the competition with the Soviet Union. In part this was a result of historic Chinese exclusivity: China considers itself a separate civilization. Its experience with imperialism was very different from the Third World's: though victimized for a little more than a century before the revolution brought the communists to power in 1949, it was never a colony, never conquered or colonized. The European powers acknowledged its sovereignty, even as they carved out spheres of influence for themselves; and Japan, despite military victories and territorial expansion, failed to consolidate its rule or influence the cultural-political values of local elites. The imperialist experience left little imprint on China. For their part, Third World countries do not want China to become a member of their exclusive institutional network or inner circles; they fear it would exert too much influence and see it more as a nascent superpower than a fellow LDC. Realizing it would be unwelcome, China has not pushed for admission to the Nonaligned Movement (NAM).

Recourse to grand strategy to explain Soviet policy in South Asia obscures more than it illumines. The importance of India in Soviet

---

[61] An example of Beijing's pragmatism in reaching agreements with a bourgeois-nationalist regime at a time when it was preaching the need for revolution and struggle can be seen in relations with Burma. Shen-Yu Dai, "Peking and Rangoon," *China Quarterly*, no. 5 (January–March 1961), 131–44.

policy does not validify the assumption that the principal consideration underlying Moscow's courtship is its desire to enlist the support
of the strongest power in South Asia in the containment of China.[62]
The USSR's courtship of India was initiated before the rift had begun,
and it was intended to counter U.S. power, not China's. Also, despite
India's festering territorial problem with China (which frustrates India's effort at a reconciliation with China and keeps it oriented toward
the USSR), Moscow knows that India has neither the power nor the
inclination to play a role in containing China in areas that are not on
its border. India's obsession is with Pakistan, not China; and, lacking
friends in the region—indeed, it does not have a close and friendly
relationship with any country on its border—India prefers to keep a
low profile in NAM and elsewhere to forestall regional realignments
that might weaken it in relation to Pakistan. It is certainly unlikely to
join with Moscow in an anti-Chinese alliance. Adam Ulam said it well:
"For all of China's temporary weakness and the confusion in its coun-
cils, the Soviets could not delude themselves that militarily or otherwise their alliance with India could in the long run dispose of the
Chinese danger."[63] The Soviet Union finds benefit enough from its
strengthened ties with India: it demonstrates the value of a Soviet connection and reinforces New Delhi's attachment to nonalignment.

Uneasiness over the Sino-American rapprochement was one of the
reasons why the Kremlin sought détente with the United States in the
early 1970s,[64] but it was not the spur to Soviet activism in the Third
World in the mid-1970s.[65] That activism was not new, but was
prompted by the same combination of opportunism and desire to undermine U.S. influence that had been so important for Khrushchev in
the mid-1950s.

Soviet professions of concern about China ought not be accepted at
face value. As Harry Gelman says,

It is reasonable to suppose that despite their repeated expressions
of concern about the Sino-American relationship in private con-

[62] For example Robert C. Horn, *Soviet-Indian Relations: Issues and Influence* (New York:
Praeger, 1982); Robert H. Donaldson, *Soviet Policy towards India: Ideology and Strategy*
(Cambridge, Mass.: Harvard University Press, 1974); Harish Kapur, *The Embattled Tri-
angle: Moscow, Peking, New Delhi* (New York: Humanities Press, 1973); Bhabani Sen
Gupta, *The Fulcrum of Asia: Relations among China, India, Pakistan, and the USSR* (New
York: Pegasus, 1970).

[63] Adam B. Ulam, *Dangerous Relations: The Soviet Union in World Politics, 1970–1982*
(New York: Oxford University Press, 1983), 72.

[64] Ibid., 59–60, 75. There is extensive literature on this proposition.

[65] See William G. Hyland, *Soviet-American Relations: A New Cold War?* R-2763-FF/RC
(Santa Monica, Calif.: Rand Corporation, May 1981).

tacts with U.S. leaders, the Soviet leaders were well aware of the
evidence that the Kissinger-Nixon policy toward China was a limited one, and that it was amply balanced by American interests in
reaching agreements with the Soviet Union.

It should also be remembered that even as late as November
1974, when détente had already begun to decline, the Chinese
leaders were dealt a humiliation when the United States con-
sented to hold a summit meeting with Brezhnev at Vladivostok.
The Soviets had chosen this site, adjacent to China, with precisely
that effect in mind, and can only have been gratified and reassured by the Ford administration's acquiescence to this slight to
Beijing.[66]

In the final analysis, the Western notion that Soviet policy in the
Third World is motivated by a desire to encircle and isolate China may
be a projection of what the West would like to be able to do to the
Soviet Union. Unlike old soldiers, the strategy of containment not only
does not die, but does not even fade away.

Central Strategic Balance

Attempts to connect the central strategic (that is, nuclear) balance with
Soviet activism and risk-taking in the Third World face conceptual
and methodological difficulties in determining what data and criteria
are relevant for assessing the strategic balance. American and Soviet
perceptions and calculations of the "strategic balance"—or (the Soviet
preferred term) "correlation of forces"—are inherently asymmetrical,
thus complicating any comparison and opening the way to contentious
assessments. Fundamentally, the Americans stress the military component, whereas the Soviets consider it only one of several variables;
and U.S. analysts devote preponderant attention to the nuclear dimension, whereas published Soviet commentaries speak more about
conventional forces—an emphasis that may, apart from the USSR's
historical experience, geographic situation, internal system, and im-

---

[66] Harry Gelman, "Rise and Fall of Détente," *Problems of Communism* 34, no. 2 (March–
April 1985), 58. Gelman believes "that a much more potent factor in reinforcing the
Politburo inclination to seize on the opportunities that began to open up in the Third
World after 1975 was the December 1974 passage by the U.S. Congress of the Stevenson
Amendment to the Export-Import Bank bill, an action that limited to U.S. $300 million
the total that the Bank could guarantee in loans to the Soviet Union over the following
four years without seeking further Congressional approval, and that banned the use of
any of this money for the development or production of energy. From the Soviet perspective, this event was a real turning point abruptly ending hopes that America might
furnish decisive help to the Soviet economy."

perial foreign policy, stem also from a very different response to nuclear weapons and to "NATO's incapacity for protracted conventional conflict," and the premium that Soviet military leaders place on "staying power."[67] Moreover, it is obvious that their approaches to the arms races that each of them fuels differ markedly: the U.S. conceives of them as ancillary adjuncts of a military policy geared to the preservation of the status quo, whereas the USSR, operating at multiple levels to acquire incremental advantages it believes will over time bring about qualitative shifts in regional and strategic balances, sees them as integral to the prosecution of political and military struggle, as a way of eventually restructuring the status quo.

There is no convincing evidence that the Kremlin's perception of the central strategic balance played a constraining role of any consequence in decisions affecting its willingness to become involved in the Third World, to runs risks, or to mount interventions. Even in the late 1950s and early 1960s, when the USSR was clearly inferior to the United States in nuclear weapons and delivery systems, it was actively pushing in key regions. Nuclear inferiority was no bar to high risk-taking, as the Cuban missile (mis)adventure showed. Moscow's failure to intervene in crises such as the 1956 Suez War, the 1957 Syrian-Turkish crisis, the 1958 Lebanon crisis, and the 1967 June War (a mixed bag of disparate types of crises) was due primarily not to uncertainty over "what the American position would be" or to the USSR's "fear of nuclear escalation,"[68] but to the USSR's lack of a suitable conventional power projection capability and absence of any Soviet commitment to intervene on behalf of any of the parties. By the late 1960s, when Moscow had assumed extensive political-military commitments and developed its PPC, its direct military interventions and forcefulness in periods of crisis affecting prized clients rose sharply.

Considerations concerning the central strategic balance are no more likely to inhibit Soviet Third World activism in the present era of nuclear equivalence than they did in the past. It is possible, in fact, that Moscow may be tempted to venture more often into situations of marginal value, knowing the United States is not going to escalate to the nuclear threshold over them. This does not, however, mean that the Soviet Union intends to use its nuclear muscle to wrest a local advantage from the United States or precipitate a nuclear confrontation by

[67] James M. McConnell, "Shifts in Soviet Views on the Proper Focus of Military Development," *World Politics* 37, no. 3 (April 1985), 318.

[68] For example Francis Fukuyama, "Nuclear Shadowboxing: Soviet Intervention Threats in the Middle East," *Orbis* 25, no. 3 (Fall 1981), 603, 596.

threatening some interest vital to the West, such as Arabian Peninsula oil.

DIRECTIONS

Everything the Soviets have done since the mid-1950s points to their being in the Third World for the long haul. They broadened their sights and commitments, adjusted their modus operandi, and came to terms with the limitations, inherent in the Third World environment, on their ability to control developments or extract advantages. But, as heirs to an imperial tradition, they have their basic objectives clearly in mind and approach each situation with an essential realpolitik.

They have continued Khrushchev's old strategy of acquiring clients catch-as-catch-can, of responding quickly to the prospects that are spawned by regional politics and upheavals (especially when the candidate is anti-American).[69] There is no "new strategy" that constitutes a shift away from reliance on bourgeois-nationalist leaders to "minor political figures who owe their political status to Soviet backing" and who could be removed at will if they resisted Soviet inroads.[70] It is not ideological affinity that binds Moscow to regimes. Be they radical, revolutionary or rogue, Soviet support of them depends on their importance to Soviet strategic aims and to the USSR's ability to meet their requirements for staying in power. Nor is the contention accurate that "the new element in the Soviet strategy is to help communist parties gain state power": "Then via friendship treaties, arms aid, and Soviet, Cuban or East European advisers, the Soviets will help the local communists hold onto and consolidate power. Ultimately, the aim of this strategy is to establish a new alliance system for the Russians in Africa and Asia, a looser eastern version of the Warsaw Pact."[71]

[69] This does not mean that Soviet leaders always effectively exploit every opportunity that arises or that they commit all the resources needed to secure a potential bridgehead; for example, though "Grenada received by far the greatest per capita economic aid given by the Soviet bloc nations," its request in July 1983 for an emergency loan or grant of $6 million was refused by Soviet officials "on the bizarre grounds that they had heard the French were going to make such a grant, a claim that appeared to be totally baseless. If the Soviets had made this loan, Grenada would probably have been able to surmount the short-run economic difficulties that led to the upheavals of October 1983." Frederic L. Pryor, *Revolutionary Grenada: A Study in Political Economy* (New York: Praeger, 1986), 53. Also in the early 1980s, unwillingness to provide long-term economic assistance almost cost the Soviets a firm political presence in Madagascar.

[70] Richard Pipes, "Soviet Global Strategy," *Commentary* 69, no. 4 (April 1980), 37.

[71] Donald S. Zagoria, "Into the Breach: New Soviet Alliances in the Third World," *Foreign Affairs* 57, no.4 (Spring 1979), 738. For an earlier version of this idea of "extended

There are weaknesses in this thesis. The record shows that Moscow was not responsible for the accession to power of the regimes in Cuba, Ethiopia, the PDRY, Mozambique, and Nicaragua that became pro-Soviet. In the cases of Laos and Kampuchea, it was Vietnam and not the USSR that sired the communist offspring, just as it is to Hanoi and not Moscow that Vientiane and Phnom Penh look for orders. Only in Angola and Afghanistan did Soviet power play a decisive role in bringing a communist party to power. Also, it is an oversimplification to put the communist rulers of Cuba, Ethiopia, and the PDRY in the same category as the rulers of Vietnam, East Germany, Bulgaria, and so on. In the latter group, the communist party is the ruling elite; in the former it is not. Thus, Castro, who publicly proclaimed himself to be a Marxist-Leninist in 1961, may be a communist, but his rule rests on personal control of the military and secret police and not on the reconstituted shell that is the Cuban Communist Party, a dummy organization Castro manipulates and never permits a measure of power. For far-reaching and important policy reasons, one should avoid ascribing an institutionally entrenched communist character to a regime that may, in fact, be only superficially communist in its internal structure, albeit fully pro-Soviet in its foreign policy. The distinction needs to be made lest the Soviet Union's influence be exaggerated and its client's independence of action be underestimated. Neither friendship treaties nor voting patterns in the United Nations are enough to warrant labeling a regime communist: pro-Soviet, definitely; communist, only perhaps.

Moscow's New Imperial Policy regards the Third World as composed of three general types of regimes: first, those that are members of the Nonaligned Movement and maintain friendly, even dependent, relations with the Soviet Union, often with a congenial anti-Americanism and occasionally with a decided "socialist orientation" domestically (in the late 1980s these would include Cuba, Ethiopia, India, Angola, the PDRY, Algeria, and Nicaragua); second, the swing states that are formally nonaligned but that have shifted, as a result of the vagaries of internal politics or priorities, from an obviously pro-Soviet tilt to one more pleasing to the United States, but which might one day swing as abruptly back to Moscow (Ghana, Guinea, Egypt, Somalia, Indonesia, Iraq, and the Sudan); and, third, those countries that are closely oriented toward the United States but whose alignment has weakened in ways assiduously encouraged by Moscow (Greece, Tur-

empire" or "collective security" system see Avigdor Haselkorn, *The Evolution of Soviet Security Strategy 1965–1975* (New York: Crane, Russak, 1978).

key, Morocco, Iran until the fall of the Shah, and Pakistan at different times in the 1970s). Clearly, any Soviet leadership will strive to improve relations with the countries in the latter two categories in the hope of edging them into the first category.

NIP functions better with congenial "nonalignment" than with militant communism. Basically, its success consists of achieving the combination of strategic denial, military privileges, and political influence that fosters Third World behavior ranging from open anti-Americanism, through avoidance of criticism of the Soviet Union, to lobbying in international forums for systematic changes such as the New International Economic Order (NIEO) and the New Information Order (NIO)—the effect of which is to put the West under additional pressure and give the Soviet Union new opportunities for carrying on its diplomatic offensive. There is nothing unexpected or sinister in this; the Soviet leadership simply regards the United States as its main adversary.[72] Only the United States has the capability to destroy the Soviet Union; only the United States can frustrate Soviet goals and aspirations not just in the Near East, as Britain did in the nineteenth century, but globally; and only the United States has the means and urge to complicate the management and stability of the Soviet imperial order.

The USSR's commitment to a forward policy is not only manifested at the state-to-state level. It also finds expression in support for revolutionary movements seeking the overthrow of colonial and "neocolonial" regimes, as was stated in the new Soviet Constitution, adopted under Brezhnev on October 7, 1977: Article 28 commits the USSR to "supporting the struggle of peoples for national liberation and social progress," thus formalizing what had always been a feature of Soviet foreign policy.

By any criterion of foreign policy behavior—economic and military assistance, new commitments,[73] and (as we shall have occasion to see

[72] According to a memoir written by the highest-ranking Soviet diplomat ever to defect, this view is held, for example, by Andrei Gromyko, who was Foreign Minister from 1957 to 1985, and who was pushed by Gorbachev in July 1985 into accepting the largely honorific post of President (Chairman of the Presidium of the Supreme Soviet) of the Soviet Union. Arkady N. Shevchenko, *Breaking with Moscow* (New York: Knopf, 1985), 151.

[73] For example, in January 1982 Moscow committed itself to a ten-year, $2 billion economic aid package to Angola, and in 1983 delivered about $800 million in military hardware. Peter Clement, "Moscow and Southern Africa," *Problems of Communism* 34, no. 2 (March–April 1985), 48.

In April 1986, *Granma*, the official Cuban newspaper, reported that Moscow had agreed to increase its five-year aid and trade package by 50 percent. *Washington Post*, April 12, 1986. The package included $3 billion in credits, mainly for projects in the energy, machine construction, chemical, and pharmaceutical sectors.

in the chapters to come) a readiness to deploy Soviet military power, the utilization of surrogates, participation in the establishment of reliable instruments for institutionalizing power, opposition to U.S.-backed initiatives to resolve regional conflicts—the Soviet leadership's resolve to retain and strengthen its position must be seen as undiminished.

Vietnam, too, is to be a major recipient of increased economic assistance during the 1986–1990 period. In December 1986, during a visit to Hanoi, Yegor Ligachev, a member of the Politburo and Secretariat, assured the Vietnamese of economic aid that would equal that given over the previous thirty years. However, while in Hanoi in March 1987, Soviet Foreign Minister Eduard Shevardnadze apparently expressed Moscow's dissatisfaction to Vietnamese Foreign Minister Nguyen Co Thach over Vietnam's "wasting Soviet economic aid, which according to the Soviet Union amounts to more than 2 billion dollars annually." Radio Liberty, RL 103/87 (March 13, 1987), 4. See also Robert C. Horn, *Alliance Politics between Comrades: The Dynamics of Soviet-Vietnamese Relations*, Joint Report S-02 (Los Angeles: Rand Corporation and University of California at Los Angeles, August 1987), 28–36.

CHAPTER THREE

Backing Liberation Movements

At the time Khrushchev's forward policy rolled into high gear, national liberation movements were not the centers of international attention they became in the 1960s and 1970s. Moscow focused on diplomatic normalization and avoided any activities that might reanimate old fears of its unconventional extra-state operations through the world communist movement, especially among those who had experienced the Stalin-inspired communist rebellions in the late 1940s. The new nations were preoccupied with domestic stabilization and with fashioning a role for themselves in world affairs. Euphoria over the decolonization that occurred in the decade after World War II had not yet given way to annoyance over the erratic pace of the final stages of the process. Third World leaderships—for the most part moderates who were not averse to working closely with the former ruling power provided this did not extend to formal military alliance—were disposed to accept the slower granting of independence to the remaining colonies. For the time being, therefore, Moscow generally kept a low profile.

WARS OF NATIONAL LIBERATION IN SOVIET POLICY

In the struggle for independence of subjugated peoples, Soviet doctrine has upheld the right of recourse to violent means in uprisings against colonialism and imperialism, in what are generally called wars of national liberation or national liberation struggles. While these terms have been applied to diverse situations by Soviet (and Western) writers, as used here they will refer to the armed struggle of Third World groups who are out of power and who can be characterized as being motivated by one or more of the following:

- anticolonialism;
- anti-imperialism;
- a desire rooted in ethnic or religious preferences for autonomy or independence from an indigenous pro-Soviet leadership or a regime with which Moscow has, or is seeking, good relations;

• a desire to overthrow an indigenous Western-oriented, anti-Soviet leadership.[1]

Used in this way the term is more restrictive than its occasional application, in Soviet and Western writings, to a regime *in* power, where it conveys approval of what Moscow sees as an ongoing struggle against either internal or external imperialist forces.[2]

Soviet scholars have written little about the specifics of national liberation movements,[3] and virtually nothing on the USSR's commitments, connections, and operational involvement. Less information is to be found in Soviet sources on the USSR's relations with national liberation movements than on any other aspect of its policy in the Third World (the matter of the KGB's involvement with terrorist groups is beyond the scope of this study). Accordingly, an analyst of Soviet policy has nothing more to rely on than the fragmentary data he can piece together from Western and Third World sources.

Definitions of national liberation movements/revolutions have varied according to the priorities of different Soviet leaders. Under Stalin the CPSU considered "wars of liberation" to be of three general types: those "waged to defend the people from foreign attack and from attempts to enslave them; or to liberate the people from capitalist slav-

---

[1] Soviet writers also use "national liberation struggle" to cover the following: the anti-imperialist policy of a Third World regime; the efforts of a country to break the remaining economic and political bonds tying it to the West (what the Soviets call "neocolonialism"); and a leadership's effort to carry out a socialist revolution. See for example, Rostislav Ulyanovsky [Ulianovskii], *National Liberation* (Moscow: Progress Publishers, 1978); Karen N. Brutents, *National Liberation Revolutions Today*, vol. 1 (Moscow: Progress Publishers, 1977), chapter 5; A. A. Ivanov, *Sotsialisticheskii vybor v Afrike i ideologicheskaya bor'ba* [The Socialist Option in Africa and Ideological Struggle] (Moscow: International Relations Publishing House, 1984), chapters 1 and 5.

[2] For a Soviet example, see *Pravda*, July 21, 1965; for a Western example, see Wallace Spaulding, "Checklist of the 'National Liberation Movements,'" *Problems of Communism* 31, no. 2 (March–April 1982), 77–82.

[3] The Palestinian issue is an exception. Since the early 1970s, the Soviet media have written extensively on the subject; and, more important, Palestinian commentaries on dealings with the Soviet Union, captured documents of the Palestine Liberation Organization (PLO), Western reporting, and records of active diplomatic contacts between the Soviets and Palestinian factions have provided a body of material from which the essentials of the USSR's position on various aspects of the Palestinian struggle emerge. See for example Galia Golan, *The Soviet Union and the Palestine Liberation Organization: An Uneasy Alliance* (New York: Praeger, 1980); Mohamed Heikal, *The Road to Ramadan* (London: Collins, 1975); Raphael Israeli, ed., *PLO in Lebanon: Selected Documents* (New York: St. Martin's Press, 1983); and material in different issues of the *Journal of Palestine Studies*.

ery; or, lastly, to liberate colonies and dependent countries from the yoke of imperialism."[4]

Under Khrushchev, a heavily revised and de-Stalinized party history, reflecting the USSR's struggle during the Second World War, gave new emphasis to Stalin's dichotomy between just wars and unjust wars: "Wars of the oppressed class against the oppressing class, the slaves against the slaveowners, the serfs against the landowners, hired labor against the bourgeoisie, wars of the victorious proletariat in defense of socialism against imperialist governments—such wars Marxists recognize as just wars."[5] P. H. Vigor informs us that "the basic Soviet criterion for approving or condemning a war of whatever kind . . . is whether the war in question does, or does not, further the cause of communism":

> In Marxist terminology, the expression "a war of national liberation" [often called insurgencies or rebellions by Western writers] is invariably one of approval: therefore it is only possible to bestow it on those struggles for the freedom of subject peoples or communities which *do* further the cause. . . .
>
> [However], movements directed against the rule of a communist party can never be regarded by communists as "wars of national liberation." In order to qualify for this title, a given war must be directed against a feudal or "bourgeois" subjugator. But when it is indeed against such a subjugator that the war in question is directed, then *in modern times* (i.e., since the October Revolution) it is invariably termed "a war of national liberation" and is given automatic approval by the Soviet Communist Party.[6]

A definition supplied in Brezhnev's time by Karen Brutents, a leading Soviet scholar on the Third World (and in the late 1980s an important official under Gorbachev), focuses the issue nicely:

> National liberation revolutions are revolutions stemming from national liberation movements and aimed to do away with foreign political, economic and ideological domination and oppression (including national colonial subjugation), and to set up sovereign states. Considering the question of the "national uprising," Lenin said: "It is an uprising aimed at achievement of *political* indepen-

[4] Central Committee of the cpsu, *History of the Communist Party of the Soviet Union (Bolshevik): Short Course* (New York: International Publishers, 1939), 167–68.

[5] B. N. Ponomarev, ed., *Istoriia Kommunisticheskoi Partii Sovetskogo Soyuza* [History of the Communist Party of the Soviet Union] (Moscow: Politizdat, 1959), 175.

[6] P. H. Vigor, *The Soviet View of War, Peace and Neutrality* (London: Routledge & Kegan Paul, 1975), 41–42.

dence of the oppressed nation, i.e., the establishment of a *separate national state*."[7]

Up until the end of the Stalin period, the extensive Soviet writings on the colonial and national question, of which wars of national liberation were a small part, proved of little practical value to communist parties in the colonies. Based on the Bolshevik experience before and after the revolution, they were highly didactic and composed of generalities that bore little relevance to the situation of the individual parties. In no instance in the Third World was Moscow able to provide a national liberation movement with a strategy for mounting a successful struggle. Neither in China nor in Vietnam—the two examples of a communist party carrying out a successful revolution—did the leaderships look to Moscow for strategy or tactics.[8] The fundamental difficulty lay in the philosophical and political incompatibility of nationalism and Moscow's variant of Marxism-Leninism.[9] The more ecumenical Moscow's pretensions, the less germane its prescription.

Traditionally, Soviet doctrine considered every colonial area and liberation movement that Moscow viewed favorably to be a "nation" and as such invested with "national sovereignty"; from this it followed that every such subject people or group was axiomatically a victim of "aggression" and therefore entitled under international law to take whatever measures were necessary to resist and overcome the aggression. After the Second World War, with the Soviet Union's liberation struggle against the Nazi aggression in mind, Soviet jurists argued that in prosecuting "just wars" every action against the aggressor was justifiable. In effect, this placed national liberation struggles beyond the legal norms of warfare previously established by the Hague Conventions. The Soviet position conferred "total immunity on the party said to be waging a just war, irrespective of its actual behavior on the battlefield and behind the front—to giving it *carte blanche* to act as it wishes, while sentencing its opponent to suffer every indignity without

[7] Brutents, *National Liberation Revolutions Today*, 25–26.

[8] Moscow did once propose a strategy that was partially successful to the extent that it was followed: in January 1933, the Chinese Comintern representative in Moscow, Chen Shaoyu (Wang Ming), urged the establishment of a United Front in Manchuria, but this policy was adopted only by some few communist elements, with the result that factional and personal disputes precluded effective opposition to the Japanese. Chong-sik Lee, *Revolutionary Struggle in Manchuria: Chinese Communism and Soviet Interest 1922–1945* (Berkeley: University of California Press, 1983), chapter 6.

[9] Walker Connor, *The National Question in Marxist-Leninist Theory and Strategy* (Princeton: Princeton University Press, 1984), 5.

recourse."[10] In the process, Moscow arrogated unto itself the right to determine whether a war was just or not.

There is an inevitable tension between national liberation struggles—which are people's wars, hence just wars and permitted to transcend the traditionally accepted norms of international law—and the concept of peaceful coexistence. The Soviets say that "peaceful coexistence" concerns relations between states and "does not touch upon relations within states; it does not touch upon the revolutionary struggle for the transformation of society."[11] And, as George Ginsburgs explains, peaceful coexistence, "the virtues of which the Kremlin so assiduously sings today and which it endlessly extols as a key to a better world, does not stand exempt from the basic reservation that it must give precedence to 'just' wars, a superior instrument for 'progress' in the dialectical scheme of history, if the interests of the two collide."[12] Moscow espouses peaceful coexistence and affirms its desire for better relations with the United States, but, as long as it allows wars of liberation to take precedence, tensions between the two countries will be inevitable and enduring. U.S. leaders have repeatedly interpreted peaceful coexistence to imply commitment to a more cooperative relationship based on essential adherence to an approximation of the status quo in the international system; they do not accept Soviet vitiation of peaceful coexistence in the name of a collateral attachment to the concept of just war, especially since the latter is used as an open hunting license to prey on *intra-state* conflicts in the Third World at the expense of Western interests. John Hazard puts the matter well:

[10] George Ginsburgs, " 'Wars of National Liberation' and the Modern Law of Nations—the Soviet Thesis," *Law and Contemporary Problems* 29, no. 4 (Autumn 1964), 935–36. An analysis of Soviet doctrine on national liberation, including discussion of the relationship between national liberation and the world revolutionary process, attitudes toward national, regional, and racial particularism, and the role of violence, is presented in S. Neil MacFarlane, *Superpower Rivalry and Third World Radicalism: The Idea of National Liberation* (Baltimore: Johns Hopkins University Press, 1985), chapter 3.

[11] "Mirnoe sosushchestvovanie" [Peaceful Coexistence], *Diplomaticheskii slovar'* [Diplomatic Dictionary], vol. 2 (Moscow: Politizdat, 1961), 299. In the 1985 edition the term is, by contrast, defined more benignly and accorded less than one-sixth as much space. There is no elaboration of its historical and ideological significance in the struggle between the capitalist and socialist (that is, communist) systems or effort to single out the national liberation movement in the Third World for particular attention. While maintaining that peaceful coexistence means "neither preservation of the social and political *status quo* in the world, nor weakening of ideological struggle," still the 1985 usage is linked to international détente (*razriadka mezhdunarodnoi napriazhennost*), which the earlier was not.

[12] Ginsburgs, " 'Wars of National Liberation,' " 938.

"If peaceful coexistence is to be a reality . . . the concept of a 'just' intervention or war will have to be put aside."[13]

None of these refinements had emerged in Stalin's time. For the most part, his ventures in Third World liberation struggles after World War II were failures.[14] His first and most direct involvement—and biggest setback—was in Iran. At the end of the war, Soviet troops, who in August 1941 had occupied the country in collaboration with Great Britain in order to end the regime's flirtation with Nazi Germany and ensure the flow of war supplies to Soviet forces through the Caucasus, did not leave as they were supposed to in accordance with the 1942 Soviet–Iranian-British treaty. On the contrary, they prevented the Iranian government from reimposing its authority in the northern part of its country and shielded the two Soviet-sponsored separatist movements—the noncommunist Democratic Party of Kurdistan, under the leadership of Mulla Mustafa Barzani; and the communist movement in Iran's Azerbaijani province, under Jafar Pishevari, a veteran communist and Comintern agent. Stalin created two puppet republics in Iranian Azerbaijan: in December 1945, the Azerbaijani Republic, with its capital in Tabriz; and, a month later, the Kurdish Republic, with its capital in Mahadabad, in the western part of the province, along the Iraqi border.[15] Encouraged by the Western powers, Iran brought a complaint to the U.N. Security Council, charging the Soviet Union with interfering in its internal affairs and jeopardizing the peace. The United States strongly supported Iran, and President Harry S Truman hinted at the use of force if Soviet troops were not withdrawn.

That Stalin pulled back and relinquished two choice pieces of strategically important real estate seems, in retrospect, to have been due to miscalculation. At a time when he was still consolidating Soviet rule in Eastern Europe, Stalin, understandably, did not want to precipitate a confrontation with the United States and may well have taken Truman's tough talk more seriously than was warranted, given the United States' inability to challenge the Soviet Union militarily in northwest-

[13] Quoted ibid., 939.

[14] The term "Third World" refers to those countries and areas lying outside the Western and Soviet security communities. It is an imprecise term, but generally is considered synonymous with the "less-developed countries"—the 1960s refinement of the previously used term "underdeveloped countries." Before 1945 Soviet writings included China in the colonial world, but today neither Soviet nor Western writers, as a rule, consider China a part of the Third World, though the Chinese themselves do.

[15] William Eagleton, Jr., *The Kurdish Republic of 1946* (New York: Oxford University Press, 1963), 60–67.

ern Iran. Nor, in 1946, was Truman in a strong-enough military position to have risked a crisis in Europe over Iran. Even more influential on Stalin's decision was probably his having been fooled (as were Western diplomats) by Prime Minister Qavam Saltaneh's diplomacy of dissimulation.[16] A reform-minded, wealthy landowner who was considered pro-communist by many Western officials, Qavam convinced Moscow that, subject to ratification by the Majlis (parliament), he would accede to its demands for economic and political concessions, the effect of which would have been to institutionalize Soviet influence in Tehran—in return for the withdrawal of Soviet forces and the formal return of all the territory controlled by the two pro-Soviet puppet regimes to the authority of the Iranian government. Stalin agreed, the troops were pulled out, and the two "republics" collapsed. Months later, in December 1946, the Majlis rejected the treaty that Moscow had expected, and Stalin came up empty-handed. For his services, Qavam was dismissed by the Shah in the kind of court intrigue that was to destroy Pahlavi rule a little more than thirty years later.

In India, Burma, Malaya, Indonesia, and the Philippines, the Cominform's hardline strategy ending the United Front phase of postwar cooperation with bourgeois-nationalist leaderships brought disaster. The communist parties in South and Southeast Asia discarded moderation and opted for militancy. They took Zhdanov's peroration at the end of the conference creating the Cominform, that "the chief danger to the working class at the present juncture lies in underestimating its own strength and overrating the strength of the enemy," as a call to action.[17] The results were disastrous: abortive coups, isolation from mainstream nationalist groups, persecution, and suspicion of the Soviet Union. For their attempts to emulate Vietnamese successes against the French and their slavish obedience to words from Moscow, regional communist parties paid a heavy price.

Stalin's only success in backing a liberation struggle was in Palestine. By supporting the Zionist struggle for a Jewish state, he helped a movement which, though bourgeois-nationalist, was from his perspective objectively anti-imperialist—in this instance, anti-British. In addition to forcing Britain to relinquish a major stronghold in the eastern Mediterranean, Stalin had reason to expect that the left-socialist outlook of the heavily Russian and East European Jewish leadership would result in close relations with the Soviet Union.

[16] Lewis V. Thomas and Richard N. Frye, *The United States and Turkey and Iran* (Cambridge, Mass.: Harvard University Press, 1951), 238–43.

[17] Quoted in J. H. Brimmell, *Communism in South East Asia* (New York: Oxford University Press, 1959), 254.

Stalin's assistance—diplomatic, political, and military—was of critical importance. Soviet-bloc votes in the U.N. General Assembly ensured the two-thirds majority required for adoption of the resolution calling for partition of Palestine and with it the establishment of an independent Jewish state; after the mandate ended on May 15, 1948, the Soviet Union was the first to extend *de jure* recognition. Stalin permitted Jews to emigrate from Eastern Europe, thereby providing much-needed manpower resources to the new state; and in late 1947 and early 1948 he allowed Czechoslovakia (already under Soviet influence even before the communists seized power in February 1948) to sell arms to the Yishuv (the Jewish community in Palestine) and approved their transit through Hungary, Yugoslavia, and Romania for clandestine shipment through the British blockade to Palestine. Jewish military cadres, especially pilots, were trained in Eastern Europe. Once the state of Israel was proclaimed, its survival was made possible by the weapons that it purchased from the Soviet bloc.[18] Stalin was the midwife who expedited the birth of Israel as a nation state. That this was his only success in the Third World was doubly ironic, given his harsh antisemitic campaign at home and the Kremlin's courtship of Arab regimes shortly after his death.

The Third World was not important to Stalin. Much has been made of hints of possible change in Soviet foreign policy in two essays of his that were published seven months apart in 1952.[19] But any insinuated change was irrelevant to Third World developments. Stalin offered no assistance to LDCs, either bilaterally or in the United Nations, only anticolonial rhetoric. Ignorance of local conditions, the absence of meaningful contacts with national liberation movements, a preoccupation with Soviet-bloc stability and orthodoxy, and military caution, all militated against policy probes in areas outside his hegemonial sphere.

THE KHRUSHCHEV INTERREGNUM: BOLD TALK

When Khrushchev reached out to Third World regimes, he evinced little interest in national liberation movements seeking independence, and not until the new wave of decolonization brought Africa into the

[18] Yaacov Ro'i, *Soviet Decision Making in Practice: The USSR and Israel 1947–1954* (New Brunswick, N.J.: Transaction Books, 1980), 25–33, 149–60.

[19] The essays appeared in Joseph Stalin, *Economic Problems of Socialism in the USSR* (New York: International Publishers, 1952). Two Western assessments of this view are: Marshall D. Shulman, *Stalin's Foreign Policy Reappraised* (Cambridge, Mass.: Harvard University Press, 1963), chapter 10; Donald S. Carlisle, "Stalin's Postwar Foreign Policy and the National Liberation Movement," *Review of Politics* 27, no. 3 (July 1965), 350–56.

limelight in the early 1960s did his policy begin to address this issue. However, inevitably, from the mid-1950s on, as part of their new diplomatic activism, Soviet officials had begun to establish a wide variety of contacts with liberation groups operating abroad. The principal connections were made through four main networks:

1. the United Nations and its many committees dealing with colonial issues;

2. Third World intermediaries, such as Nasser and Nkrumah;[20]

3. West European communist parties, especially the French and Italian, which maintained close ties to African movements; and

4. Soviet-sponsored cultural and scientific meetings, such as the twenty-fifth International Congress of Orientalists, held in Moscow in August 1960, the frequent gatherings of the Afro-Asian Solidarity Committee and other Soviet-front organizations, and the Patrice Lumumba Friendship University, established in Moscow in 1961.

New York was an important center of contact; so was Cairo, Mecca of Middle Eastern and African revolutionaries in the late 1950s and early 1960s. In these unfamiliar settings, Khrushchev moved cautiously. For fear of angering France and compromising the prospects of a Franco-Soviet rapprochement, he did not make the grand gesture that would have brought the USSR instant acclaim in Third World circles: he failed to make Moscow the first power to grant diplomatic recognition to ripening independence movements such as the Algerian Front de Libération Nationale (FLN). Nor was he freer with arms or funds in amounts that would have had an impact. Like Stalin, Khrushchev championed anticolonialism and inveighed against imperialism, but did little. In no instance was he important to any liberation struggle. His bark lacked bite.

But, being a skillful propagandist, Khrushchev appreciated the value of the United Nations as a forum. In 1960, which marked a high tide of decolonization as seventeen new nations—sixteen of them African—emerged on the international scene, he spoke out boldly. Along with a number of other members, Khrushchev offered a draft declaration whose substance was subsequently adopted in modified form as U.N. General Assembly Resolution 1514 (xv)—"Declaration on the Granting of Independence to Colonial Countries and Peoples." The declaration denounced colonialism in all its aspects and de-

---

[20] See Tareq Y. Ismael, *The UAR in Africa: Egypt's Policy under Nasser* (Evanston, Ill.: Northwestern University Press, 1971), 90–91.

manded immediate independence for all subjugated peoples. The Soviet proposal stood in sharp contrast to the abstention of the Western powers and enhanced Moscow's prestige. The following year, at Khrushchev's request, the General Assembly established the Special Committee on the Situation with Regard to the Implementation of the Declaration on the Granting of Independence to Colonial Countries and Peoples (known informally as the Special Committee of Twenty-four) to monitor implementation of Resolution 1514. In U.N. forums, the USSR supported radical Afro-Asian resolutions calling for an end to colonialism but shied away from demands for direct intervention by the U.N. Security Council: in brief, Moscow's declarations were not matched by deeds.

At this time Khrushchev's quarrel with Mao was worsening, and each side felt impelled to stake out "correct" doctrinal positions on the Third World, including attitudes toward liberation struggles. The distinguished orientalist Academician E. M. Zhukov was assigned the task of demolishing the Chinese arguments that criticized the USSR's assistance to regimes such as India and Indonesia (both of which were at odds with Beijing) and Egypt, which suppressed local communists. Zhukov's commentary appeared in *Pravda* on August 26, 1960. Citing Lenin on the progressive and historical significance of the creation of the national state, he upheld the USSR's support for new nations and national liberation movements headed by bourgeois-nationalist leaders, and upbraided "dogmatists and sectarians" for stressing their nonsocialist character and woefully underestimating the importance of what they had already achieved politically in breaking with imperialism: "The doctrinaires and 'leftists', permitting themselves to snicker at forms of the national liberation movement that do not fit into the usual sociological patterns, forget that no 'pure' revolutionary processes take place in nature. In a national liberation anti-imperialist movement, the front of participants is naturally far broader than in a social revolution."[21]

According to Zhukov, the anti-imperialist orientation of the new nations and liberation movements was substantial and sufficient to bind them to the socialist camp, and their shared opposition to colonialism and imperialism justified Soviet assistance and friendship. It was utopian to believe that revolution or a particular kind of social system could be exported: each had to emerge as a product of internal devel-

---

[21] E. Zhukov, "Znamenatel'nyi faktor nashego vremeni: O nekotorykh voprosakh sovremennogo natsional'no-osvoboditel'nogo dvizheniya" [A Significant Factor of Our Time: Some Problems of the Contemporary National Liberation Movement], *Pravda*, October 26, 1960, 3.

opment. He also cautioned that socialist transformations would take a long time and be complex affairs. A few months later, Khrushchev added his imprimatur.

A conference of communist and workers' parties convened in Moscow in November 1960 failed to close the rift between the Soviet and Chinese party leaderships. On January 6, 1961, Khrushchev delivered a major speech to party cadres at a meeting of Party Organizations of the Higher Party School, the Academy of Social Sciences, and the Institute of Marxism-Leninism of the CPSU's Central Committee. To ensure maximum exposure, the speech was published in *Kommunist* immediately afterwards.[22]

Taking the high ground of prudent concern for the cohesion of the world communist movement and the well-being of all peoples, Khrushchev quoted Leninist scripture to buttress his attacks on revisionism and dogmatism, the polar extremes to which opponents are relegated in doctrinal jousts: "It is essential to learn the indisputable truth that a Marxist must take account of life, of the exact facts of reality, and not go on clinging to yesterday's theory, which, like all theory, at best outlines fundamentals, generalities, and only approximates a total comprehension of the complexities of life."[23] He warned against threat from "revisionism which tries to wipe out the revolutionary essence of Marxism-Leninism, white-wash modern capitalism, undermine the solidarity of the Communist movement, and encourage Communist Parties to go their separate national ways."[24] But he was particularly bitter in attacking "dogmatism and sectarianism" (that is, Maoism) as irresponsible and dangerous: "They lead to the isolation of Communists from the broad strata of the workers; they condemn them to passive temporizing or leftist adventurist activities in the revolutionary struggle; they prevent full use of all opportunities in the interests of the victory of the working class and all democratic forces."[25] He implied that the Chinese leaders were adrift from reality and willing to risk nuclear war in order to promote world revolution. Khrushchev's speech was primarily a defense of his policy of improving relations with the West, of revising doctrine to make it clear that in a nuclear

[22] For Khrushchev's 20,000-word speech of January 6, 1961, and comments of American specialists on it, see "Analysis of the Khrushchev Speech of January 6, 1961," *Hearing before the Subcommittee to Investigate the Administration of the Internal Security Act and the Internal Security Laws*, Committee of the Judiciary, U.S. Senate, 87th Congress, 1st session (Washington, D.C.: U.S. Government Printing Office, 1961).

[23] Ibid., 75.

[24] Ibid.

[25] Ibid.

age Moscow no longer regarded war between capitalism and communism as "fatalistically inevitable," and of trying to isolate the Chinese and restore unity in the rest of the world communist movement.

Prior to his discussion of wars of national liberation, Khrushchev identified four general categories of war, in the process redefining Stalin's threefold classification of wars of liberation: world wars, which would be nuclear and involve the superpowers; local wars, which are limited wars fought by an imperialist power against a Third World country (as in the Anglo-French–Israeli attack on Egypt in 1956), or between two capitalist countries; wars of national liberation, which are struggles for independence from foreign rule; and popular uprisings, which are internal struggles pitting "progressive" groups against "reactionary" groups tied to the camp of imperialism. The difference between a local war and a war of national liberation is a political one. As one Western analyst observed, the determination depends on which side Moscow favors:

> In short, recourse to war by Western powers or their allies is condemned as local–limited war; recourse to arms by the newly-independent or "colonial" peoples, or by communist states or guerrilla forces in opposition to Western or Western-oriented regimes, ordinarily receives Soviet approval as a war of liberation. The same war may be labeled a war of liberation by the Soviets when referring to the belligerent that the USSR supports, but may be classified as a local-limited war when reference is made to the Western-oriented combatant.[26]

Similarly, an uprising may be defined as popular or counter-revolutionary depending on the Soviet attitude toward the particular group seeking to topple the regime.

Taking wars of national liberation out of the category of local wars and proceeding on the assumption that only the latter could escalate to world war theoretically left the Soviet Union free to help colonial peoples fight against the yoke of imperialism, give "all-round" support to liberation movements and still contend they were adhering to a policy of peaceful coexistence.

Relatively little attention was devoted to national liberation struggles, little more than 2 percent of Khrushchev's speech. He did cite the struggles in Vietnam and Algeria as examples of national liberation wars, calling them uprisings against foreign rule that had devel-

[26] Stephen P. Gibert, "Wars of Liberation and Soviet Military Policy," *Orbis* 10, no. 3 (Fall 1966), 843.

oped into guerrilla wars: "These are revolutionary wars"; they "are not only admissible but inevitable." He said that in the case of Vietnam the United States did not intervene directly for fear that if it did Vietnam would get aid from China and the Soviet Union and this could "lead to a world war." By implication, he took some credit, well after the fact, for the victory of the North Vietnamese over the French. In his brief reference to the struggle in Algeria, then in its seventh year, he noted that the United States and the NATO countries were helping France, whereas "we help and will help the peoples striving for their independence," in what is "a sacred war."[27] However, in light of China's diplomatic recognition of Algeria in April 1960 and the USSR's unwillingness to take this step, plus its generally unimpressive record of assistance to the Algerians, this part of the speech had a hollow ring. With respect to Cuba, Khrushchev had even less to say: he noted the overthrow of the tyrannical Batista regime, but said nothing about supporting Castro. That was still in the future.

In none of these three liberation struggles that Khrushchev singled out for attention had the Soviet Union played a key role. Nor did he specify the circumstances in which national liberation struggles might expect assistance from the Soviet Union. Although the formulation of a strategy for the Third World was not at the heart of his presentation, the Kennedy administration unfortunately thought it was, with momentous consequences for U.S. foreign policy and the subsequent tragic involvement in Vietnam. In light of the profound effect his words had on the Kennedy administration, the paragraph in which Khrushchev envisioned future wars of national liberation bears quoting:

> Can such wars flare up in the future? They can. Can there be such uprisings? There can. But these are wars which are national uprisings. In other words, can conditions be created where a people will lose their patience and rise in arms? They can. What is the attitude of the Marxists toward such uprisings? A most positive one. These uprisings must not be identified with wars among states, with local wars, since in these uprisings the people are fighting for implementation of their right for self-determination, for independent social and national development. These are uprisings against rotten reactionary regimes, against the colonizers. The Communists fully support such just wars and march in the front rank with the peoples waging liberation struggles.[28]

[27] Khrushchev, in "Analysis of the Khrushchev Speech," 64.
[28] Ibid., 65.

A close reading of Khrushchev's entire speech suggests that

1. far from advocating a militant line or mounting new challenges to the West in the Third World, his purpose was to restore some unity in the communist world and promote détente;

2. he was intent on countering Mao's calls for intensification of pressure on the United States and wanted to convince communist parties that the ideological fervor and inexperience of the Chinese could trigger a nuclear war;

3. he was trying to reassert Moscow's leadership over the world communist movement and counter Mao's challenge to Moscow's authority; and

4. in proclaiming the USSR's principled support for national liberation struggles and the end of colonialism, far from saying anything new or presaging a new militancy in the Third World, he was merely reaffirming standard Soviet doctrine.

All of this needs to be emphasized because it is so at variance with the interpretation given in Washington at the time; and it is difficult to reconcile the speech with the furor it created in the new Kennedy administration.[29] But without question it had a profound effect on Kennedy, prompting him to read parts of it "to the first meeting of his National Security Council" and to instruct the "assembled agency heads to study it and circulate it among their staffs"; and from this meeting emerged the Kennedy administration's fixation with developing a counterinsurgency strategy to handle the perceived Soviet threat to Western interests in the Third World.[30]

[29] One Kennedy appointee, who first served as Director of the Bureau of Intelligence and Research in the Department of State and later as Assistant Secretary of State for Far Eastern Affairs, has written, " 'What are we doing about guerrilla warfare?' was one of the first questions Kennedy asked his aides when he became President. . . . The President meant Vietnam, but he was convinced that what was happening there had wider implications—that guerrilla warfare was a new form of aggression for which we needed a new strategy." Kennedy, already aware of Mao's writing on revolutionary warfare, noted that Khrushchev's speech on January 6, 1961 had directed attention to this kind of war and spoken of his determination to support wars of national liberation. "Seeking its significance, President Kennedy directed that all the members of his new administration read the speech and consider what it portended." Roger Hilsman, *To Move a Nation: The Politics of Foreign Policy in the Administration of John F. Kennedy* (New York: Doubleday, 1967), 413–14.

[30] Douglas S. Blaufarb, *The Counter-Insurgency Era: U.S. Doctrine and Performance 1950 to the Present* (New York: Free Press, 1977), 52; see chapter 3 for a chilling analysis of how misperceptions and exaggerated notions of the uses of power distorted U.S. foreign policy and led to the tragic involvement in Vietnam. For a Soviet view of the ideological

Far from being revolutionary, Khrushchev's policy toward national liberation struggles was one of calculated caution. The case of Algeria is instructive. The Algerian war of liberation started in November 1954 under a noncommunist leadership and spanned most of the decade of Khrushchev's rule, during which time the Soviet press castigated French colonial rule and upheld the right of the Algerians to independence. But when it came to providing assistance—diplomatic, economic, or military—Khrushchev showed himself a sunshine partisan, leery of taking risks. On the third anniversary of the revolt, a leading French journalist and specialist on the Soviet Union pointed out that the Soviet media rarely reported on the two main resistance organizations—the FLN and the Mouvement National Algérien (MNA); he attributed this neglect to Moscow's reluctance to see the influence of a weak France replaced by that of a strong United States in Algeria.[31] In February 1958, the Soviet government announced its first contribution of any kind to the Algerian struggle—a shipment of food and medical supplies to Algerian refugees in Tunisia and Morocco. Seven months later, during a visit to Egypt by Nuritdin A. Mukhitdinov, a member of the CPSU's Presidium and Secretariat, a Soviet official met for the first time with representatives of the Algerian provisional government which had recently been established in Tunisia to enhance the FLN's bargaining position.[32] But in December an FLN mission visiting Moscow was refused diplomatic recognition and left empty-handed, even its request for arms rejected.

When Charles de Gaulle returned to power in the fall of 1958, Khrushchev saw opportunities to exploit Paris's differences with London and Washington and curbed his criticisms of French policy in Algeria, with the exception of the occasional comment that independence was inevitable. When, in mid-September 1959, de Gaulle stated for the first time that Algeria had a right to self-determination, Khrushchev spoke approvingly of his statesmanlike position. But still Moscow would not assist the Algerians for fear of angering de Gaulle, whose policies were causing serious strains in NATO and the European Economic Community (EEC) and inadvertently complementing Soviet objectives in Europe. Indeed, there was a report that Moscow had gone so far as to bar a shipment of Chinese arms for the Algerians from crossing the Soviet Union.[33]

---

and economic impetus underlying Kennedy's "new frontier" approach to the Third World, see K. Brutents, *A Historical View of Neo-Colonialism* (Moscow: Novosti, 1972), 67–121; 229–51.

[31] Michel Tatu, *Le Monde*, November 30, 1957.

[32] *Egyptian Gazette*, September 28, 1958.

[33] *New York Times*, September 28, 1959.

Chinese gibes at Moscow's lack of support for the Algerian cause touched the Soviets on a sensitive issue: whereas Moscow waffled on recognition for the Algerian provisional government, Beijing extended *de facto* recognition shortly after it was set up and formal recognition in early 1960; whereas Moscow was chary of providing arms or funds, the Chinese were not, though even they were less forthcoming than they intimated; and, whereas Moscow welcomed French gestures aimed at a negotiated settlement, Beijing called for revolutionary struggle till victory was achieved. Sino-Soviet polemics on the Algerian issue intensified in 1960, a reflection of worsening Sino-Soviet relations and the failure of the international communist conference in Moscow in November 1960. Moscow's concern was "that China, by adopting an irreconcilably anti-French stand in sharp contrast to Moscow's middle-of-the-road stance, would be able to increase its own influence with the Algerian rebels, and ultimately with the independent Algerian government, at the expense of the Russians."[34]

Khrushchev had his reasons for keeping a distance from the FLN:

1. he wanted to avoid any action that might distract de Gaulle from downgrading France's military relationship with NATO and the United States or that might damage the budding Franco-Soviet rapprochement;

2. the priority he accorded peaceful coexistence in Europe transcended the sympathy he may have had for a revolution in a Third World area remote from Soviet interest;

3. both French and Algerian communists had ambivalent feelings about the FLN, partly because in France the working-class constituents of the French Communist Party were anti-Algerian and partly because in Algeria many communists were Jews, whose French citizenship and European origins made them suspect in the eyes of the FLN leadership, which was Muslim and Arab in outlook and culture; and

4. the FLN, which was a nationalist, not communist organization, was intensely suspicious of communist participants.[35]

Khrushchev's position on Algeria changed very slowly. Thus, when Ferhat Abbas, the first president of the Algerian provisional govern-

[34] Donald S. Zagoria, *The Sino-Soviet Conflict 1956–1961* (Princeton: Princeton University Press, 1962), 274.

[35] Alistair Horne, *A Savage War of Peace: Algeria 1954–1962* (London: Macmillan, 1977), 405; see also Henry F. Jackson, *The FLN in Algeria: Party Development in a Revolutionary Society* (Westport, Conn.: Greenwood Press, 1977), 29; and Emmanuel Sivan, *Communisme et nationalisme en Algérie 1920–1962* (Paris: Presses la Fondation Nationale des Sciences Politiques, 1976), passim.

ment (he was replaced in 1961 by Ahmed Ben Bella), stopped in Moscow on his way back from China in late September 1960, he received a great deal of attention, but no diplomatic recognition and no arms, only a promise of them at such time as the FLN controlled "a piece of 'liberated' Algerian territory—a highly unlikely prospect in the prevailing military state of the war."[36] More frequent criticism of France and de Gaulle appeared in the Soviet press, but it was relevant to Moscow's cancellation of the planned summit conference in Paris in May 1960 and Khrushchev's attention to the world conference of communist parties in November and the challenge from the Chinese.[37] At the twenty-second congress of the CPSU, in October 1961, Khrushchev spoke of how "the Soviet Union, in fulfilment of its international duty, has been helping the peoples who struggled against imperialism and colonialism"—though he gave no examples.[38] None of this, however, was translated into military assistance. By the time Moscow extended *de jure* recognition to the provisional government of the Republic of Algeria on March 19, 1962, de Gaulle had agreed at Évian to a cease-fire and accepted the inevitability of independence by agreeing to a referendum on the subject in Algeria.[39] When Algeria became independent in July 1962, it did so without ever having received anything other than token support from the Soviet Union. Four months later, such was its suspicion of the communists that the leadership banned the Parti Communiste Algérien, a move that evoked "profound regret" in Moscow, but no tough response.[40] One year later, Moscow sold Algeria heavy arms on generous terms, the start of a close but correct diplomatic relationship between the two countries, one based on national interest, not ideological affinity.

On a number of occasions after Algeria became independent, Khrushchev, usually in the context of an overseas tour or interviews with Afro-Asian journalists, spoke of the USSR's support for national liberation movements and of how the USSR had sent the Algerians "large quantities of weapons" free of charge to help in their "bloody armed struggle" against the French.[41] But there is no evidence for his

[36] Horne, *A Savage War of Peace*, 405.

[37] For example, *Izvestiia*, October 27, 1960.

[38] N. S. Khrushchev, *Communism—Peace and Happiness for the Peoples*, vol. 2 (Moscow: Foreign Languages Publishing House, 1963), 24.

[39] *Le Monde*, March 20, 1962.

[40] *Pravda*, December 4, 1962, translated in *Current Digest of the Soviet Press* 14, no. 49 (January 2, 1963), 17.

[41] See for example, on December 21, 1963, his reply to a series of questions on the national liberation movement submitted by two Algerian newspapers, one Ghanaian, and one Burmese. *Soviet News*, no. 4934 (December 23, 1963), 157.

claims. Nonetheless, Soviet writers, perhaps proceeding on the assumption that something written often enough will in time be accepted as fact, invariably mention the "all-round assistance" or "the significant support" extended by the Soviet Union to Algeria as a contributory reason for the success of the Algerian liberation struggle.[42]

When Khrushchev was deposed in October 1964, the Soviet Union was only on the periphery of national liberation struggles, in marked contrast to its expanding relationship with Third World governments. Courtship of anti-American regimes, not involvement in the efforts of non-ruling revolutionary movements, dominated Soviet policy in the Third World.

BREZHNEV ENGAGES

Liberation struggles came to the forefront of international attention in the mid-1960s. After the early waves of decolonization had swept away most of the European overseas empires, leaving only Portugal unscathed (for one more decade, as events turned out), the unfinished anticolonial struggles intensified, notably in South Vietnam, South Yemen, and Rhodesia; and new areas of turbulence developed, inspired by the principle of national self-determination. The impulses underlying these struggles were varied: opposition to control by a Western power; political differences with the ruling pro-Western regime; dissatisfaction of an ethnic, religious, or racial group with the prevailing policy. In most cases, the struggles were generated for the purposes of overthrowing and replacing the group in power; in some cases, a redistribution or greater sharing of power was sought (as by the Kurds in Iraq); and, in a few instances, a minority fought to secede and establish its own country (the Eritreans in Ethiopia, the Biafrans in Nigeria).

Within six months after Khrushchev's deposal, the new Kremlin leadership, headed by the duumvirate of Leonid Brezhnev and Aleksei Kosygin, was drawn deeply into the liberation struggle in Vietnam. Pressed by considerations of intra-communist world politics to expand their support when the United States bombed North Vietnam and landed the first major contingent of combat forces in South Vietnam in March 1965, they promised "all-round assistance" to strengthen the

[42] For example V. Cherniaev, "Osvoboditel'naya voina alzhirskogo naroda" [The Liberation War of the Algerian People], *Voenno-istoricheskii zhurnal*, no. 11 (November 1974), 81; and N. Mel'nik, "V bor'be za nezavisimost: K 30-letiyu natsional'no-demokraticheskoi revolyutsii v Alzhire" [The Struggle for Independence: 30 Years of the National Democratic Revolution in Algeria], *Voenno-istoricheskii zhurnal*, no. 11 (November 1984), 53–60.

military capability of the Democratic Republic of Vietnam (DRV) and enable the Hanoi government to rebuff the "imperialists"; and they recognized the National Front for the Liberation of South Vietnam as the "sole representative" of the people of South Vietnam, signifying support for Hanoi's policy of overturning the 1954 Geneva agreements that partitioned Vietnam and of trying to unify Vietnam by force.[43] While the United States waged war against a communist country, Brezhnev and Kosygin were not willing to stand idly by and leave the Chinese a clear field in which to challenge Soviet leadership of the bloc and tarnish Soviet prestige abroad.

Competition with China spurred the USSR's assistance to liberation struggles in the Arab East and Southern Africa. The advantage lay with Moscow. Beijing lacked resources to compete seriously for prime clients, and from 1966 to 1970 was wracked internally by the "Great Proletarian Cultural Revolution," which was neither great nor proletarian nor cultural nor a revolution, but simply a struggle for power between Mao and his opponents. By the early 1970s China concentrated more on stymying the advances of Soviet-oriented regimes and movements than on contributing to the success of a liberation struggle: thus it courted the anti-Soviet Shah of Iran, who was helping Oman to resist an insurgency backed by the pro-Soviet PDRY, and ceased its aid to the PDRY; and it opted to back UNITA rather than the MPLA in Angola. As a result of such twists-and-turns in Chinese policy, the Soviet Union was able to command the high and principled ground in the Sino-Soviet maneuvering for influence among major liberation movements and their Third World supporters and to achieve a string of victories over the Chinese all through the late 1960s and 1970s.

It was in Vietnam that Moscow saw the advantages of raising the ante, and it committed more resources there than to any other liberation struggle. In a lengthy statement on June 28, 1965, *Pravda* set the tone. It noted that the downfall of the colonial system led to a weakening of imperialism and that national liberation struggles reinforced this process. Accordingly, "the Soviet Union advocates the use of every form of struggle for national liberation" and is helping the DRV "to strengthen its defense capacity," because every liberation struggle was an integral part of the world revolutionary process and was bound up with the general struggle against imperialism and for peace.[44] A few

[43] *Current Digest of the Soviet Press* 17, no. 16 (May 12, 1965), 13.

[44] *Pravda*, June 28, 1965. An interesting perspective on the Kremlin's perception of possible advantages is provided by a former Hungarian diplomat: see Janos Radvanyi, "Vietnam War Diplomacy: Reflections of a Former Iron Curtain Official," in Lloyd J.

weeks later, Soviet officials took the unusual step of replying directly to a series of articles that had appeared in early July in the *New York Times* in which the Soviet Union was blamed for wars of national liberation. In an attempt to downplay the contention that the Soviet Union was responsible for the intensifying struggle in South Vietnam, they denied that the USSR "exports revolutions"; that national liberation struggles can be imported from abroad or are anything but the product of primarily home-grown and popularly rooted movements; and, indeed, that communist parties were in the forefront of most liberation struggles.[45]

Be that as it may, Moscow reaped a political-military windfall from the American entanglement: discord in NATO; unrest and bitter divisiveness in the United States; diversion of the United States away from European and Far Eastern affairs and the core issues that were Moscow's concern; the rise of anti-Americanism as an important factor in international politics; enhanced prestige for the USSR among nonaligned countries and anti-war groups in the West; and a frittering away of U.S. power. Quite a return on Moscow's modest outlay of arms and economic assistance. At the twenty-third congress of the CPSU, a cocky Brezhnev declared that "there can be no peaceful coexistence when it comes to the internal processes of the national liberation struggle."[46]

By the late 1960s, Soviet writers were once again faced with the task of squaring theory with reality. The complexity and proliferation of conflicts in the Third World required refinement of the term "national liberation struggle." This time the impetus came from the military, who sensed that Vietnam's stalemating of the United States and the Soviet Union's achievement of essential equivalence at the strategic nuclear level had opened up new possibilities for fighting imperialism (the United States) without lowering the threshold of nuclear or conventional war between the superpowers.[47] The prospects for strategic gain with minimal risk were bright.

The ensuing years saw the introduction of a number of doctrinal changes. Thus, one Soviet military analyst noted that, in the general area of national liberation struggles, local wars and military conflicts

Matthews and Dale E. Brown, eds., *Assessing the Vietnam War* (Elmsford, N.Y.: Pergamon-Brassey's 1987), 57–66.

[45] See G. Starushenko, "Vymysel i pravda ob osvoboditel'nykh voinakh" [Fiction and Truth About Liberation Wars], *Kommunist*, no. 12 (August 1965), 94–95.

[46] *Pravda*, March 30, 1966.

[47] Mark N. Katz, *The Third World in Soviet Military Thought* (Baltimore: Johns Hopkins University Press, 1982), 43–51.

can "occur between individual young national governments, as for example the Indo-Pakistan wars in 1965 and 1971, and the Algerian-Moroccan border conflict in 1963."[48] Greater attention was also devoted to civil wars—that is, conflicts within countries. The net result was the expansion by the mid-1970s of the scope of what was meant by the term "wars of national liberation." Henceforth, such wars were not only wars "between Third World nations or groups and the Western imperialist nations," but also conflicts "between and within Third World nations which did not necessarily involve Western nations."[49]

Soviet writings also began to include criticisms of communist uprisings that misused violent means in the interest of liberation struggles and failed, as in Indonesia, where the pro-Beijing communist party was decimated in 1965. This, plus reiterations that revolutions cannot be exported, led some Western observers to conclude that the Soviets basically call for an evolutionary approach to the seizure of power;[50] and others to believe that Moscow, disappointed with its limited influence on developments in the Third World, was inclining to an "obvious downgrading of the national liberation movement" in its overall strategy.[51] Such approaches to Soviet policy ignore Soviet adaptability.

Soviet writers on revolution and national liberation struggles may defend the use of violent means for overthrowing foreign masters and internal reactionaries, on the grounds that no exploiter ever willingly relinquishes power; but they modify this with recognition that independence is to be won by means of both armed struggle and nonmilitary means depending on the conditions specific to each country. Thus, to select one Soviet tactic or one set of Soviet quotations leads to biased conclusions about Soviet policy, with its usual use of opportune means, be they evolutionary or revolutionary. Colonel E. Dolgopolov, who has written extensively on the subject, observes that "special conditions" caused armed struggle to become the main form of the liberation movement in China, Algeria, and Cuba, among others, but goes on to say that "the existence of the socialist world system" means that many new nations will be able to "take the road of progress by peaceful means, without having to resort to armed struggle."[52]

[48] G. Malinovskii, "Lokal'nye voiny v zone natsional'no-osvoboditel'nogo dvizheniya" [Local Wars in the Context of the National Liberation Movement], *Voenno-istoricheskii zhurnal*, no. 5 (May 1974), 94–95.

[49] Katz, *The Third World in Soviet Military Thought*, 43.

[50] For example Raymond H. Anderson, *New York Times*, September 15, 1968.

[51] For example Morton Schwartz, "The USSR and Leftist Regimes in Less-Developed Countries," *Survey*, no. 2 (Spring 1973), 220.

[52] See Colonel Ye. Dolgopolov, "National Liberation and Armed Struggle," *Soviet Mili-*

Then, to protect himself against criticisms of revisionism or sectarianism, he denounces both "bourgeois-pacifist views . . . the so-called non-violent approach" and "the leftist line," which presents "armed struggle as the only and universal method of the liberation forces." What is required, says Dolgopolov, is "sober political calculation, composure and self control" and a strategy that draws "on scientific analysis of the balance of forces within each country and in the international arena." No one could quarrel with this commendable, if elusive, formula. In practice, whatever approach the Kremlin adopted toward a particular liberation struggle was hailed as wise and farsighted, whether it was support of the Vietnamese or criticism of the Indonesian communists.[53] From the mid-1960s on, certain national liberation struggles received considerable support; others did not. An incessant meddler, Moscow is also a skilled accommodationist.

THE SOVIET RECORD IN THE 1970S AND 1980S

The number of liberation struggles on the international stage has, paradoxically, increased since the early 1970s, notwithstanding the virtual end of European colonialism. In Africa, a few movements still seek to end the last vestiges of the European hegemony. For the most part, however, struggles against the territorial and political status quo by groups who believe they have not been fairly treated by indigenous rulers or who simply seek power for themselves have replaced the earlier quest for independence from foreign rule as the dominant type of war of national liberation in the Third World. Colonialism may be almost dead, but its legacy—arbitrary and disputed boundaries, divided peoples, and unstable political systems—is very much in evidence. As long as the struggle against colonialism was the prevailing form of conflict in the Third World, Soviet analysts were on familiar doctrinal and political ground. But the eruption of civil wars or people's wars complicated their task. They could no longer use "imperialism" as the explanation for wars in newly independent countries that were often friendly and embarked on a noncapitalist or even socialist path of development; and, indeed, in the mid-1970s some analysts did acknowl-

tary Review, no. 9 (September 1968), 46–50. He develops his ideas further in Natsional'no-osvoboditel'nye voiny na sovremennom etape [National Liberation Wars in the Modern Age] (Moscow: Voenizdat, 1977).

53 In reality, the deposal of Sukarno, like the destruction of the PKI (Indonesian Communist Party), "caused little concern" in Moscow, which welcomed Jakarta's break in diplomatic relations with Beijing. P. H., "Moscow, Jakarta, and the PKI," Mizan 11, no. 2 (March–April 1969), 106.

edge that wars stemmed from "the contradictions born of the territorial disputes that arise between new nations" or "born of the
differences in their socio-political, ethnic, or religious social order."[54]

One comment before we turn to an assessment of the Soviet record
in the 1970s and 1980s and the trends that can be adduced from Soviet policy. It has been proposed that strong support for liberation
movements has a link to factional rivalry in the Kremlin,[55] and it is
certainly possible that those who favored improved relations with the
United States for the purpose of obtaining much-needed technology
and credits did adopt a firm position opposing imperialism and aiding
liberation struggles so as to forestall allegations from their opponents
that they were "soft on imperialism." We know that by the late 1960s
the Politburo was convinced that the Kosygin economic reforms of
September 1965 would not be enough to overcome technological and
productivity problems at home and that the Soviet Union would have
to look to the West and Japan for help.[56] Accordingly, the argument
goes, Brezhnev, wanting to ensure a consensus on seeking détente—
and yet to ward off accusations of "sectarianism" or "revisionism"
from opponents in the party—carried on a highly competitive policy
with the United States in the Third World, in spite of the obvious adverse effect on détente. If the argument is valid, Gorbachev, too,
might have to adopt the same strategy to counter allegations of ideological laxity from those opposed to his domestic reforms or negotiations with the West. The gap between what the leader says and what
he does is as noticeable as it was under Brezhnev. Thus, although Gorbachev paid far less attention to liberation movements and Third
World issues in the new party program that he presented in October
1985 (the first since 1961) and in his report to the twenty-seventh congress of the CPSU, in February 1986, they, in fact, show no signs of
being any less supported and promoted than previously.[57]

Every liberation movement with which the USSR has been linked,

[54] Malinovskii, "Lokal'nye voiny," 93.

[55] According to Raymond L. Garthoff, "While Western observers have usually seen Soviet statements in support of national liberation and progressive revolutionary movements as reflecting an offensive thrust in Soviet foreign policy, Soviet leaders have in fact
usually made such statements in a defensive context that related to internal controversies
within the world communist movement and domestic Soviet politics." *Detente and Confrontation: American-Soviet Relations from Nixon to Reagan* (Washington, D.C.: Brookings Institution, 1985), 48.

[56] Harry Gelman, *The Brezhnev Politburo and the Decline of Detente* (Ithaca, N.Y.: Cornell
University Press, 1984), 130.

[57] Francis Fukuyama, "Gorbachev and the Third World," *Foreign Affairs* 64, no. 4
(Spring 1986), 715–31.

TABLE 2
National Liberation Struggles in the Third World in the
1970s and 1980s

Country	Period	The USSR's role in bringing independence or in sustaining a struggle
AFRICA		
Angola	1970–1975	Valuable
	Post-1975, ongoing and anti-Marxist	None
Chad	1975–1987	Negligible
Ethiopia	Ongoing	None
Guinea-Bissau	1970–1975	Negligible
Mozambique	1970–1975	None
	Post-1979, ongoing and anti-Marxist	None
Namibia	Ongoing	Valuable
Somalia	Ongoing	None
South Africa	Ongoing	Useful
Sudan	1968–1973	None
	1983–, ongoing	None
Uganda	1970–1978	None
	1980–1986	None
Zaire	1977	Negligible
	1978 (Shaba province)	Negligible
Zimbabwe	1965–1980	Negligible
SOUTHERN ASIA		
Burma	Ongoing	None
Indonesia	1976–, ongoing	None
Kampuchea	Post-1979, ongoing	None
Pakistan	1972–1977	None
Philippines	Ongoing	None
Sri Lanka	Ongoing	None
Thailand	Ongoing	None
South Vietnam	1960–1975	Valuable
Malaysia	1950–1980	None
LATIN AMERICA		
Columbia	Ongoing	Negligible
Argentina	1970–1983	None
Bolivia	Ongoing	None
Chile	Ongoing	None
Guatemala	Ongoing	None

TABLE 2 (*cont.*)

Country	Period	The USSR's role in bringing independence or in sustaining a struggle
Nicaragua	1970–1979	None
	1981–, ongoing and anti-Marxist	None
El Salvador	Ongoing	Negligible
Peru	1980–, ongoing	None
Uruguay	Ongoing	None
Venezuela	Ongoing	None
THE MIDDLE EAST		
Afghanistan	1979–, ongoing and anti-Marxist	None
Bahrain	Ongoing	Negligible
Iran	Until 1979 and overthrow of the Shah ♠	None
Iraq	Ongoing	Negligible
Lebanon	Ongoing	None
Morocco	Ongoing	Negligible
Oman	1965–1975	Useful
Palestinian National Resistance	Ongoing	Useful
Turkey	Ongoing	None
Yemen Arab Republic	Ongoing	None

even marginally, is listed in Table 2. No attempt has been made to include all self-styled liberation movements, because many of them—the National Liberation Front of Qatar, for one—are insignificant and their inclusion would misleadingly downgrade the extent of the USSR's actual involvement. Moscow's importance to individual movements seeking to overthrow established governments is assessed as either "valuable," "useful," "negligible," or "none."

The Soviet Union has supported national liberation struggles in four types of situation. The first involved its commitment to anticolonialism. From 1945 on, this theme figured prominently in the USSR's championing of colonial peoples in international forums and in the myriad of peace groups and anti-American, Soviet-sponsored organizations. By the late 1980s, colonialism was a spent force, its last hurrah centering on the struggle led by SWAPO (the South West Africa People's Organization) for an independent Namibia.

The second type of situation eliciting Soviet advocacy is the national liberation struggle that is linked to anti-imperialism. Actually, most of the time that the decolonization process was in high gear, "anti-imperialism" and "anticolonialism" were used to describe the same phenomenon—in both cases the Soviet Union being attracted by the anti-Western animus of the liberation struggle. Linking the two was logical and convenient as long as there were many colonies. Now, with few colonies remaining, "anti-imperialism" has become a kind of general calumny to cover putative Western, especially U.S., intrigues and interventions intended to weaken or destroy liberation movements backed by the USSR. The Palestinian struggle and Arab-Israeli conflict since the June War is an example in which Soviet analysts emphasize the anti-imperialist rather than anticolonialist aspect of the struggle in order to stress that the enemy is not just Israel but, more important for the Soviets, the United States. According to Yevgeny Primakov, a leading Soviet scholar on the Middle East and director of one of Moscow's prestigious research institutes, the Soviet Union regards the Arab-Israeli conflict "not as a clash of two nationalisms, but as a manifestation of a conflict between imperialism, on the one side, and national liberation movements, on the other. The conflict is in essence such a confrontation."[58]

The third and fourth types of situations attracting Soviet attention include what Khrushchev called "popular uprisings." They are confined to one country, though external assistance may be sought, and they pit one group of the population against another. In the third situation, an ethnic or religious minority in a pro-Soviet regime or a regime with which Moscow is trying to improve relations seeks autonomy or a state of its own, as in the current struggle of the Kurds in Iraq, the Eritreans in Ethiopia, and the Sahraoui of the Western Sahara in Morocco. In the fourth situation, the struggle is directed against a regime hostile to the USSR and friendly to the United States. Generally subsumed under the rubric of national liberation struggles, popular uprisings have received little systematic attention from Soviet writers. One rare piece touching on the subject was written by V. Andrianov, a military analyst. In a discussion of partisan wars, particularly the kind that appeared in Europe during World War II, he maintained that partisan operations could develop into a national liberation

[58] Ye. Primakov, *Anatomiya Blizhnevostochnogo Konflikta* [The Anatomy of the Near East Conflict] (Moscow: Mysl, 1978), 345.

struggle, but only if they acquired a broader political dimension, as was the case in Algeria (1954–1962), Cuba (1956–1959), West Irian (part of Indonesia; 1961–1962), South Yemen (1963–1967), and several other instances.[59] His list includes thirty-one Third World partisan struggles during the 1950–1974 period. Though not comprehensive (his key omissions are the Eritrean and Biafran struggles), it closely matches the struggles that were operating in the early 1970s (Table 2).

For the Soviet leadership, each of the first three general types of situation had its complications. In the first, there was the dilemma of which anticolonialist movement to support when more than one (other than a local communist party) was in the field. In general, Moscow opted for the group that looked to the Soviet Union rather than China; that had a Marxist or socialist orientation, with a congenial ideological outlook; that tolerated communists; and that was critical of the West. In the two main instances in Africa in the 1970s—Angola and Zimbabwe—Moscow had one success, the Soviet and Cuban-backed MPLA in Angola; and one failure, in Zimbabwe, where Moscow aligned itself with Joshua Nkomo rather than Robert Mugabe.

By the early 1970s Africa was the target of anticolonialism. Until 1974 the scale and character of Soviet commitments to liberation movements in Southern Africa were relatively unimportant. The region was dominated by South Africa and Portugal, the independent black African states were weak, and the prospects for the various liberation movements based in Zambia, Tanzania, and Zaire were unpromising. However, from the early 1960s on, the Soviet Union and its bloc associates did help to train guerrillas and to channel a trickle of arms to favored national liberation groups, often through second parties such as Algeria and Egypt and occasionally through the Liberation Committee of the Organization of African Unity (OAU). As a rule though, Moscow preferred bilateral contacts: in the Portuguese colonies, its matériel went surreptitiously to Marxist-oriented movements—to the Movimento Popular para a Libertação de Angola (MPLA) and the Frente de Libertação de Moçambique (FRELIMO). Except for the MPLA, whose communist antecedents and pro-Moscow orientation date back to 1955, most of the liberation movements in Southern Africa found it easier to work with the Chinese, and Moscow wielded little clout in the region. Southern Africa was not important in Soviet global strategy, which seemed geared to using the simmering

59 V. Andrianov, "Partizanskaya voina i voennaya strategiya" [Partisan War and Military Strategy], *Voenno-istoricheskii zhurnal*, no. 7 (July 1975), 29, 31.

situation to exacerbate the West's relations with African countries by polarizing alignments and issues, and to counter the challenge from the Chinese.

The overthrow of the decades-old military dictatorship in Portugal on April 25, 1974, transformed the political situation in the region with dramatic suddenness, and Moscow quickly intensified arms shipments, especially to the MPLA. Until then, none of the Angolan liberation groups had been effective: neither the MPLA nor its rivals, the FNLA (Frente Nacional de Libertação de Angola) led by Holden Roberto and UNITA (União Nacional para a Independência Total de Angola) headed by Jonas Savimbi. Indeed, the MPLA could not even wrest the tiny enclave of Cabinda from the Portuguese. Only a year before, Moscow had suspended aid to Agostinho Neto, the leader of the MPLA, "believing that, without an active military wing, he would not be able to counter growing Chinese support for the FNLA and, to a lesser extent, for UNITA": "As part of this policy shift, the USSR began to ship small amounts of material to Chipenda [the head of still another liberation group]. In the aftermath of the April coup, however, the Soviet Union performed a diplomatic *volte-face*, apparently on the advice of the Portuguese Communist Party."[60]

Then, in late 1974 and early 1975, the Soviets stepped up their assistance to Neto's MPLA, thereby giving it an edge in the civil war that broke out in the spring and early summer among the three main protagonists. South Africa's military intervention in support of UNITA brought victory for the anti-Marxist forces within reach. But Savimbi's unwillingness to advance UNITA's forces beyond the Ovimbundu tribal areas, where his support was largely concentrated, and his inability to coordinate military moves with the Zaire-backed FNLA gave the MPLA time to organize, entrench itself in Luanda, and await the influx of Soviet arms and Cuban troops, both of which arrived in significant numbers in late summer and early fall. Soviet arms, shipped in moderate quantities in late 1974 and early 1975 to the MPLA in anticipation of the formal end of Portuguese rule, flowed in freely after mid-1975. The USSR's intervention carried the day for the pro-Soviet MPLA.

In Zimbabwe, on the other hand, the Soviets blundered. From the early 1960s, when the armed struggle against the white-dominated regime of Ian Smith took form, a number of liberation movements, clustered largely around tribal loyalties, vied with each other for suprem-

[60] Charles K. Ebinger, "External Intervention in Internal War: The Politics and Diplomacy of the Angolan Civil War," *Orbis* 20, no. 3 (Fall 1976), 688. See also John A. Marcum, *The Angolan Revolution*, vol. 2 (Cambridge, Mass.: MIT Press, 1978), 251–53.

acy. By the 1970s Moscow had opted for Joshua Nkomo's ZAPU (Zimbabwe African People's Union, whose base was among the Ndebele in the Matabeleland region), providing arms and advisers for the cadres trained in bases in neighboring Zambia. Nkomo's chief rival was Robert Mugabe, whose ZANU (Zimbabwe African National Union) relied on aid from China and, when the post-Mao succession crisis led to a falling-off of assistance, also from Yugoslavia, Iraq, and Romania.[61] Mugabe's political base was among the Shona, the largest component of the population, concentrated around Salisbury and along the eastern border with Mozambique. He was the more aggressive in waging guerrilla operations, having decided early on that only armed struggle would bring independence. His relations with Moscow, already frosty, steadily worsened after the Soviets sought written statements from him acknowledging Nkomo as the head of the Patriotic Front, the umbrella organization established to unite all groups opposed to the Smith regime.

Though Mugabe was a Marxist committed to the establishment of a one-party state, Moscow chose to back Nkomo, probably for a combination of reasons: (1) whereas Mugabe sought aid from China, Nkomo was its critic; (2) whereas Mugabe insisted on control of his forces and their deployment, Nkomo seemed willing to rely on Soviet and Cuban advisers, who assumed responsibility for training his 6,000 man army in Zambia;[62] (3) whereas Mugabe was unmistakably determined to run his own show, Nkomo was a more accommodating client, who was possibly receptive to an active role for the communists.

In both Angola and Zimbabwe, Moscow gave substantial support to liberation groups that relied on it for arms and advice, that upheld its line on international issues, and that were cool to China. The failure of Nkomo was a consequence of internal faction-fighting over which the Soviets had no control.

The last major anticolonial struggle is taking place in Namibia. Moscow's policy has been to follow black Africa's lead: in the United Nations, it supports Security Council Resolution 435, though it remains skeptical of a number of provisions; it echoes the OAU's recognition of SWAPO and repeated calls for an end to South Africa's occupation; and it is in active contact with SWAPO's external wing, whose leader, Sam Nujoma, made his first visit to Moscow in 1976. South Africa has re-

<hr/>

[61] David Smith and Colin Simpson, with Ian Davies, *Mugabe* (London: Sphere, 1981), 109. Also Keith Somerville, "The Soviet Union and Zimbabwe: The Liberation Struggle and After," in R. Craig Nation and Mark V. Kauppi, eds., *The Soviet Impact in Africa* (Lexington, Mass.: Lexington Books, 1984), 199–204.

[62] *New York Times*, June 7, 1978.

fused to relinquish the mandate given to it by the former League of Nations in 1918, despite repeated calls to do so and condemnation of its stand by the United Nations, which voted to terminate the mandate in 1966.

Moscow has become an important patron of SWAPO. According to Assistant Secretary of State Chester A. Crocker, the Soviet Union supplies SWAPO with about "90 percent of its military aid and 60 percent of its overall aid."[63] In doing so it has aligned itself with a liberation movement recognized by every African country except South Africa; demonstrated political and ideological solidarity with Africa's leaders; highlighted the utility of ties with the USSR rather than China; and occasioned inevitable comparisons with U.S. equivocation on this emotional issue and its relationship with the much-reviled apartheid regime in South Africa.[64] Without Soviet and Soviet-bloc assistance, SWAPO would be in even more difficulty than it is, because the frontline African states are no match for South Africa and no military threat to its control of Namibia. But, short of a quantum increase in Soviet involvement, of which there is no sign at all, SWAPO's future depends primarily on diplomatic efforts to bring independence. Moscow's sustaining level of support is intended to keep SWAPO in the field against South Africa, as a "policy of provocation and propaganda" that pushes the United States into alliance with South Africa and makes the Soviet Union appear "the natural ally of all black Africans."[65] To weaken U.S. influence in Southern Africa is adequate motive for Moscow.

The second situation—in which the USSR aids liberation struggles against imperialism—also has its problems. This situation is exemplified in Soviet policy toward the Palestine Liberation Organization (PLO). The Soviet Union came into contact with the PLO shortly after its founding in 1964, but, even after the June War, Moscow still had little time for it, lumping the PLO with other "leftist adventurist" groups that sought to provoke another war as the way of dealing with Israel. Soviet experts such as G. I. Mirskii argued that "guerrilla warfare cannot redeem the seized territories . . . political factors must be

[63] New York Times, March 23, 1982.

[64] For example, see Yu. I. Gorbunov and A. V. Pritvorov, Namibiya: problemy dostizheniya nezavisimosti [Namibia: The Problems of Achieving Independence] (Moscow: Nauka, 1983). In the late 1970s, when Moscow's attention to the SWAPO movement increased, Soviet writers looked at the experience of other African armed struggles for independence. See A. M. Pegushev, Povstantsy Mau Mau: istoriya antikolonial'nogo vooruzhennogo vosstaniya 1952–1956 v Kenii [The Mau Mau Insurrection: The History of the Anti-Colonial Military Rebellion in Kenya, 1952–1956] (Moscow: Nauka, 1978).

[65] Seth Singleton, " 'Defense of the Gains of Socialism': Soviet Third World Policy in the mid 1980s," Washington Quarterly 7, no. 1 (Winter 1984), 114.

brought into play."[66] In July 1968, however, Nasser took PLO Chairman Yasser Arafat to Moscow to acquaint the Russians with him.[67] By the end of the year, an arms relationship was started, and the Soviet media "began referring most positively and frequently to the Palestine resistance movement, specifically Fatah," largest of the Fedayeen organizations comprising the PLO.[68] Though serious differences existed,[69] after the October War Moscow periodically upgraded the relationship, taking care to keep in step with the pace of the Arab world and international moves. In October 1981, Moscow officially recognized the PLO as "the sole legitimate representative of the Palestinian people." Nevertheless, it continues to have disagreements with PLO leaders over, among other things, the Soviet position that Israel has the right to exist and that the PLO's use of violent means of struggle should be confined to the occupied territories and Israel proper.

Since the early 1970s, the Soviet Union has provided the PLO with "intelligence, weapons, funds, and training at camps in the Soviet Union and elsewhere in Eastern Europe."[70] Palestinian officials acknowledge that "hundreds" of senior Palestinian officers have graduated from Soviet military academies.[71] Confirmation of this extensive military relationship is embodied in PLO documents captured by Israeli forces during their invasion of southern Lebanon in June 1982.[72]

From the beginning, Moscow's attitude toward the PLO was a function of its perceived need to adapt to the policies of the Arab states it courted. As the PLO acquired higher status in the Arab world and a more central position in the conflict with Israel, so its importance to Moscow rose. But, though the Soviet Union provided arms and training, as it has for other liberation movements, it has not undertaken any obligation, moral or legal, to defend the PLO. Hence it did nothing when PLO forces were defeated by Israel in Lebanon in 1982.

Soviet influence in the PLO is minimal: on no significant issue has Arafat acceded to Moscow's preferences—not in a willingness to ac-

---

[66] G. I. Mirskii, "Illusions and Miscalculations," New Times, no. 39 (October 2, 1968), 7.

[67] Heikal, The Road to Ramadan, 62–65.

[68] Golan, The Soviet Union and the PLO, 9.

[69] For a discussion of differences between Soviet officials and Syrian communists over how to deal with Israel, see "The Soviet Attitude to the Palestine Problem: From the Records of the Syrian Communist Party, 1971–72," Journal of Palestine Studies 2, no. 1 (Autumn 1972), 187–212.

[70] This is according to Director of the CIA (1981–1986) William J. Casey, "The International Linkages—What Do We Know?" in Uri Ra'anan et al., Hydra of Carnage: International Linkages of Terrorism (Lexington, Mass.: Lexington Books, 1986), 8.

[71] New York Times, February 18, 1981.

[72] Israeli, PLO in Lebanon, 103–11.

cept the right of Israel to exist with secure and recognized boundaries in accordance with U.N. Security Council Resolutions 242 and 338, and not in the matter of curbing terrorist activities in favor of intensified political initiatives.

Still, apart from reasons pertaining to its ambitions in the Arab world, Moscow is a willing patron because of the PLO's policy of anti-imperialism and its support for Moscow's position on issues such as Afghanistan—a type of political recompense the PLO can offer at little cost. The PLO's hostility to the United States is reinforced through close ties to the most anti-American leaderships in the Third World (Syria, Libya, the PDRY, Iraq until 1982, Cuba, North Korea, and Nicaragua); its policies have the effect of undermining the stability of those regimes in the Middle East whose basic interests lie in a pro-American orientation.[73] There is little doubt that Moscow derives advantages from its connection with the PLO:

> The intimate Soviet-PLO relationship is beneficial in building linkages with wars of national liberation in many other parts of the world. The PLO is useful in its capacity as a resource center for terrorist organizations seeking to subvert non-Communist regimes anywhere. In carrying on low-intensity warfare, these organizations serve basic Soviet geopolitical interests of creating instability and unrest in nations where the Communists have a chance to gain political power.[74]

The third kind of situation that has proved troublesome for Soviet leaders is one in which the liberation struggle is directed against a regime with which Moscow already has or seeks good relations. Moscow tries to straddle the fence and avoid alienating either side. Its position is especially complicated if it supported the insurgents in an earlier period when its relations with the government were not too cordial, as in the 1960s in Ethiopia and Iraq. When state-to-state relations improved, Moscow's backing of the rebels diminished, even while it retained a measure of sympathy for their cause.

Illustrative is Moscow's position on the Kurds, a non-Arab Muslim people scattered through Iraq, Iran, Turkey, Syria, and the USSR.

[73] Aryeh Y. Yodfat and Yuval Arnon-Ohanna, *PLO: Strategy and Tactics* (New York: St. Martin's Press, 1981), 128.

[74] Ray S. Cline and Yonah Alexander, *Terrorism: The Soviet Connection* (New York: Crane Russak, 1984), 62. See also Yonah Alexander and Richard Kucinski, "The International Terrorist Network," in Georges Fauriol, ed., *Latin American Insurgencies* (Washington, D.C.: Centre for Strategic and International Studies, and National Defense University, 1985), 56–59.

Encouraged by President Woodrow Wilson's call for national self-determination, they hoped for independence when the Ottoman Empire was dismantled in 1918, but the nation states that were created left them divided and bitter. As long as Iraq was headed by British-dominated Hashemite rulers, Soviet leaders nurtured Kurdish aspirations. In late 1945 Moscow established a Kurdish Republic in the Kurdish part of Iran, but it collapsed when Soviet troops withdrew in mid-1946.[75] Mulla Mustafa al-Barzani, head of the Democratic Party of Kurdistan (DPK) and symbol of Kurdish nationalism, found sanctuary in the Soviet Union. When the Hashemite rule was ended in July 1958, the new Iraqi military regime under Abdel Karim Qasim allowed the Kurds to return. Barzani and thousands of his followers were repatriated in Soviet ships and expressed their loyalty to the Iraqi Republic.[76]

The halcyon period was brief. By late 1960, reports were appearing in the Western press of a rift between Qasim and the Kurds, and by the summer of 1961 full-scale hostilities had broken out.[77] On a number of occasions, Moscow criticized Qasim for persecuting the Kurds, saying that their movement was "basically of a general democratic nature . . . aimed at ensuring the national rights" guaranteed by the constitution; and it chastized Baghdad for misrepresenting "the legitimate demand of the Kurds for autonomy within the framework of the Iraqi Republic as a separatist movement allegedly aimed at the secession of Kurdistan from Iraq" and misnaming "the courageous leaders of the movement agents of imperialism."[78] During the next two years, as the fighting escalated, so, too, did Soviet criticisms of Qasim. There were, however, limits to what Moscow was prepared to do: it suspended military assistance to Iraq, but its "support of the Kurds did not go as far as providing arms either for the Kurds or the communists [who were also being persecuted]."[79] In May 1963 the Soviet government even had the Kurdish question placed on the U.N. agenda by Mongolia, but it was withdrawn a few months later.

Although Qasim was overthrown in February 1963, the Ba'athists who seized power persisted in the attack on the Kurds, prompting the USSR, on July 9, to warn Iran, Turkey, and Syria against becoming involved in the suppression of the Kurds. Intended primarily as a

---

[75] Eagleton, *The Kurdish Republic of 1946*, passim.

[76] S. E. van Rooy, "The Struggle for Kurdistan," *Survey*, no. 43 (August 1962), 113.

[77] Ibid., 115.

[78] *Current Digest of the Soviet Press* 15, no. 8 (March 20, 1963), 28.

[79] Sa'ad Jawad, *Iraq and the Kurdish Question 1958–1970* (London: Ithaca Press, 1981), 309.

warning to Iraq, the Soviet Note said that "what is happening in northern Iraq means . . . genocide, a policy of the mass extermination of people because of race, nation or religion, which is condemned by all mankind and described by the United Nations as the gravest international crime."[80] Throughout this period of considerable strain in Soviet-Iraqi relations, Moscow never referred to the Kurdish struggle as a national liberation movement. To have done so would have meant recognition of the right of the Kurds to a state of their own, and cast doubt on Moscow's commitment to the inviolability of post-colonial Third World boundaries. Such a position would have weakened its own case for the permanence of the USSR's borders, especially against active Chinese and Japanese claims. More to the point, Moscow did not want the Kurdish issue to prevent an improvement in state-to-state relations with Iraq, in which it saw a leading Arab actor, anti-American, hostile to a pro-U.S. Iran, and able to advance Soviet objectives in the region.

By the mid-1960s, after a series of coups and counter-coups, a Ba'athist group took power and sought accommodation with the Kurds, to the relief of the Soviets. In August 1966, during a visit to Moscow by an Iraqi delegation, the two sides signed a communiqué in which the Soviets expressed "satisfaction in connection with the positive steps the Iraqi government has taken to end the fraticidal armed struggle and to settle the problem of Northern Iraq within the framework of a single state."[81] Convergent strategic-military interests that led to a friendship treaty on April 9, 1972, prompted Moscow to downgrade the Kurdish question and accept the Ba'ath's asserverations of a willingness to offer autonomy. Despite the Ba'ath's crackdown on the Iraqi Communist Party at the end of the 1970s, its criticisms of irregular Soviet arms deliveries during the first three or four years of the Iran-Iraq War (which started in September 1980), and its resumption of diplomatic relations with the United States in the fall of 1984 for the first time since June 1967, Moscow has maintained a quiescent attitude toward Iraq's handling of the Kurds. Once again, as so often in their recent history, the Kurds have turned out to be dispensable pawns in the big-power game.

The changing Soviet attitude toward the Eritreans illustrates even more vividly the transcendency of strategic considerations and opportunism over support for a national liberation struggle. At the end of World War II, Eritrea was taken from Italy, which had ruled it since

[80] *Soviet News*, no. 4870 (July 10, 1963), 21.
[81] *Current Digest of the Soviet Press* 18, no. 31 (August 24, 1966), 25.

the 1890s, and placed under Ethiopia's administration. During the U.N. discussions in the early 1950s, Moscow had advocated independence for Eritrea, if only to prevent its being given to pro-Western Ethiopia. In the late 1950s, convinced that Emperor Haile Selassie did not intend to provide the autonomy called for in the 1952 agreement between the United Nations and Ethiopia, Eritrean students and political exiles established the Eritrean Liberation Front (ELF) in Cairo, and armed struggle began in 1961. Instead of seeking a political solution, in November 1962 the Emperor declared the federation of Ethiopia and Eritrea null and void and made Eritrea Ethiopia's fourteenth province.[82] Throughout the decade the Eritreans groped for a strategy, all the while conducting hit-and-run attacks which, though failures, drained Ethiopian resources, forcing growing commitments of men and matériel at a time when other parts of the country were growing restless over the anachronistic imperial rule and lack of modernization.

Factional divisions have, from the beginning, haunted the Eritrean struggle: "There is, more precisely, neither a profound sense of nationalism nor a shared ideological experience to help activists in overcoming clan, class, linguistic, regional, religious, and personal differences. Nor is there a single charismatic leader."[83] After internecine rivalries split the movement in 1970, the Eritrean People's Liberation Front (EPLF) was founded, as a rival to the ELF. Haile Selassie's skillful diplomacy contributed to a sharp reduction in outside support for the Eritreans. He normalized diplomatic relations with China, extending recognition in return for an end to its assistance to the ELF; improved relations with the Soviet Union, thus inducing Moscow to stay aloof from the Eritrean struggle; and, in late 1971, worked out a series of agreements with the Sudan, leading to a reduction of arms-smuggling across the border. Finally, civil war broke out between the ELF and the EPLF in early 1972 and ended only after a military coup on September 12, 1974, toppled the Emperor and presented them with a rare opportunity for gaining independence.

However, the Coordinating Committee of the Armed Forces, more generally known as the Derg, determined to keep the empire intact and poured thousands of troops into Eritrea in an attempt to reestablish central control. In 1976 and early 1977 the Eritreans were on the

[82] Richard Sherman, *Eritrea: The Unfinished Revolution* (New York: Praeger, 1980), 29.

[83] Tom J. Farer, *War Clouds on the Horn of Africa*, 2d (revised) ed. (New York: Carnegie Endowment for International Peace, 1979), 37. See also Sherman, *Eritrea*, chapter 2; and Bereket Habte Selassie, *Conflict and Intervention in the Horn of Africa* (New York: Monthly Review Press, 1980), 67–73.

threshold of a military victory, but Somalia's invasion of Ethiopia's Ogaden province in July 1977 changed the politics and alignments on the Horn of Africa with dramatic suddenness, and with them the fortunes of the Eritreans. Briefly, in 1977, a complex series of policy probes and gambles on everybody's part ended with the Soviet Union shifting its support from Somalia to Ethiopia and supplying massive military assistance that enabled the Derg, headed by Mengistu Haile Mariam, to repel Somalia's invasion and stymie the ELF-EPLF bid for independence.[84]

The degree of Soviet involvement in the Eritrean liberation struggle is difficult to fix. In the late 1960s the head of the ELF said, "The Soviet Union does not assist us. We have high hopes of aid from Cuba, though we have not received any yet."[85] Soviet arms did reach the Eritreans, but there is no evidence of a direct connection: sympathetic Arab states such as Syria, Iraq, the PDRY, and the Sudan could have shipped different kinds of weapons from their own stockpiles of Soviet arms. Paul Henze, who served with the U.S. Embassy in Addis Ababa in 1968–1972 and on the National Security Council during the Carter administration, acknowledged that "by and large, Russian support for the Eritrean dissidents was not direct," but he found it "impossible to believe" that the sustained assistance provided by Cuba and Arab states tied closely to the USSR "could have persisted and gained momentum if the Kremlin had found it distasteful"; he argued that "Soviet encouragement of the Eritrean insurgency paid off handsomely, for the situation there became a major contributing factor to the destablization of the pro-Western imperial system in Ethiopia. Without the strain Eritrea represented, it is conceivable that the pressures which produced the 1974 revolution could have been accommodated by accelerated reform."[86] In a monograph published two years later, he is less equivocal about the Soviet role, though noting that "the Soviets were still cautious [after the June War] about appearance of direct intervention": "They maintained proper relations with

[84] See below, Chapter Four, for details of Soviet policy in Ethiopia after 1975. The Eritreans' determination to continue their struggle is evident in the formation in January 1985 of an umbrella organization, the Eritrean Unified National Council, uniting three Eritrean groups, other than the EPLF, which declined to participate: "These are Osman Saleh Sabbe's Eritrean Liberation Front–Popular Liberation Forces (ELF-PLF), Abdallah Idris's ELF-Revolutionary Council (ELF-RC) and Abdul Qadir Gailani's ELF Revolutionary Committee." Andrew Lycett, "Eritrean Factions Unite," *New African*, no. 212 (May 1985), 44.

[85] *Christian Science Monitor*, April 5, 1969.

[86] Paul B. Henze, "Communism and Ethiopia," *Problems of Communism* 30, no. 3 (May–June 1981), 61–62.

the government in Addis Ababa and disavowed support of growing insurgency in the Eritrean countryside. . . . By the end of the 1960s the Soviets and Chinese were competing for influence with Eritrean rebels and both were supplying arms and equipment in increasing amounts through a wide variety of channels—across the Red Sea from the Yemens, down the Red Sea from Egypt."[87]

It can be argued that a more important role for the Soviets is implied in Henze's analysis than is warranted by evidence or inference. First, while the weapons were Soviet, they came from Arab supporters, not the Soviet Union. Nothing indicates that the Arabs were acting on behalf of the Soviets. True, some were dependent on the Soviet Union, but all of them had their own reasons for intervening, and, moreover, the quantity and type of weaponry given were such as to be readily available to any moderately armed state.

Second, and even more significant, it was not Soviet encouragement or weaponry that generated the Eritrean liberation struggle, but the Emperor's obduracy and unwillingness to consider a political solution. Revolutions are made at the center, not the periphery. Instead of the Soviet Union's having played a key role in the destabilization of the Ethiopian monarchy, it may be the Emperor who was primarily responsible for weakening the center: by persisting with an archaic style of rule; by tolerating a corrupt aristocracy and bureaucracy that was unresponsive to social restiveness and economic catastrophe, including a famine in 1972; and by political obtuseness in resorting to military means to settle a genuine national grievance that arose from his reneging on a promise to the United Nations of federal status for Eritrea, with the substantial autonomy this implied. Haile Selassie was an autocrat, and his one aim in pursuing the Eritrean campaign in the early 1970s, when economic conditions were poor in the heartland of the country, may have been to mobilize the Amharic sector of the population behind his policy of preserving the empire. The aging Emperor was a man of the nineteenth century, out of touch with his people and national and regional currents. In the early 1970s, he stumbled badly in handling the famine in the northern provinces, the uncertainty over the succession occasioned by his son's stroke, and the

---

[87] Paul B. Henze, *Russians and the Horn: Opportunism and the Long View* (Marina del Ray, Calif.: European American Institution for Security Research, Summer 1983), 17–21. After several more years, Henze wrote that up through 1976 the Soviets "kept supplies flowing to the Eritrean rebels," clearly implying that Moscow was a major arms supplier during the early 1970s. Paul Henze, "The Dilemmas of the Horn," *The National Interest* 1 (Winter 1986), 70.

unresponsive bureaucracy. His decision to pursue the corrosive war in Eritrea in such an environment contributed to his downfall.

The extent of Moscow's support for the Eritrean liberation struggle remains a subject on which different interpretations are inevitable, but a number of features of Soviet policy are clear. At no time after the United Nations sanctioned the federation of Eritrea with Ethiopia did Moscow openly espouse the Eritrean claim to independence; and at no time did it designate the Eritrean insurgency a "national liberation struggle." Throughout the 1960s and 1970s it "preferred instead to utilize the historical and religious links between Russia and Ethiopia to try to gain a foothold in Ethiopia and woo Haile Selassie away from his U.S. benefactors."[88] Its shift in alignment from Somalia to Ethiopia has entailed support for Mengistu's policy of dealing with Eritrea, which is similar in every respect to his predecessor's. Members of the OAU accept the official Soviet explanation that the USSR acts to uphold the territorial integrity of Ethiopia, the position of the inviolability of existing boundaries adhered to by African states. But Moscow also has its strategic reasons to oppose efforts "to tear Eritrea away from it [Ethiopia] and set up there a reactionary Moslem state which would be dependent on neighboring Arab states and the NATO countries,"[89] as well as its ideological affinity with Mengistu's Marxist-Leninist regime. None of this precludes the Soviets' efforts to maintain clandestine or unofficial links with different Eritrean groups—witness the visits to Moscow of ELF Chairman Ahmed Nasser in 1978 and 1980;[90] and the discussions in East Berlin between Soviet officials and members of the EPLF.[91]

For the moment, however, Moscow has found in Ethiopia a kindred state on the continent of Africa. It is sympathetic to the imperial out-

[88] Raymond Watson, "Eritreans and Moscow" (letter to the editor), *Problems of Communism* 35, no. 4 (July–August 1986), 102.

[89] V. Yefremov, "Lessons of Ogaden," *Soviet Military Review*, no. 6 (June 1978), 50–51. A study by an Israeli scholar notes that "an Eritrean war was a problem the Soviets wished to avoid. They had always considered the leftist-oriented Eritrean organizations an asset. . . . The ideal solution from the Soviet point of view would have been the implementation of the National Democratic Revolution, modified in a way that would permit Eritrea to be an entity federated with Ethiopia enjoying political, cultural, and administrative autonomy." Such a solution, however, would require a political compromise, and Mengistu determined on a military approach and destruction of the Eritrean movement. Haggai Erlich, *The Struggle over Eritrea, 1962–1978: War and Revolution in the Horn of Africa* (Stanford: Hoover Institution Press, 1983), 111–12.

[90] Mekalh Harnet (pseudonym), "Reflections on the Eritrean Revolution," *Horn of Africa* 6, no. 3 (1983/84), 13.

[91] Watson, "Eritreans and Moscow," 103.

look in Addis Ababa, in somewhat the same way as the late-nine-teenth-century czars, who established a close relationship with the au-tocratic Christian kingdom that the Amhara had fashioned through the conquest and incorporation of diverse tribal peoples.

A final example of the diplomatic complications that can arise out of the USSR's position on liberation struggles is its stand in relation to the Popular Front for the Liberation of the Saguia el-Hamra and Rio de Oro. POLISARIO seeks to establish the Saharan Arab Democratic Republic (SADR) on territory that was formerly Spanish Sahara but was seized by Morocco (and, for a brief time, Mauretania) after Spain relinquished its rule in late 1975. From the very beginning, the USSR has supported the position of pro-Soviet, nonaligned Algeria against Morocco, backing its motions in the United Nations in favor of self-determination for POLISARIO. It has echoed Algeria's call for a referendum on the future of the area, noting that the SADR is recognized by the majority of African states and is a member of the OAU.[92] But this has been the full extent of its support; it has not sent military or economic aid directly to POLISARIO[93] nor given diplomatic recognition. One important reason for Soviet restraint is its courtship of Morocco, whose pro-U.S. orientation proves no bar to extensive economic relations. The basic commodity exchange is Moroccan phosphate for Soviet oil and machinery.[94] Morocco's knowledge that, though POLISA-RIO's weapons are Soviet, the suppliers are Algeria and Libya, permits both Morocco and the Soviet Union to pursue their mutually advantageous relationship. Indeed, by strengthening commercial ties, Morocco hopes to restrain the USSR from a greater degree of involvement on behalf of POLISARIO. And Moscow has managed to maintain this balance for more than a decade.

The fourth situation, the popular uprising or people's war in which the internal struggle is against pro-Western, anti-Soviet regimes, as might be expected is relatively problem-free for Moscow. In these cases, Moscow's policy seeks the weakening, eventual overthrow and replacement of the regime by one prepared to improve relations with the Soviet Union. For this reason, it is favorably disposed toward lib-

[92] *Current Digest of the Soviet Press* 36, no. 47 (December 19, 1984), 17.

[93] On January 6, 1978, the *New York Times* reported that the Moroccan Navy had seized a Soviet freighter carrying weapons and having Algerian military officers on board. Cited in Daniel S. Papp, *Soviet Policies toward the Developing World during the 1980s* (Maxwell Air Force Base, Ala.: Air University Press, 1986), 269. The incident occurred prior to the consummation of the massive Soviet-Moroccan economic deal in 1978, and there has been no evidence to suggest that it is part of a recurring pattern.

[94] David Lynn Price, *The Western Sahara* (Washington, D.C.: Sage, 1979), 63–65.

eration struggles in El Salvador, Chile, Zaire, and South Africa. Threatening to U.S. interests, distant from Soviet borders and marginal to its vital interests, these struggles are low-risk, low-cost, and of high political potential. They could hardly be better suited to Soviet diplomacy. The outlawed African National Congress (ANC) may have little prospect of seizing power through armed struggle, but it is continually mobilizing hostility to U.S. and South African policies and thereby serves Soviet strategy by persuading the remainder of Africa, "to the extent it needs persuading, that an unholy alliance had been struck between the two countries."[95] However long it persists, the ANC's struggle has already weakened U.S. influence on the continent and aligned the USSR on the side of those struggling against apartheid. It does not require much in the way of arms, "AK-47's, pistols, limpet mines, grenades, rockets," from the Soviet bloc, which ships them "through the Organization of African Unity, and directly"; and the cost is negligible, far less than the $12 million coming from the Scandinavian countries.[96] If Moscow fosters an image of official hostility to the South African regime by providing military training and arms to Unkonto We Sizwe (The Spear of the Nation), the ANC's military wing, it at the same time secretly carries on "a discreet and fabulously profitable relationship" with South Africa's power structure "for the marketing of gold, diamonds, and other precious minerals":

> Through an accident of politics and geology, these two enemies possess much of the world's supply of many strategic minerals. For example, DeBeers Corporation of South Africa pays the Soviet Union just under a billion dollars a year for its supply of gem-quality diamonds. This lucrative pact to keep mineral prices and profits high has not stopped the Soviet Union from criticizing South Africa's Western trading partners, particularly the United States, for doing business with apartheid.[97]

All this suggests that the USSR's self-interest is a shrewd mixture of public relations and surreptitious dealing for advantage. Thus, far from throwing itself wholeheartedly behind the ANC, Moscow has exercised restraint in supplying arms, recognizing the ANC's limited ability to wage an armed struggle; meanwhile, business with South Africa

[95] Robert Legvold, "The Soviet Threat to Southern Africa," in Robert I. Rotberg et al., *South Africa and Its Neighbors* (Lexington, Mass.: Lexington Books, 1985), 44.

[96] ANC spokesman Johnny Makhatini told this to Flora Lewis, *New York Times*, August 16, 1985.

[97] Kurt M. Campbell, "Kremlin's South Africa Influence Magnified," *Boston Globe*, September 15, 1985, A25, A28.

goes on as usual. From past experience, Moscow knows that liberation movements receiving its assistance will overlook the inconsistencies in its policy.

OBSERVATIONS

The Soviet Union has not been a major actor in national liberation struggles. During the 1970s and 1980s, it did influence the outcome of several anti-American, pro-Soviet armed struggles, but a larger number of Marxist and/or anti-American regimes seized power without Soviet inputs. Thus, Moscow's assistance was crucial in Angola and South Vietnam, and it enabled Vietnam to extend its dominion over Kampuchea and Laos. But it played no role in the coming-to-power of leftist, Marxist, anti-American regimes in Mozambique, Guinea-Bissau, Ethiopia, Zimbabwe, Grenada, and Nicaragua. Nor did it contribute in any way to the overthrow of pro-American rulers in Iran and Nicaragua in 1979, the Sudan in 1985, or the Philippines and Haiti in 1986. Indeed, Moscow was so intent on safeguarding its close ties to Philippine President Ferdinand Marcos that it egregiously misjudged the groundswell of opposition to his twenty-year-old dictatorship and supported him to the very end. Throughout the hotly contested election campaign, which brought Marcos a pyrrhic victory on February 7, 1986, Soviet commentaries ignored his fraudulent electoral tactics and widespread use of violence against the coalition headed by Mrs. Corazon Aquino, and rarely mentioned the opposition's views and activities. Instead, they criticized U.S. interference and attempts by the United States to retain its military bases at Subic Bay and Clark Field.[98] When Marcos suddenly fled the country on February 25, the Soviet government was taken by surprise. Its strategy now is to establish a working relationship with the Aquino government and to strengthen ties with the weak Moscow-dominated Philippine Communist Party and the Maoist-inspired, militantly nationalist and anti-American Communist Party of the Philippines (CPP), whose military arm—the New People's Army (NPA)—is a very real threat to the Aquino government.[99]

[98] Pavel Demchenko, *Pravda*, February 21, 1986.

[99] An excellent account of the CPP and the NPA is Leif Rosenberger, "Philippine Communism and the Soviet Union," *Survey* 29, no. 1 (Spring 1985), 143–44. In January 1987, two spokesmen for the CPP "disclosed that Moscow offered unlimited arms and money to the communist New People's Army. They did not say if the offer was accepted." *Washington Times*, March 24, 1987, 1. However, there has been no convincing evidence to corroborate this allegation.

Most of the insurgencies listed in Table 2 are neither communist-generated nor Soviet-supported. They are for the most part spawned by revolts against injustice or foreign rule—eruptions of impatience with the path and pace of modernization. More of them are financed by extortion of one kind or another (as in the case of the NPA in the Philippines,[100] and that of the Sendero Luminoso in Peru) than by contributions from sympathetic governments (as in the cases of SWAPO and UNITA in Southern Africa). Not one liberation struggle is financed primarily by the Soviet Union.[101]

There is nothing principled about the USSR's attitude toward liberation struggles. Lenin did deride as chauvinists those who failed to stand for the right of self-determination,[102] but that was at a time when he was not in power and did not have to make a choice between the interests of the Soviet state and those of the world communist movement or bourgeois-nationalist revolutions. Soviet rulers exalt liberation struggles when they are "progressive" and apt to weaken a country's ties to the West, especially the United States. This consideration supersedes a movement's attitude toward indigenous communists, China, or even the Soviet Union. Conversely, any struggle for liberation from a pro-Soviet regime is defined as counter-revolutionary, an attempt by imperialism to regain a foothold; and it is condemned and resisted. In Ethiopia and Afghanistan, Soviet forces function as instruments of repression against these "unjust" liberation struggles.

The Soviets also criticize separatism: that is, violent activity by ethnic

---

[100] "In some of the more remote areas of the Philippine archipelago, the NPA brazenly extracts protection money from Marcos's own men. American sources say they know of a Philippine constabulary commander in northern Luzon who signed a 'contract' with the local NPA leader. The agreement: local loggers pay the NPA five cents a board foot, in return for which the rebels refrain from attacking a 16-mile stretch of logging road built (with U.S. aid money) by Philippine Army engineers." *Newsweek*, February 17, 1986, 20; also, *New York Times*, November 1, 1985.

[101] According to David Scott Palmer, Sendero's ideology and strategy are, if anything, Maoist. "Rebellion in Rural Peru: The Origins and Evolution of Sendero Luminoso," *Comparative Politics* 18, no. 2 (January 1986), 141. The Sendero Luminoso (Shining Path) movement scorns Moscow's line: "it is highly unlikely that Sendero receives aid from the Soviet bloc." Soviet policy has backed "Peru's traditional Marxist parties—particularly the Moscow-line Communist Party. Recent Soviet and Cuban foreign policy in most South American countries had emphasized the need for unity among Marxist leftist groups. Sendero disagrees. . . ." Moreover, Moscow would jeopardize the amicable relations that it has developed with Peru since the late 1960s, if it supported Sendero. Cynthia McClintock, "Sendero Luminoso: Peru's Maoist Guerrillas," *Problems of Communism* 32, no. 5 (September–October 1983), 23.

[102] V. I. Lenin, *Collected Works*, vol. 21 (Moscow: Progress Publishers, 1964), 316.

and religious groups, encouraged by "home reaction and hostile external forces" who seek "to weaken the country and make it vulnerable to external pressure"—as in the case of India, where "extremist members of the Sikh community," with support from abroad, are responsible for "a vast terror campaign under the slogan of separation from India and establishing an 'independent Sikh state of Khalistan' in Punjab."[103] Soviet writers sometimes link separatist movements with terrorism and deny such groups the imprimatur of national liberation movements, which are lauded because of their anti-imperialist outlook: whereas the latter are considered capable of advancing Soviet aims, the former are seen as benefiting only the "imperialists."[104] This position is congenial to most Third World regimes, who fear separatism as an ever-present threat to the very existence of the state system that upholds their independence. Indeed, one key to Moscow's prestige and continued attraction as prospective patron is its determination to uphold the inviolability of international frontiers, not only in Europe and the Far East where its own interests are directly engaged, but everywhere else as well.

Since armed struggles against pro-Soviet regimes are new features of the Third World landscape, the first Soviet allusion to them did not appear until 1978. Colonel Yevgeny Rybkin, an influential military writer, referred to the defense against internal insurgents put up by "countries which have gotten on, or are getting on, a socialist path of development" as a new type of war, as "wars in defense of socialism."[105] He located the opposition in externally generated forces and assistance, ignoring the strong undercurrent of mass discontent which is prevalent in all of these instances. According to Mark Katz, this was in sharp contrast with Rybkin's assessment in 1968 to the effect that the source of many internal conflicts "lay within the politics of the Third World itself," in ethnic, religious, and cultural animosities rather than in class struggle, the orthodox Marxist-Leninist diagnosis.[106]

Anti-Soviet insurgencies have drained Moscow in various ways and

[103] Vladimir Ryabinin, "India: Defending National Unity," *International Affairs*, no. 12 (December 1986), 119.

[104] For this insight I am indebted to Peter Vigor.

[105] Ye. Rybkin, "xxv s'ezd kpss i osvoboditel'niye voiny sovremennoi epokhi" [The Twenty-fifth Congress of the CPSU and Liberation Wars in the Contemporary Epoch], *Voenno-istoricheskii zhurnal*, no. 11 (November 1978), 12, 16.

[106] Katz, *The Third World in Soviet Military Thought*, 49.

degrees:[107] in Afghanistan 120,000 Soviet troops are fighting a bitter war; in Angola 25,000 Cubans keep the MPLA in power; in Kampuchea the Vietnamese are fighting anti-Vietnamese forces, but with generous amounts of Soviet arms and supplies; in Nicaragua Moscow helps the Cubans and a melange of Soviet-bloc and anti-American Third World militants act as girders for the Sandinista structure; and in Mozambique a beleaguered regime has almost been left to its own devices, Soviet-bloc security and economic assistance being minimal. How Moscow responds to the threats posed to these and other pro-Soviet Marxist regimes in the years ahead will tell a great deal about the kind of policy that Mikhail Gorbachev intends to follow in the Third World. Thus far, he has met clients' essential requirements for retaining power in much the same way as his predecessors did.

   The Soviets' record of fostering Third World liberation struggles turns out, on close examination, to be a modest one. Their weapons have been important but not their advisers or tactics. Thus, since 1945 the USSR "has probably been the major supplier to insurgent forces, establishing the AK47 automatic rifle as standard form of guerrilla equipment from Vietnam to the Middle East and Southern Africa," with copious quantities of "Soviet rockets, grenades, machine-guns, mortars, and artillery" provided as well;[108] and it also trains, equips, and assists various groups, many of whom engage in terrorism.[109] In so doing, the USSR helps make some armed struggles militarily viable: for example, that of SWAPO in Namibia, that of the PLO in Lebanon, and in South Africa that of the ANC, which in the mid-1980s obtains "roughly half" of its overall support (military and other) from the Soviet bloc.[110] However, with the exception of the MPLA in Angola, the

[107] Mark Katz, "Anti-Soviet Insurgencies: Growing Trend or Passing Phase?" *Orbis* 30, no. 2 (Summer 1986), 365–91.

[108] Robert O'Neill, "Insurgency and Sub-National Violence," in Robert O'Neill and D. M. Horner, eds., *New Directions in Strategic Thinking* (London: Allen & Unwin, 1981), 214. In early 1986, a Sudanese political commentator accused the Soviet Union, Cuba, and Ethiopia of providing Sudanese rebels with modern weapons. Radio Liberty, RL 135/86, March 21, 1986, 2.

[109] Shlomo Elad and Ariel Merari, *The Soviet Bloc and World Terrorism,* Jaffee Center for Strategic Studies, paper no. 24 (Tel Aviv: Tel Aviv University, 1984), 5. The diary of Nidia Diaz, a Salvadoran Marxist guerrilla commander, indicated that many of her comrades in arms had been trained in the Soviet Union, East Germany, Bulgaria, and Vietnam. James LeMoyne, "The Guerrilla Network," *New York Times Magazine,* April 6, 1986, 16, 18.

[110] Mark A. Uhlig, "Inside the African National Congress," *New York Times Magazine,* October 12, 1986.

men who led successful armed struggles developed their own strategies and tactics: they accepted Soviet weapons (mostly through third
parties), but conducted their own campaigns. Amilcar Cabral in Portuguese Guinea,[111] Samora Machel in Mozambique, and, of course, Ho
Chi Minh and Vo Nguyen Giap in Vietnam all followed this course.
Nor were pro-Moscow communist parties very helpful. In Latin
America, for example, the "Communist parties in coalition with other
forces of the Left" all too often blundered tactically, "or were perceived as responsible for holding back revolutionary processes," as the
Colombian, Cuban, and Nicaraguan cases suggest.[112]

Moscow prefers to funnel assistance to national liberation movements through third parties, finding in such an approach maximum
flexibility for the conduct of its multidimensional diplomacy. It can
assume a principled position, align itself with leading Third World
governments in international forums and appear to be the superpower champion of progressive liberation struggles. However, if the
armed struggle is directed against a government that, though closely
linked to the United States, is nevertheless not averse to better relations with the Soviet Union, Moscow is able to disclaim any responsibility for the struggle to topple the government, and even convey the
impression of its readiness to use its "good offices" to help improve
the situation (as was its approach at various times with Iraq, Pakistan,
Morocco, and the Sudan)—all the while working behind the scenes to
establish ties with the leadership of the liberation movement.

Despite its spotty record of reliability to national liberation movements, Moscow has fared reasonably well with them politically. By
aligning itself with popular struggles, such as those of the ANC, SWAPO,
and the PLO, which enjoy widespread support in the Third World,
Moscow is seen as part of an international consensus, as a mainstream
participant. Should the Soviet position show up well against the U.S.
stand, Moscow's credentials are enhanced among those who are the
prime targets of its diplomacy. When it arms Libya, Syria, Cuba, the
PDRY, and Nicaragua, it knows that they are actively aiding armed
struggles (and terrorist activities) detrimental to U.S. interests; and
their anti-American animus is all the reason Moscow needs. And it
accepts situations where pro-Moscow communists defer to noncom-

[111] Patrick Chabal, "National Liberation in Portuguese Guinea, 1956–1974," *African Affairs* 80, no. 318 (January 1981), 90; and Richard Gibson, *African Liberation Movements*
(New York: Oxford University Press, 1972), 257.

[112] Fernando Lopez-Alves, "Soviets and Insurgents in Latin America: A Third World
View," in Augusto Varas, ed., *Soviet–Latin American Relations in the 1980s* (Boulder, Colo.:
Westview, 1987), 84.

munist leadership, in the interest of avoiding splits in the liberation movements and of working toward a common goal.[113]

As they look ahead, Soviet leaders may be less sanguine about the prospects of national liberation movements and their ability to advance "the world revolutionary process"—and the interests of the Soviet Union—than they were at the beginning of the 1980s, when the head of the Central Committee's International Department, Boris Ponomarev, noted with obvious satisfaction that world politics had changed in the 1970s in a number of far-reaching ways:

- the correlation of forces in the international arena had improved in favor of socialism and national liberation;

- the policy of détente had had major successes, such as seriously restricting the so-called "freedom of maneuver" of the most aggressive imperialistic forces;

- the scope of the anti-imperialist struggle had broadened, in the process drawing into it practically all regions of the national liberation struggle.[114]

In the late 1980s, the prospect for national liberation movements are not promising. Anticommunist insurgencies show considerable strength and staying power in Afghanistan, Angola, Ethiopia, Mozambique, and Kampuchea, and Soviet leaders might be hard-pressed to identify possible new triumphs for armed insurrection with an anti-

[113] According to a leading South African scholar, the ANC is not communist-dominated or tied to a Soviet-designed strategy. Tom Lodge, "The Second Consultative Conference of the African National Congress," *South Africa International* 16, no. 2 (October 1985), 80–97. An American counterpart concurs: "The allegation of outright Communist control over the ANC cannot be substantiated, and estimating the degree of Communist influence in the ANC is nearly as difficult. Though the Communists' ideological convictions and long-range agenda distinguish them from many in the ANC, at this stage of the struggle for national liberation Communists and non-Communists in the ANC have no significant differences on policy or strategy. Furthermore, the Communists and the ANC share an anti-imperialist stance, condemnation of many aspects of U.S. foreign policy, and embrace of all who support the ANC." Thomas G. Karis, "South African Liberation: The Communist Factor," *Foreign Affairs* 65, no. 2 (Winter 1986/87), 268. On the other hand, a U.S. State Department report noted that "Dependence on Moscow for military assistance will continue to entrench [communist] Party influence in the ANC and its strong representation in the ANC hierarchy." *New York Times*, January 9, 1987. This thesis is reinforced by detail provided in Michael Radu, "The African National Congress: Cadres and Credo," *Problems of Communism* 36, no. 4 (July–August 1987), 58–75.

[114] B. Ponomarev, "Sovmestnaya bor'ba rabochego i natsional'no-osvoboditel'nogo dvizhenii protiv imperializma, za sotsial'nyi progress" [The Joint Struggle of the Working Class and the National Liberation Movement against Imperialism and for Social Progress], *Kommunist*, no. 16 (November 1980), 32.

American impetus. But this is not too important for evolving Soviet strategy, since the value of such movements is more symbolic than strategic. Sufficient mileage can still be gotten from "progressive" liberation struggles in Namibia, South Africa, Chile, and El Salvador to warrant their continued support, since anticolonialism, anti-imperialism, and the promotion of "socialism" are intrinsic to the CPSU's self-legitimation and propagation of the mythology of world socialism internationally.

CHAPTER FOUR

Intervention

The Soviet Union's use of its armed forces on behalf of clients in the Third World is the logical extension of Khrushchev's forward policy and an outgrowth of three developments: the USSR's emergence as a credible nuclear superpower; its ability for the first time in its history to project power into areas lying far beyond the immediate environs of its imperial system (something that the Russian Empire could never do); and its willingness to bear costs and run risks, unrelated to the preservation of vital Soviet state interests, on a hitherto unknown scale. The step has profoundly affected U.S.-Soviet relations, regional rivalries, and domestic leadership outcomes in a number of key countries. Above all, it has marked the advent of Soviet globalism.

In a sense, all Soviet activity in the Third World before the recourse to direct military intervention was prologue. The quest for diplomatic normalization, the establishment of a multifaceted presence, the commitment of resources and support to diverse regimes in a variety of circumstances—these were necessary but preliminary moves in a determined drive for strategic advantage. What links Soviet interventions to Soviet aims is the quest to deny the United States unchallenged reign in the Third World and to assure a central role for the Soviet Union. With the accretion of military power, the Kremlin leadership has resorted to intervention with increasing frequency.

OPERATIONALIZING A CONCEPT

Definitions of "intervention" abound.[1] To explore its many possibilities is to enter a terminological maze. Intervention may be viewed as interference in the internal or external affairs of a state; as coercive or

[1] For example, "Intervention and World Politics" (special issue), *Journal of International Affairs* 22, no. 2 (1968); Yair Evron, "Great Powers' Military Intervention in the Middle East," in Milton Leitenberg and Gabriel Sheffer, eds., *Great Power Intervention in the Middle East* (New York: Pergamon, 1979), 17–45; S. Neil MacFarlane, *Intervention and Regional Security*, Adelphi Papers, no. 196 (London: International Institute for Strategic Studies, Spring 1985); James N. Rosenau, "Intervention as a Scientific Concept," *Journal of Conflict Resolution* 13, no. 2 (1969), 165–76; and Michael Walzer, *Just and Unjust Wars* (New York: Basic Books, 1977), chapter 6.

125

noncoercive intrusion; or as a threat to elicit compliance. In truth, almost any behavior, depending on the context and the analyst's criteria, can be regarded as intervention. In international politics the line where it begins is difficult to establish. As Talleyrand, a French foreign minister who served both Napoleon and the Bourbons, once artfully observed, "Nonintervention is a political and metaphysical term and means about the same thing as intervention."

As used here in reference to Soviet policy in the Third World, "intervention" is the direct and overt deployment of military power on behalf of a client for a political purpose. It differs from "involvement" in a number of ways. Intervention is not just the transfer of arms and some advisory staff but also the commitment of combat or combat-support personnel. Accordingly it accepts the risk of escalating a conflict or of confrontation with a third party, whereas involvement is comparatively free of danger. Unlike involvement, which is likely to be extensive and have a longer-term perspective, intervention is issue-specific or time-specific, and unmistakably politically purposive in its concentration of military force. Its greater significance inheres in the intensive concern that it manifests for a client's security, possibly for his very survival. And it is more likely to bring the patron privileges as a reward for his effort. Finally, being overt and easily monitored, it differs markedly from subversion or covert activities, which may be considered an unconventional type of involvement in the Third World.

Interventions are either low-risk or high-risk. If one or more of the following circumstances prevail, they are regarded as low-risk:

- the intervening power did not initiate the introduction of military power but responded to requests from the legitimate government;
- the intervention was mounted to preserve the national sovereignty and territorial integrity of an internationally recognized government;
- the intervention was regulated by norms that typify interactions between independent governments and was arranged through proper diplomatic channels or procedures;
- the forces deployed were not used to alter the internal or regional situation existing prior to the crisis that triggered the intervention in the first place;
- the intervening power was not indiscriminate in its use of force, but deployed only forces appropriate to the actual threat facing

the client and in ways that sought to allay the concerns of its superpower rival and avoid confrontation or exacerbation of tension.

Viewed in the context of Soviet activity in the Third World, a high-risk intervention would, by contrast, entail the use of Soviet forces to do one of the following:

- acquire a decided advantage over the United States;
- extend the USSR's control over the client state;
- change the client's leadership;
- enable a client to undertake disruptive activities aimed at altering the existing balance of power or fostering major changes of regime in the region.

The line between low-risk and high-risk intervention is not a sharp one, but a workable distinction is that high-risk behavior heightens the danger of confrontation between the Soviet Union and the United States, lowers the nuclear threshold, and affects the stability of areas lying outside the specific confines of the interventionist activity. Categorization is determined by observable consequences. The ample data available since the 1960s lend themselves to a consensus on the instances and types of interventions and make it possible to arrive at some policy-relevant generalizations about Soviet behavior.

Soviet military interventions increased in the 1970s and took place in regions and situations that challenged the interests, credibility, and commitments of the United States. The result was not just intensification of the U.S.-Soviet global rivalry but complication of efforts to reach agreement in other spheres of Soviet-American interaction as well, notably arms control and trade.

The shift in Soviet policy from inhibiting and undermining pro-Western alignments and positions to forcefully pressing its own ambitions is easier to identify than to date. It took place gradually, was initially tentative and piecemeal, but gained in assertiveness so that by the CPSU's twenty-sixth congress, on February 23, 1981, Brezhnev could proclaim, "No one should have any doubts, comrades, that the CPSU will consistently continue the policy of promoting cooperation between the USSR and the newly free countries, and consolidating the alliance of world socialism and the national liberation movement."

Soviet readiness to intervene is presumed to be the result of deliberations that weighed certain considerations: (1) the opportunity factor, which derives from regional instability and the alacrity with which local actors have turned to the Soviet Union in order to secure or advance their own aims; (2) the inability or unwillingness of the United States to use its power to bring about a more favorable strategic-political environment in the Third World; (3) the role that clients can play in advancing Soviet objectives; and (4) the coming on line of a power projection capability (PPC) favoring greater assertiveness.

The growth in the Soviet Union's conventional power projection capability is impressive, especially in respect of the enhanced mobility of its forces. This has been achieved by a variety of means, including the development of a long-range airlift capacity, airborne divisions, and roll-on, roll-off merchant ships, designed to operate in Third World ports that are poorly equipped with machinery for fast unloading.[2] By such means Moscow has acquired an effective global reach, manifest in Angola in 1975 and Ethiopia in 1977. Whereas prior to the late 1960s Moscow's limited PPC hampered its ability to mount military interventions of a consequential character, since then its options have increased significantly.

On a number of occasions, Moscow's PPC has convincingly demonstrated all the requisite traits for long-term policy significance. It conveys *credibility*, the assurance that necessary forces will be used; *deliverability*, the capacity for transporting the forces needed; *relevance*, the appropriateness of the forces available to the threat faced; and *effectiveness*, the high probability of success. Over the years, it has become organizationally better adapted to Third World environments and logistically increasingly well run: witness its more impressive performance in Ethiopia than in Angola, especially in relation to command and control functions.

Besides improvement of its PPC, Moscow's strength derives from a set of politically coherent and consistent priorities; a tenacious and unsparing pursuit of its aims, irrespective of foreign opinion; a historical

---

[2] Details on the systematic Soviet buildup of its power projection capability are readily available in a variety of authoritative sources, including *The Military Balance*, published annually by the London-based International Institute for Strategic Studies; *World Armaments and Disarmament: SIPRI Yearbook*, an annual of the Stockholm International Peace Research Institute, as well as other of SIPRI's publications; and reports issued by the U.S. Arms Control and Disarmament Agency. See also John M. Collins, *U.S.-Soviet Military Balance 1980–1985* (Elmsford, N.Y.: Pergamon-Brassey's, 1985), part IV, chapters 11 and 12; Dennis M. Gormley, "The Direction and Pace of Soviet Force Projection Capabilities," *Survival* 24, no. 6 (November–December 1982), 266–76; Rajan Menon, *Soviet Power and the Third World* (New Haven, Conn.: Yale University Press, 1986), chapter 3; Daniel S. Papp, *Soviet Policies toward the Developing World during the 1980s* (Maxwell Air Force Base, Ala.: Air University Press, 1986), chapter 6; and Bruce D. Porter, *The USSR in Third World Conflicts: Soviet Arms and Diplomacy in Local Wars, 1945–1980* (Cambridge: Cambridge University Press, 1984), chapter 3.

perspective that helps keep the leadership focused on an array of seemingly disparate but interlinked and complementary objectives; and a commitment to the maintenance of an extensive intelligence and research capability, which includes thousands of linguistically competent experts.

By the mid-1950s, the Soviet leadership determined that it needed conventional forces capable of protecting and promoting "state interests" in areas that "do not lie immediately within the boundaries of the bloc and the USSR."[3] Admiral Gorshkov has confirmed that the task of building "a powerful oceanic nuclear missile fleet" was begun "roughly from the middle of the fifties" to service the diverse range of "state interests."[4] Like the long-range airlift capability, the "blue water" fleet took more than a decade to become a force to be reckoned with.[5]

After Stalin's death, there was disagreement at the top over which weapons to build.[6] The conventional force structure needed for a PPC was not pushed as a defense priority, whereas strategic nuclear forces were, and in 1959 a separate branch of the armed services was established for the Strategic Rocket Forces. By the late 1950s, however, there was a surge in Soviet expenditures for both strategic and conventional forces.[7] Thus, we can discern in Khrushchev's tenure the desire for a "balanced force structure," and the conceptual link between the spate of diplomatic, political, and economic moves toward competitive engagement in the Third World and defense expenditures designed to give Soviet leaders the wherewithal to conduct such a policy credibly.

Soviet leaders are imbued with a belief in the value of military power for securing political interests. Once it had adopted a policy of

[3] James M. McConnell, "Doctrine and Capabilities," in Bradford Dismukes and James M. McConnell, eds., *Soviet Naval Diplomacy* (New York: Pergamon Press, 1979), 6; and see above, Chapter One.

[4] S. G. Gorshkov, *The Sea Power of the State*, trans. from Russian (Annapolis: Naval Institute Press, 1979), 179–180.

[5] In addition to data mentioned in note 2 above, there is a fund of information in John M. Collins, *U.S.-Soviet Military Balance: Concepts and Capabilities 1960–1980* (New York: McGraw-Hill, 1980).

[6] N. S. Khrushchev, *The Last Testament*, trans. and ed. Strobe Talbott (New York: Bantam Books, 1976), 47. Chapter 2 sheds light on disagreements over naval construction; chapter 3, on aircraft and missiles, with a bit on the army.

[7] David Holloway, *The Soviet Union and the Arms Race*, 2d ed. (New Haven, Conn.: Yale University Press, 1984), 127–28; McConnell, "Doctrine and Capabilities," 15–20; and Thomas W. Wolfe, *Soviet Power and Europe 1945–1970* (Baltimore: Johns Hopkins University Press, 1970), chapters 7–9.

penetrating the Third World and making expensive investments in clients there, Moscow had to give increasing attention to the problem of how to protect the client (and its investment)—to safeguard him against being overthrown or attacked. At first, in 1955, it may have been uneasy over the sale of arms to Egypt, hence the shipments of Czech rather than Soviet weapons and the screen of secrecy behind which the operation was conducted. According to Mohamed Heikal, when Nasser was asked what would happen if the United States decided to stop the weapons shipments he replied that that was a Soviet problem;[8] and indeed it was and not one that the Soviets would be likely to overlook for long. It was more than a matter of securing access by sea: the natural sequence of things was to proceed from protecting an investment *during* delivery to protecting it *after* delivery and keeping the client a going concern.[9]

Moscow was circumspect, because very soon Third World requests for, and receptivity to, all kinds of Soviet military support and demonstrations of force on their behalf outpaced Soviet capabilities or inclinations for risk-taking. Diplomatic gestures were carefully controlled so as not to trigger a U.S. military response. Thus, during the 1956 Suez crisis, Moscow proposed that the Soviet Union and the United States jointly send their armed forces to the Middle East, knowing there was no chance that Washington would accept—particularly since Soviet troops had invaded Hungary a week earlier and were in the process of crushing the Hungarian revolution. Despite the Soviet Union's obvious inability to act independently on behalf of Nasser, its proposal enhanced Moscow's standing in Cairo and the Arab world without risking a thing.[10] The Syrian-Turkish crisis a year later provides another manifestation of Moscow's prudence. Two Soviet warships put in at Latakia, in a demonstration of support for Syria, apparently at the behest of Minister of Defense Marshal G. K. Zhukov. However, in an atmosphere of rising tension, he was summarily stripped of his government and party posts two days after Tirana Radio quoted him during his visit to Albania as having assured Syria that, "if war is declared, the Soviet Union will not remain with its arms folded. We are all ready to strike at any military adventure organized

---

[8] Mohamed Heikal, *The Sphinx and the Commissar: The Rise and Fall of Soviet Influence in the Middle East* (New York: Harper & Row, 1978), 63.

[9] I owe this insight, and awareness of its implications, to James M. McConnell of the Center for Naval Analyses.

[10] Oles M. Smolansky, *The Soviet Union and the Arab East under Khrushchev* (Lewisburg, Pa.: Bucknell University Press, 1974), 48–49.

by the United States near our southern borders."[11] Khrushchev quickly squashed this incipient adventurism (and, incidentally, rid himself of a potential rival): the USSR lacked the PPC for credible deterrence on behalf of a potential client.

Khrushchev continued to exercise restraint. In July 1958, when the pro-Western regime in Baghdad was toppled, Nasser flew to Moscow to ask him to support the Iraqi revolution against a possible Western intervention, but Khrushchev refused: "He was not prepared to take any risks that could lead to war"; the most that he was prepared to do was to increase the scale of military maneuvers along the Bulgarian-Turkish frontier.[12] However, when Nasser stopped in Damascus he announced that "the Soviet Union is fully behind us," conveying an impression of commitment that was unwarranted but that nonetheless may have served his purpose, which was to make the United States think twice before attempting a counter-coup.

Moscow learned from such experiences what its clients wanted and how it could improve its standing with them, but its capabilities were not good enough. Several years later, it provided advisers and troops to help Indonesia man some of the Soviet planes and ships Sukarno had bought, but did so secretly, to avoid the danger of a confrontation with the West.[13] Taking a leaf out of Nasser's book, Sukarno leaked word of an alleged Soviet pledge to furnish military personnel to help fight against the Dutch if need be.[14] Once again, Moscow saw not only how important a link to the Soviet Union could be for a Third World leadership, but also how a client could exploit that connection to engage in brinksmanship with potentially serious consequences. (The Netherlands finally relinquished control over West Irian, ending the conflict with Indonesia.) The covert character of Khrushchev's despatch of combat personnel disqualifies it as an "intervention" as defined in this study, which is why the incident is not included in the list of Soviet interventions provided in Table 3.

By the mid-1960s, the official Soviet doctrine on local wars was beginning to undergo modifications reflecting the USSR's new circum-

[11] J. M. MacKintosh, *Strategy and Tactics of Soviet Foreign Policy* (London: Oxford University Press, 1962), 229. For the sequence of events that led to Zhukov's fall, see McConnell, "Doctrine and Capabilities," 6–10.

[12] Mohamed Heikal, *Nasser: The Cairo Documents* (London: New English Library, 1972), 132; and Anwar el-Sadat, *In Search of Identity: An Autobiography* (New York: Harper & Row, 1977), 153.

[13] The reports of Soviet troops operating Indonesian equipment in 1962 were confirmed in 1971 by Indonesia's foreign minister, Adam Malik. *The Statesmen*, January 7, 1971.

[14] Khrushchev, *Last Testament*, 370–71.

stances—its growing experience in the Third World, commitments, and PPC. Heretofore absorbed with nuclear issues and the technological revolution in military affairs, Soviet leaders had held that any local conflict "could" escalate but that escalation would be "inevitable" if the nuclear powers were involved. As far as Soviet military thought was concerned, this meant that the USSR should not become involved in a local conflict in the Third World unless its vital interests were at issue. But, since it had few vital interests there, the net effect was to leave the Soviets with no local war doctrine suitable to their forward policy. However, as James McConnell and Bradford Dismukes have noted,

> in late 1965 this formula was qualified in a major way by General Colonel N. Lomov, when he declared that escalation was inevitable only in "certain circumstances." These circumstances may have been specified in Marshal M. V. Zakharov's 1968 statement that "escalation is more likely with the participation in the local war of states having nuclear weapons, and *especially when the vitally important interests of these states are infringed upon in such a war.*" The implication is that escalation is less likely if vital interests are not at stake; this would generally be the case in the Third World.[15]

Lomov and others used phrases such as "might escalate," "threatens to escalate," and the "possibility" of escalation to distinguish between "possible" wars and "inevitable" wars and provide the doctrinal underpinnings for a diplomacy of force in the Third World. Though rarely mentioned in the reasoning that went into them, the Cuban missile crisis, which exemplifies the danger of a confrontation between the superpowers turning nuclear, was probably the existential watershed that occasioned the distinction between local wars that might become nuclear and those that were unlikely to do so.

The change in doctrine kept pace with Soviet policy and with new perceptions of reality. Faced with the possibility that they might be called upon to fight in a Third World environment, Soviet military planners sought to define the nature of the wars that might arise, the circumstances, and the implications for the Soviet Union.[16] With pro-

[15] James M. McConnell and Bradford Dismukes, "Soviet Diplomacy of Force in the Third World," *Problems of Communism* 28, no. 1 (January–February 1979), 21. See also Mark N. Katz, *The Third World in Soviet Military Thought* (Baltimore: Johns Hopkins University Press, 1982), 39. He makes the point that the Soviet military itself, and not the party, was instrumental in altering views on conflicts, and the possibilities of conflicts, in the Third World (43–55).

[16] According to one analyst, "it is the military nature of the war that gives Soviet doctrine and capabilities their actual meaning"—namely, the ability to affect the outcome of

liferating local wars an increasing probability, by the end of the 1960s and early in the 1970s Soviet writings regularly included Soviet interests in the Third World in the military's longstanding mission of "protecting state interests." With respect to the Third World, the long-avowed "international duty" of the USSR underwent expansion in frequent references to "broadening the international obligations of *the Soviet armed forces*" beyond the area of the Warsaw Pact.[17] A remarkably unequivocal statement of official policy appeared in 1972 in a book edited by the influential military analyst Colonel V. M. Kulish:

> In connection with the task of preventing local wars and also in those cases wherein military support must be furnished to those nations fighting for their freedom and independence against the forces of internal reaction and imperialist intervention, the Soviet Union may require mobile and well-equipped armed forces. In some situations, the very knowledge of a Soviet military presence in an area in which a conflict situation is developing may serve to restrain the imperialists and local reaction. . . .[18]

Kulish's analysis was given the official imprimatur in 1974 when Minister of Defense Marshal A. A. Grechko wrote,

> At the present stage the historic function of the Soviet Armed Forces is not restricted to their function in defending our Motherland and the other socialist countries. In its foreign policy activity the Soviet state purposefully opposes the export of counter-revolution and the policy of oppression, supports the national liberation struggle, and resolutely resists imperialists' aggression in whatever distant region of our planet it may appear.[19]

By the 1970s, Kulish and Grechko, among others, were merely putting in writing what Soviet combat forces had already demonstrated on Third World battlefields about the USSR's readiness to intervene

---

a conflict; and "the military nature of a given local war" is determined by the interaction "of the following five interconnected factors: the operational nature of the war; the scale of the war; the composition of the opposing local armies; the duration of the war; and the general course of belligerent operations." Efraim Karsh, *The Cautious Bear: Soviet Military Engagement in Middle East Wars in the Post-1967 Era* (Boulder, Colo.: Westview, 1985), 23–24.

[17] McConnell, "Doctrine and Capabilities," 25.

[18] V. M. Kulish, ed., *Voennaya sila i mezhdunarodnye otnosheniya* [Military Force and International Relations] (Moscow: International Relations Publishing House, 1972), 137.

[19] Cited in Harriet Fast Scott and William F. Scott, *The Armed Forces of the USSR* (Boulder, Colo.: Westview, 1979), 57.

in regional conflicts. Once again doctrinal innovation followed practice.

CASES

Soviet interventions started at the end of the Khrushchev period. For
the most part they have been well documented, and a coherent picture
of the essentials of Soviet foreign policy emerges from the record: why
the Soviet Union intervened, the characteristics of its diplomacy, and
what criteria are likely to shape its future interventions. Each of the
following thirteen case studies will look at several aspects of the interventions:

- What was its purpose?
- What was the relationship between the intervention and Mos-
  cow's power projection capability? Did the Soviet Union have the
  means appropriate for the task?
- What forces were used?
- What was the effect on relations with the United States?
- What was the outcome?

Congo (Zaire)

In July 1960, less than a week after the Congo had gained its independence from Belgium, a mutiny triggered a breakdown of civil order
and eruption of separatist activity that prompted the new government
in Leopoldville to appeal to the U.N. Security Council for assistance.
Under the leadership of U.N. Secretary-General Dag Hammarskjöld,
a peacekeeping operation was quickly mounted—the ONUC (Organi-
sation des Nations Unies au Congo). Its activities were complicated by
the struggle for power between the top Congolese leaders—President
Joseph Kasavubu and Premier Patrice Lumumba, long-time antagonists. Amidst the spreading of tribal violence and breakdown of order,
the Soviet Union shifted from supporting ONUC to courting Lumumba. At the end of August, ostensibly in line with U.N. resolutions
calling for assistance to the government, it put "about 100 military
trucks and some [10] Ilyushin transport planes together with about
200 technicians" at the personal disposal of Premier Lumumba.[20] In

[20] James Mayall, *Africa: The Cold War and After* (London: Elek, 1971), 118. According
to Brian Urquhart, then deputy to Ralph Bunche, the chief U.N. official supervising
U.N. operations in the Congo (and a deputy secretary-general), Western diplomats
feared that the Soviet assistance would "tilt the balance in the capital" in Lumumba's
favor: the Soviets had started "a strong propaganda effort . . . to promote Soviet prestige

aligning itself with this charismatic figure and hero of the movement for independence, Moscow was helping a prominent African nationalist and positioning itself to influence internal developments in a huge and potentially rich country, but in the process it badly misjudged the local situation—specifically, it underestimated the ability of the United Nations to act forcefully in an unsettled and fluid domestic upheaval, the substantial African support for the U.N. operation, and the complexity of the Congo's tribal alignments;[21] nor did it realize that Lumumba was erratic and politically incapable of maneuvering in the jungle of internecine rivalries.

The Soviet role was short-lived. On September 5, 1960, President Kasavubu removed Lumumba, with the tacit approval of U.N. officials who were responsible for the ONUC peacekeeping operation and who viewed with suspicion Lumumba's attempt to use Soviet pilots to suppress separatist movements in Kasai and Katanga provinces.[22] Nine days later the military seized power, arrested Lumumba, and closed the Soviet embassy, ending Moscow's direct role in the Congo's domestic politics. In February 1961, Lumumba was murdered. Opponents of the Kasavubu government, spearheaded by Egypt and Ghana, recognized the Prague-trained Antoine Gizenga, who had been a vice-premier under Lumumba, and his separatist group in Stanleyville, in Oriental province. Khrushchev supported Nasser, supplying arms and aircraft, but the logistical problems of sustaining Gizenga were enormous. Egypt's effort could do little more than sustain the rebels until early 1965, when U.N. forces helped restore the central government's control.

The episode can barely be labeled an intervention. Moscow expended little effort on behalf of Lumumba or Gizenga. Yet it did show its willingness to become involved in the quest for influence, and its ability to respond quickly with some logistical support. Had Lumumba retained power, Soviet assistance might have become substantial. As it was, neither the Soviet Union nor the United States was in the forefront of developments, so most of the sparks between them were struck in U.N. debates.

---

and undercut United Nations activities, and this in turn made the remaining Europeans uneasy." Brian Urquhart, *A Life in Peace and War* (New York: Harper & Row, 1987), 165–66.

[21] Waldemar A. Nielsen, *The Great Powers and Africa* (New York: Praeger, 1969), 194–95.

[22] Christopher Stevens, *The Soviet Union and Black Africa* (New York: Holmes & Meier, 1976), 17–18.

Laos

A nationalistically motivated young paratroop captain, Kong Le, led a coup in Vientiane on August 9, 1960, which resulted in the resignation of the U.S.-oriented rightist premier and his replacement by the centrist Souvanna Phouma, who favored a nonaligned policy. In his search for an alternative to reliance on the United States, Phouma established diplomatic relations with the Soviet Union. Moscow's first ambassador arrived in October; and its active, highly successful intervention, in the form of an airlift, followed two months later.

Moscow regarded Souvanna Phouma as a promising alternative to the Hanoi-dominated hard-line Pathet Lao, over which it had no influence.[23] Aware that Souvanna Phouma and Kong Le faced an imminent attack by the pro-Western Phoumi Nosavan, who was supplied by a CIA that was not controlled by the U.S. ambassador,[24] Moscow mounted an airlift—the first of the planes, redeployed from the Congo, arriving with a load of oil on December 3.[25] A week later, General Phoumi Nosavan's troops prepared their assault on the capital. On December 11, Soviet Ilyushins dislodged six 105 mm howitzers, complete with ammunition and North Vietnamese gun crews, on the runway of Vientiane airport—in full view of U.S. observers.[26] The subsequent battle for Vientiane lasted from December 13 to 16, ending with the orderly withdrawal of Kong Le toward the Plaine de Jarres. He captured it at the end of the month with the assistance of the Pathet Lao and, of course, Soviet air resupply, which was improvised "with amazing rapidity."[27]

The Soviet Union's policy in Laos differed from Vietnam's and China's. It supported the "centrist" Souvanna Phouma, who still had a legal case for remaining the head of the internationally recognized government of Laos, whereas Vietnam and China backed the "Red Prince" Souphanouvong, who headed the Pathet Lao and espoused violent revolution. Moscow followed a low-risk policy of aid to a neu-

[23] For this and other insights, I am indebted to G. W. Bailey, "In Like a Lion, Out Like the Lamb: The Soviet Intervention in Laos, December 1960–December 1962" (unpublished paper). See *Pravda*, October 15, 1960.

[24] Thus, the United States was actively supporting rebels attacking a government with which it maintained diplomatic relations.

[25] Arthur J. Dommen, *Conflict in Laos* (New York: Praeger, 1964), 164. *New York Times*, December 14, 1960.

[26] Dommen, *Conflict in Laos*, 167; and Shelby L. Stanton, *Green Berets at War: U.S. Army Special Forces in Southeast Asia 1956–1975* (New York: Presidio, 1985), 20–21.

[27] Douglas S. Blaufarb, *The Counter-Insurgency Era: U.S. Doctrine and Performance* (New York: Free Press, 1977), 137; Bailey, "In Like a Lion."

tralist government far from the locus of Soviet power, whereas the regional communist powers pursued a high-risk national liberation struggle.

Neither the Americans nor China and Vietnam were prepared for a test of strength in Laos, so negotiations involving the superpowers and regional actors were started in Geneva in May 1961 and dragged on until July 1962. As co-chairman of the Geneva Conference, the USSR was able to advance the cause of the neutralist Souvanna Phouma, and a compromise formula was adopted calling for him to head a tripartite government of national unity—with representatives of the neutralist, pro-Western, and pro-communist groups. Khrushchev lauded the settlement; the United States made the best of a bad bargain.

Moscow's aim in Laos was to exploit a flawed U.S. policy. The means were limited to the airlift and supplies for the forces of Kong Le: no Soviet combat forces were committed. Over the approximately eighteen months of the operation, Khrushchev was able to influence events in the country, counter Chinese criticisms and demonstrate Soviet support for a liberation struggle. Moscow had entered the arena with minimal outlay and little risk. However, by mid-1962 it had terminated the airlift and withdrawn from the center of the Laotian stage, partially because of absorption with developments in other areas and partially out of a growing realization that it lacked the ability to affect the outcome of events. The tension with China, the missile gap, the Berlin crisis, and the Cuban situation all drew Khrushchev's attention elsewhere. Once again, as in the Congo, the unidimensionality of the USSR's power had restricted Moscow's options in an area far from its locus of interest and effective sway. Its influence on developments was important—but for a brief period only; and whatever peaceful intent and reasonableness it had succeeded in conveying at Geneva in the settlement negotiations were soon dissipated by the crisis in Cuba. Nonetheless, Moscow had learned it could at little cost or risk thwart U.S. policy, a lesson it applied again and again with considerable success.

Cuba

The Soviet interventions in Cuba were of two kinds: the projection of a deterrent force, and a quest for strategic advantage. In May 1960, the Soviet Union and Cuba formally established diplomatic relations. The low-risk phase began with heavy shipments of Soviet weapons several months after the failure in late April 1961 of the CIA-organized attempt at the Bay of Pigs to topple Castro by landing émigré Cubans to raise a revolt. A year later, there were approximately 20,000 Soviet troops on the island, manning an impressive array of conventional weapons, including "24 batteries of surface-to-air missile (SAM) launchers, each of which was supplied with 24 missiles with a firing range of 25 miles; more than 100 jet planes, including at least 42 MiG-21's, Moscow's most sophisticated supersonic fighter; short-range harbor defense missiles; and missile-equipped coastal patrol boats."[28] As long as only conventional forces were used, the intervention was low-risk, intended to protect the internationally-recognized government of Fidel Castro from possible invasion and deter any further U.S. military action, but this dispatch of combat forces did mark the first time that Moscow committed itself to the defense of a non-communist regime in the Third World.

The second intervention, the attempt to implant nuclear-tipped medium and intermediate-range ballistic missiles in Cuba in September–October 1962, was a high-risk intervention that represented a quantum escalation of Soviet aims, having nothing to do with the protection of a client or deterrence against a potential aggressor. Whether it was Khrushchev's perception of Kennedy as indecisive and weak, a desire to offset Soviet strategic inferiority by a "quick fix" of IRBMs in Cuba, an attempt to compensate for political setbacks in Lebanon, the Congo, and Berlin or to counter the pressure of those in the leadership who favored a costly buildup of the Strategic Rocket Forces, the move was a dangerous gamble that sought to exploit Third World real estate for the promotion of Soviet strategic objectives at a time of nuclear inferiority to the United States.

The missile crisis erupted on October 22, 1962, with President Kennedy's announcement that "unmistakable evidence has established the fact that a series of offensive missile sites is now in preparation" on the island of Cuba; and it ended on October 27, when it was clear that both sides wanted to pull back from the nuclear brink. Work on construction of the sites ceased, existing facilities were dismantled, and nuclear warheads en route were returned to the Soviet Union.[29] After

[28] Morton Schwartz, "The Cuban Missile Venture," in James B. Christoph and Bernard E. Brown, eds., *Cases in Comparative Politics*, 3d ed. (Boston: Little, Brown, 1976), 318. Schwartz writes that there were between 15,000 and 20,000 Soviet troops on the island. According to McGeorge Bundy, by October 1962 there were between 21,000 and 40,000 troops. "The Brigade's My Fault," *New York Times*, October 23, 1979. In an interview with CBS television on September 30, 1979, Fidel Castro put the number of Soviet troops at 40,000. Mose L. Harvey, *Soviet Combat Troops in Cuba* (Coral Gables, Fla.: Advanced International Studies Institute, 1979), 6.

[29] According to Raymond L. Garthoff, who was at the time Special Assistant for Soviet Bloc, Office of Politico-Military Affairs, Department of Defense, "no nuclear warheads

this near-confrontation, U.S.-Soviet relations took a dramatic upturn in 1963 with an easing of tensions over Berlin, the signing of a limited nuclear test-ban treaty, and the start of negotiations on a range of issues. The Cuban experience showed that in 1962 the Soviet Union possessed a PPC that could transfer arms and troops great distances to help a client, but was dependent on transport by sea; and, in a region so far from home, Soviet naval power was not capable of interdicting U.S. operations. Furthermore, Moscow's airlift capability was still too limited to be relied on for resupply in time of crisis.

Egypt after the June War

The Soviet courtship of Egypt, started by Khrushchev, was pursued by Brezhnev, urged on by his military. They wanted access to Egyptian ports and permanent naval facilities to compensate for what they had lost when Albania evicted them in May 1961. In 1964, 1965, and 1966, economic and military assistance were increased, confounding Western expectations of curbed Soviet commitments. In May 1967, Nasser bungled a good diplomatic hand and blundered into a confrontation with Israel that resulted in a stunning defeat of Egypt, Syria, and Jordan. Unable to render any assistance to the Arabs during the fighting because of the rapidity of Israeli advances and the collapse of the Egyptian Army, the Soviet government mounted a major diplomatic campaign in the United Nations and pledged "all necessary material assistance" to help the Arabs out of their plight. On June 12, two days after the ceasefire took effect, Moscow began a massive resupply by air. Its airlift capability was greatly enhanced by overflight and refueling privileges in Yugoslavia, and resulted in a rapid rearming of the Egyptian Army and the introduction of an air defense system.[30]

On July 10, 1967, to underscore its commitment to Nasser and intention to shield Egypt from any further Israeli attacks or military

---

were ever identified in Cuba, but there was evidence of preparation for their transfer from the Soviet Union, and some may even have been transferred." Raymond L. Garthoff, "The Meaning of the Missiles," *Washington Quarterly* 5, no. 4 (Autumn 1982), 81.

There is an enormous literature in the West on the Cuban missile crisis. Particularly valuable in shedding light on Khrushchev's approach are the following: Herbert S. Dinerstein, *The Making of a Missile Crisis: October 1962* (Baltimore: Johns Hopkins University Press, 1976), chapters 5 and 6; and Arnold Horelick and Myron Rush, *Strategic Power and Soviet Foreign Policy* (Chicago: University of Chicago Press, 1965).

On the Soviet side, two carefully argued essays written by Anatolii A. Gromyko appeared in successive issues of *Voprosy istorii* in 1971: see *Soviet Law and Government* 11, no. 1 (Summer 1972).

[30] Details of Tito's cooperation were revealed by Mohamed Heikal on the occasion of Tito's eightieth birthday. *Cairo Press Review*, no. 5593, May 19, 1972.

pressure—Israeli artillery was in a position to shell Port Said and cities along the western bank of the Suez Canal—Moscow sent units of its Mediterranean fleet to Port Said and Alexandria. These were the first Soviet combat forces openly committed in the Middle East to the defense of a client. The ships left in late September. But, soon after the sinking of the Israeli destroyer *Eilat* on October 21, "the Soviets responded to Israeli retaliatory air strikes and threats of further retaliation by again dispatching surface combatants to Port Said and Alexandria. . . . The result: there were no further Israeli attacks on Port Said. This occasion was the beginning of the continuous presence of Soviet ships in Egyptian ports, which lasted until the Soviets were totally expelled on April 14, 1976."[31]

The use of its naval forces also opened a new channel for Soviet diplomacy. Henceforth, through naval deployments, Moscow could alert Washington to impending danger. Since 1967 the naval instrument has permitted Moscow to conduct a "diplomacy of force" in Third World areas, thereby significantly altering "the political shape and complexion" of superpower relations.[32]

Yemen

The Soviet intervention in Yemen in late 1967 and early 1968 was an outgrowth of five years of logistical support for Nasser's campaign to spread his influence in the Arabian Peninsula. He had become involved shortly after a group of Yemeni military officers, with support among diverse urban social and economic groups who favored modernization and an end to traditional rule by the Zaidis, overthrew the imamate at the end of September 1962 and proclaimed the Yemen Arab Republic (YAR). But the revolution, which "was neither a mass movement nor homogeneous in its objectives once the monarchy was overthrown, feared a counter-coup by Zaidi tribesmen in the north," aided by the Saudis or by the British in the neighboring South Arabian Federation (after its independence in 1967 known as the People's Republic of South Yemen, and from 1970 as the People's Democratic Republic of Yemen) or by both, and called on Nasser for help.[33] The first contingent of several thousand Egyptian troops arrived in early October.

Notwithstanding the presence of upwards of 70,000 Egyptian

---

[31] Abram N. Shulsky, "Coercive Diplomacy," in Dismukes and McConnell, eds., *Soviet Naval Diplomacy*, 119; also 269.

[32] McConnell and Dismukes, "Conclusions," ibid., 300.

[33] Robert W. Stookey, *Yemen: The Politics of the Yemen Arab Republic* (Boulder, Colo.: Westview, 1978), 230–31.

troops, the tribal war dragged on inconclusively for five years. Moscow subsidized Nasser's intervention, providing the arms and logistical assistance without which the Egyptian Army could not have continued to operate so far from home. The Soviet Union gave this support for a number of reasons: to demonstrate solidarity with Nasser and enhance its prestige among "progressive," anti-American groups in the Arab East; to increase Nasser's dependence on the USSR, in the hope of receiving naval privileges in Egypt; to acquire a foothold in Yemen and familiarize Soviet intelligence agents with the area, with a view toward eventual subversion of the oil-rich rulers of the peninsula; to intensify pressure on the British to abandon their naval base in the colony of Aden and the South Arabian Federation; and to establish close ties with the Yemeni military officers.[34]

Defeat in the June War forced Nasser to withdraw from his "Vietnam." The last Egyptian soldier left in early October. The Royalists, backed by the Saudis, closed in on San'ā' and appeared on the verge of recapturing the capital. At this point, Moscow intervened directly, not just with massive amounts of arms and ammunition, but also with "combat aircraft with technicians and ground crews"—and Soviet pilots to fly combat missions: "This was a measure of some desperation, but a royalist victory would have meant the loss of a considerable investment and of a strategic position on the Red Sea coast. (It would also have left exposed the most recent and vulnerable addition to the 'progressive' Arab states, the People's Republic of South Yemen, proclaimed on November 30, 1967)."[35]

The Soviet intervention tipped the balance in favor of the Republicans. In particular, it was control of the air by Soviet combat pilots that enabled them "to defend the open plain between the city and the superior Royalist forces in the surrounding hills" and survive the two-and-a-half-month siege.[36] The Republicans persevered, and in February 1968 a Soviet-organized relief column lifted the siege. By the end of the year, the Republicans, well-armed by the Soviets, were in control, and a settlement was worked out ending the civil war.

Ironically, as a result of domestic politics the YAR turned away from dependence on the Soviet Union, in important measure because Moscow was simultaneously giving heavy support to the rival regime in South Yemen. By 1970 the Soviets were left with little tangible benefit to show for their effort. Still, the Yemeni experience was useful in the

---

[34] Porter, *The USSR in Third World Conflicts*, 72; Vladimir Sakharov, *High Treason* (New York: Ballantine, 1980), 139–40.

[35] Stephen Page, *The Soviet Union and the Yemens* (New York: Praeger, 1985), 6.

[36] Porter, *The USSR in Third World Conflicts*, 83.

evolution of Soviet policy. The Yemeni civil war produced "the first confirmed instance in the postwar period of Soviet fighter pilots engaging in combat in the Third World"; it was "one case in which Soviet arms shipments reversed a local balance of power and achieved a decisive political outcome in a Third World conflict"; and it strengthened the USSR's reputation "in the Middle East as a reliable and powerful ally."[37] Nowhere has the Soviet use of arms as an instrument of diplomacy and penetration of a strategic area been more patent. As an enduring manifestation of the Soviet Union's quest for influence in the Arabian Peninsula, it is also a constant source of tension with the United States, for whom the YAR is the back door to Saudi Arabia.

Egypt's War of Attrition

After Israel's victory in the 1967 June War, the USSR mounted a costly effort to rebuild the Egyptian and Syrian armed forces. By the fall of 1968, Nasser felt strong enough to start a series of low-level military actions along the Suez Canal against the Israeli occupiers of Sinai. Within a year, Nasser's "war of attrition"—his interim answer to a no-war, no-peace stalemate—backfired, escalating to a major conflict, with Israeli air power flying virtually unchallenged over Egypt's now exposed heartland and threatening another debacle. In this setting and after an urgent secret visit from Nasser in late January 1970, the Soviet leadership upped their ante and intervened on a massive scale to save their client.

Moscow's operational objectives were, first, to bring an end to Israeli deep-penetration raids over Cairo, Port Said, and other cities; second, to force the fighting in the air back to the Suez Canal zone; and, third, to provide Egypt with an effective air defense system which would assure an approximate balance of power between the Egyptians and the Israelis. In early March 1970, an estimated 1,500 air defense personnel began installing SAM-2 and SAM-3 sites and large numbers of antiaircraft batteries around Cairo and Alexandria and in the Nile Valley.[38] Soviet MiG-21J interceptors (the most advanced in the Soviet arsenal), approximately one hundred combat pilots, and ground support crews were soon operating out of six airfields; and Soviet-piloted aircraft, which at first restricted "their patrols to the Nile Valley"

---

[37] Ibid., 23–24, 83, 88. This is the most complete analysis of the Soviet intervention in the 1962–1968 Yemeni civil war. See also Mark N. Katz, *Russia and Arabia: Soviet Foreign Policy toward the Arabian Peninsula* (Baltimore: Johns Hopkins University Press, 1986), 24–32; and, for a perspective on the intra-Yemeni tribal and political infighting, Robert W. Stookey, *Yemen: The Politics of the Yemen Arab Republic* (Boulder, Colo.: Westview, 1978), 225–60.

[38] Roger F. Pajak, "Soviet Arms and Egypt," *Survival*, 17 (July–August 1975), 167.

steadily extended "their operations forward to areas on the flanks of the Canal front."[39] By the end of June, the number of Soviet air defense personnel had risen to about 8,000; by the end of the year, the number was almost double this figure. As the thick Soviet air defense system made Israeli attacks more costly and intensified the fighting along the canal, the United States succeeded in arranging a ceasefire agreement, which took effect on August 7, 1970.

The cease-fire came before the point at which the Soviet intervention might have assumed a high-risk character—that is, have drawn Soviet forces into support for an attempt to cross the canal and change the status quo prevailing before the war of attrition. Soviet leaders had once again saved Nasser from the consequences of his miscalculation. Their intervention had been decisive: it denied Israel a victory, kept Egypt a credible belligerent, seemingly secured Soviet privileges, avoided a confrontation with the United States yet evidenced the USSR's determination to play a prominent role in the Arab-Israeli conflict, and demonstrated a vastly expanded PPC.

Sudan

Soviet interest in developing closer ties with the strategically important Sudan picked up after the June War, when most Arab governments broke off diplomatic relations with the United States. But it took a leftist-oriented military coup on May 25, 1969, to whet the appetite of both parties. The new regime, under Colonel Gaafar Muhammed al-Nimeiry, included communists in the ruling Revolutionary Command Council and in the cabinet and courted leftist groups to offset the influence of "conservative, traditionalist, religious, and pro-Western forces."[40] Moscow saw this as an opportunity and as evidence of Nimeiry's progressive outlook. One of his main problems was a civil war in the south against the Anyanya—the military force of an amorphous coalition of black Christian tribes and clans of the southern Sudan—who had been fighting since 1963 for autonomy.[41] Nimeiry's request for arms did not cause Moscow to worry about becoming enmeshed in a civil war, because his promise of regional autonomy for the southern areas was accompanied by the appointment of "a prominent southerner (the Communist lawyer, Joseph Garang) to the newly created

[39] Jon D. Glassman, *Arms for the Arabs: The Soviet Union and War in the Middle East* (Baltimore: Johns Hopkins University Press, 1975), 77–78.

[40] Haim Shaked, Esther Souery, and Gabriel Warburg, "The Communist Party in the Sudan, 1946–1971," in Michael Confino and Shimon Shamir, eds., *The USSR and the Middle East* (New York: Wiley, 1973), 56.

[41] Robert O. Collins, *The Southern Sudan in Historical Perspective* (Tel Aviv: Shiloah Center for Middle Eastern and African Studies, 1975), passim.

Ministry of Southern Affairs in June 1969," and by other conciliatory moves toward the Anyanya.[42]

Soviet arms and advisers began to arrive in late 1969. During the buildup and modernization of the Sudanese armed forces in the next eighteen months, the Soviets' long-term aim of a strategic presence superseded their disappointment with Nimeiry's hardening attitude toward Sudanese communists and lack of progress in finding a solution to the southern problem.[43] The Soviet equipment was composed of armored personnel carriers, tanks, and a range of aircraft—fighters, transports, and helicopters, including sixteen MiG-21 short range supersonic fighters, six Antonov-12 heavy cargo planes, capable of transporting about one hundred troops, and different types of helicopters, ideally suited to counter-insurgency operations. The bulk of the planes were delivered from mid-July 1970 on, when Nimeiry's campaign against the Anyanyas gathered momentum.[44] However, the number of missions flown by Soviet pilots in search-and-destroy type counter-insurgency actions was probably quite low.

Soviet-Sudanese relations turned sour in July 1971, when Nimeiry barely survived a communist-led attempted coup. Although there was no evidence that Moscow had engineered the coup, its prompt support for the government proclaimed by the putschists and its attempt to pressure Egyptian President Sadat to follow suit were proof enough to Nimeiry. Soon afterwards, he worked out a settlement with the southerners (which held for a decade, until he broke the accord by pushing a policy of Islamicization) and ended his reconciliation with the USSR.[45]

Egypt during the 1973 October War

At the time of the ceasefire of August 7, 1970, the USSR's military position in Egypt was at its peak: the air defense system, the best in

[42] Peter K. Bechtold, *Politics in the Sudan* (New York: Praeger, 1976), 263.

[43] Information is drawn from Alvin Z. Rubinstein, "Air Support in the Arab East," in Stephen S. Kaplan, ed., *Diplomacy of Power: Soviet Armed Forces as a Political Instrument* (Washington, D.C.: Brookings Institution, 1981), 492–94.

[44] According to Kenneth R. Whiting, "There seems to be good evidence that the Russians not only supplied MiGs, TU-16s, and tanks but also advised Khartoum on how to conduct its war against the Anya-Nya rebels in the southern part of Sudan." *Soviet Air Power* (Boulder, Colo.: Westview, 1986), 186.

[45] Since deposing Nimeiry in April 1985, his successors have faced an escalation of the insurgency in the south because of neighboring Ethiopia's support for the rebels. In looking for a way out of the impasse, they have improved relations with the USSR and, during a visit to Khartoum in February 1987 by a parliamentary delegation, asked Moscow to help mediate an end to the war. Radio Liberty, RL 85/87 (February 27, 1987), 10.

the Middle East, was Soviet-operated; the advanced fighter aircraft were Soviet-piloted and only Soviet personnel worked on them; Moscow enjoyed extensive air and naval privileges; and Soviet advisers functioned from the battalion level to the highest echelons of the Egyptian High Command. In brief, the Kremlin thought it had a dependent client capable of resisting but not defeating Israel and therefore sensitive to its wishes and goodwill.

After Nasser's death on September 28, 1970, the continuity the Soviet leadership expected became instead a succession struggle that in May 1971 ended with the virtual elimination of Nasser's entire entourage. Concerned over the unanticipated turn of events and the preservation of its strategic assets in Egypt, Moscow pressed for a formalization of the Soviet-Egyptian relationship, and a friendship treaty was signed on May 27, 1971. Despite the treaty, it found working with Sadat difficult: not only did he help suppress the communist-inspired coup in the Sudan in July, but he cracked down on Egyptian communists and put out feelers to the United States for better relations. The ultimate indignity came in July 1972 when Sadat abruptly terminated the mission of all Soviet military personnel (between 15,000 and 20,000); and only the naval privileges were permitted to continue more or less as before. A limited reconciliation at the end of the year preserved the Soviet-Egyptian relationship intact until the 1973 Arab-Israeli war.

The decision to go to war on October 6, 1973, was made in Cairo and Damascus. The conflict was one Moscow did not want but did nothing to prevent. Three days after the outbreak of fighting, the Kremlin launched its biggest air supply operation in the Third World up to that time (the 1977–1978 airlift to Ethiopia would be even larger) on behalf of Egypt and Syria. Antonov-12 and Antonov-22 transports flew more than 900 sorties, bringing much-needed supplies of "sagger" anti-tank missiles, tanks, SAMs, and ammunition.[46] The Soviets delivered more than four times as much matériel by sea and, alert to the potential of U.S. forces to influence the outcome, they deployed a sizable fleet that "reached a peak of 96 ships, including 34 surface combatants and 23 submarines"; the fleet served as a warning against any interference with the Soviet sealift, as a way of gathering intelligence and keeping tabs on U.S. naval operations, and as a protective chain to safeguard Soviet forces in the event that large numbers would

[46] Lieutenant-General Saad El-Shazly, *The Crossing of Suez: The October War* (San Francisco: American Mideast Research, 1980), 274–75. Shazly, one of Egypt's military heroes, was Chief of Staff during the October War; he was removed from his post two months later because of outspoken disagreement with President Sadat.

have to be sent to fight in Egypt or Syria or both.[47] Finally, after the ceasefire of October 22 broke down because of Israel's decision to press its advantage, Moscow placed its seven airborne divisions on high alert for rapid deployment in the event of their being needed to relieve the surrounded Egyptian Third Army. The Soviet Union's power projection capability had come of age.

According to Bruce Porter, Soviet military personnel performed essential noncombat functions, such as driving tanks from port offloading to the battlefront, operating radar equipment, and reassembling and repairing tanks and other military hardware, but "there is no evidence that any Soviet troops or advisers participated in military operations on the front," though "there was some secondary involvement in combat":

> Soviet advisers accompanied Syrian air-defense units and ground units everywhere except on the front line, and Soviet advisers were reported to have been assigned to Syrian command posts, from the battalion level up, at a ratio of one per post. Soviet soldiers actually controlled and operated air-defense systems at Latakia and Damascus, apparently to deter Israeli air strikes against the resupply operation. It is possible that Soviet personnel also assisted in the firing of the scud missiles [by the Egyptians] on October 22.[48]

Though starting out as a low-risk intervention, Soviet policy moved to the threshold of high risk, because of a determination to shield clients from defeat, even if this meant a confrontation with the United States. As Jon Glassman noted, several Soviet moves were departures from previous practice—"resupplying Arab belligerents during the conflict, urging other Arab states to assist the fighting parties, long postponing the establishment of a ceasefire, and employing physical threats associated with possible application of [nuclear] weapons which were strategic in the Middle East context."[49] Possessing a credible PPC, Moscow seemed to be taking a quantum leap toward intervention that suggested it was prepared (1) to commit whatever forces were necessary to save a client from defeat; (2) to go to extraordinary lengths to

---

[47] Dismukes and McConnell, *Soviet Naval Diplomacy*, 193–210; William B. Quandt, "Soviet Policy in the October Middle East War: II," *International Affairs* 53, no. 4 (October 1977), 590–601.

[48] Porter, *The USSR in Third World Conflicts*, 134. See also Galia Golan, *Yom Kippur and After* (New York: Cambridge University Press, 1977), 89; and Glassman, *Arms for the Arabs*, 138.

[49] Glassman, *Arms for the Arabs*, 173.

deny victory to an American-supported client; and (3) to jeopardize détente with the United States if need be in order to safeguard a prized Third World client or military position.[50]

Iraq, October 1974 to March 1975

Soviet relations with Iraq improved in the late 1960s and early 1970s, and a treaty of friendship and cooperation was signed on April 9, 1972. The Ba'ath Party leadership calculated that the combination of the treaty, expanded trade, arms purchases, their toleration of Iraqi communists, and anti-imperialist foreign policy would give Moscow a stake in the stability of their regime and lead it to use its influence with the Kurds and the Iraqi Communist Party to help find a settlement of the Kurdish problem. The Kurds, in revolt for autonomy since 1961, were being armed by Iran, Iraq's powerful neighbor and regional rival.

Soviet arms deliveries to oil-rich Iraq increased in the spring of 1974, in time for a new Iraqi offensive against the Kurds, who in March had rejected the Ba'athist proposal for self rule. From June on, Kurdish claims that Soviet pilots were flying bombing and intelligence missions against them seemed plausible, because Iraq was not known to have any pilots trained to fly advanced MiG-23 fighter-bombers or TU-16 reconnaissance planes. By late fall, the Iraqi offensive had squeezed the Kurds into a narrowing strip along the Iranian border but could not manage a knockout blow because Iranian protective artillery barrages and supplies of weapons stiffened Kurdish resistance.[51] At this point, concerned by the growing strain on the Ba'ath government and the covert U.S. aid to the Kurds, Moscow quickly upgraded Iraq's military capability, a move which, combined with sorties by Soviet-piloted aircraft, played a crucial role in the settlement reached between Iraq and Iran on March 5, 1975.

Moscow had shown what it could do for a client and successfully brought about a settlement between historic adversaries without having to take sides or disrupt its courtship of both countries. This may explain its effort two years later to reconcile Somalia and Ethiopia. (Its initial venture as "honest broker" in January 1966 at the Tashkent Conference had helped end the 1965 Indo-Pakistani War and may have encouraged it to think of filling the nineteenth-century British role of great-power mediator and crisis-manager in the region.)

[50] Alvin Z. Rubinstein, *Red Star on the Nile: The Soviet-Egyptian Influence Relationship since the June War* (Princeton: Princeton University Press, 1977), 277–81.

[51] Rubinstein, "Air Support in the Arab East," 505–7.

Angola 1975

The overthrow of the decades-old dictatorship in Portugal on April 25, 1974, brought an end to Portugal's 500-year old African empire. In Guinea-Bissau, the Cape Verde Islands, São Tome and Principe, and Mozambique, the transition from colony to sovereign nation was peaceful. However, in Angola there was a civil war and a superpower intervention.

In January 1975 the Portuguese agreed to grant Angola independence on November 11, and the struggle for power among the various groups intensified. By March the Soviet Union started major arms shipments to the Marxist MPLA via Congo-Brazzaville. Crucial to the MPLA's victory was the arrival of Cuban troops, starting with 1,000 in August, increasing to 5,000 at the end of November and 11,000 by early 1976; they were flown across the Atlantic in Soviet transports.[52] This interventionary effort, which was buttressed by a substantial Soviet sealift with Soviet naval protection, was a cooperative Soviet-Cuban effort. The impetus came from Castro, who was determined to show continued solidarity with the MPLA; the means, from Moscow, whose PPC proved decisive. In addition, "the disinclination of the United States to intervene, made evident by strong Congressional opposition to such action in December 1975," reinforced Moscow's resolve and assured military success.[53]

During the period before independence officially took effect, aware that it "was openly defying the authority of the OAU and potentially jeopardizing its standing in Africa" by shipping arms to the MPLA and ferrying Cubans into the country, Moscow developed three main arguments to justify its policy:

1. "Soviet assistance to the MPLA was said to be a continuation of aid given during the colonial period at the request of the OAU";

2. after November 11, the Soviet Union insisted that the Democratic Republic of Angola, led by the MPLA, was the legitimate government, and aid to help defend it against outside intervention was legal; and

---

[52] For details of the Cuban involvement, see Arthur Jay Klinghoffer, *The Angolan War: A Study in Soviet Policy in the Third World* (Boulder, Colo.: Westview, 1980), 110–20; Edward Gonzalez, "Cuba, the Soviet Union, and Africa," in David E. Albright, ed., *Communism in Africa* (Bloomington: Indiana University Press, 1980), 145–67; W. Raymond Duncan, *The Soviet Union and Cuba: Interests and Influence* (New York: Praeger, 1985), chapter 5. See also below, Chapter Five.

[53] Gonzalez, "Cuba, the Soviet Union, and Africa," 153.

3. the Soviet Union's actions were taken in accordance with U.N. resolutions.[54]

On the eve of independence, when South Africa's intervention was threatening Luanda and the MPLA's control was not yet so secure that recognition of its legitimacy as the legal government was at all certain, *Pravda* denounced the involvement of foreign forces (by which it meant South African troops and covert U.S. arms shipments to UNITA and the FNLA), declaring that "the armed intervention in Angola is a gross violation of international law and defies the U.N. declaration on the granting of independence to colonial countries and peoples."[55] Had Pretoria refrained from interfering in the civil war, "it is doubtful that the USSR would have been quite so successful, at least diplomatically."[56]

Angola was a landmark intervention in two respects: first, it witnessed a Soviet intervention to determine the outcome of a civil war and ensure the triumph of a Marxist, pro-Soviet regime; second, success depended on the availability of surrogate forces for use in combat: in order not to alienate the Africans or, more importantly, provoke a sharp U.S. response, Moscow did not use its own combat forces, but rather relied on a willing accomplice to handle the bulk of the combat operations on land. Over the years, however, Soviet advisers have themselves helped the MPLA conduct operations against UNITA and overseen the use of aircraft, tanks and counter-insurgency campaigns.[57]

Ethiopia 1977

Moscow had courted a receptive Somalia in the late 1960s and early 1970s, building up its armed forces and, in turn, obtaining military and communications privileges at Berbera and Mogadishu. Shortly after the two countries signed a friendship treaty in July 1974, America's loss of interest in Ethiopia, coupled with the revolutionary transformation that Ethiopia experienced after the overthrow of Emperor Haile Selassie in September 1974, whetted the Kremlin's interest in expanding its presence in the region. Throughout 1975–1976 it proceeded tentatively to develop ties with the Derg (Armed Forces Coor-

---

[54] Porter, *The USSR in Third World Conflicts*, 154–55.

[55] *Pravda*, November 8, 1975.

[56] Porter, *The USSR in Third World Conflicts*, 155.

[57] Jonas Savimbi, "The War against Soviet Colonialism," *Policy Review*, no. 35 (Winter 1986), 23.

dinating Committee), headed by Major Mengistu Haile Mariam, all the time being careful not to jeopardize Soviet bases in Somalia.

President Mohammed Siad Barre's irredentist ambitions, however, frustrated the USSR's broad regional design. Long covetous of the Somali-populated Ogaden region of Ethiopia, aroused by the weakened internal condition of its larger, more populous neighbor, and heavily armed by the Soviet Union, Somalia began to infiltrate the Ogaden. A visit by Fidel Castro in March 1977 failed to persuade Siad Barre of the benefits in some kind of federation of Somalia, Ethiopia, Djibouti, and the PDRY. As Somali pressure along the border grew, Mengistu, unable to obtain weapons from the United States and feeling increasingly isolated, flew in early May to Moscow, where he signed a major arms agreement. The Somalis launched an all-out offensive in July and came close to a decisive victory. However, Siad Barre, who went to Moscow in late August, could not persuade the Russians to stay on the sidelines.

Even with their substantial assets in Somalia, Soviet leaders could not resist the prospect of alignment with the revolutionary regime in Addis Ababa—or else they thought down to the last minute that they could somehow retain footholds in both countries. Soviet arms flowed into Ethiopia, in response to Mengistu's parlous situation on the battlefield. The massive airlift that began in November (a senior Soviet general arrived in Addis Ababa at this time) and continued through January 1978, after which most arms and supplies came by sea, brought approximately 1,500 Soviet advisers and combat personnel, 15,000 Cuban troops, and $1–2 billion worth of weaponry—the largest amount ever shipped in such a brief period to a Third World country.[58]

The intervention achieved its aims: the withdrawal of the Somalis from the Ogaden, the strengthening of the Mengistu regime, and the establishment of close relations with Ethiopia, epitomized by the signing of a friendship treaty on November 20, 1978. In terms of the criteria suggested earlier for evaluating Soviet interventions, the Soviet-Cuban action must be adjudged a low-risk enterprise, because the

[58] For information on the Soviet-Cuban intervention in the Ogaden conflict see Paul B. Henze, "Getting a Grip on the Horn," in Walter Laqueur, ed., *The Pattern of Soviet Conduct in the Third World* (New York: Praeger, 1983), 150–86; Porter, *The USSR in Third World Conflicts*, chapter 9; Bereket Habte Selassie, *Conflict and Intervention in the Horn of Africa* (New York: Monthly Review Press, 1980), 116–46; Marina Ottaway, *Soviet and American Influence in the Horn of Africa* (New York: Praeger, 1982) chapters 6 and 7; Zbigniew Brzezinski, *Power and Principle* (New York: Farrar, Straus, Giroux, 1983), 178–90.

Soviet Union was upholding internationally recognized borders and not trying to alter the territorial status quo.

Afghanistan, December 1979

Over a generation, Moscow had provided generous economic and military assistance, had trained hundreds of Afghan army officers, and had emerged as the leading foreign influence in Afghanistan. In international affairs, Afghanistan was nonaligned, but deferential to Soviet wishes—for example, in approving of Brezhnev's 1969 proposal for an Asian collective security system and tilting toward the Soviet side on Sino-Soviet issues. With the advent of a communist regime in Kabul on April 27, 1978, Afghanistan's nonaligned status ended. Geographically in the shadow of Russian power since the latter half of the nineteenth century, it now found itself caught politically as well.

The new communist government was headed by Nur Mohammed Taraki, one of the founders of the People's Democratic Party of Afghanistan (PDPA). The party had split in 1968, with Taraki leading a major faction known as the Khalq and Babrak Karmal heading the smaller, more pro-Soviet group known as the Parcham. For a time the two groups cooperated, but three months after the coup Taraki purged the Parchamis and Babrak Karmal went into exile in Eastern Europe. Taraki zealously pressed radical reforms, alienating tribal and religious leaders, as well as the small urban middle class. On December 5, 1978, he concluded a twenty-year treaty of friendship and cooperation with the Soviet Union, greatly expanding its assistance and advisory personnel—and Afghanistan's dependence.

However, Taraki's forced pace of modernization and alienation of the countryside brought open rebellion. Concerned over the deteriorating situation, Moscow tried surreptitiously to effect a reconciliation between Taraki and Babrak Karmal and a return to the former Khalq-Parcham collective leadership. The intrigue apparently called for the removal of Hafizullah Amin, Taraki's deputy prime minister, making him the scapegoat "for all that had gone wrong in the country since the Great Saur Revolution" in April 1978.[59] On September 14, 1979, there was a shoot-out in Kabul between Taraki and Amin, in which the latter, however, came out on top. Three days later, not enthusiastic but unabashed, the Kremlin congratulated Amin on his "election" to the posts of General Secretary of the PDPA, Chairman of the Revolutionary Council, and Prime Minister. And in early October, being for

[59] Anthony Arnold, *Afghanistan's Two-Party Communism: Parcham and Khalq* (Stanford: Hoover Institution Press, 1983), 88–89.

the moment without an alternative, Moscow even swallowed his accusations of Soviet complicity in the bungled September coup.

Amin proved to be even more aggressive in pressing for change and in trying to destroy the growing numbers of Mujahideen ("the Holy Warriors"). Like Taraki, he was confident of Moscow's support and welcomed the heavy flow of Soviet arms and advisers. But Moscow had other plans. On December 27, 1979, three days after Soviet transports—landing and taking off at fifteen minute intervals—had airlifted about 5,000 troops to the Bagram airbase north of Kabul, Soviet forces murdered Amin and his entourage, installed Babrak Karmal as the head of the PDPA and a new Revolutionary Council, and pushed an open program of Sovietization.

Afghanistan is a distinctive case in the list of Soviet interventions in the Third World, because it marks the first time that Soviet troops were used to replace one pro-Soviet faction with another in order to institutionalize ultimate Soviet authority. Contiguity was a crucial catalyst, and it could occasion a similar Soviet response in Iran, if Iran's revolution were to veer to the pro-Soviet left—a most unlikely occurrence as long as the mullahs' rule is well-entrenched—and then be threatened with destabilization and counter-revolution. The particular contiguity of Afghanistan, with its relative isolation from easily accessible sources of outside assistance, limits its use as a model on which to predicate the possibility of other high-risk Soviet moves in the Third World.

Syria, Fall 1982

After the October War, when Sadat looked to Washington for help in regaining Egyptian territory from Israel, Moscow made Syria the centerpiece of its Arab policy. Syria was armed and encouraged in its opposition to U.S. efforts to fashion a settlement of the Arab-Israeli conflict. The repolarization of the Arab world that occurred after Sadat concluded a peace treaty with Israel in March 1979 gave Moscow a new importance and intensified the ongoing rivalry with the United States. In October 1980, at President Assad's importuning, a friendship treaty was concluded, deepening Moscow's involvement and providing the Syrian leader with added insurance in his high stakes' interventionist policy in Lebanon and struggle against Israel.

In June 1982, Israeli Prime Minister Menachem Begin, urged on by his hawkish Defense Minister, Ariel Sharon, invaded Lebanon, ostensibly in retaliation for the PLO's attempted assassination of Israel's ambassador in London, but in reality to destroy the PLO's growing military presence in southern Lebanon and help the anti-Palestinian Christian Phalange Party gain power in Beirut. Besides defeating PLO units, Israeli forces gave the Syrians a severe drubbing, especially in the air over the strategically important Bekaa Valley of eastern Lebanon, downing ninety aircraft in the first few days of fighting.

Since there was no immediate danger to Syria, the Kremlin proceeded quite deliberately. Israel's invasion had set in motion a series of dynamic and unpredictable forces which could embroil Israel and Syria in a war. Moscow responded with a steady arms buildup throughout the summer of 1982, but made its main move in late fall, with the installation of SAM-5 missile batteries. Possessing a slant range of about 150 miles and a straight-up range of 95,000 feet and thus capable of interdicting reconnaissance and battle-management aircraft, the SAM-5s, when combined with low- and medium-altitude SAMs and new electronic jamming equipment, provided Syria with an air defense system that severely limited Israel's ability to operate freely over Lebanon or attack Syrian targets; in the event of a Syrian decision to launch a preemptive attack, such as in October 1973, the thickened air defense system would provide maximum protection from Israeli air power and enhance the likelihood of achieving the initial objectives. This interlocking grid of missiles, manned by approximately 6,000 Soviet troops,[60] greatly strengthened Syria's deterrent capability. It demonstrated Moscow's unwavering commitment to Assad and, crucial to any understanding of why the Soviet Union arms Syria to the teeth, destroyed Washington's chances of forging a peace settlement without Soviet participation.

PURPOSES

From what is known about Soviet interventions, it is possible to adduce the motives underlying the Kremlin's projection of power in the Third World. Most of the cases require multicausal explanations, and in some the experts disagree on which were salient. The most contentious case remains Afghanistan, where the Soviet decision to intervene is seen variously as

1. a defensive reaction to the growing concern about possible instability spilling over into the Soviet Uzbek and Tadjik union republics;
2. fear that the United States and China would exploit a Soviet setback and acquire increased influence in the Muslim world;
3. a desire to install a more compliant satrap;

[60] *New York Times*, March 16, 1983. Two years later, there were reports that more than a third of the Soviet air defense personnel had been withdrawn. Radio Liberty, RL 145/85 (May 3, 1985), 3. Presumably, it is now Assad's finger on the trigger.

4. a shedding of restraint occasioned by the deterioration in relations with the United States;

5. a belief that the United States by its passive acceptance of the April 1978 coup had recognized Afghanistan as being in the Soviet sphere of influence;

6. a necessary step toward turning the country into a stepping-stone for an advance to the Indian Ocean;

7. a manifestation of traditional Russian imperialism, which has always sought to acquire and establish control over additional territory along the empire's periphery; and

8. a refusal by ideologues in the Politburo such as Mikhail Suslov to abandon a "progressive" movement to "reactionaries" or to allow it to fall victim to its own ultra-leftist excesses.

Whatever are thought to be the controlling considerations, all accept Brezhnev's word that "it was no simple decision."[61]

Still, for the most part, there is substantial agreement that when circumstances required it, the Soviet leadership has committed its own combat personnel to protect prime clients or coveted positions. Its objectives have been overwhelmingly political and military. The frequency of response in the 1970s was a function of opportunity (and an increased PPC); in the 1980s, the USSR has not been required to come as often to the aid of endangered clients and there have been fewer strategically attractive situations to occasion new commitments.

As demonstrated in Table 3, the purposes of the interventions can be identified as follows:

- deterrence;
- quest for strategic advantage;
- preservation or protection of a prized regime from defeat;
- strategic denial: decreasing the influence and narrowing the options of the United States;
- installation of a leadership more compliant to Soviet control;
- determination of the outcome of a civil war;
- alignment with an ideologically promising development.

Soviet writers do not use these terms to explain Soviet policy. The only one of the above purposes that has been alluded to, and then only elliptically, is deterrence. Moscow believes that its deterrent capability both constrains adversaries and attracts clients. In 1972 Colonel Ku-

[61] *Pravda*, January 13, 1980.

lish declared that "the very knowledge of a Soviet military presence" could restrain "the imperialists and local reaction"; as an example, he cited the "role that ships of the Soviet Navy are playing in the Mediterranean."[62] Three years later, General of the Army I. E. Shavrov was not quite as direct as Kulish, but he said that Soviet assistance—meaning direct military involvement—could be important in affecting the outcome of a war in the Third World.[63] The importance of military means and the use of force to achieve political goals and determine the outcome of local wars were stressed in an important study published by General Shavrov and a team of thirteen military analysts.[64] It ranges from the Spanish-American War of 1898 to Indonesia's civil war in East Timor in 1975, and focuses on wars between Western powers and Third World countries, and between Third World countries. Unfortunately, there is nothing on the USSR's military role in any of the conflicts. More recently, Soviet academic specialists openly ascribe a deterrent affect to the USSR's interventionary capability. A study on U.S. policy toward developing countries noted that Vietnam showed the limits of direct military intervention by the United States and went on to say,

> In the most common view, it can be said that these opportunities [for intervention] still persist but by no means without limits. Presently, the imperialist circles when planning any interventionary action are obliged to take into account not only factors such as the particulars of the internal situation of the potential target of aggression, the extent of their economic and strategic interests, the military possibilities, and the possible internal repercussions of the actions but also a whole group of different considerations. *And among the most important of these is the possible reaction of the Soviet Union* and other socialist governments to any such adventure.[65]

Also present in most Soviet interventions is the quest for strategic advantages, generally in the form of basing privileges. Through the

[62] Kulish, *Voennaya sila*, 137.

[63] I. Shavrov, "Lokal'nye voiny i ikh mesto v global'noi strategii imperializma, II" [Local Wars and Their Place in the Global Strategy of Imperialism, II], *Voenno-istoricheskii zhurnal*, no. 4 (April 1975), 96.

[64] I. E. Shavrov, ed., *Lokakl'nye voiny: istoriia i sovremennost'* [Local Wars: History and Contemporaneity] (Moscow: Voenizdat, 1981).

[65] V. A. Kremenyuk, V. P. Lukin, and V. S. Rudnev, *S.Sh.A. i razvivayushchiesya strany 70-gody* [The USA and the Developing Countries in the 1970s] (Moscow: Nauka, 1981), 266. For a slightly oblique, but specifically military assessment, see A. I. Sorokina, ed., *Sovetskiye vooruzhennye sily v usloviyakh razvitogo sotsializma* (Moscow: Nauka, 1985), 232–33, 261.

TABLE 3
Soviet Interventions in the Third World

Target	Affinity	Purpose	Scale and nature	Outcome	Risk
Congo (Zaire), Aug.–Sept. 1960	Newly independent country that is object of a U.N. peacekeeping operation	To support government of Patrice Lumumba	Minimal: transport aircraft, trucks, small arms	Expulsion of Soviets and coming to power of pro-Western, anti-Soviet government	Low
Laos, Dec. 1960–Jan. 1961	Country undergoing internal power struggle	To support a neutralist faction against a pro-Western one	Minimal: airlift of supplies to Kong Le, military head of Souvanna Phouma's neutralist government	Establishment of a tripartite government headed by Souvanna Phouma	Low
Cuba, Apr.–Oct. 1962	Radical, anti-American regime	After the Bay of Pigs affair (Apr. 1961), to deter a U.S. invasion; to overcome strategic inferiority through the installation of IRBMS	Major: 20,000 Soviet combat troops, several thousand of which remained after the 1962 missile crisis	Dismantling of Soviet missile sites in return for a U.S. agreement not to invade	High
Egypt, summer–fall 1967	Principal client in Arab world	Deterrence	Minimal: stationing of naval ships in Alexandria and Port Said	No further Israeli attacks on the two ports	Low

Case	Nature of regime	Soviet objective	Soviet involvement	Outcome	
					Low
Yemen, Nov. 1967–Feb. 1968	Revolutionary republic aligned to Nasser	To preserve a pro-Soviet radical regime from Saudi-backed royalist forces; strategic denial	Modest: airlift of arms and flying of combat missions to prevent fall of capital	Survival of the republican regime	Low
Egypt, War of Attrition, spring 1970	Principal client in Arab world	To prevent Israeli victory; to restore status quo ante Sept. 1969; to protect Egypt west of the canal	Major: installation of thick air defense system; 20,000 air defense personnel plus a contingent of Soviet combat pilots	Ceasefire in Aug. 1970	Low
Sudan, July 1970–July 1971	Anti-American Arab regime, friendly to USSR	To help the regime wage a counter-insurgency campaign	Minimal: military reconnaisance; helicopter missions against the insurgents	Soviet-Sudanese cooperation ended by abortive communist-led coup	Low
Egypt, October War 1973	Principal client in Arab world, linked by a friendship treaty (1971)	To prevent destruction of surrounded Third Army; to forestall victory of U.S.-backed regional rival	Major: airborne divisions on alert; deployment of naval forces near Egyptian coast	Sadat saved from major military defeat	High
Iraq, fall 1974–spring 1975	Radical Arab regime, linked by friendship treaty (1972)	To deter Iran from aiding Kurdish rebellion against Iraq	Modest: air operations, Soviet-piloted aircraft	Iraq-Iran agreement ends Kurdish ability to sustain rebellion	Low

TABLE 3 (cont.)

Target	Affinity	Purpose	Scale and nature	Outcome	Risk
Angola, fall 1975	Marxist-Leninist party	To help a Marxist-Leninist faction gain power; to repel invasion of South African-backed insurgents	Major: Soviet airlift of arms and Cuban troops; naval deployment to assure flow of supplies	MPLA retains power and consolidates control	Low
Ethiopia, fall 1977–early 1978	Radical revolutionary regime	To protect Mengistu regime against Somali aggression; to enable him to consolidate power and cope with separatist rebellion	Major: Soviet advisers and Cuban troops	Somalis repelled; Mengistu consolidates power	Low
Afghanistan, Dec. 1979	Communist regime, linked by friendship treaty (1978)	To install more compliant leadership; to end civil unrest	Major: over 100,000 Soviet troops invade	Babrak Karmal faction put in power; ongoing war against Mujahideen	High
Syria, fall 1982–winter 1983	After 1973, principal Arab client, linked by friendship treaty (1980)	Deterrence; to frustrate U.S. policy in Lebanon	Major: air defense forces	Assad secure from Israeli atack and enabled to affect events in Lebanon	Low

accretion of local privileges, Moscow seeks to strengthen its diplomatic hand in the quest for a wide range of political and military objectives. This is most often acccomplished in the course of protecting clients, the principal impetus behind most Soviet interventions, as in Cuba, Egypt (on three occasions), Angola, Ethiopia, and Syria. The comple-mentary aspect of the quest for strategic advantage is strategic denial. A number of separate but mutually reinforcing purposes are sub-sumed under this broad category: to undermine the position of the United States; to prevent a U.S.-backed client from benefiting by re-gional instability or conflict; to limit and complicate U.S. policy op-tions; and to forestall any "demonstration effect" that might redound to the U.S. advantage.

There are several instances—the Congo, Laos, Yemen, and An-gola—of interventions whose primary purpose was to affect the course of an ongoing civil war. In Afghanistan we have the only instance, thus far, of a Soviet intervention to replace one leadership by a more com-pliant one. Finally, the ideological purpose, which is proclaimed in such phrases as the Soviet government's "fulfillment of its internation-alist duty" and support of "progressive forces," is the most difficult to ascertain in any given intervention, because we simply do not have access to Soviet decision-makers and are in no position to know what really prompted their behavior.[66] The elusiveness of the ideological factor accounts for the range of interpretations of Soviet behavior and magnifies the tendency to treat Soviet actions as arcane or the outcome of an international conspiratorial mentality or predictably determin-istic, none of which has ever proved helpful in understanding what the Soviets do and why or in speculating meaningfully about the prob-able circumstances of future interventions.

PATTERNS

A great deal has happened between the USSR's feeble intervention in the Congo in 1960 and its deployment of a powerful air defense sys-tem on behalf of Syria in 1982: Moscow has become an integral factor in the politics of the Third World. Its interventions have been varied and extensive enough to permit some generalizations about the oper-ational considerations guiding Soviet policy. The unavoidable excep-tions are far outweighed by the similarities and symmetries, so that a

---

[66] Such considerations may have been important to some Politburo members in the discussions leading up to the interventions in Ethiopia and Afghanistan. For a careful look at the Afghan crisis, see Henry S. Bradsher, *Afghanistan and the Soviet Union*, new and expanded ed. (Durham, N.C.: Duke University Press, 1985), chapter 8.

number of distinguishable policy-relevant patterns emerge to contribute to speculation about future Soviet interventions.

First, Soviet interventions have been responses to existing regional politics and rivalries, and not manufactured targets of exploitation, except in the case of Afghanistan.[67] They are expressions of a differentiated policy that has developed from a keen sense of local realities and a sharp eye for opportunity and strategic advantage.

Second, the level and character of the intervention have been determined by the Third World country—again, except for Afghanistan. Soviet forces have entered by invitation, not imposition, and have then proceeded to use whatever instruments were needed to cope with a given situation. Considerations of cost have never been a serious constraint on Soviet patronage.

Third, the Soviet Union has generally proved a reliable, effective patron-protector. It has demonstrated an impressive capability and determination to render satisfactory assistance—significantly, irrespective of whether the client had been attacked or was the initiator of the conflict (Egypt in 1970 and 1973, by way of example). Moscow has intervened on behalf of clients threatened by external attack, by internal opposition aided from outside, or by pressure from a U.S.-armed regional rival. (Even in the case of Afghanistan, Amin himself not only continued to rely on Soviet aid but also requested additional armed Soviet assistance.) There is no longer any doubt of the USSR's military capability to affect the outcome of any regional conflict. Once committed, Moscow has shown a readiness to stay the course, to persist until it has achieved the original or primary purpose(s) of the intervention—or, at least, has done what it can in the circumstances at the time.

Fourth, the interventions have shown Moscow to be sensitive to regional and global political considerations in that the forces committed have been relevant to the crisis or challenge faced by the client. Moscow has not, except in Cuba in 1962 and Afghanistan since 1980, sought to upset the existing regional configuration of power or effect a sudden alteration in its strategic competition with the United States in a Third World region. Except in Afghanistan, the interventions since 1967 have been mounted with skill, sensitivity for the concerns of local actors and the United States, and a desire to manage rather than inflame the situation; and they have avoided military overkill.

[67] For an African scholar's view that Soviet policy in Africa is best understood by referring to local conditions and not the contriving of the USSR, see Sam C. Nolutshungu, "African Interests and Soviet Power: The Local Context of Soviet Policy," *Soviet Studies* 24, no. 3 (July 1982), 397–417.

Fifth, the Soviets have intervened to preserve and strengthen re- gimes that are anti-American. The most prominent single thread run- ning through the fabric of all the interventions is the anti-American bent of the client's policy or outlook. It is this that prompted Moscow, which has long shown a flair for international public relations, to be- stow the designation of "progressive" on the regimes. Actually, they were a mixed lot. Only the PDPA was Moscow-dominated and com- munist; a few of the others (Lumumba in the Congo, Castro circa 1960 in Cuba,[68] and the MPLA in Angola) were "socialists" in the sense of being imbued with a belief in the philosophical and socio-economic doctrines of Marxism-Leninism. Of the rest, perhaps some weight was given in Soviet decision-making circles to their professed commit- ments to "socialism," but it takes a leap of imagination to call the lead- ers of Laos, Egypt, Yemen, Sudan, Iraq, Ethiopia, and Syria "social- ists" in a way that links them ideologically to Soviet "socialism." More probably, opportunism, anti-Americanism, and a chance for strategic advantages shaped Soviet policy. In each of the cases, the Soviet lead- ership expected the interventions to result in closer ties. If relations later soured, as they did with the Congo, Yemen, and Egypt after the October War, or failed to fulfill initial hopes, the reasons for the di- minished strategic-political gains were unanticipated, rooted in local conditions, and beyond Moscow's control.

Sixth, interventions have generally enhanced Soviet prestige among the members of the nonaligned movement, especially in Africa and the Arab East. Even regimes that are anticommunist have commended Moscow for upholding national sovereignty and internationally rec- ognized territorial boundaries. That its interventions are no longer undifferentiatedly condemned, at least not in Africa, by "regimes who have difficulty in mounting resistance to intrusion by outsiders," or by "parties to internal conflicts [who] solicit outside assistance against their rivals," or by regimes whose survival is threatened and want an external benefactor, is persuasively argued by S. Neil MacFarlane.[69]

Finally, Soviet leaderships have often been willing to undertake in- terventions irrespective of possible adverse effects on the U.S.-Soviet relationship. To Washington's repeated surprise, the prospect of im-

---

[68] Castro's embrace of Marxism-Leninism entailed the creation of his own communist- party apparatus; his power has always been personal not institutional. See Duncan, *The Soviet Union and Cuba*, 25–33; Carlos Franqui, *Family Portrait with Fidel: A Memoir* (New York: Random House, 1984), 149–54; Tad Szulc, *Fidel: A Critical Portrait* (New York: William Morrow, 1986), passim.

[69] S. Neil MacFarlane, "Africa's Decaying Security System and the Rise of Interven- tion," *International Security* 8, no. 4 (Spring 1984), 129–30, 143.

proved relations with the United States has not automatically taken precedence over the quest for strategic and political advantages from key Third World clients on whose behalf Moscow has been prepared to commit Soviet power. This has been feasible militarily even in situations where the United States has enjoyed preponderant power in the region, because the Soviet Union's interventions have been mounted on behalf of internationally recognized governments—thus defining them, under international law, as exercises in support of national sovereignty, and ensuring access to the land-based facilities crucial to the success of Soviet power projection. In such circumstances Moscow has not encouraged resolution of regional conflicts as an alternative to an intervention from which it could expect tangible benefits as a reward for its partisanship.

PROSPECTS

Interventions have become an integral part of Soviet policy in the Third World. A formidable power projection capability makes it possible for Soviet troops to lend assistance wherever they can be assured of access facilities; once on the scene, the USSR is able to hold territory in support of a client. The uncertainty is no longer whether the Soviet Union can intervene, but rather under what circumstances and on whose behalf it is apt to do so.

At present, Moscow has Soviet or Soviet-surrogate forces deployed in Afghanistan, Angola, Cuba, Ethiopia, the PDRY, and Syria. From its point of view, they are valuable clients. Their leaderships share a number of key characteristics, though not all apply in each case: they are anti-American; threatened by or at war with a U.S.-backed regional rival; assertive, ambitious, heavily armed by the USSR, and linked to it by treaties of friendship or, in the case of Cuba, elaborate military "understandings"; and strategically important to the Soviet Union. Based on past experience, there is every reason to assume that Moscow takes seriously its defense arrangements with these often-troublesome, costly, unpredictable regional actors, and that it would expand its combat presence if required for their survival.[70] It has invested enormously in these clients—each of which, in its own way, challenges America's diplomacy, interests, and friends. As long as a central principle of Soviet diplomatic strategy is to prevent the establishment of *Pax Americana* in the Third World, Moscow is unlikely to

---

[70] In a number of other cases—for example, Mozambique and Nicaragua—there are Soviet or Soviet-surrogate personnel present; but Moscow is unlikely to intervene militarily, if that should be necessary, to defend these clients.

be a passive bystander and allow any U.S.-backed regional actor to achieve a victory over a Soviet-supported client. It has staunchly protected and upheld existing leaderships in the past and there is no reason to believe it will equivocate in the future. If change were to occur in their relationships it would most likely reflect some calculation of the client's—as in Sadat's turn to Washington after the October War or Siad Barre's rupture of ties over Moscow's aid to Ethiopia.

Less certain, and a subject of understandable interest, are the circumstances under which the Soviet Union would be prepared to undertake new interventions. Based on Soviet behavior, two very different kinds of situations bear watching: one in which Moscow might be called upon to render combat assistance to a regime with which it already has close relations; and one that might induce a high level of risk-taking because of the intrinsic strategic value of the prospective suitor.

The potential for the first kind already exists in Nicaragua, Libya, and Mozambique (which, though the only one of the three to have a friendship treaty with the USSR, is the least anti-American). All three are threatened by internal opponents, Nicaragua and Mozambique by insurgents supported from outside the country. Mozambique would seem to meet the criteria of ideological affinity—a Marxist-Leninist regime that is pro-Soviet and has a friendship treaty—and have the greatest need. Its economy, devastated in the early 1980s by drought and afflicted by flawed governmental policies, is further destabilized by the guerrilla campaign waged by the Mozambique National Resistance (RENAMO), which receives assistance from South Africa. Yet visits to Moscow yield little, neither economic aid nor meaningful commitments of arms and advisers. Moscow's reluctance to become deeply involved may stem from several considerations: its already heavily stretched resources; unwillingness to commit its own troops so far from assured lines of supply and so close to South Africa, which might invade Mozambique if there is any sign of a Soviet or Soviet-backed Cuban combat deployment (whether Castro is prepared to get involved in Mozambique in a major way is not yet clear); a limited strategic interest or stake; and the meager mileage to be gotten from the regime's attenuated anti-Americanism. Clearly, the risks outweigh the prospects for gain. As a result of Moscow's unresponsiveness, Mozambique has looked to the West for economic and military assistance and tried to reach an accommodation with South Africa (epitomized by the 1984 Nkomati Accord, a nonaggression pact under which Mozambique agreed to shut down ANC operations on its territory in return for South Africa's pledge not to aid RENAMO, but one that has been violated more than upheld); and it has sought better relations with the United States (in September 1985 President Samora Machel visited Washington, as did his successor in October 1987). For the moment, Moscow hopes, by encouraging Mozambique to explore different alternatives, to avoid having to face "a moment of truth" with respect to the defense of the Marxist-Leninist regime of Joaquim A. Chissano, who assumed the presidency when Machel was killed in an airplane crash on October 19, 1986. Moreover, as long as Moscow is absorbed in the costly defense of the MPLA, it makes sense to limit direct involvement elsewhere in Southern Africa.

Like Mozambique, Nicaragua is threatened by anti-Marxist forces supported by an external power, in this instance the United States. Since the Sandinista regime came to power in July 1979, it has attracted Soviet support—some of it open, much of it covert or channeled indirectly through Cuba. The Marxist, anti-American, pro-Soviet, restlessly revolutionary character of the Daniel Ortega leadership is a low-risk boon to Moscow. Though providing assistance, the Soviet leadership would be most unlikely to commit its own combat troops to the preservation of the Sandinista regime. Geographic remoteness from the Soviet Union and proximity to the United States make Nicaragua an improbable candidate for a Soviet interventionary force. Indeed, distance, strategic marginality to Soviet interests, and risk of confrontation with the United States might well serve to make the entire Western Hemisphere—except for Cuba—a realm into which Moscow will not venture with its combat forces in quest of advantage. Support for Cuban-generated activities is a different matter entirely.

A more complex and potentially dangerous situation could arise with respect to the regime of Colonel Muammar Qaddafi. The Soviet-Libyan relationship developed slowly after Qaddafi seized power in September 1969. At the urging of President Sadat, Qaddafi began to buy Soviet weapons in 1972–1973. After the October War, Qaddafi's quarrel with Sadat over Egypt's pro-U.S. turn led him to expand military relations with the Soviet Union. Since 1974, Moscow has sold Libya upwards of $20 billion worth of advanced weaponry, and hundreds of Soviet-bloc advisers, technicians, and security police (mostly drawn from East Germany) help keep Qaddafi's arsenal in order. Though it has not acquired any major military privileges, Moscow benefits from Qaddafi's hostility to U.S. peace initiatives in the Middle East and his fueling of anti-American sentiment and activities, as well as from significant hard-currency earnings. However, it has been careful to keep him at arm's length, refusing to sign a friendship treaty lest he embroil the Soviet Union in unwanted confrontations with the United States.

Gorbachev has continued to funnel new weapons to Qaddafi, seemingly indifferent to the uses to which they are put. He does not seem bothered by the political conundrum of seeking better relations with the United States while selling Qaddafi sophisticated weapons that aggravate strained U.S.–Libyan relations. In April 1986 tensions rose to the point where U.S. planes bombed Libyan military installations in Tripoli and Benghazi in retaliation for Qaddafi's giving the "green light" for terrorism against U.S. servicemen in a West Berlin night club and for firing on U.S. planes in the Gulf of Sidra. Gorbachev went out of his way to show political support, canceling Foreign Minister Eduard Shevardnadze's scheduled May visit to Washington, but he very carefully refrained from any move to back up Qaddafi militarily. Nor is he likely to take risks on his behalf: Qaddafi is too erratic, and Libya too peripheral an actor in the Arab world.

Of all the inviting targets around the Third World, Iran might, if the conditions were promising, be the one apt to attract another major Soviet intervention. However, the prospects seem dimmer at the end of the 1980s than they did at the beginning. At that time, Iran was in turmoil, intensely anti-American and facing a fraticidal struggle for power with the well-organized leftists capable of capturing the revolution.

If the past record of Soviet interventions in the Third World has any predictive value, then the indications are that two preconditions would be essential to induce Soviet leaders to move into Iran. First, a friendly regime would have to emerge in Tehran. All previous Soviet interventions were mounted on behalf of friendly regimes, which took the initiative in inviting greater and greater Soviet commitments on their behalf. As long as Khomeini lives, Moscow seems reconciled to strained relations and sporadic anti-Soviet outbursts. However, faced with increasing Soviet arms sales to Iraq in the protracted Iran-Iraq War, by late 1984 Tehran came to realize that aggravating the tense relationship with Moscow redounded to its enemy's advantage. It encouraged a modest expansion of diplomatic contacts and trade, and in late 1986 the two sides agreed to a resumption of natural-gas deliveries by 1990 (an eventuality that depends on Iran's ability to increase oil production, since natural gas is produced as part of the process of pumping oil); and in August 1987, during a visit by Yuli Vorontsov, the USSR's First Deputy Foreign Minister, prospects for long-term economic cooperation were discussed, including oil and natural-gas exploration in the Caspian Sea and a pipeline across Soviet territory

to the Black Sea.[71] Second, even in the event that the government in
Tehran expanded economic ties, purchased larger quantities of Soviet
and Soviet-bloc weapons, and aligned itself with the Soviet position on
various international issues, it would still have to intensify interactions
at the political and military levels. In the strongly xenophobic atmosphere in Khomeini's Iran this might still occur if there were a serious
and immediate external threat to the very survival of the fundamen-
talist Islamic regime in Tehran. Barring a sudden magnification of the
military threat from Iraq or an American attempt to topple Khomeini
or his successors, Iran's danger comes primarily from within, not from
without. Without a request from a courted client, and with no friendship treaty to provide a legal cover, Moscow is unlikely, judging from
the case studies presented earlier, to intervene.

The absence of the above-mentioned circumstances does not, however, entirely eliminate the possibility of Soviet intervention. Since history plays a significant role in Moscow's thinking about its relations
with neighboring countries, Iran may have a special importance for
Soviet leaders, who remember that for most of the century prior to
World War I northern Iran was a virtual Russian protectorate and
pro-Russian Iranians generally reigned in Tehran. A state of quasi-
anarchy or a weak central authority in Tehran might tempt some form
of intervention under the terms of Articles 5 and 6 of the 1921 Soviet-
Iranian treaty, periodic Iranian abrogations of which Moscow has chosen to ignore. Under the treaty, Soviet forces may unilaterally intervene in Iranian affairs in the interests of self-defense if a third country
threatened to attack the Soviet Union from Iranian territory or if Moscow considered its border threatened. Moscow might exploit the
treaty's provisions to encourage, as it did in 1945–1946, the establishment of separatist regimes in the Kurdish and Azerbaijani provinces
of Iran; or to occupy Tehran and northern Iran—but not southern
Iran and the oilfields—under the pretext of intervening temporarily
to restore "law and order"; or to occupy northern Iran in response to,
or in anticipation of, an American seizure of Khuzistan, the strategically salient naval base at Bandar Abbas on the Strait of Hormuz near
the entrance to the Gulf, or the smaller naval base (and surrounding
territory) at Chah Bahar in Iranian Baluchistan, near the Pakistani
border. In any of these scenarios, the Soviet intervention would be
restricted to northern Iran, that part of the country that had been
under czarist influence in the nineteenth and early twentieth centuries. Although only one step toward an eventual foothold on the Gulf,

[71] FBIS/SOV, August 6, 1987, E1; FBIS/SOV, August 25, 1987, E3.

it would, as a czarist minister of foreign affairs wrote at the turn of the century, seek to make Iran "politically an obedient, i.e., sufficiently powerful, instrument in our [Russian] hands, and, economically, to preserve for ourselves the large Persian market for a free application of Russian labor and capital."[72] Southern Iran would be negotiable, depending on the U.S. response. The Soviet leadership might well reason that, if it did not threaten the oil areas of the Gulf, the United States would not go to war and that a "deal" could be struck.

Under the worst case scenario—a sudden and unprovoked Soviet invasion of Iran—a Soviet-American confrontation becomes a near certainty. Such a contingency, however, is the least likely to occur, if only because, having been bogged down in a costly war in Afghanistan, Moscow would hardly want to tackle a country whose land mass is two-and-a-half times larger and whose population is more than four times as numerous. Moreover, Iran's resistance to Iraq's invasion shows the power of the mullahs to mobilize the country against an invader. The prospect of an intervention against a hostile Iranian population sounds like a Kremlin planner's nightmare.

The wave of Soviet interventions that swept through the Third World in the 1970s seems to have crested, but this does not foreclose the possibility of a new surge in the 1990s. There are two good reasons for this—in addition to the USSR's development of an ever-more-powerful power projection capability: the availability of surrogates prepared to venture where the Soviets prefer not to go, and the vulnerability of most Third World regimes, whose principal aim is survival. Both of these developments enhance the attractiveness of the Soviet Union as a prospective patron-protector; and both account for Moscow's continuing good prospects in the Third World.

[72] Cited by Firuz Kazemzadeh, "Russian Imperialism and Persian Railways," in Hugh McLean, Martin E. Malia, and George Fischer, eds., *Harvard Slavic Studies* 4 (Cambridge, Mass.: Harvard University Press, 1957), 365.

*

CHAPTER FIVE

Surrogates

The USSR's use of surrogates in the Third World represents a new stage in the development of the Kremlin's "forward policy." The surrogates fill military, police, and economic functions and, most significant, serve to keep in power pro-Soviet client leaderships. First introduced in Africa in the 1970s, they have since chalked up notable successes in Angola and Ethiopia and demonstrated remarkable adaptiveness in a variety of sensitive but promising situations.

Surrogates have enabled Moscow to fashion preferred political outcomes and affect the character of political, social, and economic change in the Third World, in ways that undermine long-established Western positions. Their flexibility and reliance on Soviet approval, explicit or tacit, make them an ideal instrument of foreign policy in an arena where tactical inputs and maneuver can improve the overall environment within which the USSR conducts its foreign policy. Looked at from the perspective of more than three decades of Soviet involvement in the Third World, the development of surrogates as military-political strike forces has been an important step in the advancement of Soviet objectives and ambitions. Up till now, the costs have been modest and the risks low.

In foreign policy, the term "surrogate" (literally, one who fills the role of another) indicates a function in the relationship between two governments, in which government A, the surrogate, defers to the preferences of government B and acts on its behalf or in support of its policy in pursuance of shared though not necessarily identical goals and in circumstances that otherwise might require B to assume higher costs and/or higher risks.

Though surrogates have shown themselves to be a useful instrument of Soviet policy, they are by no means the major one; nor, for that matter, even a new one. Their role in the advancement of Soviet objectives in the Third World and in the array of available policy instruments is, for the most part, secondary, supportive, and limited, and not primary or possessed of unlimited potential. However, the Soviet leadership, though cautious, is restlessly drawn to opportunities for improving its strategic position, and has found in surrogates—whose use complements involvement and intervention—a flexible, less costly, and more regionally suitable instrument (besides subversion and covert activities) for defending Third World clients and promoting the "class struggle" against "imperialist" states.

Since our focus is on the circumstances that facilitated the use of surrogates, the manner and extent of their use, and the short-term benefits and costs to the Soviet Union, as well as the probable long-term ones, no extensive examination will be made of the phenomenon from the standpoint of the objects of Moscow's diplomacy—the Third World clients or the surrogates themselves.

PERSPECTIVE ON SOVIET USE OF SURROGATES

The Soviet use of surrogates is not a new phenomenon: it is as old as the Comintern and the establishment of pro-Moscow foreign communist parties and communist front organizations. During the Lenin and Stalin periods especially, these parties and organizations invariably toed the Kremlin's line and zigged and zagged according to signal. The excommunication of Yugoslavia from the Cominform in June 1948 and the emergence of a communist regime on the mainland of China in 1949 changed all that and set in motion the polycentric—some would say acentric—character of the world communist movement that has epitomized the situation under Khrushchev and his successors. There are, of course, still pro-Moscow foreign communist parties and communist front organizations willing to follow Soviet cues for political behavior, but they are not the surrogates we seek to analyze. Today's key surrogates differ in essential ways:

- organizationally, they are not parties, but governments and therefore have international legitimacy;
- they are not non-establishmentarian or isolated splinter groups functioning overtly or covertly in a society, but are the power elite and command the resources of the nation state they rule;
- they are not parties or front organizations assigned the role of mobilizing domestic opinion on behalf of Soviet initiatives within their own countries, but regimes who provide cadres and resources for promotion of Soviet foreign policy goals abroad;
- they do not concentrate on propaganda and psychopolitical activity, but perform extensive military, police, and economic functions as well; and
- as governments, their reasons for complicity with the Soviet Union encompass a quest for diplomatic recognition, trade, per-

sonal fulfillment, ideological legitimation, and recompense to Moscow for its assistance in furthering their national interest.

That surrogates are viewed by the Soviet leadership as extensions of national policy is an assumption that is inferential, because Soviet writings say little on the subject, other than to reiterate generalizations about the USSR's policy of helping national liberation movements and "progressive" regimes and groups.[1] Moscow's ability to exact acceptance of its preferences varies according to the relationship, formal and informal, it has with the surrogate. Preeminent military power is no automatic guarantee of political control. Foreign policy is about political influence and not just military power, which may count for a great deal but is by no means the sum of considerations to be weighed in evaluating complex political relationships: whereas surrogates may connote subordination and dependence, in practice they cover a range of relationships that may not include that of one equal to another but does include much more than that of ruler to satrap. It is not true that a surrogate is a surrogate is a surrogate.

USSR: Types of Surrogate Relationships

At present, Moscow has four kinds of surrogate relationships, varying in degrees of Soviet control and concomitant surrogate compliancy.

First, there is the USSR's relationship with communist members of the Warsaw Pact Treaty Organization (WTO). By virtue of its dominant role and many levers of direct pressure, Moscow can shape to its will on issues of importance the behavior of East Germany (the German Democratic Republic, GDR), Czechoslovakia, or other members of the WTO. This position enables it to fashion cooperation, assign areas of activity, and coordinate bloc efforts on behalf of the USSR's interests as the leader of the "socialist camp." This does not mean, however, that everything an East European member of the Warsaw Pact does in the Third World must first be approved by Moscow. Over the years, the East Europeans have pursued their own economic and political goals when they have not fallen directly into the USSR's line of stra-

[1] A major Soviet study of 143 local wars from 1898 to 1975 examines the behavior of the "imperialist" and the national liberation struggles in the Third World, but makes virtually no mention of the role of the Soviet Union or other "socialist countries" in any of these wars. For example, in the brief discussion of events in the Horn of Africa in 1977–1978, there is only one sentence on the Cuban role; in the lengthy discussion of Angola, there is nothing on the intervention of Soviet and Cuban military forces. General of the Army I. E. Shavrov, ed., *Lokal'nye voiny: istoriia i sovremennost'* [Local Wars: History and Contemporaneity] (Moscow: Voenizdat, 1981), 174, 189–200, respectively.

tegic outreach, so that, for example, Poland, Hungary, Romania, and even East Germany have considerable latitude in undertaking projects in the Third World.[2] Still, it is only here that one will find completely compliant surrogates. The three other types of surrogate relationship are more a function of shared aims and complex dependency than one of unquestioned obedience.

A second kind of surrogate relationship exists between the USSR and friendly communist governments that are not WTO members—namely, the Democratic People's Republic of Korea (DPRK) and Vietnam. Here as above the rulership is centered in the Communist Party. But neither Kim Il-Sung nor the Vietnamese leadership is a puppet of the Kremlin. Each has shown a capacity for independent action, a tenaciousness in pursuit of national objectives, and a toughness that do not make for subservient surrogates.

The Soviet Union's relationship with Cuba must be looked on as a third category because, though "socialist" (i.e., communist), Cuba is ruled by Fidel Castro not the Communist Party; it is Castro who determines foreign policy, not the communists in his entourage that do so, and he has shown himself to be very much his own man. Such leverage as Moscow possesses derives from Cuba's heavy dependence on the Soviet Union for economic assistance and protection against the United States, since its leadership is not institutionally subject to pressures from foreign communist parties.

Finally, there is the relationship that the Soviet Union has fashioned with noncommunist governments such as Libya, Syria, and the People's Democratic Republic of Yemen (PDRY), and with the Palestine Liberation Organization (PLO), a special situation arising out of the USSR's diplomacy in the Arab world. These actors, in addition to being noncommunist and unreceptive to the development of strong communist parties in their realms, have not participated with the Soviet Union in joint policy ventures: there are no analogues to Cuban-Soviet collaboration in Angola and Ethiopia. They pursue their own foreign policy objectives independently of Soviet wishes, hence cannot be called surrogates in the sense of the actors in categories 1, 2, and 3. However, since *at times* their policy benefits the Soviet Union and is in some fashion dependent on Soviet support, they may be said to perform as quasi or functional surrogates.

In all four types of surrogate relationships, the patron (USSR) and the surrogate doubtless engage in bargaining that is extremely diffi-

---

[2] See the essays on Hungary, Poland, and East Germany in Michael Radu, ed., *Eastern Europe and the Third World: East vs. South* (New York: Praeger, 1981).

cult for an outsider to discern. This is not surprising, since Soviet ties with a surrogate (or functional surrogate) involve two very sensitive and secretive aspects of Soviet foreign policy: namely, military activities and relations with internal security forces in Third World countries. From observing past Soviet dealings with Third World regimes—e.g., Ghana, Guinea, Egypt—we know that Moscow can be a trying patron, demanding and oblivious of personal sensitivities. Even more must this be the situation in the triangular relationship among patron, surrogate, and client. The more independent the surrogate, the more intense must be the bargaining over arms, burden-sharing, and benefits.

Moscow's propensity is toward diktat in dealing with subordinates. It has no tradition of sharing authority or building consensus among its communist satraps. To ensure cohesion and consistency in an operation, it prefers to concentrate decisions in its hands. Accordingly, the presumption seems reasonable that the greater the direct involvement of the USSR, the more it monopolizes, or at least dominates, the successive stages of engagement: this perception comes easily to analysts of Soviet policy in Europe. However, the Third World (with the exception of post-1978 Afghanistan), because it lies outside of the direct military control of the Soviet Union, spawns enough exceptions to require a closer look.

Being a surrogate does not mean, as will be demonstrated, that the government serving Soviet interests can be relied upon to do everything Moscow desires. The line beyond which it will not go on behalf of the Soviet Union is as variable as the actors. For example, Castro committed Cuban combat troops to assist Ethiopia in expelling the Somali invaders in the Ogaden, but he balked at counter-insurgency operations against the Eritreans.

One final observation on the operational meaning of the term "surrogate." Even when it has been a patron in the sense of providing the wherewithal for military operations in contested terrain, Moscow has not always been the party initiating or controlling an operation once it has become involved. In enabling the other party to pursue a self-determined policy option, Moscow itself has performed the function of a surrogate—for example, in Vietnam in the mid-1960s and in Yemen in 1962–1967. Thus, Egypt's intervention in Yemen in late 1962 was ordered by Nasser, without consultation with the Soviet Union. Once engaged he realized that Soviet support, logistical and military, was essential, and Moscow for reasons of its own willingly backed his move, subsidizing him for almost five years. The Soviets had nothing substantial to show for their efforts, but they were building for the future and, having committed themselves, decided not to disengage, for reasons that related more to Soviet-Egyptian relations than to Soviet policy toward Yemen. In this situation, to describe Egypt as the USSR's surrogate would be to distort cause and effect and misread the lessons to be learned about Soviet policy in the Arab world.[3] Egypt may have appeared to be the Soviet Union's surrogate, but it was pursuing its own objectives, and deciding when to engage and when to disengage; without Egypt, the Soviet Union could not have become involved. Moscow provided the material and followed the Egyptian lead, seeking in the process to bring about an outcome that would redound to the USSR's advantage, either in the form of military privileges in Egypt, or in that of a strategic foothold in Yemen, or in that of a defeat for the West.

Looking at the origins of the USSR's and Cuba's involvement in Angola in 1975, an intriguing question is, who was using whom as surrogate? It is known that the Cubans had been pursuing their own policy in Southern Africa long before the Soviets became heavily involved. Castro's support for the MPLA antedated Moscow's. He was involved in insurgency activities in Angola before the collapse of the Portuguese Empire and in the period prior to formal independence for Angola on November 11, 1975. And it was he, according to Arkady Shevchenko, the highest ranking Soviet official ever to defect, who originated the idea of sending large-scale military forces to Angola: Castro volunteered the Cuban expeditionary force; Moscow did not pressure him.[4] But it is also clear that Cuba could not have mounted a major military intervention in late 1975 on its own. Without the USSR's logistical and material assistance, and implicit military shield, there would not have been so extensive a Cuban involvement,[5] though the contrary case has been forcefully argued.[6] But this reliance on Soviet military support does not mean that the Cubans are in Angola at Moscow's bidding: they were pursuing long-cherished goals of their own, and in the process meshed efforts with the USSR. What can safely be said without contradiction is that "an organic relationship"

[3] Richard E. Bissell, "Soviet Use of Proxies in the Third World: The Case of Yemen," *Soviet Studies* 30, no. 1 (January 1978), 87–106.

[4] Arkady N. Shevchenko, *Breaking with Moscow* (New York: Knopf, 1985), 272. At the time of his defection, Shevchenko was U.N. Under Secretary-General for Political Affairs.

[5] Bissell, "Soviet Use of Proxies," 88.

[6] William M. LeoGrande, *Cuba's Policy in Africa, 1959–1980* (Berkeley: Institute of International Studies, University of California, 1980), 21–22.

between the Soviet Union and Cuba "made the accomplishment of each government's goals dependent upon the actions of the other."[7]

UsES OF SURROGATES

Soviet surrogates serve a wide range of purposes:

1. they can help keep a beleaguered client or prospective client in power;
2. they can foster receptivity to the USSR's quest for military access;
3. they can affect in decisive fashion the outcome of a civil conflict and assure the emergence of a pro-Soviet Marxist regime to power;
4. they can foster destabilization of pro-Western governments and raise the costs of U.S. responses; and
5. they can assist in the training of cadres committed to toppling pro-Western regimes.

Since the early 1970s, when the Soviet Union began to use surrogates extensively as an arm of policy in the Third World, they have performed one or more of these functions, each of which more than justifies the USSR's expenditures and efforts. For analytical purposes their uses may be evaluated under three broad categories:

1. destabilization or promoting revolution (system change);
2. keeping pro-Soviet leaderships in power (system maintenance);
3. complementing the USSR's efforts to acquire military-strategic strongholds (influence-building).

Destabilization

Destabilization is a strategy for exploiting situations of endemic instability. A logical outgrowth of unconventional diplomacy, which has been an integral part of Soviet foreign policy since the establishment of the Communist International in March 1919 and on which the Soviet government spends enormous sums every year, it has been augmented by the availability of well-positioned, well-trained, ideologically motivated surrogates. Such a strategy is geared for environments characterized by mass unrest, corrupt rulers, depressed living standards, deteriorating social conditions, violence, weak institutions, and dubious political legitimacy. The USSR's increasingly sophisticated

[7] Bissell, "Soviet Use of Proxies," 88.

means of encouraging the involvement of suitable surrogates, especially Cuba and East Germany (as well as functional surrogates, such as Libya and the PLO) suggest that the Soviets have given much thought to this tactic. Moscow appreciates that Africa and Central America are pregnant targets of foreseeable opportunity in which skilled cadres can serve as midwives in revolutionizing existing patterns of politics and administering stunning setbacks to the United States. Indeed, one may speculate that Hanoi's determination in the mid-1960s to resist the United States in Vietnam prompted the Brezhnev-Kosygin leadership to expand Soviet support for terrorism and insurgency, and involvement with noncommunist radicals. According to Brian Crozier, not only are "guerrilla and terrorist leaders from all over the world" trained in camps in countries such as Bulgaria, Czechoslovakia, North Korea, Cuba, Mozambique, East Germany, Libya, and the PDRY, as well as in the Soviet Union, but front organizations such as one in France, "known alternatively as 'Solidarité' and 'Aide et Amitié'" provide

> training in arms, explosives and secret communications to a variety of so-called national liberation movements, mainly African and Latin American but including some Far Eastern and Near Eastern extremists. The front also provides them with false documents, hiding places and other conspiratorial support facilities. It sponsors a number of allegedly charitable sub-fronts, such as the CIMADE refugee hostelry in the Paris suburb of Massy, which in turn receives support from certain religious institutions and from church-goers and other donors to charitable causes.[8]

Such organizations have proliferated, and are found throughout the Western world. Their activities often have a covert as well as overt character. Some, not all, have KGB connections.[9]

Destabilization has been promoted through civil wars, insurgencies, and terrorism. The Soviet Union has had successes and failures in each. The least-frequent form of destabilization is civil war, but it was just such an event that occasioned one of the most notable successes by a Soviet surrogate. In Angola prior to independence and wide-

[8] Brian Crozier, *The Surrogate Forces of the Soviet Union*, no. 92 (London: Institute for the Study of Conflict, February 1978), 5.

[9] For information on Soviet-supported revolutionary parties and front organizations, see Wallace Spaulding, "International Communist Front Organizations," in Richard F. Starr, ed., *Yearbook on International Communist Affairs 1982* (Stanford: Hoover Institution Press, 1982), 528–32. Dr. Spaulding provides an updated list in each new edition of the *Yearbook*.

spread African recognition of the MPLA, Cuba's intervention, assisted and complemented by that of the Soviet Union, assured the MPLA's triumph in the civil war with the FNLA and UNITA.

The greater frequency of insurgencies would appear to offer promise for Soviet surrogates, and since the early 1970s they have been active in at least fifteen of one kind or another. But till now they have not been the determining factor in the outcome of any of them.[10] In Nicaragua, it was only in the final months, when a Sandinista victory was in sight, that the Cubans played an important role:

> By the end of 1978, Cuban advisers had been sent to northern Costa Rica to train and equip FSLN [Frente Sandinista de Liberación Nacional] battalions with arms flown in from Cuba on Soviet An-26 transports—two squadrons of which had recently been supplied to the Castro regime. . . . When the FSLN's final offensive was launched in the summer of 1979, Cuban military advisers from DOE [Cuban Directorate of Special Operations], the elite commando unit that had recently assisted in the March 13, 1979, coup d'état in Grenada, accompanied Sandinista columns and maintained direct radio communications with Havana.[11]

In El Salvador, where the insurgency is replenished by arms and cadres from Nicaragua and Cuba, the involvement of surrogates, if expanded, could prove the critical mass that topples the existing government. On the other hand, a Soviet- and Cuban-backed rebellion generated by the PDRY in the Dhofar province of Oman was defeated in late 1975, with the aid of Iranian troops, British advisers, and timely reforms by Oman's Sultan Qabus; Cuban guerrilla activities in the early 1970s in the Ogaden on behalf of Somalia and in Eritrea against Ethiopia were thwarted; and in Zimbabwe the Cuban role in helping to train Joshua Nkomo's Soviet-armed ZAPU forces in Zambia proved futile, because it was Nkomo's rival, Robert Mugabe, no friend of Moscow's, and his ZANU party that emerged as the leading political force after independence in early 1980.

[10] In Africa: Angola, Guinea-Bissau and Cape Verde, Mozambique, Namibia, South Africa, Ethiopia (Eritrea), Somalia, Zimbabwe, and Zaire; in the Middle East: Oman (Dhofari rebellion), Morocco (POLISARIO), and the PLO; in Latin America: Nicaragua, El Salvador, Guatemala.

[11] Timothy Ashby, *The Bear in the Back Yard* (Lexington, Mass.: Lexington Books, 1987), 111. According to Eden Pastora, a top Sandinista commander who broke with the regime in 1982, Castro helped unify the FSLN factions and, as prospects for success brightened in 1978, "Cuba set up an operational center for distribution of weapons to the Sandinistas." Richard Shultz, "Soviet Use of Surrogates to Project Power into the Third World," *Parameters* 16, no. 3 (Autumn 1986), 37.

Soviet surrogates remain active in other insurgencies, but their role to date has been limited: in Namibia and South Africa, insurgency operations are generated by indigenous forces or by assistance from sources other than the Soviet Union and its surrogates. Even SWAPO, which in its struggle for Namibia's independence depends heavily on Soviet arms, could, if necessary, obtain enough assistance from African sources to do without any Soviet-supplied weapons and funds. Meanwhile, as South Africa continues to resist a political solution in Namibia, the Soviet bloc shows that it is willing "to provide the means of sustaining sabotage and subversion."[12]

The last mode of destabilization—terrorism—is the most difficult type of low-intensity conflict to counter. According to Ray Cline, a former intelligence analyst,

> in the past decade, the USSR and, in supporting roles, Cuba, East Germany, Czechoslovakia, North Korea, Libya, South Yemen, and Syria, have developed terrorism as an international troublemaking system. . . . The surge began in 1969, after the USSR's military occupation of Czechoslovakia, when the Soviet Politburo directed the KGB to accept the Palestine Liberation Organization as a major political instrument in the Mideast and to subsidize its terrorist policies by freely giving money, training, arms and coordinated communication. . . .
>
> The main training centers, located in Baku, Odessa, and Tashkent, enroll trainees from the Arab states, the Mideast, West Europe, Latin America, Southeast Asia, and Australasia—in fact from all parts of the Third World. The military academy at Simperopol provides special courses for Palestinians numbering 75–100 trainees per course. In recent years the KGB, directly or indirectly, has financed the trained terrorists in less permanent centers outside the Soviet Union—in Cuba, Chile, East Germany, Czechoslovakia, Libya, South Yemen, and North Korea—for specific activities.[13]

---

[12] William Gutteridge, *South Africa: Strategy for Survival?* no. 131 (London: Institute for the Study of Conflict, June 1981), 14.

[13] Ray S. Cline, "Terrorism: Seedbed for Soviet Influence," *Midstream* 26, no. 5 (May 1980), 5. Antonia Savasta, a Red Brigades terrorist captured in January 1982 when General James Dozier was rescued in Padua, related that the Red Brigades had received two shipments of weapons from the PLO. *The Times* (London), May 7, 1982. Documents captured by Israel in Lebanon purportedly buttress the Israeli contention that the PLO maintained close connections with terrorist groups and Soviet-bloc countries. *New York Times*, July 11, 1982. See also U.S. Department of State, "Central American Review," Current Policy no. 261, March 5, 1982; Claire Sterling, *The Terror Network* (New York: Holt,

The PLO, whose activities often serve Soviet aims, has been armed, trained, and supported by the Soviet Union since the late 1960s. Yet Moscow exercises little influence. The USSR's connivance with the PLO's hijackings, murders, and bombings is a function of its perceived need to align itself with the position of the hardline Arab states it courts and is facilitated by the PLO's concentration on Western targets. Thus, although it officially deplores individual terrorism, Moscow actively abets the use of violence by "national liberation movements" whose struggles are directed against pro-Western governments.

Of far greater potential significance to the Soviet Union than the PLO (or terrorist groups based in Western Europe) are Castro's campaigns of destabilization in the Western Hemisphere through terrorism and subversion, which have gone through three phases.

The first began around 1960 and gradually petered out around 1968 after the death of its most promising advocate, Che Guevara. The practice of establishing guerrilla focal-points ("*focos*") was tried in a number of countries, including Guatemala, Venezuela, Colombia, Peru and Bolivia, but nowhere did it bring much success. . . .

The second phase, which began around 1970 and lasted into the second half of the last decade, focused on the southern tip of Latin America and on Brazil. It concentrated mainly on the activities of urban terrorists, toward whom Havana was from the outset far more hesitant and cautious with its support than it had been toward the rural guerrillas of the *focos*. Nevertheless urban terrorism turned out to be far more dangerous, especially to the survival of democratic governments, than the Guevara-Debray methods had been. . . .

The third phase of Cuban subversion in Latin America began around 1978 and was obviously linked to the declining regional power of the USA under the Carter administration. . . . It is characterized by two new elements: First, in contrast to the two previous phases of infiltration and intervention, the overall political constellation in the target countries is no longer neglected. *Second, and probably more important, Cuba is apparently checking its moves with Moscow in advance and coordinating them with the Soviet bloc far better than before.*

This coordination seems to have been perfected during the various Cu-

Rinehart and Winston, 1981); Uri Ra'anan et al., *Hydra of Carnage: International Linkages of Terrorism* (Lexington, Mass.: Lexington Books, 1986).

ban mercenary actions in Africa and Asia. (Italics in last two paragraphs added)[14]

Cuban backed leftist terrorist groups have operated at various times in Guatemala, El Salvador, Colombia, Venezuela, and Peru.[15] Over the years, Castro's destabilization campaign has drawn substantial Soviet support, both for covert activities and an upgrading of Cuba's conventional military capabilities. This continues, even though in the mid-1980s, burdened by a massive indebtedness to Western creditors and a malperforming economy, Castro adopted a more moderate approach toward "many Latin American countries (though not with the English-speaking Caribbean) . . . Cuba distanced itself somewhat from insurgencies in Colombia and Peru and refrained from further large weapons deliveries to the Salvadoran guerrillas. Relations improved with Colombia, Costa Rica, Peru, and Venezuela. In 1985–86, they were reestablished with Brazil and Uruguay. They remain good with Panama and Mexico."[16]

System Maintenance

The second major category of function that surrogates fill for the Soviet Union is to help protect a pro-Soviet Third World leadership from domestic and foreign threats and make irreversible the revolution and its systemic changes. East Germans and Cubans, in particular, have been welcomed in such diverse settings as Angola, Libya, the PDRY, Guinea, and Nicaragua, because of their reputation as trusted myrmidons and internal security-police managers. For any authoritarian rulership—there are few democratic ones in the Third World— the first commandment of politics is "Thou shalt survive." It is precisely the ability to keep clients in power, irrespective of the cost, that in large measure accounts for the USSR's high credibility as a patron in Africa and the Middle East. Once committed, the Soviet Union and its surrogates stay the course, unless, of course, specifically requested to leave, as in the cases of Egypt in 1972 and Somalia in 1977. Such experiences have shown that, in the absence of the Red Army, Moscow cannot with confidence regard even its most entrenched positions as permanently secure—not in Angola, not in Ethiopia, and not in the PDRY.

[14] Robert F. Lamberg, "The Long Arms of Cuban Subversion," *Swiss Review of World Affairs* 31, no. 12 (March 1982), 8. See also Thomas O. Enders, "Cuban Support for Terrorism and Insurgency in the Western Hemisphere," *Department of State Bulletin* 82 (August 1982), 73–75.

[15] Lamberg, "The Long Arms of Cuban Subversion," 9.

[16] Jorge I. Dominguez, "Cuba in the 1980s," *Foreign Affairs* 65, no. 1 (Fall 1986), 130.

What the Soviet Union can provide Third World leaders eager to consolidate their rule is a prefabricated structure for institutionalizing power. In contrast to Khrushchev, who focused on establishing personal relationships with charismatic leaders, his successors have sought to cement Soviet–Third World relationships through an interlocking web of governmental and party organizations and treaties; and, unlike their peripatetic predecessor, they have rarely traveled to the Third World: Brezhnev went once to Cuba and twice to India; Andropov and Chernenko made no foreign visits during their brief tenures of power. Gorbachev shows signs of being a throwback to Khrushchev: he visited India in November 1986, and has accepted invitations from Mexico and Syria, among others.

The essential components of the Soviet package are a theology of self-legitimation and internal unification, an organizational model for mass control and mobilization, and a security apparatus to nip plots in the bud and eliminate opposition. The surrogates can help adapt each of these components to the particular environment, since their own experience is often more relevant to the client's needs than that of the Soviet Union. The meshing of the parts need not be perfect for the structure to be usable to the client, whose requirements and vision rarely extend beyond immediate time frames. When Somalia unilaterally abrogated the Soviet-Somalian friendship treaty in October 1977 and chose to look elsewhere for support, it was from overweening confidence and miscalculation, not from dissatisfaction with what the builder had already done.

Irreversiblity of the revolution is linked to institutionalization of political power and not to economic transformation, which more often than not has been more form than substance, with nationalizations being "the easiest part of the Revolution" and the spread of Marxist-Leninist ideas and structures very much more difficult to achieve.[17] Surrogates are brought in to help this process in countries that have made a commitment to some kind of Marxist-Leninist orientation— that is, "that have proclaimed Marxist-Leninist forms of government but are not yet officially designated Socialist by Soviet ideologists or in the foreign-trade statistics of CMEA countries, yet maintain close relations with the USSR, and receive substantial military aid from her."[18]

[17] This observation on Benin's experience is pertinent to most pro-Soviet leaderships in Africa, with the exception of Ethiopia. Samuel Decalo, "Ideological Rhetoric and Scientific Socialism in Benin and Congo/Brazzaville," in Carl G. Rosberg and Thomas M. Callaghy, eds., *Socialism in Sub-Saharan Africa: A New Assessment* (Berkeley: Institute of International Studies, University of California, 1979), 245. See also the assessment of Eden Pastora, *New York Times*, July 14, 1982.

[18] Peter Wiles believes persecution of religion is further corroborative evidence that a

Such countries are Angola, Mozambique, the PDRY, Ethiopia, the People's Republic of Congo (Congo-Brazzaville), the People's Republic of Benin, Madagascar, and Nicaragua. Libya, which relies heavily on Soviet surrogates, is so far the notable exception.

Though the USSR and its surrogates do assist in the economic transformation of prized clients, they prefer to concentrate on political institution-building. Not only are they unable to provide the resources needed to meet the economic needs of Third World Marxist-Leninist regimes, but, as consummate pragmatists and ultra-orthodox Leninists, they appreciate "that the degree of planning and state control which can be instituted by a revolutionary government shortly after coming to power in an underdeveloped country is severely limited by the usual objective constraints of underdevelopment."[19] The fact of the matter is that the Soviet leadership "no longer sees Soviet and African interests in terms of introducing the socialist management of the economy and of ousting the West. Current Soviet development theory does not regard backwardness as an asset permitting a speedy transition to socialism. Rather, it stresses the sequential nature of growth as well as the material prerequisites essential for steady and genuine progress."[20] It maintains that the Afro-Asian and Latin American countries (Cuba is an exception) are still part of the capitalist world economy, rebuffs overtures for their admission to CMEA, and encourages continued utilization of foreign capital and expertise, provided that these do not compromise the political monopoly of power. Thus, at a time when multinational corporations still shy away from participation in Marxist-oriented systems, such as Zimbabwe and Mozambique, the USSR counsels these countries to deal with the multinationals, albeit on terms that will not compromise their political independence. Moreover, in adapting policy to capability, it is just possible that the Soviets are coming to recognize that economic assistance does not automatically bring political influence.

Building Influence

The third category of function—and the one surrogates are least able to fill—is to help the USSR to acquire influence and tactical strongpoints. The commitments are too weighty, the stakes too high, and the

---

regime is genuinely Marxist-Leninist. His criterion would, however, raise questions about the depth of the PDRY's commitment. Peter Wiles, ed., *The New Communist Third World* (New York: St. Martin's Press, 1982), 14, 19.

[19] Ibid., 17.

[20] Elizabeth Kridl Valkenier, "Great Power Economic Competition in Africa: Soviet Progress and Problems," *Journal of International Affairs* 34, no. 2 (Fall 1980–Winter 1981), 264.

risks of confrontation with the United States over regional conflicts too great for responsibility to be assigned to subordinates or close associates. Thus the heart of Soviet efforts to acquire strategic assets in the Third World still depends on the USSR's bilateral relationships with important courted countries.

It is Moscow's willingness to intervene militarily on behalf of clients threatened by defeat at the hands of U.S.-backed regional rivals, and not the activities of Soviet surrogates, that accounts for most of the military and strategic benefits that Moscow has acquired during the 1970s and 1980s. Regardless of the many uses to which Moscow puts surrogates in promoting its objectives, any overall assessment of the USSR's imperial policy must recognize that this readiness to project its own military power is crucial to its acquiring influence, both directly in a target country and indirectly in shaping the outcome of the environment within which policy is pursued. Perhaps too much has been made of Cuba's role, admittedly important, in Angola and Ethiopia: even there, it was the military power and shield of the Soviet Union that ultimately decided the outcome. Cuba's involvement demonstrated how the burden could be shared, how a surrogate's own aims could mesh with and be exploited by the USSR, and how the presence of Soviet personnel was thus made easier for the client; but Cuba could not have accomplished what it did on its own, whereas the Soviet Union could.

THE RECORD OF KEY SURROGATES

The number of effective surrogates is fewer than at first blush appears to be the case. In theory, the members of the Warsaw Treaty Organization are the most readily orchestrated. In actuality, only East Germany has played an important role in complementing the USSR's aims, particularly in carrying out functions pertaining to system maintenance—that is, helping to keep pro-Soviet regimes in power. Poland, Hungary, Czechoslovakia, and Bulgaria have, for the most part, been long on gestures and short on performance. Except for a few years in the mid-1970s when they significantly increased their exports of arms to oil-rich customers and helped to train Third World military personnel at their military academies, they have concentrated on trying to assure themselves of raw materials, oil, trade, and markets, proceeding "independently and often at each other's expense."[21] Romania has

---

[21] Janos Radvanyi, "Policy Patterns of Eastern European Socialist Countries Toward the Third World," in Radu, ed., *Eastern Europe and the Third World*, 338–39. See also Mi-

gone its own way. Burdened by heavy indebtedness to the West, internal unrest, low productivity, buyer resistance to shoddy products, and growing foreign trade deficits, the East European countries have little interest in poor Third World countries, much less in providing them with long-term credits and development assistance. To the extent that they are active at all, it is out of economic necessity not political ambition or ideological commitment.

East Germany is the prominent exception. Prior to 1972–1973, when it received widespread diplomatic recognition and admission to the United Nations, its principal aim in the Third World was diplomatic recognition as an independent nation state, to acquire legitimacy; since then, as ties with the Soviet Union have increased and deepened, it has been a willing and active participant in the USSR's strategy of penetrating and establishing tactical areas of influence in the Third World. This " 'socialist division of labor' achieved under Brezhnev and Honecker has served, in effect, to place important reserves of proverbial German technical know-how and organizational efficiency at the disposal of Soviet foreign policy," and the "unconditional" support of East Germany's ruling communist party, the Sozialistische Einheitspartei Deutschlands (SED), for African national liberation movements was affirmed at its 1976 party congress, "in marked contrast to what had transpired at the immediately preceding Eighth SED Party Congress of 1971" at which Africa had hardly figured at all.[22] The East German leadership has prepared well for its surrogate role. Especially impressive have been the "organizational contacts, dating back to the early sixties, between the SED and various national liberation movements, particularly the Angolan MPLA, Frelimo in Mozambique, and the African Independence Party of Guinea-Bissau and the Cape Verde Islands (PAIGC)," and "the training of selected East German cadres as well as individual academic specialists in African affairs."[23] From the early 1960s on, the East Germans have worked assiduously through missions, treaties, cultural and economic activities, technical institutes, and medical programs to consolidate relations with the key targets of their effort: Ethiopia, Mozambique, Angola, Congo-Brazzaville, Guinea-Bissau, Benin, the PDRY, Somalia, Libya, and the PLO.[24]

chael Boll, "The Soviet-Bulgarian Alliance: From Subservience to Partnership," *Parameters* 14, no. 4 (Winter 1984), 47–54.

[22] Melvin Croan, "A New Afrika Korps?" *Washington Quarterly* 3, no. 1 (Winter 1980), 24.

[23] Ibid., 25.

[24] Details can be found in Croan, ibid.; Michael Sodaro, "The GDR and the Third

East Germany has earned a well-deserved reputation in Africa for its assistance in system maintenance. Useful though it has been to black African insurgencies, to terrorist and subversive organizations, and to groups trying to destabilize pro-Western regimes, as in the second invasion of the Shaba province of Zaire in 1978,[25] its skill in helping Marxist leaderships to stay in power is what has drawn Third World clients and plaudits.

The essential components for retaining power are a strong and reliable army and an efficient internal security system. After signing its first military agreement in 1973 with Congo-Brazzaville, East Germany quickly assumed an important role in helping create effective military establishments for prime Soviet clients. Supplies of military hardware are provided, and much assistance is extended in the form of instructors, advisors, and communications specialists. GDR military experts—numbering several thousand, though no accurate figures are available—are active in training armies in Mozambique, Angola, Ethiopia (all of whom signed friendship treaties with East Germany in 1979), Libya, and the PDRY. Prior to Zimbabwe's independence, they trained Zambian troops in the use of Soviet artillery and ground-to-air missiles to protect Nkomo's ZAPU insurgents against Rhodesian airstrikes.[26] The East Germans (unlike the Cubans, who hold public reviews of their troops) maintain a low military profile in Mozambique, with which they are especially close, having provisioned FRELIMO during its struggle against Portugal and having signed a treaty in 1979 that, unlike the GDR-Ethiopian treaty, calls specifically for "cooperation in the military sphere." Working in tandem with Moscow is intrinsic to East Germany's "forward policy" in the Third World. Alone among the members of the Soviet bloc, East Germany has its national army "officially directly subordinated to Warsaw Pact, i.e. Soviet, com-

World: Supplicant and Surrogate," and Jiri Valenta and Shannon Butler, "East German Security Policies in Africa," in Radu, ed., *Eastern Europe and the Third World*; and John M. Starrels, *East Germany: Marxist Mission in Africa* (Washington, D.C.: Heritage Foundation, 1981).

[25] Starrels, *East Germany*, 26; Valenta and Butler, "East German Security Policies," 153–55. According to the West German specialist Dr. Henning von Lowis, there is sufficient circumstantial evidence to support the hypothesis that East Germany was implicated in the second Shaba invasion: General Heinz Hoffmann, the East German Minister of Defense, and Lieutenant-General Helmut Poppe, the East German Deputy Defense Minister, apparently left Angola only a few hours before the invasion started on May 11, 1978; Hoffmann visited the Angolan provinces of Lunda and Moxico, whence the attack began; and Poppe was responsible for the training of the rebels who took part in the attack. Editorial, "East Germany's Role in Africa," *East-West Digest* 14, no. 15 (August 1978), 565.

[26] *Financial Times*, July 12, 1979.

mand. This relic from East Germany's past means that military coordination between the Soviet Union and the GDR is far easier to achieve than between the Soviet Union and the more tetchy national armies of, say, Poland or Hungary. The distinction is more than a formality."[27]

The East Germans were instrumental in establishing security services in Mozambique and Angola after their independence,[28] and in improving Ethiopia's domestic intelligence system. They provide a much-feared presidential bodyguard for the leaders of Mozambique and Ethiopia. In Mozambique they also train "border troops and assist them in carrying out anti-guerrilla operations" against the RENAMO.[29] In the Arab world, East Germans advise Libya's Mukhabarat (intelligence service) and staff Qaddafi's Praetorian Guard; and on a number of occasions they have helped put down attempted coups.[30] They are well-entrenched in the PDRY, where their role in the security system and in training Palestinian commandos "has become almost legendary and is rumored to include the administration of a concentration camp."[31] In Kampuchea, while the Soviets train the politically unreliable army, the East Germans help organize the intelligence service.[32]

How well East Germany has served Soviet purposes is evident from the following two incidents. When Somalia abrogated the Somalia-USSR friendship treaty in October 1977 and gave the Soviets a week to withdraw their military personnel and advisers, it specifically requested the East German security advisers to remain, and, at least as of early 1981, small contingents of them continued to operate in Mogadishu and elsewhere,[33] presumably with Moscow's blessing, leaving open a line for a future return. Six months later, when Werner Lamberz, SED Politburo member and top African specialist, who had

[27] Edwina Moreton, "The East Europeans and the Cubans in the Middle East: Surrogates or Allies?" in Adeed and Karen Dawisha, eds., The Soviet Union in the Middle East: Policies and Perspectives (London: Heinemann for the Royal Institute of International Affairs, 1982), 77.

[28] In Mozambique there are two security organizations: SNASP (National Service for Popular Security) and PIC (a criminal-investigation agency that focuses on uprooting labor unrest). In Angola there was one, DISA (Department of Information and Security of Angola), but it was dissolved by Agostinho Neto before his death in September 1979, presumably because it "had been exposed to a considerable degree of Eastern influence—especially from the GDR." Winrich Kühne, "Black Africa and the Soviet Union," International Affairs Bulletin, 5, no. 1 (1981), 36.

[29] Starrels, East Germany, 31.

[30] John Cooley, Libyan Sandstorm (New York: Holt, Rinehart and Winston, 1982), 282.

[31] Croan, "A New Afrika Korps," 32.

[32] David Watts, The Times (London), April 23, 1985.

[33] Interview with a British diplomat in May 1982.

played a key role in coordinating military aid to Ethiopia during the worst days of the Somalian invasion, was killed in a helicopter explosion on a visit in Libya, Mengistu "interrupted his speech at a mass rally" to announce Lamberz' death, "whereupon the Revolutionary Council declared a period of national mourning."[34]

Cuba is Moscow's most important military surrogate. Though not a WTO member, it has worked hand-in-hand with the Soviet Union since 1975 to promote destabilization, system maintenance of Marxist regimes, and strategic access for Moscow in Africa, the Middle East, and Latin America. Its policies are in the main congruent with Moscow's.

Cuba's transition from maverick to surrogate has been gradual. It is a function of Fidel Castro's restless, egoistic romanticism, of his consuming ambition to spearhead Third World revolutions against the "capitalist imperialism" of his main enemy and threat, the United States, and of his profound dependency on Soviet economic and military assistance.[35] Without the USSR's protection and provisioning, Castro would become the Che Guevara of the 1980s—a revolutionary symbol but political impotent, a Cuban *narodnik* endlessly exhorting unresponsive peasants to revolt, a quixotic adventurer performing in obscure byways. However, with the Soviet Union behind him, Castro can command a leading role on the international stage. (Cuba is too small for Castro, and I believe it may not be too facetious to say that hormones explain behavior as well as doctrine.)

Misperceptions of what motivates Castro keep manifesting them-

[34] Leopold Unger, "E. Germany Reaps African Harvest," *International Herald-Tribune*, March 19, 1979. "A member of the East German Communist Party's politburo, less than 50 years old when he died in a Libya helicopter crash on March 6, 1978, bright, fluent in several languages, cynical, tough and a realist, Lamberz was both an ideologist and one of the principal pillars of the Soviet African policy, as well as one of the spearheads of the East German penetration of the black continent."

[35] According to two American experts on international relations who met with Cuban officials in Havana in April 1982, the Cubans came across as intensely nationalistic and devoted "to Marxist-Leninist revolutionary principles, especially to 'internationalism' and to 'solidarity' with revolutions elsewhere; they believe that time works in Cuba's favor, and they have a deep animosity toward the U.S." Yet the Americans reported that "the Cubans were eager to put more distance between themselves and the Soviets," and though they seem to believe that the Cubans are free agents they imply exactly the opposite twice in their article: namely, "With regard to Afghanistan, the Cubans say they voted with the USSR on the U.N. resolution because *they had no choice*"; and "It appeared, at least, that Cuba's desire *for some degree of autonomy from the USSR* might be greater than is generally recognized. No doubt the expansionist aims of the Soviet Union and the convictions of the Cubans often coincide or overlap." Seweryn Bialer and Alfred Stepan, "Cuba, the U.S., and the Central American Mess," *New York Review of Books* 29, no. 9 (May 27, 1982), 17–18 (italics added).

selves in proposals to wean him away from his dependence on the Soviet Union—as if Castro really wants to unhitch Cuba from the Soviet
supply train. In the main, these proposals are historically flawed and
politically ingenuous. For example, they argue that it was U.S. pressure that "forced" Castro to embrace Marxism-Leninism and a close
relationship with the Soviet Union, ignoring the 1962 Khrushchev-
Kennedy understanding that effectively ended the likelihood of a U.S.
attack on Cuba;[36] they note that Cuba is hurting economically and believe that Castro would welcome improved economic and political ties
in order to ease the burden on the Cuban people, but ignore not only
his own primary responsibility for Cuba's economic plight and his
stubborn unwillingness to make reforms that might turn the economy
around, but also the fact that political melioration of tensions is a pre-
requisite for economic expansion—and not vice versa;[37] and they call
for understanding and toleration of Castro's revolutionary policy, ignoring that what impels Castro's interventionism is not a belief in socialism and a commitment to fight injustice and poverty, but a deep
hatred of the United States: according to José Luis Llovio Menéndez,
who before his defection was chief adviser to the Cuba State Committee for Finance from 1977 to 1980 and chief adviser to the Minister of
Culture from 1980 to 1982, "Fidel hates totally the United States of
America. He hates its institutions. He hates its policies. He hates everybody here. He speaks of the United States of America in the lowest
terms you can imagine."[38] Castro is no captive of the Kremlin; he benefits from the relationship, which is very much an advantageous one
given his oceanic ambitions and the deep current of anti-Americanism
that are inherent in them.[39]

Angola was the high-water mark of Soviet-Cuban collaboration in
Africa. Prior to that there had been some overlap in support of the
MPLA, but each had essentially gone its own way and cultivated its own
ties with anticolonialist movements, and, "when the Portuguese
Armed Forces Movement overthrew the Caetano regime in April
1974, Soviet and Cuban policies in Africa were not only operating un-

[36] For example, Joseph J. Sisco, "Test Castro to Learn if He Would Negotiate," *New York Times*, August 9, 1983.

[37] For example Mark N. Katz, "The Soviet-Cuban Connection," *International Security* 8, no. 1 (Summer 1983), 110–11; Wayne S. Smith, "Dateline Havana: Myopic Diplomacy," *Foreign Policy*, no. 43 (Fall 1982), 157–74.

[38] *New York Times*, November 19, 1984.

[39] See W. Raymond Duncan, *The Soviet Union and Cuba: Interests and Influence* (New York: Praeger, 1985). See also Joseph Whelan and Michael J. Dixon, *The Soviet Union in the Third World: Threat to World Peace?* (Elmsford, N.Y.: Pergamon-Brassey's, 1986), 305–18.

der different assumptions, but in the case of Angola were at odds (though not belligerently so)."[40]

For his part, Castro encouraged insurgencies in Latin America and Africa, sent small numbers of combat troops to Syria (an armored battalion deployed near Damascus following the October War), to the PDRY (advisers in 1973 to train the People's Militia), Somalia, and Guinea-Bissau, and ran camps for revolutionaries in Cuba.[41] At the same time, Moscow nurtured and subsidized him, at first because of his anti-Americanism and valuable real estate for gathering intelligence on U.S. military operations; after 1968, because of his value as a defender of its intervention in Czechoslovakia and general support for the Soviet line in foreign policy among the nonaligned countries; and, from 1975 on, because of the availability of his troops for the protection and promotion of Soviet clients and strategic objectives. The diverse strands of Cuban and Soviet policy in the Third World connected in Angola; it was there that the two fashioned a new pattern of cooperation that was to have far-reaching consequences for them and their relations with the United States.

Castro's military involvement in Angola began in May–June 1975, when Cuban military advisers to the MPLA "were reported to be involved in combat" in Caxito, Lobito, Quibala, Cola, Sá da Bandeira, and the Cabinda enclave.[42] In August, more Cubans were sent, in response to pleas from the MPLA for immediate help in countering South African aid to rival FNLA and UNITA forces.

> At this point, Cuban-Soviet coordination in Angola was still relatively limited. Each country continued to follow its historic policy of aiding the MPLA, and the level of aid provided by each had been growing gradually since early 1975. The policies of both were essentially reactive: each increase in aid came at the request of the MPLA in response to escalations by the MPLA's opponents—domestic and foreign.[43]

Valenta observes that "the Soviet-Cuban intervention assumed substantial proportions only in late September, when Cuban ships, followed by Soviet ships and aircraft, began to deploy hundreds of Cuban soldiers. . . . The Soviet decision to go for broke in Angola was

[40] LeoGrande, *Cuba's Policy in Africa*, 15–16.
[41] See William J. Durch, "The Cuban Military in Africa and the Middle East: From Algeria to Angola," *Studies in Comparative Communism* 11, nos. 1–2 (Spring–Summer 1978), 34–74.
[42] Jiri Valenta, "The Soviet-Cuban Intervention in Angola, 1975," ibid., 11.
[43] LeoGrande, *Cuba's Policy in Africa*, 18.

probably made, however, only after the Soviet leadership had reassessed the situation in Angola some time in late August or early September."[44] The escalation that was undoubtedly emboldened by U.S. passivity and quickly assumed major proportions by January 1976, by which time 12,000 Cuban troops had arrived, ushered in the new era of Soviet-Cuban collaboration and assured the triumph of a Marxist-Leninist regime in Angola.[45]

Very different was the Cuban involvement in Ethiopia. Cuba had no cultural, linguistic, or racial affinities with Ethiopia, no tradition of political support (indeed, it had aided the Eritrean insurgents seeking independence from Ethiopia), no national interest, and no autonomous, distinctive role to play. Nonetheless Castro placed Cuban troops under Soviet military authority, insisting apparently only that they be used in the Ogaden and not in Eritrea, and publicly hailed strongman Mengistu as a real revolutionary, a man "with clear political ideas, of audacious and energetic character, the expression of the most advanced and solid thinking in the midst of the political and social whirlwind created by the unexpected and extraordinary events of the Ethiopian Revolution," ignoring the brutal and repressive aspects of the Ethiopian Revolution.[46]

Unlike Angola, Ethiopia showed Cuba to be a camp-follower of the Soviet Union. The deposal of the pro-U.S. Emperor Haile Selassie in 1974 and the subsequent internal upheaval that convulsed Ethiopian society had attracted Soviet attention. By December 1976, the ruling Derg's announcement that "a new system of Marxist-Leninist leadership" was in operation coincided with the signing of a secret arms agreement with the Soviet Union. On February 3, 1977, Mengistu's emergence as the victor from a palace showdown brought immediate Soviet and Cuban recognition and reaffirmations of support. Castro and the Kremlin sought to consolidate their relationship with Ethiopia without jeopardizing long-nurtured and (for Moscow) strategically valuable ties with Somalia. In March–April 1977, both Castro and Soviet President Nikolai V. Podgorny visited the principals and tried unsuccessfully to interest them in a confederation, which would also include Djibouti and the PDRY, and which would have established

[44] Valenta, "The Soviet-Cuban Intervention in Angola," 13.

[45] For discussions of Cuba's involvement in Angola, see Durch, "The Cuban Military in Africa and the Middle East"; Valenta, "The Soviet-Cuban Intervention in Angola"; John A. Marcum, *The Angolan Revolution*, vol. 2 (Cambridge, Mass.: MIT Press, 1978).

[46] Quoted in Marina Ottaway, *Soviet and American Influence in the Horn of Africa* (New York: Praeger, 1982), 140.

Soviet strategic domination in the Horn of Africa.[47] However, events now overtook them. Somalia, made overconfident by Ethiopia's seeming internal disintegration, decided to seize the Somali-populated Ogaden province, using the war machine that Moscow had built. Through the façade of the Western Somali Liberation Front, it infiltrated the Ogaden in May 1977 and openly invaded in July. Mengistu turned to Moscow for assistance and was not disappointed, because, as a Soviet embassy official reportedly observed to a Somali counterpart over vodka in Mogadishu, "If socialism wins in Ethiopia we will have 30 million friends there plus the ports of Assab and Massawa. You Somalis are only 3 million."[48]

Cuban troops and technicians played an important part in the massive Soviet military intervention in late 1977 and early 1978: 2,000–3,000 in January 1978; 17,000 by May; and a peak of about 24,000 in 1979, of whom 11,000 (estimates differ widely) were still in the country in 1987, nine years after the Somali drive was blunted and thrown back.[49] As Ethiopia's counter-offensive, aided by Soviet and Cuban armor, airstrikes and battlefield direction, defeated the Somalis, Moscow informed Washington that Cuban forces would be substantially reduced, and Addis Ababa declared that its army would not invade Somalia.[50] The threat from Somalia long since having ended, the continued Cuban military presence in Ethiopia is suspect, as is Castro's alleged autonomy of action. Castro is no puppet, but neither is he the free–spirited revolutionary of the 1960s. Until recently, his troops functioned to help maintain Mengistu's self-professed "Marxist-Leninist" regime in power, but there are now signs that the Cubans may also be abetting an Ethiopian effort to destabilize Somalia. An Ethiopian-organized group, the Somali Democratic Salvation Front, backed by Libya, the Soviet Union, and Cuba, launched a series of local offensives in early June 1982, intended to topple President Mohammad Siad Barre and bring in a "friendly," less pro-U.S.-oriented regime in Mogadishu.[51] The probes, however, were limited, as have been subsequent ones. Preoccupied with ongoing insurgencies in Eritrea, Tigre, Bale, and other provinces, and with the lingering socio-political consequences of the 1984–1985 and 1987–1988 droughts in the north,

[47] New York Times, April 7, 1977.

[48] "The Model Socialist State that Prays Five Times a Day," The Economist, May 14, 1977, 65.

[49] Pamela S. Falk, "Cuba in Africa," Foreign Affairs 65, no. 5 (Summer 1987), 1085.

[50] For example, New York Times, March 11 and February 12, 1978.

[51] New York Times, August 1, 1982.

Mengistu has let the situation with Somalia simmer; he also would not want to alienate the OAU at this juncture by invading another country.

Despite serious economic difficulties at home, there has been no flagging in Castro's penchant for promoting revolutionary change and facilitating strategic access for the Soviet Union in the Third World. He has cast his net far and wide: for example, in June 1966 in Congo-Brazzaville, where "the combined efforts of the Cuban palace guard and the [Cuban-trained] Civil Defense Corps crushed a military coup against the Massamba-Dabat government" and kept that pro-Cuban anti-Western dictatorship in power till 1968;[52] in Equatorial Guinea, where Cubans helped maintain the harsh rule of Nguema Biyoto Masie from 1968 to 1979;[53] in Zambia, where Cubans trained Joshua Nkomo's insurgent forces in the mid-1970s;[54] in Angola, where they (and East Germans) retrained in the use of Soviet weapons exiled Katangan troops, who had fought with the MPLA from 1974 on and who tried in 1977 and 1978 to destabilize Zaire;[55] in the PDRY, where Cubans trained Dhofari rebels and flew PDRY MiG-21 aircraft;[56] and, of course in Mozambique, Ethiopia, and extensively in Latin America. Castro's deployments in Africa may have reached their feasible political and military outer limit, especially if new opportunities closer to home should, once again, capture his imagination.

The activities of North Korea, Syria, Libya, and the PDRY call for comment in that, though none are surrogates in the sense that East Germany or Cuba is, each can be said to have functioned, at some time

[52] Michael A. Samuels et al., *Implications of Soviet and Cuban Activities in Africa for U.S. Policy* (Washington, D.C.: Georgetown Center for Strategic and International Studies, 1979), 45.

[53] *New York Times*, September 12, 1979.

[54] *New York Times*, June 7, 1978.

[55] Morris Rothenberg, *The USSR and Africa: New Dimensions of Soviet Global Power* (Coral Gables, Fla.: Advanced International Studies Center, 1980), 52. For a commendable effort to piece together all the bits of evidence, see Michael Radu, "The Foreign Policies of the African Peoples' Republics: Angola, Benin, Congo, and Mozambique 1975–1982" (Ph.D. dissertation, Columbia University, 1982), 170–74. Radu observes, "Not only did the Katangans have almost exclusively Soviet equipment, but for them to be able to use it properly after a decade of being armed with Portuguese-provided Western arms involved thorough training during 1975–1976, a training they could only have received from Soviet bloc personnel—Cubans, East Germans and probably Soviet advisers as well. In turn, such training and the necessary presence of Soviet bloc advisers in the Katangan camps made it extremely unlikely that the latter were not fully aware of Mbumba's plans, movements, and intentions."

[56] J. E. Peterson, *Oman in the Twentieth Century: Political Foundations of an Emerging State* (New York: Barnes & Noble, 1978), 193.

or other, as if it were. The evidence is ambiguous, episodic, and inferential, yet nevertheless provocative.

Communist North Korea (the DPRK) is perhaps the most interesting
of the lot—and the least studied. In some ways its experience is similar
to East Germany's: the quest for recognition to match the international status of its rival other part; the search for markets, hard currency, and assured supplies of raw materials and oil; and the courtship
of the nonaligned Third World countries. However, North Korea has
balanced the tugs of Moscow with those of Beijing, seeking thereby to
maximize its freedom in foreign affairs: thus it condemned the Soviet-
backed Vietnamese intervention in Kampuchea as an act of "domina-
tionism" and refrained from criticizing China's punitive action against
Vietnam in 1979, but upheld Soviet interventions in Southern Africa
and Afghanistan; and in 1976 at the Colombo Conference it became
a full member of the Nonaligned Movement.

Pyongyang has responded to Third World requests for military assistance on a number of occasions, none of which appears to have been
as a consequence of Soviet intercession or pressure. The most significant was Egypt's request in 1973. After Sadat's expulsion of Soviet military personnel in July 1972, Egypt was short on combat pilots. According to the former Egyptian Chief of Staff, General Saad el-Shazly,
during a visit to Egypt of North Korea's Vice-President, in March
1973, he recommended to Sadat that Egypt ask for Korean assistance.

> Korean pilots—all highly experienced, many with more than
> 2,000 hours—arrived in Egypt in June and were in operation by
> July. Israel or her ally soon monitored their communcations, of
> course, and on August 15 announced their presence. To my re-
> gret, our leadership would never confirm it. The Koreans were
> probably the smallest international military reinforcement in his-
> tory: only 20 pilots; eight controllers, five interpreters, three ad-
> ministrative men, a doctor and a cook. But their effect was dispro-
> portionate: they had two or three encounters with the Israelis in
> August and September, and about the same during the [October]
> war.[57]

In August 1978, during a visit to North Korea, Major Jalloud, Qad-
dafi's lieutenant, requested that combat pilots be seconded to Libya.
Early the following year U.S. intelligence reported that more than 100
North Korean pilots were in Libya flying Soviet-built aircraft.[58] In

---

[57] Lieutenant-General Saad El-Shazly, *The Crossing of Suez: The October War* (San Francisco: American Mideast Research, 1980), 83-84.
[58] *New York Times*, February 12, 1979.

1980, Egypt's Vice-President Hosni Mubarak visited Pyongyang and asked the North Koreans to withdraw their pilots from Libya, with which Sadat had troubled relations, and some phasing-out apparently did occur, though precise figures are difficult to find. The North Koreans have also been engaged by the Malagasy Republic to train its air force in the use of Soviet MiGs.[59] In addition, since August 1981, they have been training Zimbabwe's army and selling weapons, including Soviet-styled T-55 tanks and 122 mm rocket-launchers;[60] in July 1982, Prime Minister Dom Mintoff announced that North Korea will provide Malta's armed forces with weapons and military training;[61] and a defecting North Korean ship captain said that the DPRK secretly sells Third World countries arms disguised as farm equipment.[62] North Korea has become a major exporter of arms, with Zimbabwe, Iran, Nicaragua, Benin, and Togo some of the buyers.[63] Given its record of bristly independence, North Korea is probably running its own arms policy in the Third World, though doing so with Moscow's acquiescence, since it manufactures weapons under Soviet license.

The growing presence of North Korean military personnel and weapons in Africa and Latin America (the two vast regions where Moscow has made maximum use of surrogates), the treaty of friendship and cooperation North Korea signed with Cuba (1986), and the military agreements it concluded with Uganda (1980), Ghana (1981), Libya (1982), Ethiopia (1983), Burkina Faso (formerly Upper Volta; 1984), and Zambia (1987), all bear careful monitoring to determine whether they are mainly a manifestation of assertiveness by an economically beset regime seeking to exploit lucrative markets for its military wares or whether they are an evolving stage in the web of cooperative relationships between the Soviet Union and its ideologically motivated allies.[64] What may heighten Moscow's interest in the selective use of North Koreans is the information supplied by Brigadier-General Rafal del Pino Diaz, a high-ranking Cuban officer who de-

---

[59] *The Guardian*, November 16, 1978.

[60] *Straits Times*, February 18, 1982.

[61] *The Times* (London), July 6, 1982.

[62] *Straits Times*, February 18, 1982.

[63] *Washington Times*, February 19, 1985; also *New York Times*, November 27, 1983. By 1987, "though estimates vary," North Korean arms sales to Iran, for example, "have been conservatively valued at more than $1 billion." *Insight*, July 20, 1987, 30.

[64] P. Chaigneau and R. Sola, "North Korea as an African Power: A Threat to French Interests," *ISSUP Strategic Review* (Pretoria), December 1986, 5–8, and "La France face à la subversion nord-coréenne en Afrique," *Defense nationale* 43 (January 1987), 111–34. The North Koreans have at various times undertaken to ensure the personal security of leaderships in Benin, Madagascar, and Mozambique.

fected in June 1987. He speaks of widespread domestic opposition to Cuba's intervention in the Angolan civil war: "only Fidel and Raul Castro [Cuba's First Vice President] have any faith in victory."[65]

The Arab world has a long tradition of complex political maneuvering. Everything hinges on personalities and tactics. Developing surrogates in such an environment, and with such tough candidates as the PDRY, Syria, and Libya, is extremely difficult. If, for reasons of their own, they serve a surrogate's function at some time or other, it is always briefly. Thus, it may well be that the PDRY sent a small contingent to fight in Ethiopia as a gesture of solidarity toward another revolutionary Marxist-Leninist regime, as a show of support for Moscow's attempt to promote unity among the "anti-imperialist" countries of the region, and at the behest of Werner Lamberz;[66] but "these troops were later withdrawn, partly because of opposition to such an involvement within South Yemen itself."[67] Syria served as a conduit for covert Soviet support to Iran against Iraq and shipped "several shiploads of heavy war supplies," because, as one diplomat in Damascus observed, "the Syrians could not and would not have undertaken this kind of resupply without either direct or indirect Soviet approval."[68] Episodic occurrences are, however, the lowest level of functional surrogacy and hardly a reliable instrument of foreign policy.

SOVIET-SURROGATE TENSIONS

What has been remarkable so far about Soviet-surrogate relationships is not the absence of disagreements—there have been some—but the expeditious handling and confining of them so that they do not jeopardize the broader and convergent policy objectives. The relationships have worked. From the open literature, one can glean at least three instances of Soviet-Cuban tugs of purpose—in Angola, in Ethiopia, and in Grenada—and occasional asymmetries between the USSR and countries described here as functional surrogates, but none in the Soviet-GDR relationship.

In Angola, on May 27, 1977, Havana and Moscow found themselves on opposing sides in a struggle for power within the MPLA between party leader Agostinho Neto and Nito Alves, respectively. The root cause lay in the widespread resentment of black leaders over the par-

---

[65] David S. Hilzenrath, *Washington Post*, July 1, 1987.

[66] *Washington Post*, January 25, 1978.

[67] Fred Halliday and Maxine Molyneux, *The Ethiopian Revolution* (London: Verso, 1981), 235.

[68] *New York Times*, May 25, 1982.

ty's domination by the mestiços (mulattos and whites numbering about 100,000 out of a population of 6 million), led by Neto, who espoused multiracialism but effectively kept power in their own hands. Neto's militant and radical rivals, Nito Alves, José van Dunem, and others, had been dismissed a week earlier for accusing the leadership of catering to petit-bourgeois tendencies, departing from the revolution, giving preferential treatment to whites and mestiços in the government, failing to follow a strict pro-Soviet line, and engaging in "fractionalism"; they were unsuccessful "because of poor planning, a lack of coordinated popular support, and the intervention of Cuban troops."[69] Not only did they fail to "mobilize the very inhabitants of Luanda's sprawling slums whose interests they claimed to represent," but, according to Gerald Bender, "they also seriously miscalculated that the Cubans would refuse to intervene on Neto's side. It is not clear whether Alves and van Dunem assumed that the Soviets would aid them openly, but Alves clearly believed that he had the Soviets' blessing for the coup."[70] But Castro, though a long-time supporter and advocate of multiracialism, sided with Neto, who would most likely not have survived without the active assistance of Cuban troops and who immediately after victory implicated the Russians.[71]

Moscow reacted cautiously, withholding judgment for more than a week, and then, the outcome having become clear, praised the Neto government for thwarting "reactionary attempts to undermine the patriotic forces from within."[72] Its relationship with Neto had been a checkered one,[73] but prior to his death in September 1979, while in Moscow for medical treatment, it was good, albeit not without

[69] Kevin Brown, "Angolan Socialism," in Rosberg and Callaghy, eds., *Socialism in Sub-Saharan Africa*, 314.

[70] Gerald J. Bender, "Angola, the Cubans, and American Anxieties," *Foreign Policy*, no. 31 (Summer 1978), 25.

[71] Arthur Jay Klinghoffer provides valuable detail: "Two hours after pro-government forces regained control of the Luanda radio station, Neto went on the air to say: 'At a time when we are fighting forces attacking us from abroad, it is very strange that the leftists and ultrarevolutionaries should attack us.' On May 28, the MPLA Politburo released a statement on factionalism which claimed that the Nitists distorted Marxist-Leninist concepts and had a 'feigned dedication to some friendly country.' It was obviously the Soviet Union." *The Angolan War: A Study in Soviet Policy in the Third World* (Boulder, Colo.: Westview, 1980), 129.

[72] Ibid., 130. However, some, including those in UNITA, while agreeing that Alves was "an extreme-leftist nationalist, irritated by the highhandedness of foreign troops and the mulatto elite," dismiss allegations of Soviet complicity in the plot, noting that, "If the Russians supported Alves, he would have succeeded." Flora Lewis, *New York Times*, September 16, 1979.

[73] Marcum, *The Angolan Revolution*, vol. 2, 252–53.

strains.[74] Neto's successor, José Eduardo dos Santos, is a black who has a pro-Soviet orientation, but the MPLA–Worker's Party hierarchy is still dominated by mestiço Netoites, and the underlying tensions that triggered the 1977 affair persist. It is possible that the leadership's need for a sizable Cuban presence is linked to fear not only of South Africa, but also of domestic opponents, both in and out of the party. Moreover, the MPLA may not be able to send the Cubans home, even if it so desires; its autonomy of action is narrowing. Cuba's involvement in helping to run Angola—and since 1984 there has been a major influx of Soviet arms and Cuban troops—has become so extensive that "its aims come to dominate over host-country objectives."[75]

Soviet and Cuban involvement in Ethiopia and the change in alignments in the Horn of Africa wrought a dramatic turnabout in the fortunes of the Eritrean separatists who have been battling with Addis Ababa for more than a generation. From the 1960s to the mid-1970s, the Soviet Union and Cuba covertly provided arms and training to Eritrean secessionist movements, most of whom profess a commitment to Marxism-Leninism.[76] However, as strategic and ideological considerations impelled them to support Mengistu, they tried to fashion a confederation that would end the Eritrean civil war. This was rejected by the Eritreans, who saw victory for their cause within reach, as the centrifugal forces in Ethiopian politics tore the country apart and threatened the Derg with catastropic defeat.[77] But the buoyant expectations of the Eritreans were short-lived; they vanished as Soviet and Cuban weapons and troops poured into Ethiopia at the end of 1977 and reversed the situation on the battlefield.[78]

For a brief period, Cubans were reported fighting the Eritreans, whose cause they had only recently assisted. Moscow made the switch from one client to another with characteristic ruthlessness, quickly accusing the Eritreans of being a "band of separatists" and of fostering "imperialist designs."[79] Havana, however, found itself on the horns of a dilemma: during Mengistu's visit in late April 1978, Castro announced full support for Ethiopia's struggle against "imperialism"

[74] For example, Leonid Fituni, "Five Years on the Path of Socialist Orientation," *Asia and Africa Today*, no. 1 (January–February 1981), 45.

[75] Falk, "Cuba in Africa," 1091–92.

[76] Rothenberg, *The USSR and Africa*; Haggai Erlich, *The Struggle over Eritrea, 1962–1978: War and Revolution in the Horn of Africa* (Stanford: Hoover Institution Press, 1983), chapter 8.

[77] David B. Ottaway, *International Herald-Tribune*, June 9, 1977.

[78] *Washington Post*, May 9, 1978.

[79] *Pravda*, March 11, 1978, 5.

(i.e., the Somali invasion of the Ogaden), but conspicuously refrained from saying anything about continuing with help in ending the Eritrean rebellion.[80] By late June, Castro had decided to avoid involvement, and Eritrean spokesmen confirmed that Cuban (and PDRY) contingents were no longer fighting with the Ethiopians to crush the Eritrean insurgency.[81] Mengistu's successes in driving the Eritreans out of Keren, reopening Addis Ababa's national outlet to the sea via Asmara and Massawa, and reestablishing control over the key centers and lines of communication in the Eritrean province were due to Soviet, not Cuban, assistance.

Cuba still, however, helps Mengistu. Many years have passed since Somalia's unsuccessful invasion of the Ogaden, but the Cubans remain in Ethiopia in force. Castro's protracted military involvement may be the result of his commitment to revolution and to Soviet pressure. First, as a staunch supporter of the Ethiopian Revolution, which he thinks is not yet secure, Castro is receptive to Mengistu's request for continued Cuban expertise to train Ethiopia's new army and militia in the use and maintenance of Soviet weapons, and to provide the technical know-how essential for the consolidation of his power. Second, Mengistu's occasional attacks on Somalia may foreshadow an effort, backed by Moscow and Havana, to topple Siad Barre and bring to power a "friendly" regime with which a settlement could be fashioned. The prospect of undermining the present Western-oriented government in Mogadishu and carrying the revolution there must be attractive to Castro. Finally, he may be acceding to Soviet arguments that a continued Cuban role is essential. In contrast to his Angolan policy, in Ethiopia he follows in the Soviet wake; whatever may have been the aims that prompted his original decision to commit Cuban troops to

[80] *Christian Science Monitor*, April 28, 1978; *Washington Post*, April 28, 1978.

[81] *New York Times*, June 22, 1978. At the same time, Iraq had second thoughts about the Soviet-Cuban role in Eritrea, and, "because of its support for the Eritrean cause, would not allow [Soviet] supply planes bound for Ethiopia to use Iraqi air space." *Washington Post*, June 22, 1978. For Eritreans, the about-face of the Cubans was difficult to explain. According to one Eritrean scholar, "there is ample evidence that Cuban officers trained and led Ethiopian militia in their campaigns to recapture Eritrea, though Cuba has vehemently denied any involvement in Eritrea. What is beyond question, however, is Cuba's past association and championing of Eritrean independence forces. . . . Even as late as 1978, Carlos Rafael Roderiguez, Cuba's Foreign Minister, underlined the justness of the Eritrean struggle for independence as well as Cuba's support for that struggle. So why did the Cubans turn their backs on Eritrea? . . . There are at least two possible explanations; either the Cubans were acting as surrogates of the Soviet Union against their own convictions, or they succumbed to the socialist and anti-imperialist rhetoric of the ruling junta." Tekie Fessehatzion, "The International Dimensions of the Eritrean Question," *Horn of Africa* 6, no. 2 (1983), 22.

combat, Castro now serves policies that are made in Moscow and Addis Ababa, not Havana.

In Grenada, a micro-country of palm trees and beaches in the Caribbean, Moscow and Havana found themselves at variance over approaches to the New Jewel Movement (NJM), led by Maurice Bishop, a London-trained "lawyer who had seized power on the island in a bloodless coup in March 1979."[82] Until he and his movement were overthrown in October 1983 after a leadership struggle set off a chain of events that resulted in a U.S. intervention, Bishop had concluded a series of economic, political, and military agreements with the Soviet Union that placed the island squarely in the Soviet camp. Still Moscow was not satisfied, possibly viewing with suspicion Bishop's overture to the United States for improved relations, and sided with his rival, Bernard Coard, a Brandeis University-educated economist, who took power on October 13 and murdered Bishop on October 19. Moscow's preference may have been for a more orthodox Marxist-Leninist.[83] By contrast, Castro "took a more eclectic approach to revolutionary leadership, choosing out of friendship to support Bishop, whose orientation could be called more Caribbean than Leninist. He condemned Coard's actions and tried to save Bishop's life."[84] When the United States intervened militarily on October 25, imprisoning Coard, the Soviet government did nothing, "limiting itself to low-key denunciations of the action," whereas "Cuba actively sought to prevent the U.S. invasion and ordered its soldiers in Grenada to fight."[85]

THE COSTS AND BENEFITS OF SURROGATE RELATIONSHIPS

Judging by Soviet policy, Moscow is bullish on surrogates as an instrument in its quest for influence and promotion of revolutionary change in the Third World. In assessing their net political utility to Moscow,

[82] Robert Rand, "Grenada's Links with the USSR and Cuba," Radio Free Europe–Radio Liberty, RL/401/83 (October 26, 1983), 2.

[83] For example, see Jiri and Virginia Valenta, "Leninism in Grenada," Problems of Communism 33, no. 4 (July–August 1984), 1–23.

[84] W. Raymond Duncan, "Castro and Gorbachev: Politics of Accommodation," Problems of Communism 35, no. 2 (March–April 1986), 49. For a comprehensive account of Soviet-Cuban involvement in Grenada and the events of 1983 see Jiri Valenta and Herbert J. Ellison, eds., Grenada and Soviet/Cuban Policy: Internal Crisis and U.S./OECS Intervention (Boulder, Colo.: Westview, 1986).

[85] Duncan, at the time of the U.S. invasion, there were 784 Cubans and about 100 military personnel and advisers from the Soviet Union, North Korea, East Germany, and Bulgaria on the island; twenty-four Cubans were killed in action. Washington Times, January 25, 1984.

it is important not to impute to Soviet leaders the same yardsticks of costs and benefits (or failures and successes) that seem reasonable or compelling to us. My own assessment derived from the Soviet record is based on certain assumptions that I believe are crucial to understanding Moscow's attitude toward the Third World. First, there are no isolationists in the Kremlin. The Soviet Union has paid dearly for its status as a superpower. Having driven itself to the center of the world stage, Moscow is not going to retire to the wings soon or gracefully. In its determination is a willingness to bear the cost of an imperial policy. Second, as befits the style of a calculating and toughminded elite, Soviet leaders will continue to respond pragmatically and opportunistically to developments, weighing the risks and rewards, careful to minimize the danger of direct confrontation with the United States, but unlikely to forgo cheaply the advantages which they have obtained or which they perceive in evolving situations. Soviet resources are limited and the Soviet economy has its troubles, but the Kremlin has the wherewithal and the will to make such commitments to ventures in the Third World as are required in support of its imperial policy and outlook.[86] Both these assumptions imply a continuation into the Gorbachev era of the Khrushchev-Brezhnev policy.

It is not always easy to say which elements in a cost-benefits analysis are direct, which, indirect; which, bilateral, regional, or international; which, short- or long-term. Components often overlap and are disparate. In this process, costs are probably easier to assess than benefits.

First, at the bilateral level, Cuba is Moscow's costliest surrogate, requiring about $4–5 billion a year to stay economically afloat.[87] Most of this takes the form of subsidies for the purchase of Cuba's sugar and nickel at above world market prices and the sale of oil at a generous discount. The USSR's subsidies "now amount to over 40 per cent of Cuba's GNP."[88] In addition, Cuba has already accumulated a debt to the Soviet Union of more than $20 billion, and Castro admits the situation is worsening, so Moscow has to gird itself for a continuing burden, adding to its difficulties at home and in Eastern Europe. The military costs of sustaining Cuba's present role are also considerable. Moscow provides all of Cuba's military hardware virtually cost-free and maintains about 6,000 military personnel in the country. According to W. Raymond Duncan, Soviet civilian and military personnel in-

[86] Charles Wolf, Jr., K. C. Yeh, Edmund Brunner, Aaron Gurwitz, and Marilee Lawrence, *The Costs of the Soviet Empire* (Santa Monica, Calif.: Rand Corporation, September 1983), passim.

[87] Duncan, "Castro and Gorbachev," 46.

[88] Moreton, "The East Europeans and the Cubans in the Middle East," 72.

clude "about 7,000 civilian advisers, a 2,800-man military brigade, 2,800 military advisers, plus approximately 3,100 technicians at the Lourdes electronic intelligence installation."[89] The Soviets train the Cuban armed forces and bear the expense (perhaps upwards of $1 billion annually) of provisioning and supplying logistical support for the sizable Cuban combat contingents in Africa.

Given Moscow's desire to foster Cuba's surrogacy, these economic and military subsidies appear to be of indefinite duration and they have undoubtedly been factored into long-term Soviet planning; they could not be significantly reduced without calling into question Castro's reliability and the future of Soviet-Cuban relations. Moscow started to assume this burden long before Cuba became so valuable a surrogate, having subsidized Castro in the 1960s, even when the two did not see eye-to-eye on many issues.

Second, there are costs to the USSR at the regional level, both in Eastern Europe and in Africa. Soviet-bloc economic relationships are strained as a consequence of financing Cuba (as well as Vietnam and Afghanistan, the two other high-price ventures in the USSR's overall policy in the Third World). By providing cheap oil to Cuba, Moscow creates a situation in which it must respond to the requests of energy-poor Eastern Europe for comparable concessions that weigh heavily on its already pinched energy sector; or the East European countries are forced to look increasingly to hard-currency areas for their oil requirements. In either case the end result is an exacerbation of strains on the Soviet economy.[90]

In Africa, Soviet surrogates may engender excessive expectations among those they help to preserve in power. If they prove unable to generate economic development and social change, these compradores of communism could occasion second thoughts in their clients, so that, as one skeptic says, in the end their "only value may be to prove the irrelevance of European Marxism-Leninism to the developing world."[91]

Moscow may discover that too prominent a presence can arouse resentment. Thus, in periodic allusions to the Soviet-Cuban forces in Angola and Ethiopia, African leaders have already counseled Moscow not to overstay its welcome.[92] The more Moscow uses surrogates to

[89] Duncan, "Castro and Gorbachev," 46.

[90] Moreton, "The East Europeans and the Cubans in the Middle East," 80.

[91] Ibid., 81.

[92] For example, at the OAU meeting in Khartoum in July 1978, Lieutenant-General Olusegun Obasanjo of Nigeria said the Russians and "their friends" ran "the risk of being

manipulate a Third World client, the more it will incur nationalist resentment and resistance, with attendant adverse consequences for its overall political position; the more it presses clients for military privileges as a quid pro quo for the assistance rendered by it and its surrogates, the greater will be the suspicions of Third World countries.

A final cost, impossible to measure but in many ways the most significant of all, relates to Soviet relations with the United States. The USSR's military presence in Cuba is a constant irritant, and its use of surrogates in conjunction with projections of power in Africa and the Middle East aggravates Soviet-American tensions and undercuts its simultaneous quest for detente and agreements on nuclear issues and trade. Though repeatedly asserting that there should be no linkage in negotiations on the latter subjects, the Soviet leadership cannot be oblivious of the unanticipated costs it has incurred in relations with the United States since the mid-1970s, when surrogates became an important component of its policy in the Third World.

Let us turn to the benefits. A suitable surrogate is first and foremost an economical instrument. Thus, for example, "Cuban troops can use Soviet equipment with no additional training so that they can be flown in to pick up *matériel* ferried directly from Russia or a forward stockpile; Cubans are technically in advance of manpower skills of many Third World countries; and Cubans can be used to stiffen up local forces, to provide staff and communications personnel and, when necessary, engage in combat. In short, Cubans are essential to provide the nervous system without which many Third World armies are little more than a collection of poorly motivated and ill-disciplined individuals."[93] Moreover, because of cultural and racial affinities with many Third World elites, they are useful go-betweens in facilitating Soviet access. Castro justified the Cuban intervention in Angola by pointing out that Cubans were not just Latin Americans but also Latin Africans: "The blood of Africa flows abundantly in our veins, and from Africa many of our ancestors came as slaves to this land, and many of them fought in the independence struggle."[94]

---

dubbed a new imperial power" if they remained once their military presence was not needed. *New York Times*, July 20, 1978.

[93] Jonathan Alford, "The New Military Instruments," in E. J. Feuchtwanger and Peter Nailor, eds., *The Soviet Union and the Third World* (London: Macmillan 1981), 25.

[94] Castro used this racial connection to drum up enthusiasm for the Angolan regime and organize a mass mobilization of the country, providing "a new danger to which to react and a new boost for Cuban pride, and a new set of myths." Quoted in A. M. Kapcia, "Cuba's African Involvement: A New Perspective," *Survey* 24, no. 2 (Spring 1979), 148, 157.

The availability of surrogates increases Soviet options, as in Angola. It opens a convenient and politically effective channel for funneling assistance to clients. It could become particularly important in any future expansion of Soviet involvement in the Western Hemisphere, where Cubans would take the point, permitting the Soviets to remain in the rear and escalate aid or not, depending on U.S. reactions. This was the situation in Grenada, and it seems to be Moscow's approach in Nicaragua.

Use reinforces dependability. By encouraging East Germany and Cuba to pursue their ambitions, Moscow fosters their dependency, and in the process shapes more reliable policy instruments. True, dependency is an interactive process, and once committed Moscow must either support them, adding to its costs, or risk losing their services. But the upper hand is Moscow's. Without Soviet logistical backing, Castro's major overseas ventures would be impossible. Nor need Moscow worry that he will turn inward. His sense of mission—which suits Soviet strategic purposes—shows no signs of flagging, judging by a speech on January 1, 1978: "We're now helping and we'll go on helping Angola. We're now helping and we'll go on helping Mozambique. . . . And not only are we helping the government of Angola, Mozambique, Ethiopia, and other governments in Africa, but we're also helping the liberation movements in Namibia, Zimbabwe, and South Africa. We're helping them now and we'll go on helping them."[95]

Likewise, in a speech in May 1985, during a visit by U.N. Secretary-General Javier Pérez de Cuéllar, he affirmed, "Not a single Cuban soldier will be withdrawn from Angola until real steps are taken towards the independence of Namibia. Indeed, if more Cuban soldiers have to be sent, we will send more."[96] And in a speech on September 2, 1986, at the eighth summit of the Nonaligned Movement, held in Harare, Zimbabwe, he pledged himself to keep Cuban troops in Angola "for as long as apartheid exists in South Africa."[97]

Surrogates and functional surrogates also benefit Soviet diplomacy by defending Soviet actions among the Third World constituencies that Moscow courts. Thus, as head of the Nonaligned Movement from 1979 to 1982, Castro worked to muffle criticisms of the Soviet occupation of Afghanistan—as did the PLO. In a more general vein, cooptation of the Cubans was a political godsend to the Soviets.

[95] Quoted in Hugh Thomas, "Cuba in Africa," *Survey*, 23, no. 4 (Autumn 1977–Winter 1978), 182.
[96] *The Times* (London), May 31, 1985.
[97] FBIS/The Middle East and Africa, September 3, 1986, L11.

The latter regularly face the danger in the Third World of being outdone in revolutionary zeal by the Chinese. The Cubans help Moscow by bridging the cultural and psychological gap between the bureaucratised Soviet leadership and the leaders of the revolutionary movements in the Third World. Clearly revolutionary, black-Hispanic and reliably pro-Soviet, they frequently take the lead in denouncing the Chinese.[98]

And Castro regularly speaks out in nonaligned forums against attempts to link the Soviet Union with the United States as an "imperialist."

Another benefit is the training of Third World revolutionaries and cadres—the human fuse of political change—in Cuba, East Germany, Bulgaria, and Czechoslovakia. This training is more cost-effective and probably more durable politically than that provided at, for example, Lumumba Friendship University in Moscow. This situation arises from certain paradoxes that hamper Soviet cultural-political diplomacy. Thus, whereas anti-Americanism is de rigueur in the Third World, Americans are usually well-received and things American are coveted; they epitomize material well-being and a modern outlook. By contrast, whereas more Third World countries now pursue pro-Soviet policies than a decade ago, on a personal level the Russians do poorly, constrained by their morbidly suspicious rulers (and omnipresent KGB overseers) from cultivating meaningful social contacts, which are so valuable for getting things done and influencing events in societies run by small elites. The USSR is generally regarded with a mixture of distrust and contempt: Soviet culture is largely ignored, including the study of the Russian language; Soviet civilian wares are ignored if there is a Western alternative. These political realities and the frustrations they occasion increase Moscow's interest in surrogates who are able to strengthen the links it is trying to forge with Third World regimes.

Finally, another unquestionable benefit—perhaps the most important of all to Soviet leaders—is the way the use of their surrogates complicates U.S. diplomacy. Surrogates divert U.S. resources to areas having little intrinsic importance to the Soviet Union, and to this extent limit the ability of the United States to affect developments in the Soviet empire or in areas that are strategically significant in Soviet thinking. They strengthen the Kremlin's global reach and thus contribute to its New Imperial Policy.

Surrogates have come into their own as a policy instrument of the

[98] *Financial Times,* June 29, 1977.

USSR only relatively recently and have not played a critical role in helping it to acquire military facilities or influence.[99] In most of the Third World areas where the Soviet Union has at one time or another obtained valuable military privileges—whether in Egypt, Somalia, Cuba, Vietnam, the PDRY, Syria, or Guinea—it has done so because of the direct military/security assistance that it rendered to the host country. Only in Angola and Ethiopia did surrogates help; and only in the former situation was the surrogate's participation essential to the acquisition of subsequent military dividends. Overall, the military payoffs from surrogates—as distinct from their political value—while useful to the Soviet Union, should not be exaggerated.

In terms of their functions, surrogates have been most valuable, so far, in system maintenance—that is, in trying to consolidate the Marxist-Leninist character of a regime and the political changes it seeks to institutionalize. Moscow benefits from the endemic vulnerability to deposal of most Third World regimes and their readiness to turn to it for assistance in helping them stay in power.

[99] The USSR does have extensive military privileges in Cuba: the use of airfields for refueling Soviet reconnaissance planes; access to port facilities for Soviet naval ships, including the Cienfuegos submarine-tender installation; a satellite-tracking station; and electronic stations for gathering intelligence on U.S. military activities. But they are an outgrowth of Cuba's post-1961 reliance on the Soviet Union for protection against the United States, and were granted to the Soviets by 1970; they are not the result of Soviet-Cuban collaboration in Africa since 1975 or Cuba's growing dependency. These privileges were accorded because of Cuba's vulnerability and to ensure continued Soviet protection.

CHAPTER SIX

Managing Vulnerabilities

Moscow's New Imperial Policy is viable because vulnerabilities have increasingly impinged on the policies and politics of ruling Third World elites and resulted in an environment suited to Soviet aims and resources. As defined here, the condition of vulnerability derives from a leadership's perceived need the satisfaction of which is potentially conducive to the USSR's acquisition of tangible gains, influence, or other advantages. The vulnerability may be psychological—the drive of a well-entrenched leader to augment his available options; or it may be the desperation of a leader whose security and survival are actually at stake. In either case, he is prompted to seek Soviet assistance and, in return for commitments, to make concessions on a far greater scale than was previously characteristic of the relationship, which nevertheless is and remains a voluntary one. Vulnerability is not tantamount to being without bargaining chips.

While in theory the Soviet Union may acquire gains and advantages even though no vulnerability is present or evident, in practice no Third World regime that is not vulnerable makes concessions or grants of privileges. Nor need a regime be objectively weak to be vulnerable: India, for one, was strong enough to cope with its security and domestic problems, but the outlook and ambitions of Prime Minister Indira Gandhi led to the reliance from which the Soviet Union profited. As a rule, the vulnerability of an LDC is a function of its pursuit of goals in foreign and domestic affairs for which it lacks a matching capacity.

PERSPECTIVE ON THIRD WORLD VULNERABILITY TO THE USSR

All relationships between a Third World country and a superpower are inherently unequal. However, what accounts for the complexity and variations in the interactive processes is the asymmetry in aims and not the disparity in capabilities. The reasons that impel A to turn to B for assistance are not the same as lead B to commit resources to the defense of A. It is precisely this asymmetrical character of their aims that permits the weaker party to promote its own goals, even during a period of maximum vulnerability. And the USSR, though unable to impose its preferences on the domestic or foreign policy of a Third World regime, may nonetheless be quite satisfied with the trade-off, because facilitating the regime's general policy orientation will, it believes, result in the accretion of regional and global advantages and an overall improvement in the strategic context within which it seeks to advance its broader objectives.[1] Syria's opposition to U.S. policy and U.S. formulations for an Arab-Israeli settlement is enough to elicit massive Soviet military support, regardless of the risk of another war; and Castro's bedeviling Washington in Central America compensates very adequately for the heavy subsidizing of his troubled economy.

The ability of a Third World regime to exploit its relationship with a superpower is an important feature of the present international system. Great powers are not totally immune from influence by the weak nations, and weak nations are able to obtain the support of stronger states in order to foster their own ends, usually without compromising their independence.[2] There is little evidence to justify the assumption that vulnerability is a way-station to satellitization or that being heavily dependent on a superpower for protection means that a regime is fated to become a puppet.

Third World vulnerability is an outgrowth of the post-World War II period. Carried along by the groundswell of decolonization, heady developmental plans, and the decomposition of the bipolar international system, Third World leaderships looked to their own ambitions. They came to the position that to normalize relations with the Soviet Union would enable them to maintain an equal distance from both superpower blocs and also to increase their political options by exploiting the competitive courtship of the two superpowers. From the perspective of many developing countries, the Soviet decision to embark on a foreign economic aid program in the mid-1950s proved advantageous in that it forced the United States to expand its own efforts.

Initially, Third World regimes did not rely heavily on Soviet aid programs, because the amounts were modest and not crucial to their economies or developmental budgets. By the mid-1960s, Afghanistan, Egypt, and Cuba became exceptions, as their economies grew dependent on Soviet markets, trade, and credits—though only Cuba granted any privileges in return. Assistance did bring the Soviets ready access to the leaderships in Guinea, Mali, and Ghana (until Nkrumah's deposal in 1966). In the main, however, Third World regimes took aid

[1] Alvin Z. Rubinstein, *Red Star on the Nile: The Soviet-Egyptian Influence Relationship since the June War* (Princeton: Princeton University Press, 1977), 340.

[2] See for example, Michael Handel, *Weak States in the International System* (London: Frank Cass, 1981), 129–30.

without the ensuing Soviet presence resulting in any inordinate dependency on their part.

The situation in recent decades has been very different, the vulnerability of Third World leaders being conducive to enhanced relations and Soviet gains. No two instances are exactly alike, but there are sufficient resemblances to permit the identification of five types of situations in which particular Third World vulnerabilities can be linked to improvements in the Soviet position; and some circumstances in which certain vulnerabilities resulted in no Soviet gains.

THE RECORD OF RELATIONSHIPS BETWEEN VULNERABILITY AND SOVIET GAINS

Short of outright Soviet military intervention such as occurred in Afghanistan, five types of situations can be identified in which a Third World vulnerability can result in gains and enhanced relations for the Soviet Union:

1. when leaders' ambitions exceed their capabilities;
2. when leaders fear defeat at the hands of a regional rival;
3. when leaders are—or fear they are—domestically insecure and unable to quell externally supported insurgent groups;
4. when leaders seek help for system maintenance;
5. when leaders seek to demonstrate regional solidarity or respond to issues not directly affecting their own vital interests.

(In the subsequent development of these situations some overlap is inevitable given the frequency of multiple causation.)

In the first situation, Third World leaders become vulnerable when their grasp exceeds their capability. Rather than rein in their foreign policy ambitions, they seek the support of the USSR, making concessions, or holding out the prospect of them, in order to enlist its assistance for the promotion of their national goals. Most of the Third World leaderships that have granted the USSR an assortment of tangible advantages were impelled to do so because their ambitions required the assistance or assurance of protection of a superpower patron: Cuba, Egypt, Afghanistan, Iraq, Somalia, Syria, and Libya are prominent examples. Blunders aggravated the vulnerability, prompting additional concessions, it being easier to persist in a line of policy than to acknowledge error and shed the ambitions that brought on the situation in the first place. Nasser could continue to wage war in Yemen for five years and refuse to reach an agreement with Israel after June 1967 only because he was supported and shielded by the USSR.

Some of Moscow's greatest successes in the Third World—Cuba, Afghanistan, Syria, and Somalia—stemmed from the ample support it provided: for example, assistance enabled Daoud to foster unrest among the Pathan tribes in Pakistan in the 1960s, and Siad Barre to plan for war against Ethiopia in the 1970s. Without Soviet support these two leaders could not have pursued the foreign policy they did—policies that ultimately led to their downfall and defeat, respectively. The Soviet Union gave assistance, because like a banker extending credit to a high-risk client, it expected some return, though when was not certain; and it did not want the client to look elsewhere or adopt a different policy, lest it lose a potential future operation. Though the payoffs for Moscow were not immediately forthcoming, the consequent closer alignment of leaders such as these created an environment congenial to the advancement of Soviet policy in all Third World regions.

Afghanistan, Egypt, Indonesia, and Ghana were the leading early recipients of large-scale Soviet arms transfers; Syria, Iraq, and Cuba followed soon after.[3] Without Soviet arms they could not have undertaken the threatening, tension-producing policies that polarized regional rivalries and necessitated increased reliance on the Soviet Union, closer relations and even the granting of tangible privileges.

In their restless search for leverage to promote their foreign policy goals and for a counterweight to U.S.-supplied regional rivals, Third World leaders originally set out to enmesh the USSR in the advancement of their regional objectives by playing on Moscow's desire to undermine U.S. influence, become aligned with "progressive" forces, and acquire forward positions in the Third World; but in the end they became dependent on the Soviet Union. Though attracted by Moscow's willingness to accept repayment in local currency and goods, price was only part of the Soviet appeal. More important was the prospect of a supplier who was politically motivated to help them match the military power of their rivals; this was especially true in periods when Third World leaders found themselves bogged down in conflicts they would indeed have lost had it not been for Soviet backing. By the 1970s, no Third World leadership could risk being without a major

---

[3] Vietnam and North Korea are not treated in great detail in this study. Both are unmistakably communist countries closely allied to the USSR, but their key role in Soviet strategy inheres primarily in the context of Moscow's China policy; neither can really be classified under the general category of the Third World countries that are being actively courted by the USSR.

supplier, given the importance of high-technology weapons, rapid obsolescence, spare parts, and assured lines of resupply.

Impatient for triumphs and oblivious of consequences, Third World leaders were lured to disaster by the exaggerated sense of power that Soviet arms gave them. With these arms, they embarked on policies whose failure deepened their vulnerability. For example, Nasser's five-year war in Yemen was made possible by the USSR's continued supply of weapons and logistical support; and Nasser and the Syrian leadership stumbled with cavalier obtuseness into the crisis that resulted in their defeat in June 1967, because they believed that Moscow would back their every move, regardless of risk, out of its desire to curry Arab friendship. In Afghanistan, the availability of Soviet arms deluded Daoud for far too long into pushing policies that never had any chance of success and into relying on leftists in the military whose aims he misinterpreted egregiously. In Somalia, Siad Barre was emboldened to go to war by the military machine the Soviets had built for him. In Iraq, Saddam Hussein invaded Iran in September 1980 to seize territory from an internally divided regime. Believing military power would achieve cherished political goals, all of these leaders were trapped by their excessive reliance on the military instrument that Moscow had given them.

For the most part, Third World recipients of Soviet arms did not show any particular gratitude. Prior to the June War, Nasser repeatedly refused requests to allow "Soviet warships to make regular calls at Egyptian ports without having to obtain permission for each visit."[4] He felt no need to compromise Egypt's sovereignty or to manifest so blatant a favoritism toward the Soviet Union—to be the first Arab leader to do so might have weakened his prestige in the xenophobic Arab arena. Like all recipients, once an arms connection had been established, he proceeded as if he had acquired a measure of leverage over the supplier, whose willingness to assume the role signified that it attached considerable political importance to the relationship and would persist even if the benefits were not all it had hoped for originally.[5] Moreover, as Third World officials habitually emphasize, Soviet arms are not gifts; they are paid for, albeit generally on very favorable terms. Egypt's former Foreign Minister, Ismail Fahmy, tells of a meeting with Leonid Brezhnev in Moscow on January 23, 1974, at which

---

[4] George S. Dragnich, "The Soviet Union's Quest for Access to Naval Facilities in Egypt Prior to the June War of 1967," in Michael MccGwire, Ken Booth, and John McDonnell, eds., *Soviet Naval Policy: Objectives and Constraints* (New York: Praeger, 1975), 257.

[5] Rajan Menon, "The Soviet Union, the Arms Trade and the Third World," *Soviet Studies* 34, no. 3 (July 1982), 391.

Brezhnev, in a "three-hour tirade," declared that "the Soviet Union was not so wealthy that it could give large amounts of financial aid without achieving anything" and, "pounding on the table," noted that Moscow had given the Arab countries almost $21 billion worth of aid during the previous eighteen years. To all of this Fahmy replied that "Iraq and Algeria paid in full for everything they received," that the assistance extended to Egypt and Syria did not "even come close" to the amount mentioned by Brezhnev, and that whatever Soviet assistance had been given "was being repaid and would be fully reimbursed in the future."[6] Under Idi Amin in the 1970s, a former high-ranking Ugandan military officer relates, "Uganda's coffee, cotton, and copper" were used to pay for Soviet weapons: "There is no truth in Amin's frequent statements that the Soviet Union provided free military aid to Uganda."[7]

The mere acquisition of large quantities of arms seldom results in the grant of extensive privileges: Somalia was the single case of a major arms recipient that provided the Soviet Union with tangible military advantages (unrestricted access to the port of Berbera, use of airfields for reconnaissance, and missile handling and storage facilities) without any noticeable risktaking or extraordinary effort on the part of Moscow. Algeria may depend on Soviet weapons—MiG-25 aircraft, T-72 tanks, SAMs, artillery, and so on—but it has yet to accord the Soviet Union any special status.[8] India's own impressive industrial capability reduces any likelihood of undue reliance on Soviet arms; Iraq, Libya, and other oil-rich countries can, if need be, find alternative suppliers in the international marketplace.

In instances where a Third World regime granted the USSR military privileges or other advantages, it needed the Soviet Union for more than only the supply of arms: it depended for its survival and security on combat forces of the USSR or Soviet surrogates. And as a result of such help it provided Moscow with extensive benefits. For example, Castro, who had sought Soviet military aid as early as September 1960,[9] gradually supplied facilities for electronic intelligence-gathering air reconnaissance, and naval visits, but only after the Soviet Union had risked war on its behalf during the 1962 missile crisis and

[6] Ismail Fahmy, *Negotiating for Peace in the Middle East: An Arab View* (Baltimore: Johns Hopkins University Press, 1983), 126, 130.

[7] Colonel Gad W. Toko, *Intervention in Uganda: The Power Struggle and Soviet Involvement*, UCIS Occasional Working Paper Series, no. 1 (Pittsburgh: University of Pittsburgh Press, 1979), 75.

[8] *New York Times*, November 2, 1979.

[9] Arkady N. Shevchenko, *Breaking with Moscow* (New York: Knopf, 1985), 106.

continued to demonstrate its commitment to Cuba's defense. And the PDRY permitted the Soviets firm access to its air and port facilities only after Moscow had given valuable logistical support for the PDRY-generated insurgency in Oman's Dhofar province.

The striking common denominator in all these developments was the initiatory role of the Third World leaders and the reactive role of the USSR. Third World elites were at first the manipulators, not the manipulated. Their ambitions drew them to Moscow, which, ju-jitsu style, yielded for a time and then, at the propitious moment when Third World leaders found themselves out of control, reacted to exploit its advantage.

The second most prevalent type of situation in which vulnerability brings the USSR tangible gains is that in which a Third World leadership fears defeat at the hands of a regional rival. In seven major instances Moscow heeded the call of clients and committed combat forces, including those of its allies, to their defense: (1) Cuba after the Bay of Pigs, especially in the spring and summer of 1962; (2) Egypt (and to a lesser extent, Syria) after the June War; (3) Egypt in the spring of 1970; (4) Egypt and Syria during the October War; (5) Angola in the latter half of 1975 and early 1976; (6) Ethiopia in the 1977–1978 period; and (7) Syria after the Israeli invasion of Lebanon in the summer of 1982.[10]

In each of these cases of extreme vulnerability, Moscow's client believed he required more than guns. Without the dispatch of Soviet (and Cuban) combat forces, his regime faced defeat or serious weakening of its domestic credibility. And every time the Soviet Union responded with the necessary military power.

In Cuba, a major part of the contingent of Soviet combat forces was sent before any decision was taken by the Kremlin to implant nuclear-tipped IRBMs and before the sudden surge in July–August 1962 of Soviet personnel and shipments. This suggests that Khrushchev was determined to provide Castro with a strong and politically symbolic shield against another U.S.-instigated attempt to overthrow him well before being granted substantial military privileges. Since then the Soviet Union has maintained a continuous military presence in Cuba, notwithstanding periodic tensions (especially between 1965 and 1969).

As for Castro, absolutism and age are breeding the growing paranoia typical of long-ruling dictators. Although far less threatened today by the United States than in the early 1960s, Castro retains a large

---

[10] Details of these seven Soviet military interventions, as well as one other major and five minor interventions, are provided in Chapter Four.

Soviet contingent: about 2,500 military advisers, a combat brigade, and 6,000–8,000 civilian technicians. He does so to deter the United States, whose hostility toward him he sees as unabated. "The CIA is hunting me everywhere," he told an American journalist.[11] Throughout Reagan's presidency, he braced himself for an invasion; indeed, in the summer of 1984, on the eve of Reagan's reelection, Castro orchestrated a mass mobilization and expansion of territorial troop militias to back up the regular army and ready reservists.[12] His suspicion may extend to the Soviet Union as well, and if so he may believe that the presence of Soviet troops is more effective than any friendship treaty in forestalling the possiblity of a U.S.-Soviet "understanding" at his expense, as in October 1962.

Moscow has used Castro's sense of vulnerability to extract substantial political and military benefits. The military privileges are part of the premium he pays for his regime's insurance policy and the hefty annual dividends that come in the form of economic subsidies and cost-free weapons. Soviet privileges include the largest intelligence-collection facility of its kind in the world, a 28-square-mile facility that expanded by more than 60 percent in size and capability during the 1973–1983 period. In addition to this installation, which is manned by 1,500 Soviet technicians in Lourdes in western Cuba, the USSR has an airfield that it can use freely for its own long-range reconnaissance missions, and from which, in March 1983, two Soviet antisubmarine warfare planes started operating.[13]

Egypt, Ethiopia, and Syria are examples of regimes that turned to the Soviet Union, irrespective of previous indifference, disagreements, or low levels of economic interaction, not only for their political survival but also to manipulate its strength for their own national purposes. In this way they were able to transform a bleak situation into one with prospects for major improvement.

In Egypt, the need for protection by Soviet forces brought Moscow long-coveted privileges. Following the June War the USSR was given extensive port facilities, including control over repair shops and warehouses needed for the storage, repair, and provisioning of the Soviet Mediterranean Fleet, and permission to use a number of airfields to maintain surveillance over the U.S. Sixth Fleet and Israeli positions. Then, in the spring of 1970, deepening vulnerability led Nasser to accede to Soviet conditions for the dispatch of 15,000–20,000 combat

[11] Joseph B. Treaster, *New York Times*, August 5, 1985.

[12] *Washington Post*, July 8, 1985; *New York Times*, October 8, 1984.

[13] President Ronald Reagan's speech on March 23, 1983. *New York Times*, March 24, 1983.

missile and air defense personnel to blunt and force back Israeli deep-penetration raids: he gave the Soviet military exclusive jurisdiction over large sections of six airfields (which they had heretofore merely had the use of) and a free hand to deploy their forces.[14] The Soviet Union's position in Egypt reached its apogee. Its commitment of personnel in a combat role against the Israelis was the first time that it took such a step outside the Soviet bloc.[15]

Regime vulnerability in Ethiopia, as in Angola two years earlier, enabled the Soviet Union to realize important returns. By committing Soviet and Cuban forces, Moscow ensured the triumph of two pro-Soviet, Marxist regimes. Complementing these political gains are some military advantages that, if not impressive, are nonetheless useful for the time being: Soviet aircraft fly reconnaissance missions out of Angola, and Ethiopia's Daklak Islands are available to Soviet naval ships. Though Moscow's military privileges in Ethiopia are not as extensive as those it formerly had in Somalia, the Daklak Islands are adequate to probable operational needs and, being isolated, permit the Soviets to function in greater secrecy.

Realizing that Ethiopia is the key country of the Horn, Moscow looked for ways to strengthen political ties. The Ethiopian leadership, despite its dependency on Soviet and Cuban military assistance, has little personal rapport with the Russians and Cubans and keeps them away from centers of power.[16] Nonetheless, after several years of pressuring Mengistu and trying to penetrate his mass political organization, COPWE (Commission for Organizing the Party of the Working People of Ethiopia), Moscow persuaded him to establish a vanguard Marxist-Leninist party. In September 1984, Mengistu convened a congress of the newly established Workers' Party of Ethiopia (WPE); the following year, he proposed the adoption of a constitution that shows all the hallmarks of having been written in Moscow;[17] and on February 22, 1987, Mengistu announced that the country would henceforth be called the People's Democratic Republic of Ethiopia, with a Marxist

[14] Muhammad Hasanayn Haykal [Mohamed Heikal], then Editor of *Al Ahram* and Nasser's confidant, was the first to provide details. See translation of his weekly article, as cited in *Cairo Press Review*, no. 5599 (September 18, 1970). See also Robert G. Weinland, "Land Support for Naval Forces: Egypt and the Soviet Escadra 1962–1976," *Survival* 20, no. 2 (March–April 1978), 73–79.

[15] Jon D. Glassman, *Arms for the Arabs: The Soviet Union and War in the Middle East* (Baltimore: Johns Hopkins University Press, 1975), 74.

[16] Paul B. Henze, "Communism and Ethiopia," *Problems of Communism* 30, no. 3 (May–June 1981), 66–74.

[17] *Storm: Somali, Tigray and Oromo Resistance Monitor* 5, no. 2 (April 1985).

party as the "guiding force of the state."[18] Moscow's persistence and Mengistu's own inclinations and perceived vulnerability have drawn him to Moscow, even though from what we know his relations "with the Soviet leaders have not always been easy":

> When the spirit moved him, he has not hesitated to show them he is not one to take orders. He sent home two Soviet Ambassadors, one in 1978 and the other in 1981. But each row has been quickly patched up and he has shown Moscow consistent loyalty. The Soviet Union may be niggardly in economic aid, and unable to provide food, but it has been and continues to be lavish in supplying arms. . . .
>
> Mengistu's experience with the Soviet Union and the west during the crisis of the autumn of 1984 and 1985 must have confirmed him in his political preferences. The west pestered him about feeding starving people in the rebel-held areas, complained about lack of Ethiopian government support for emergency relief programmes and criticised the resettlement programme. The Soviet Union and its eastern European and Cuban followers did not importune him on any of these issues; they expressed no humanitarian concerns about people on the rebel side, ran no programmes for the hungry on the government side and did not protest the use of coercion in resettlement.[19]

Syria is the Soviet Union's most important client in the Arab world, more for political reasons than for privileges received. Soon after the October War, when Moscow saved the Syrian army from complete defeat, but possibly even a year earlier in the aftermath of Sadat's termination of the Soviet combat presence in Egypt and the consequent souring of Syrian-Egyptian relations, Syria's President Hafez Assad permitted Soviet ships to use Latakia for rest and recreation, refueling, and some repairs, thereby improving the USSR's ability to maintain a naval presence in the eastern Mediterranean—and, adventitiously, his ability to intrigue in Lebanon. He has not, however, granted privileges to the Soviets comparable to those they had obtained in Egypt, notwithstanding the signing of a friendship treaty in 1980 and the crucial role of their military assistance for the defense of the country against Israel in 1982–1983.

Though no Soviet combat forces were committed to Vietnam, it

---

[18] *New York Times*, February 23, 1987.

[19] David A. Korn, "Ethiopia: Dilemma for the West," *The World Today* 42, no. 1 (January 1986), 7.

merits attention because, like Cuba, it grants Moscow military privileges in exchange for protection. It had signed a friendship treaty with the Soviet Union in November 1978, but not until after China's punitive attack in February 1979 (in retaliation for its invasion of Kampuchea and overthrow of the pro-Beijing Pol Pot regime) did Vietnam turn over to the Soviets the DaNang air base and the Cam Ranh Bay naval base (former centers of U.S. power during the 1965–1975 period). The facilities give Moscow an important deployment complex between Vladivostok and Aden and give Hanoi a claim on Soviet resources and an assurance of support, if need be, against China.

A third situation in which vulnerability can improve the position of the Soviet Union is one in which domestic insecurity is heightened by possible inability to quell externally supported insurgent groups committed to the overthrow of a Third World regime. The more such insurgencies are aided by outside powers (for example, in Central America, the United States; in Southern Africa, South Africa; and, in Ethiopia, Arab aid to Eritrea), the more the beset regimes turn to the Soviet Union for assistance. The experience of Cuba, Angola, Mozambique, Ethiopia, and Nicaragua is illustrative.

The importance of the Soviet Union and its allies in keeping a particular regime in power varies. Castro first sought Soviet assistance out of fear of émigré groups dedicated to his overthrow. Now strong enough to deal with such opposition, he still retains Soviet troops as a bulwark against external attack by the United States and behind which he can with impunity fuel revolutions abroad.

Angola's MPLA depends on Soviet and Cuban assistance in its protracted counter-insurgency war against Jonas Savimbi's South Africa supported UNITA in the southern part of the country. Repeated efforts to destroy his forces have failed, notwithstanding the commitment of Soviet, Cuban and East German personnel in support of well-equipped Angolan forces;[20] and high-level MPLA delegations go frequently to Moscow to consult and to lobby for more aid.[21]

Mozambique faces an even more threatening insurgency from the Mozambique National Resistance (RENAMO), but the Soviets have not been very forthcoming. Originally created in 1977 by the white government of Rhodesia (Zimbabwe) to harass Samora Machel in retaliation for his assistance to Robert Mugabe's insurgency, the movement transferred its bases to South Africa when black majority rule won out

[20] "Military Reverses for Angolan Government," *International Defense Review*, no. 3 (1986), 271–72; *New York Times*, November 21, 1987.
[21] For example, FBIS/USSR International Affairs, January 31, 1986, J1–J4.

in Zimbabwe in 1980.[22] Together with East Germany, the USSR provides some military and security assistance, but not enough to defeat
RENAMO, which has grown stronger under South Africa's sponsorship.
In the past, the Soviets used their "connection with Mozambique to
help the liberation struggle in South Africa by furnishing assistance to
Mozambique-based members of the ANC," tried to institutionalize their
influence by a host of "party-to-party agreements and cadre training
programs that enable them to identify and cultivate future leaders,"
and created a certain dependency through the provision of much-
needed technical and advisory services.[23] But they were annoyed with
Machel's unwillingness to grant naval facilities and were also reluctant
to become too deeply involved militarily in a weak, poor country bordering on South Africa. For their part, Mozambique's leaders no
longer feel the initially strong identification with the Soviet bloc that
prevailed after their coming to power in 1975. That changed as a result of their disappointment over being refused membership in Comecon and receiving low levels of economic assistance, realization that
the Soviet economic model of development is inappropriate for Mozambique, and appreciation of the need to expand the country's ties
with Europe, especially Portugal.[24]

In Ethiopia, Mengistu, newly in power and faced by resistance from
various non-Amharic peoples (the Oromo, the Tigre, the Afar, and
the Eritreans), relied on the Soviet Union to preserve Ethiopia's multi-
ethnic imperial system intact. He keeps on the Soviets and Cubans,
using them to help train and equip his large army. Unlike Castro,
Mengistu seems to have no ambitions to play a leading role on the
international scene or to foster revolutions in his region.

Nicaragua's Marxist-Leninist leadership depends on the Soviet
Union and Cuba for military and economic assistance to institutionalize its power and defeat the threat from the U.S.-backed UNO (United
Nicaraguan Opposition) whose military arm, the FDN (Nicaraguan
Democratic Forces), is known as the "Contras." The number of Cubans and other foreigners serving in a variety of security and military
roles has fluctuated over the years, but it is in conformity with the
military buildup and the repressive apparatus required to curb the opposition. Sandinista forces are now the largest army in Central Amer-

[22] *Insight*, May 26, 1986, 26–27, and July 28, 1986, 33; *New African*, May 1985, 33.

[23] Peter Clement, "Moscow and Southern Africa," *Problems of Communism* 34, no. 2
(March–April 1985), 31.

[24] Norman MacQueen, "Mozambique's Widening Foreign Policy," *The World Today* 40,
no. 1 (January 1984), 22–23, 28. See also Winrich Kühne, *Sowjetische Afrikapolitik in der
'Ära Gorbatschow'* (Ebenhausen: Stiftung Wissenschaft und Politik, May 1986), 17–46.

ica. They are well-armed and equipped to fight a counter-insurgency war and should be able to handle the melange of anti-Sandinista forces who have no attractive political leader or political program and no discernible appeal to any mass constituency in Nicaragua. The "Contras" can strike at the government, but are unlikely to bring it down. Indeed, the harder they hit, the more deeply embedded the regime may become, argues a leading Latin American writer, because it can then draw on international sympathy and nationalist sentiment to protect the country against "the rightist counterrevolutionaries" controlled by the United States.[25] If there was any opponent who was widely respected as a patriot in the country and had the charisma to greatly increase the dissidents prepared to fight the regime's dictatorial pro-Soviet bent, it was Commandante Edén Pastora, one of the genuine heroes of the revolution.[26] Pastora broke with his former comrades in 1981 and became an active opponent. But in 1986, after countless frustrations in dealing with the CIA, which preferred the more compliant FDN, he decided to disband his Alianza Revolucionaria Democrática (ARDE) and apparently has withdrawn from the struggle.

The Soviet leadership responded to the Sandinista's sense of vulnerability by shipping arms appropriate for counter-insurgency operations—especially the long range Mi-24 helicopter gunship, the "Hind."[27] The economic assistance includes oil, a key hard-currency item the regime cannot do without. Moscow and Havana have also agreed to purchase a large portion of Nicaragua's sugar exports at prices well above those on the world market.[28] Nicaragua's vulnerability is unlikely to translate into military privileges comparable to those Moscow enjoys in Cuba, because no U.S. administration could afford domestically to ignore such a development; but for the foreseeable future Moscow need be given no tangible advantage to elicit its cooperation. It sees useful political gains in U.S. estrangement from important Latin American countries and West European social-democratic elites; in intensification of anti-Americanism among Third World crit-

[25] Carlos Fuentes, "Force Won't Work in Nicaragua," New York Times, July 24, 1983.

[26] This is the assessment of, among others, Arturo José Cruz, the former Nicaraguan ambassador to the United States, who broke with the Marxist-Leninist regime in November 1981 and who was active in the "Contra" movement until 1987. Arturo J. Cruz, "Nicaragua's Imperiled Revolution," Foreign Affairs 61, no. 5 (Summer 1983), 1038.

[27] John F. Guilmartin, Jr., "Nicaragua is Armed for Trouble," Wall Street Journal, March 11, 1985. However, the provision of Redeye portable anti-aircraft missiles by the United States quickly reduced the effectiveness of the "Hinds." For example, two years later Walter Calderón, a Contra field commander, said, "Helicopters used to be a terrible problem for us, but now we hardly ever see them." New York Times, December 6, 1987.

[28] Radio Liberty, RL 27/86 (January 10, 1986), 10; New York Times, March 24, 1985.

ics; and in the absorption of American domestic political groups with an issue that diverts attention from Soviet activities in Afghanistan, Eastern Europe, and the Middle East.

According to U.S. estimates, by 1986 the Soviet Union had invested over $1 billion in Nicaragua.[29] This commitment of resources stands in studied contrast to the relatively minimal (perhaps less than one-fifth the amount) and ineffectual aid extended to Mozambique during the same period. Though possibly unwilling to expand its disbursements any further,[30] Moscow seems satisfied with the political payoff from the one, but not with that from the other, and seems prepared to sustain past levels of support.

A fourth situation illustrative of vulnerability bringing increased leverage to the USSR arises from a Third World leadership's interest in attracting Soviet help for system maintenance. Moscow and its surrogates find ready buyers in the insecure regimes whose interest in a proven formula for institutionalizing power, suppressing opposition, and developing institutions for mass mobilization and control invariably overshadow their erratic impulses toward development. Especially in Africa, where regimes have few trained administrators, planners, or specialists in internal security, the Soviet Union and its allies have earned a reputation for their contributions.

Ideologically, most, but not all, of the regimes looking to the Soviet Union for assistance in systems maintenance are Marxist or Marxist-Leninist, anti-American, and signatories of friendship treaties with the USSR: Angola, the PDRY, Ethiopia, Afghanistan, Somalia (prior to October 1977), Mozambique, Benin, Nicaragua, and Congo-Brazzaville.

Marxist socialism has appeal in the Third World, but only in Angola, Mozambique, and Afghanistan does one find leaders who professed Marxism before coming to power. Interestingly, the main source of Marxist ideas in Africa is Western culture itself, since very little primary Marxist literature is as yet printed in Amharic, Yoruba, Hausa, or Kiswahili—let alone in the lesser-known African languages—and an African seeking to understand Marxism would have to have undergone a degree of Western acculturation.[31]

Viewed politically, the official embrace of Marxism-Leninism may

[29] President Reagan gave this figure in a speech calling for a $100 million aid package to anti-Sandinista forces. *New York Times*, June 26, 1986. Soviet economic and military aid levels were sustained, despite Western expectations of a sharp decrease, in 1987. *New York Times*, November 1, 1987.

[30] *New York Times*, August 20, 1987.

[31] Ali A. Mazrui, "Marxist Theories, Socialist Policies, and African Realities," *Problems of Communism* 29, no. 5 (September–October 1980), 47.

often be the means used by a regime, more or less cynically, for reasons of ambition and anti-Americanism arising out of its regional position, to obtain Soviet protection and patronage. Mengistu's determination to move the Ethiopian Revolution farther to the left and obtain Soviet support was evident in his announcement on April 20, 1976, launching a "national democratic revolution" that would open the way for "scientific socialism" and a "people's democratic republic."[32] By the following February, though the exact role of the Soviet Union and Cuba in his seizure of power remains unclear, there is evidence that Mengistu "had made secret contacts with Soviet and Cuban diplomats in Addis Ababa and had received assurances of immediate recognition if he took power and eliminated his adversaries within the PMAC [Provisional Military Administrative Council]."[33] The USSR's quick recognition and supply of arms rewarded his formal adherence to Marxism-Leninism. Also lending credence to the notion that a regime's commitment to Marxism-Leninism is a function of its anti-Western foreign policy orientation and desire for Soviet assistance was Siad Barre's downgrading of Somalia's Marxism-Leninism subsequent to his break with Moscow in October 1977.

Fear of internal opposition has whetted interest in Soviet expertise in security control not only among Marxist-Leninist regimes but also, at various times, in Ghana, Egypt, Syria, and Libya. What will eventuate in terms of the USSR's ability to intrigue against a leadership whom it is assisting but whom it suspects of antithetical interests, we can not yet determine from the few glimpses afforded us in events such as the anti-Neto affair in Angola or Mengistu's expulsion of two Soviet ambassadors. Moscow's intervention in December 1979 to wipe out Hafizullah Amin and his entourage in order to install a more compliant communist leadership that is hostage to its will seems not to have deterred any client; presumably, its suitors regard Afghanistan as a special case that has no bearing on their relationship with the Soviet Union. And, indeed, no independent Third World leader has publicly accused the Soviet-bloc advisers of attempted subversion.

Moscow's position in the PDRY does not seem to have suffered as a result of its limited involvement in the factional struggle for power that erupted in Aden in January 1986.[34] Surprised by the outbreak and by the sheer violence of the fighting, it switched loyalties when events indicated that the rebels were winning:

[32] Marina and David Ottaway, *Ethiopia: Empire in Revolution* (New York: Holmes & Meier, 1978), 120–21.

[33] Ibid., 168.

[34] See David Pollock, "Moscow and Aden: Coping with a Coup," *Problems of Communism* 35, no. 3 (May–June 1986), 50–70.

Several days into the fighting, Soviet assistance to the rebels was confined to provision of offshore transmission-boosting equipment for their radio broadcasts, as each side in South Yemen's civil war struggled to win the vital "battle of the airwaves." A week or so later, however, as Ali Nasir remained on the run, the Soviets apparently began providing the rebels with some intelligence and logistical support, and ultimately also with limited but useful tactical combat assistance. Reliable accounts in both Arab and Western publications refer to Soviet as well as Cuban participation in directing the insurgents' artillery fire, supplying them with ammunition and other matériel, and even bombing Aden's airport runways in order to neutralize the country's largely pro-Ali Nasir air force.[35]

Possibly, it even helped tip the scale in favor of the anti-Ali Nasir group. At a critical moment it helped to install in power "a heretofore marginal player, Haydar Abu Bakr Al-Attas," who was in India at the time the fighting erupted and who "had the foresight to fly on to Moscow instead of Beijing . . . for unscheduled crisis consultation."[36]

Third World Marxist regimes, such as exist in Ethiopia, Mozambique, the PDRY, Benin, Congo-Brazzaville, and Nicaragua, seek Moscow's help in developing a political organization that can mobilize, manipulate, and socialize the masses. But, though eager for an instrument to institutionalize control, they nevertheless resist Moscow's urging to follow a Leninist model that would permit the Communist Party free access to power, preferring to keep it marginal and tightly regulated, under the best of circumstances. Ironically, only in democratic India does the party function freely and wield power. Indeed, there are no ruling communist parties in Africa, the Middle East or South Asia, but rather "vanguard revolutionary-democratic" parties. In Latin America, Cuba is the only country officially ruled by a communist party; and even there the party is Castro's tool, not a power in its own right. According to Robert Leiken, "Fidel was not so much a Marxist-Leninist as a Fidelista" who saw in communism and close ties with Moscow the means of consolidating his political power.[37] In Nicaragua, the ruling FSLN is set up on the Cuban model and has extensive connections with Cuba and other communist governments but

[35] Ibid., 59.
[36] Ibid., 58.
[37] Robert S. Leiken, "Inside the Revolution," a review of Carlos Franqui, *Family Portrait with Fidel: A Memoir* (New York: Random House, 1984), in *New York Review of Books*, October 11, 1984, 3.

does not acknowledge itself to be a communist party;[38] indeed, the "small but vocal Communist Party" once allied with Sandinista leaders pulled out of the government-controlled coalition of political parties in 1984 and says that the Sandinistas "are not Marxists, not even close"; they are "Bonapartists"—that is, they "have taken their militaristic attitudes into government."[39]

Moscow may regard legitimation of a role for communist parties as useful for its long-term prospects but hardly a sufficient argument for jeopardizing an ongoing political relationship. However much Soviet writers theorize that vanguard parties constitute a necessary stage in the evolution toward Communist Party rule,[40] Moscow's policy toward this or that region is based on political not ideological criteria. Indeed, under Gorbachev, pragmatic adaptations to secure strategic footholds from Ethiopia to Nicaragua, from Afghanistan to Angola, are much in evidence. Soviet scholars have not only downgraded the previous attention accorded to vanguard parties but have also undertaken searching reassessments of their previous assumptions about trends in the Third World.[41] In line with Gorbachev's call for "new thinking" (*novoye myshleniye*), prominent analysts such as Mirskii and Ulianovskii have become quite dismissive of prospects for LDC's moving toward "socialism" and rule by vanguard parties,[42] and others write openly of the difficulties of following a "socialist orientation."[43]

---

[38] Robert Wesson, "Checklist of Communist Parties, 1982," *Problems of Communism* 32, no. 2 (March–April 1983), 99.

[39] *New York Times*, January 14, 1987.

[40] For example, G. I. Mirskii, *"Tretii mir": obshchestvo, vlast', armiia* ["The Third World": Society, Power, Army] (Moscow: Nauka, 1976). Mirskii writes, "To consider the army as the leading force of the anticapitalist revolution and the leader of the society in countries with a socialist orientation is a serious mistake. The only condition guaranteeing a truly democratic progressive development of nations of Asia, Africa, and Latin America is the creation of an avant-garde party that has adopted the positions of scientific socialism. Such a party must assume leadership over the army . . . in the final analysis, everything depends not on the army itself but on the society, on the level of its development, the degree of the maturity of the toiling masses and their ability to lead in the struggle for independence and progress" (385, 391). See also his article in *Voprosy filosofii*, no. 3 (March 1979), 97–108.

[41] Elizabeth Kridl Valkenier, "New Soviet Thinking about the Third World," *World Policy Journal* 4, no. 4 (Fall 1987), 651–74.

[42] G. I. Mirskii, "K voprosu o vybore puti orientatsii razvivayushchikhsia stran" [On the Question of the Choice of Orientation by the Developing Countries], *Mirovaia ekonomika i mezhdunarodnye otnosheniya*, no. 5 (May 1987), 70–81; and R. A. Ulianovskii, *Pobedy i trudnosti natsional'no-osvoboditel'noi bor'by* [The Triumph and Tribulation of the National Liberation Struggle] (Moscow: Politizdat, 1985): the section dealing with the "revolutionary process" in Afghanistan (198–226) provides an appraisal of the problems encountered by the PDPA.

[43] See N. Shmelov, " 'Tretii mir' i mezhdunarodnye ekonomicheskie otnosheniya" [The

Finally, there is the vulnerability that impels a Third World regime to show solidarity with likeminded states and, in the process, to grant Moscow special, if transient, treatment. This was instanced when Egypt permitted Soviet planes to fly supplies to Stanleyville, during the civil war in the Congo in the early 1960s; more importantly, in 1975, when Guinea granted landing privileges to Soviet and Cuban aircraft during the early stages of the Angolan civil war (by 1977, Sékou Touré withdrew them and improved relations with France and other Western countries); and in late 1977, when Iraq permitted Soviet overflights en route to Aden, whence Soviet arms were transshipped to Ethiopia at a crucial time in the Ethiopian-Somali war.

Even when privileges such as these are limited, issue-specific, and temporary, Moscow anticipates goodwill to enhance its overall position. For example, to Africans the Namibian and South African issues are of great importance; and, since on these and other key issues they regard Moscow's policy as having been valuable to their cause, the net result is they are disposed to look favorably on the Soviet Union and its role in Africa.[44] By adopting the moral posture favored by Third World regimes and contrasting its stand with that of the United States, Moscow encourages anti-Americanism and the maximalist demands that polarize issues and alignments and weaken the moderates who seek accommodation with the West.

THE LIMITS ON SOVIET GAINS

Regardless of kind or duration, vulnerability does not always bring Moscow tangible gains, influence, or other advantages. That it does not compel a client to make progressively more and greater concessions to retain the patron's support is what accounts for the ever-changing character of the bargaining process. Though a regime may have already provided significant advantages, Moscow may seek even more if it thinks this can be done without jeopardizing its existing privileged status. The following are illustrations from different spheres of Soviet–Third World relationships—military, political, economic, cultural—of the proposition that vulnerability does not necessarily enhance Moscow's position.

"Third World" and International Economic Relations], *Mirovaia ekonomika i mezhdunarodnye otnosheniya*, no. 9 (September 1987), 12–24; and R. Avakov, "Novoe myshleniye i problema izycheniya razvivayushchikhsia stran" [New Thinking and the Problems of Studying Developing Countries], *Mirovaia ekonomika i mezhdunarodnye otnosheniya*, no. 11 (November 1987), 54–57.

[44] Mazrui, "Marxist Theories," 49.

In the military sphere, there exists a reluctance on the part of even Marxist, strongly pro-Soviet regimes to grant Moscow privileged access.[45] When faced with a crisis affecting their security, they do not hesitate to upgrade Soviet access, as Angola and Vietnam did; but this is quite different from extending privileges for Moscow's strategic purposes as a matter of course. The Soviet leadership does not have all it would like from Marxist Mozambique or the PDRY, and it has even less to show from non-Marxist clients such as India, Libya, Nigeria, and Iraq. Ultimately, the infrastructure that Moscow uses to project power in the Third World must depend on the goodwill and the convergent goals of accommodating clients, and not on the physical assets it can claim at any given time.

In the political sphere, vulnerability often brings Soviet officials easy entrée to Third World leaders, but entrée is no assurance of agreement: in the late Nasser period, the Soviet ambassador could have access to him at any time, but that did not mean he could persuade Nasser to desist from his war of attrition or overhaul the Arab Socialist Union or introduce major economic reforms.[46] It also prompted friendship treaties, but, regardless of whether the intiative for one was Moscow's or the Third World regime's, the treaties seldom brought new gains. Nor were they instrumental in making regimes more pro-Soviet or more receptive to Soviet preferences; they merely put a gloss on a relationship already in place. Only Egypt's was unmistakably concluded as a result of Soviet pressure;[47] and not only did the Soviets fail to add one jot to their impressive list of advantages, but they also unwittingly exacerbated Sadat's existing distrust and dislike of them. Sadat acquiesced because, having just effected a preemptive coup that jailed, among others, such Soviet favorites as Ali Sabri, he wanted to neutralize possible opposition from Soviet agents; he had no wish to annoy his arms supplier and protective shield against Israel; and he lacked a U.S. option to fall back on.

[45] Crawford Young, *Ideology and Development in Africa* (New Haven, Conn.: Yale University Press, 1982), 268. In the case of Mozambique, the Soviet Union under Gorbachev has increased its economic and military aid somewhat, and there have been visits by Soviet warships, but it has yet to receive any naval or military privileges.

[46] See Rubinstein, *Red Star on the Nile*, chapters 2 and 3; and Mohamed Heikal, *The Sphinx and the Commissar: The Rise and Fall of Soviet Influence in the Middle East* (New York: Harper & Row, 1978), passim.

[47] Mohamed Heikal, *The Road to Ramadan* (London: Collins, 1975), 138–39. According to Heikal, Soviet President Nikolai Podgorny came to Cairo on May 25 with "a treaty ready for signature." Sadat said he was going to sign it: "He would have preferred to wait, but apparently the Soviets were in a hurry." See also, Anwar el-Sadat, *In Search of Identity: An Autobiography* (New York: Harper and Row, 1977), 225.

In the economic sphere, the bloom has faded from the Soviet rose. Time has borne out Western contentions that most of the large-scale projects undertaken with Soviet assistance in the public sector were uneconomic diversions of a regime's scarce resources.[48] No Soviet-built project anywhere operates at a profit or at approximate optimal efficiency. The reluctance of needy countries such as India, Turkey, Guinea, Nigeria, and Iraq to utilize Soviet credits reflects their disenchantment with the Soviet product and a preference for Western equipment and technology. Growing indebtedness is a heavy burden, and Moscow's insistence on repayment is a source of tension.[49] By the early 1980s, noncommunist LDCs (India, Turkey, Egypt) were paying back, in capital and interest, more than they were receiving.

As Third World governments look back over their record of economic planning and performance, they tend to blame the easy availability of Soviet credits for having induced them in the first place to embark on projects that were beyond their financial and physical capabilities.[50] The high cost of technical assistance and goods produced in Soviet-built plants, the confining character of Soviet credits, and the difficulties in negotiating minor matters with Soviet bureaucracies all militate against reliance on the Soviet developmental option or, indeed, trade with the USSR, in situations in which a Western alternative is possible. Moreover, Moscow's economic difficulties at home and in Eastern Europe act as a constraint on its ability to use economic assistance to exploit a regime's vulnerability in instances of seeming strategic opportunity. Madagascar is a good example. Strategically useful because of an excellent harbor at Diego Suarez on the northern tip of the 1,000-mile-long island off the southeast coast of Africa, it veered

[48] By the late 1960s, this was already creating difficulties in Soviet relations with India. Harish Kapur, *The Embattled Triangle: Moscow, Peking, New Delhi* (New Delhi: Abhinav Publications, 1973), 127–29.

[49] Fahmy, *Negotiating for Peace*, 144, notes that, after the October War, Gromyko kept on bringing up Egypt's indebtedness to the USSR and insisting that Cairo "must repay the debt, in annual installments of $500 million." In the early 1970s, the following joke made the rounds in Cairo. When Soviet President Nikolai Podgorny came to inaugurate the completion of the Aswan High Dam in January 1971, he demanded to see Nasser. The Egyptians were embarrassed and explained that was impossible, it being against their religion to exhume the body or reopen the tomb. But so insistent was Podgorny that they finally relented, reopened the tomb, and allowed him to enter. Five minutes passed, ten, thirty, an hour. Curious and concerned, the Egyptian leaders went in and found Podgorny busily putting Nasser's thumbprint on hundreds of old IOUs.

[50] Elizabeth K. Valkenier, "New Soviet Views on Economic Aid," *Survey*, no. 76 (Summer 1976), 26. Dr. Valkenier discusses the new realism in Soviet thinking about foreign economic assistance to developing countries: see *The Soviet Union and the Third World: An Economic Bind* (New York: Praeger, 1983).

to the left in the early 1970s, establishing extensive economic, military, and political ties with the Soviet Union and embarking on an openly anti-American tack. This was short-lived, however. By the end of the decade, faced with a massive debt, a deteriorating foreign trade situation, and a Soviet Union unable to meet the regime's economic needs, the leadership improved relations with the West and adhered to a more nonaligned course.[51]

As a general proposition, it can be said that the Soviet Union has determined that it is not in a position to use economic instruments to derive important advantages from Third World vulnerabilities. In Grenada, the Soviet Union was "slow and cautious" in committing resources. While accepting the New Jewel Movement of Prime Minister Maurice Bishop as a communist party, it "questioned Grenada's membership in the Socialist International," was reluctant to develop closer economic relations because of "Grenada's spotty record in using aid effectively," and wanted to avoid any confrontation with the United States over the Caribbean mini-state.[52] Even when the Soviets did start to provide assistance, they drove a hard bargain: there were no munificent grants. Of course, there are exceptions, and targets of opportunity such as Nicaragua do attract enough economic aid to help the pro-Soviet leadership maintain power and persist in an anti-American orientation.

Judging by the shift from economic to military assistance (noticeable in all Soviet relationships with Third World countries, except Cuba and Vietnam), Moscow has surely concluded that arms bring the diplomatic, political, and military advantages and gains it prizes; that security support not economic assistance is the key to establishing close links with those elites that really matter in Third World regimes. Given its own predisposition and surpluses, Moscow may be making a virtue of necessity.

Finally, the link between vulnerability and Soviet gains in the cultural sphere is the most difficult to assess. A focus on a regime's dearth of skilled manpower shows the complexity of the problem. Except for India, Egypt, and Cuba, Third World countries are desperately short of trained personnel in the sciences, engineering, management, and administration. They use fellowships from the Soviet Union (and Eastern Europe) to send thousands of their students there, in particular, to the Patrice Lumumba Friendship University, established by Khru-

[51] *New York Times*, July 24, 1983. There is a comparable situation in the Seychelles.

[52] Gregory Sandford, *The New Jewel Movement: Grenada's Revolution 1979–1983* (Washington, D.C.: Foreign Service Institute, 1985), 114–15.

shchev in Moscow in 1961 for that purpose. Moscow expected that graduates would return to their countries and, over time, assume leading roles and form a cadre of influential opinion-makers and intellectual pace-setters with a pro-Soviet orientation in the political, economic, and social fields. But there is much merit in the adage, "To make a person a communist, send him to London or Paris; to make him a capitalist, send him to Moscow."

There are no published studies tracing the career patterns of Lumumba graduates. My own discussions in India and Egypt lead me to believe that Soviet efforts and expenditures have an extremely limited payoff, if the aim is to educate students who will return home and become influential and advocates of better relations with the Soviet Union. First, students going to Lumumba University are generally regarded as second-rate, certainly not first-rate; the best are sent or go to the West. Second, Third World countries prize holders of Western degrees, while those from Lumumba are deprecated as having credentials of low esteem. Moscow had to work hard in India, for example, to arrange for the Ministry of Higher Education to grant official accreditation to degrees given by Lumumba University. Third, graduates of Lumumba have not achieved eminence or importance in their countries (India, Iraq, Ethiopia, Sri Lanka, Nigeria, among others) in any of the professional fields. The top personnel in engineering, medicine, business, and the social sciences are products of indigenous institutions or graduates of Western universities. Fourth, Third World leaderships, even the Marxist ones, are leery of Lumumba returnees, fearing that they have been coopted by the KGB (as undoubtedly some have been). In India, returnees are viewed with disdain and end up in unimpressive positions. Finally, there have been enough reports by returnees to indicate that for Afro-Asian students the contact with Russian culture is not a happy one. Africans are quick to recognize the deep-rooted racist attitudes of the average Russian, and they acquire a permanent resentment.[53] The experiences of the Egyptians and Sudanese with Soviet military advisers turned sour because of the ill-disguised Russian contempt for "colored" peoples—a consideration, incidentally, that militates against Moscow's attempts to win over the Pathans in Afghanistan.

Little in Soviet writing provides information or insights about actual Soviet views on the different aspects and levels of vulnerability and

[53] For example, Colin Legum, "The USSR and Africa: The African Environment," *Problems of Communism* 27, no. 1 (January–February 1978), 10; Toko, *Intervention in Uganda*, 103–4.

how these affect Soviet policy choices. Soviet writers do not discuss the USSR's multifaceted experience with Third World regimes in any detail, so specifics on the problems, processes, and prospects of military, political, economic, and cultural relations are not given. Nor do they comment on the vulnerability that led to improved relations or greater influence. Their emphasis is on the U.S. policy of "neoglobalism" and its exploitative aspects: Third World vulnerabilities are explained in terms of the legacy of colonialism, economic dependence on Western markets and capital, overreliance on single commodity exports, and the pervasive influence of multinational corporations—in a word, assumptions derived from the Leninist theory of imperialism.

In general there seem to be constraints on any inclination Moscow might have to use the leverage it possesses. Soviet leaders do not want to jeopardize already-acquired basic gains, do not want to drive Third World leaderships to reconsider the fundamentals of their policy and explore a U.S. option. They realize that in most of the countries they have targeted power is highly personalized, and to alienate a leader is to risk an abrupt reversal on his part. Moreover, communist parties are weak and at present unsuited for mounting serious challenges to those in power. Short of outright military intervention on the scale undertaken in Afghanistan, Moscow cannot force a leadership to do something it considers against its vital interests; and intervention with lesser forces is not apt to be successful. Indeed, to intervene forcefully or attempt to subvert a regime in Africa or the Arab world would make other clients in these regions suspicious, if not openly anti-Soviet, and result in a sharp reduction of Soviet advisers in the country.

More examples of counter-leverage are needed before a convincing hypothesis about the capacity of vulnerable Third World regimes to resist Soviet pressures and intrigues can be formulated. But for the moment, a healthy respect for their ability to limit or reverse Soviet gains—unless they are occupied by Soviet troops—is warranted.

VULNERABILITY: REAL OR APPARENT

What is noteworthy is not the vulnerability of Third World regimes, but rather their ability to elicit from the Soviet Union resources ranging from economic assistance and advanced weaponry to political advisers and combat troops for the promotion of their regional ambitions, national defense, or internal consolidation; and their skill in doing so without relinquishing sovereignty or freedom of action on vital issues in foreign policy.

It is also noteworthy, not that Third World regimes have accorded

advantages and privileges to the Soviet Union in return for assistance
that was essential for their political ambitions or survival, but that so
little of what they have given is of permanent or unequivocal character.

Over the years, Moscow has become reconciled to the difficulties involved in obtaining facilities from vulnerable Third World regimes. It
has not pressed its case, in part because the need for them is not urgent and in part because political objectives figure prominently in its
overall policy. It prefers not to arouse suspicions or embitter relations
unnecessarily. For the moment, the access it does have is sufficient for
its purposes, and the possibility of a steady upgrading of existing advantages and privileges makes for caution. But, looking to the longer
term, Moscow must, no matter how promising the situation in any
given country may seem, view with uneasiness the volatility of Third
World leaders and the abruptness with which they can reverse policy—or, indeed, be deposed. The Soviet Union has had its share of
setbacks in the Third World—Egypt, Somalia, Guinea, Ghana, Iraq,
Indonesia, Mali, Sudan, Uganda, and Iran.

Vulnerability is a changing condition and indications are that the
USSR's ability to exploit a regime's vulnerability will invariably be lead-
ership-specific and issue-specific. All of this adds up to an absorption
with concrete and short-term advantages and a Soviet policy that is
essentially reactive. Such an approach suits the USSR's emphasis on
military instruments and concentration on military elites. Moscow, unable to demonstrate the benefits for a regime from enmeshing its
economy with that of the Soviet bloc, and lacking the attractive power
for significant cultural penetration, rests its hopes on a Third World
regime's fixation on security-political issues and the persistence of regional conflicts and the polarization they spawn.

CHAPTER SEVEN

The Soviet Impact

The Kremlin's courtship of the Third World began, as we have seen, with a number of objectives: diplomatic normalization with its neighbors and the new nations of the Arab East and Southern Asia; strategic denial aimed at preventing the United States from acquiring and exploiting military-political advantages in the vast region to the south of the Soviet Union; establishment of footholds in heretofore hostile environments; expansion of trade; enhancement of the USSR's prestige; and the fostering of socialism. In casting a wide net and hoping for some kind of yield, it discovered that the biggest haul came from targeting regimes that were for various reasons at odds with regional rivals who were backed by a Western power. As these bilateral relationships took hold, Moscow accepted the reality that each party sought to use the other to defend and advance its own interests. Indeed, the asymmetry of their aims eased the cementing of ties; serious frictions were thus rare.

Soviet initiatives and responses unfolded within an essentially bilateral framework, and it is mainly within this framework that the Soviet Union's achievements and disappointments, advances and setbacks, have, in this study, been assessed. They have been examined thematically: the circumstances and nature of the USSR's involvement; the USSR's approach to national liberation struggles; its use of force on behalf of clients; its use of surrogates; and the vulnerability in Third World systems and behavior that elicited greater commitments and brought additional advantages. Keeping in mind the record of what Moscow wanted, did, and achieved in its relations with particular regimes, we now need to look at the broader effects of its policies on regional and global developments and trends.

The Soviet impact on the Third World has been profound. It has affected regional politics, and the character of superpower rivalry and their prospects for détente. Like other key terms in the foreign policy lexicon (such as "power," "influence," "deterrence," "threat," and so on), "impact" can have multiple meanings.[1] As used here, "impact" is

---

[1] Impact is to be differentiated from influence, which I have defined elsewhere in an attempt to assess a bilateral relationship: influence is manifested when A affects, through

a long-term phenomenon; by contrast, "influence" has been used in as limited and specific a sense as possible to describe the outcome of a given issue or situation in the context of relations between two governments or leaderships. Whereas influence waxes and wanes according to the mood and condition of individual Third World leaders, impact is more durable; its force comes from the weight of incremental change. Impact is further differentiated from influence in that it refers to consequences that are unplanned and not readily manipulable, and that are discernible beyond the confines of nation states, at the subregional, regional, or global levels of the international system. These consequences must be considered when an attempt is made to extrapolate probable future Soviet policy on the basis of the record to date, because any overall assessment of achievements must include what emerged indirectly as well as what was consciously sought. All parties may be affected in ways they did not imagine possible and were in no position to prevent. The impact that Soviet policy has had on the political environment requires that Moscow itself make adaptations in order to be able to pursue the principal aims of its strategy.

Though manifested in different ways in different countries and regions, the Soviet Union's impact on the Third World can be examined by focusing on a number of themes that cut across regional lines:

- the attitudes of Third World elites toward the Soviet Union;
- the credibility of the Soviet Union as a patron;
- the attractiveness and relevance of the Soviet/socialist model of development;
- the operation of the military factor in regional patterns of conflict and cooperation;
- the evolution of regional politics;

---

nonmilitary means, directly or indirectly, the behavior of B so that it redounds to the policy advantage of A. This definition immediately raises a semantic problem because the phenomenon of influence is both a process and a product, and no wording can completely free us of this problem. "Influence may be considered to have a number of characteristics: (a) it is a relational concept involving 'the transferral of a pattern (of preferences) from a source (the controlling actor) to a destination (the responding actor), in such a way that the outcome pattern corresponds to the original preference pattern'; (b) it is issue-specific and situation-specific: the duration of influence is restricted to the life of the issue or the situation within which it appeared and when these change so does the influence relationship; (c) it is a short-lived phenomenon; (d) it is an asymmetrical interaction process; (e) it has no fixed pattern of achievement costs; (f) it is multidimensional, manifesting itself in different spheres." Alvin Z. Rubinstein, *Red Star on the Nile: The Soviet-Egyptian Influence Relationship since the June War* (Princeton: Princeton University Press, 1977), xiv–xv.

- the modus operandi of the United States;
- Moscow's own policy.

Consideration must be given not only to Moscow's commitments, activism, and priorities, but also to the Third World's changing perceptions, agendas, and demands. The many gaps in the written record make it impossible to establish causality, and this opens the way for divergent interpretations of Soviet policies, as well as those of the United States and the leading Third World countries. Nonetheless, broad patterns can be traced, and from these a number of generalizations can be made about the Soviet impact on the developments and direction of political conflict in the Third World. Viewed in historical perspective, the record is one of surprises—of fears that never materialized and, even more, of changes that were not anticipated.

THE ATTITUDES OF THIRD WORLD ELITES TOWARD THE USSR

In the mid-1950s, as the Kremlin shed Stalin's ideological and political fetters on accommodation with bourgeois-national regimes, Third World elites began to dissociate their opposition to communists at home from their inherited suspicion of Soviet aims; and very quickly the Soviet Union "ceased to frighten, since it advocated the stability of political systems, whatever their complexions, provided they be nonaligned, that is to say, at odds with the Western world."[2] Searching for assistance and alternatives to reliance on the West and on former colonial masters, they became receptive to Soviet diplomatic overtures and offers of economic and military assistance. As experience showed that a growing Soviet presence did not subvert their rule, they came to value the many ways that ties to the USSR enabled them to pursue their preferred domestic and foreign policies.

For the Soviet leadership, the congruence between its new course and the political currents in the Third World was both fortuitous and felicitous. Moscow sought to deprive the United States of unchallenged access to Third World real estate; and leaders such as Nehru, Sukarno, and Nasser looked to counter Washington's arming of their regional rivals. In the short term, Moscow used diplomatic normalization and ambitious aid programs to promote strategic denial; however, it was attuned to the future, where prospects for more tangible military and economic advantages lay. Third World requests for assistance were generally acted on favorably during the Khrushchev pe-

[2] Hélène Carrère d'Encausse, *Ni paix ni guerre: le nouvel empire soviétique ou du bon usage de la détente* (Paris: Flammarion, 1986), 20–21.

riod. Though not knowing precisely which benefits might accrue from its largesse, Moscow could anticipate some advantage, in some sector, to one of its multiple aims.

Third World leaders approached relations with the Soviet Union with the same wariness they felt toward any great power. Once ties were established, they paid little heed to Moscow's "revolutionary" ideology or programmatic statements, treating it as a traditional power. Historical and political considerations were important to those who probed the various possibilities offered by closer ties with the Soviet Union. For one thing, Moscow came with "clean hands": it was untainted by a colonial past in the Arab world or the Indian subcontinent, much less in Africa or Latin America. This meant that Soviet aims were not seen as imperialist or as directed toward the seizure or domination of territory, and the ease with which Egypt and Somalia managed the Soviet expulsions in the 1970s served to reinforce this impression among many nonaligned countries. For another thing, Third World leaders saw the Soviet Union as a lever to pry concessions from the Western powers. It was with this in mind that Moscow was quickly made persona grata. Thus, on one occasion, when asked whether India would prefer to receive economic aid on a bilateral basis or through the United Nations, Prime Minister Nehru replied that the bilateral method was preferable since it enabled India to take advantage of the rivalry between the United States and the Soviet Union and obtain assistance from each.[3] But only a handful of rulers were able to play this kind of a bold political hand in order to extract advantage from the superpower rivalry. Iran under the Shah, Turkey, Algeria, and Nigeria managed to some extent to operate thus. For most countries, as regional rivalries worsened, the premium was on securing one superpower as patron and protector, with a consequent narrowing of opportunities for diplomatic gamesmanship.

Though Third World elites improved relations with the USSR, they did not feel impelled to change their attitude toward local communists, whom they for the most part continued to view as politically untrustworthy quasi-tools of a foreign power and to be kept distant from the centers of power. This suspicion was extended also to those of their countrymen who studied in the Soviet Union, the assumption being that the KGB would recruit, often through blackmail, from such groups.[4]

[3] Author's interview in New Delhi, December 21, 1961.

[4] For example, see Vladimir Sakharov, *High Treason* (New York: Ballantine, 1980), 147–48, 266; Aleksandr Kaznacheev, *Inside a Soviet Embassy* (Philadelphia: Lippincott, 1962), 69.

Dealing with the Soviet Union does not complicate the process of retaining power and curbing a leftist opposition. In fact, neither the rulers nor their domestic opponents find much mileage in denouncing the Soviet Union. Anti-Sovietism simply does not translate into a prescription for acquiring or exercising power; unlike anti-Americanism, it is rarely used to mobilize support behind an unpopular ruler. There are no obvious and convenient targets of Soviet "influence," comparable to American companies, schools, mores, culture, and consumer items for the leadership to single out and manipulate as an outlet for nationalist rage. Anti-Soviet outbursts are not unknown, but they tend to be expressions of official displeasure over a particular issue rather than spontaneous eruptions of popular anger. On balance, this circumstance tends to benefit those in power, because it means that domestic opponents cannot use the regime's policy toward the Soviet Union as an issue in their efforts to unseat the leadership. Thus, in the Third World, close ties with the Soviet Union are not the catalysts of controversy that ties with the United States often are.

Still, the extensive associations that many Third World elites have had with the Soviet Union over the past few decades have led to remarkably little affinity for the Russians who work in their country but who remain unknown and alien. In Egypt, for example, the Russians are thoroughly disliked. Their standoffishness is seen as disdain for things Egyptian. To the average Egyptian, they are known as "the unsmiling ones." One long-time Western observer of the Egyptian scene has written, "Russians working in Egypt tend to live in their own physical and cultural ghetto. Many of them consider Egypt a 'hardship post.' . . . They are suspicious of the average Egyptian and detest his levitous insouciance, as well as his native cynical sense of humour."[5]

The Soviets are hard to get to know because their tightly controlled political system conditions them to regard all outsiders as enemies: they do not conform in the flesh to the poster picture of the open, fresh, heroic stalwart carrying the banner of socialism and holding out a hand in friendship. Hence they cannot relate informally as do the Americans or British or French, and this is a decided handicap in societies where informal networks are often far more important than formal ones. One British journalist, returning to Vietnam to observe the tenth anniversary of the liberation and unification of the country, reported the presence of a large number of Soviets in Ho Chi Minh

[5] P. J. Vatikiotis, "Notes For an Assessment of the Soviet Impact on Egypt," in Michael Confino and Shimon Shamir, eds., *The USSR and the Middle East* (New York: Wiley, 1973), 280.

City (Saigon), but noted that the "Russians are considered boorish, humourless, and, above all, distressingly stingy."[6] In the 1980s, few among the elites in Third World countries harbor any emotional illusions about the Soviet Union or Soviet society; the Soviet Union is a "wasteland" to which no rulers would think of sending their children to be educated.

Nevertheless, the desire of Third World elites for Soviet support led them to surmount the difficulties of dealing with the Soviet Union. Their pragmatism and ambition were instrumental in opening the way for Soviet entry into the Third World, a development that was inevitable, anyway, given the size and power of the Soviet Union. Whatever the combination of reasons that led Third World governments to rapprochement with the Soviet Union, their political egoism forever changed regional and global politics. Henceforth the Soviet Union was included in the Third World as a player for all seasons and of many parts. By using the USSR, elites expanded their options and introduced new elements of complexity, peril, and divisiveness into an already dangerous and difficult environment.

In the process, they learned to treat the Soviet Union gingerly. Moscow's reputation for toughness conditioned the way even unfriendly regimes and groups behave toward it. Among Third World regimes, which are primarily authoritarian systems, a grudging respect for Soviet forcefulness and power often contrasts with a lack of sympathy for the vagaries of the democratic process—specifically, for a U.S. policy that is frequently hobbled or used against them by unpredictable Congressional actions. Consequently, fewer liberties are taken with Soviet personnel and property. For example, no minister of a friendly government would dare offend the Soviet leadership as a Zimbabwean minister in Harare offended the United States: attending the U.S. embassy's celebration of its national holiday on July 4, 1986, he denounced the U.S. government as imperialist. Such incidents are not unimportant expressions of the very different tactics used by Third World leaders in their relations with the United States and with the USSR, and of the different outlooks that each superpower engenders by its behavior. If there are few illusions operative in the approach of Third World elites to the USSR, there are also few misunderstandings about the real nature of the relationship and about what each party expects from the other.

[6] Gavin Young, *The Observer*, April 28, 1983, 7.

Soviet Credibility

The transition from pariah to partisan was an easy one for the Soviet Union to make. The establishment of diplomatic ties and readiness to provide economic, military, and political support led to its active defense of endangered clients. In the process, Moscow set an impressive record as a reliable patron. Despite difficulties and occasional policy differences, a Soviet connection remains a coveted link in the Third World.

The USSR's reputation for credibility is based on a demonstrable record of dependability, consistency, and capability. It has been a reliable patron and protector, openly supportive of major clients who request assistance against external attack, against internal threats, and against pressure from a U.S.-backed regional adversary. Once it had unequivocally committed itself, Moscow stayed the course, irrespective of military and economic costs or the adverse affect on its relationship with the United States. A client considered important was rendered assistance appropriate to the threat whether or not there was a friendship treaty; indeed, in most instances in which the USSR went to the brink of war, as in Cuba, Egypt, and Syria, no formal commitment to defend the client existed, yet Moscow did not equivocate. Up to now, its responses to situations of obvious threat to the continuity of a client's power have been forceful, unambiguous and unwavering.

There are, however, a few dilemmas in the offing that may force the Kremlin to make choices that will inevitably tarnish its hitherto unblemished record. For one, Mozambique faces a serious threat from a South Africa-supported insurgency; and the death of Samora Machel in a plane crash on October 19, 1986, and his replacement by Foreign Minister Joaquin Alberto Chissano, who has a reputation for pragmatism and political realism, may reinforce the Kremlin's reluctance to pour resources into an unstable country so far from the Soviet Union and so near to South Africa. Judging by Moscow's very limited, and not terribly relevant, assistance to date, it seems increasingly doubtful that the Soviet leadership will extend itself to live up to the spirit of the March 31, 1977, friendship treaty.

Afghanistan is another case in which Soviet adherence to the spirit of a friendship treaty may be tested. If the PDPA's leadership, suddenly faced with an imminent end to Soviet military involvement and the collapse of its regime, were to invoke the treaty, it is not likely Moscow would do much to help—something the Afghan regime of Nijibullah may already know.

None of the treaties requires an automatic armed Soviet response, but they did create an expectation among Third World signatories—and prospective signatories—that Moscow would take appropriate action to safeguard a client threatened by external enemies. Now, with the regimes in Mozambique and Afghanistan in danger of being overthrown, neither seems to expect much direct combat support from the Soviet Union. Moscow's reputation for dependability is undergoing a bit of tarnishing.

Thus far, though, Moscow has come to the aid of clients as often as necessary—in the case of Egypt, three times between 1967 and 1973. Its involvement has always been by invitation and its response has been prompt and consistently satisfying: every client on whose behalf Moscow has mounted a rescue operation has retained power and staved off the necessity of making peace with a regional rival. Moreover, as a rule, the USSR has taken care in the dispatch of arms and combat troops not to make indigenous rulers fearful of domestic meddling. It has done what had to be done discreetly, with minimum publicity and internal dislocation, and with no attempt to blackmail the client for concessions.

Basic to the USSR's credibility as a patron and protector is its ability to undertake military operations in the Third World. The USSR's continually improving conventional power projection capability can support an array of logistical and combat roles. While there has been a major buildup of the Soviet Navy, it is Soviet air power, air defense systems, armor, and artillery that have been most pertinent to the servicing of Third World clients.[7] Time and again, Moscow has demonstrated that it has the weapons and the will to shield clients and project the power appropriate to the threat.

Moscow's response to each crisis carefully distinguishes between friends and adversaries and also its own primary adversary and its

[7] For example, "during the 1970s, the Soviet Union demonstrated that it was able to fund improvements in both the quantity and the quality of its weapons systems, with the quality of its most modern systems approaching—and at times exceeding—that of their U.S. counterparts. Tank development (the T-72 and T-80), armored personnel carrier development (the BMD and air-droppable BRDM), air defense guns such as the ZSU-23, and a host of other systems—including mundane but critical items such as engineering equipment—all pointed to the tremendous advances the Soviets had made in the support of their land force operations. . . . Soviet qualitative advances in tactical aviation permitted them to assume military missions that previously were beyond their capability. . . . Soviet development of missile-armed helicopters, such as the Mi-24, has allowed them to perfect their own tactics in a field in which Western, and especially U.S., forces had always been dominant." Dov S. Zakheim, "The Unforeseen Contingency: Reflections on Strategy," *Washington Quarterly* 5, no. 4 (Autumn 1982), 161–62.

clients' adversaries, some of whom may one day look to it for improved relations. It proceeds with an eye on the future. Illustrative of Moscow's persistent regard for detail and the essential congruence between its tactics and broader strategic aims is a minor incident that occurred during the U.S.-Iranian tension over the 1979–1980 hostage crisis, when "Washington gave the impression of being afraid of the entire Islamic world." At the time of the 1,400th anniversary of Islam, President Carter decided "not to send any messages of congratulations to any Muslim leaders," presumably out of fear "of adverse domestic political reactions," while the Soviet Union flooded the Arab capitals with messages, and, as one Arab official observed, "they don't even believe in God."[8]

Moscow accepts the use of force as an integral feature of international politics and is not prone to moralize or preach to clients. It does not seriously pressure them to change even policies with which it disagrees, as when Assad expanded into Lebanon in the mid-1970s and made efforts in the 1980s to create a PLO alternative to Arafat's leadership. Given lavish Soviet arms transfers, this makes high-tension politics an allowable, indeed, a feasible, option for a protected client. As far as can be determined, there seems not to be in Soviet–Third World client relationships an analogue to U.S. pressures on its ally Turkey over the question of Cyprus, to the U.S. abandonment of Pakistan in its 1965 war with India, or to the U.S. control of arms shipments in order to force modifications in Israel's policy toward Egypt and in Lebanon. Nor does Moscow intrude itself as an "honest broker" in situations where it had intervened militarily on behalf of one of the parties to the conflict. It resists pressuring clients to accommodate to a regional rival, partially out of fear of alienating them and partially out of the perception that Soviet aims can as well be served by the perpetuation of regional conflicts. Whatever the reason, Moscow sees the advancement of its longer-term regional objectives as being dependent on the preservation of close ties with a prime client. The net result of all of this is that Moscow's credibility as a patron is high, because it goes along to get along.

Finally, credibility is a relative concept. In important measure, its political value is determined by how Third World actors compare Soviet and American performance, since there are no other patrons of consequence to be considered. If criteria of dependability and consis-

[8] William B. Quandt, "The Reasons behind America's Decline in the Middle East," *Wall Street Journal*, December 14, 1979. Dr. Quandt was head of the Middle East section of the National Security Council during the Carter administration.

tency are the benchmarks against which prospective clients in highly explosive regional settings make political judgments, it is likely the Soviet Union would rank higher than the United States. Should, however, other considerations—domestic, economic, cultural, historical— enter into the equation, the Soviet Union's ranking would be lowered. Ultimately, each client regime makes its choice of patron for a variety of reasons, including availability, but the Soviet Union's proven staying power must certainly weigh heavily.

THE RELEVANCE OF THE SOVIET/SOCIALIST MODEL OF DEVELOPMENT

The biggest casualty of Moscow's involvement in the Third World is the Soviet model of development. One would be hard put to find an elite that looks to the Soviet Union for a blueprint of how to modernize its economy. Far from advancing socialism and a desire for closer economic ties to the Soviet Union, the impact of the Soviet model and specifically of the Third World's economic experience with the USSR has been disenchantment with development and a greater concentration on institutionalizing power. It was Kwame Nkrumah who insisted, "seek ye first the political kingdom and all else will follow." This redirection, a preeminence of the political over the economic, signifies the inability of economic development to provide a successful focus for the activities of second- and third-generation post-colonial elites. The proposition that the Soviet strategy for economic development exercises "a deep influence on the underdeveloped countries"[9] is no longer credible, even if one singles out for illustration countries with promising combinations of resources and manpower such as India, Pakistan, Nigeria, and Turkey, or occasional leaderships who have attempted disastrously costly campaigns to collectivize agriculture (for example, Ethiopia, Grenada, Madagascar), or, in the case of Madagascar, taken a "great forward leap" (*investissement à outrance*) or, in the cases of both Madagascar and Grenada, foreseen the construction of a heavy industrial base.

In the 1950s and 1960s, many of the first-generation post-colonial leaders sought not only an independent path in foreign affairs but also a rapid economic development that they uncritically equated with

---

[9] For such an approach, which this writer considers flawed, see Norton T. Dodge and Charles K. Wilbur, "The Relevance of Soviet Industrial Experience for Less Developed Countries," *Soviet Studies* 21, no. 3 (January 1970), 331–32; and Bernard P. Kiernan, "The Nature of Communism in the Emergent World," *Yale Review* 59, no. 3 (Spring 1970), 321–32.

heavy industrialization: a steel mill was a symbol of modernity. Hopes for progress, social justice, and an end to poverty, as well as hostility to the capitalist colonial system that had kept them in bondage, predisposed them to socialism and to the Soviet experience. The USSR's willingness to help finance and construct industrial projects in the public sector dovetailed with their vague belief in the efficacy of a centralized, planned, highly nationalized, urban-oriented economy, which they saw as the salient characteristics of the Soviet model.[10]

The results were not successful anywhere. Moscow may not have pushed these governments along what it calls the noncapitalist path of development, but it did encourage them. Accordingly, as concerns economic development, their failure is Moscow's as well; and in their eyes the USSR's own difficulties and inability to help them overcome their backwardness are seen as indications of serious flaws in socialism (that is, the Soviet variant) itself.

Successive Soviet leaderships have asseverated the importance of economic achievements in enhancing Soviet influence in the Third World. Speaking at the CPSU's twenty-seventh congress, on February 25, 1986, General Secretary Gorbachev reiterated this theme:

> The acceleration of socio-economic development will enable us to contribute considerably to the consolidation of world socialism, and will raise to a higher level our cooperation with fraternal countries. It will considerably expand our capacity for economic ties with peoples of developing countries, and with countries of the capitalist world. In other words, implementation of the policy of acceleration will have far-reaching consequences for the destiny of our Motherland.[11]

No doubt it would. And Soviet leaders may well believe this in a fairly general sort of way. But by now the timing of these formulations has

[10] Four features of the Soviet model of economic development had particular attraction for economists and politicians in the Third World. "There is, first and foremost, the expropriation of large-scale owners of the means of production—the hallmark of Soviet-type economies. Secondly, there is the use of all-pervasive government planning and controls in preference to Adam Smith's 'invisible hand' (consumer sovereignty, the profit motive, a free price system, etc.). . . . Thirdly, there is the retreat to something near autarky, or at least the drastic reduction of dependence on foreign trade. Lastly, there is the redeployment of resources (including the labour force) in favour of industry—particularly heavy industry and construction—if need be to the detriment of agricultural production, and the consequent systematic deprivation of the consumer." Francis Seton, "Planning and Economic Growth: Asia, Africa, and the Soviet Model," *Soviet Survey*, no. 31 (January–March 1960), 38–39.

[11] Mikhail Gorbachev, *Political Report of the CPSU Central Committee to the 27th Congress of the Communist Party of the Soviet Union (February 25, 1986)* (Moscow, 1986), 31–32.

become too predictable: these linkages of economic growth with improved prospects in foreign policy are included in the rationale disseminated to justify economic reforms, the appendages to official commentaries and speeches that call for greater efficiency and growth in the Soviet economy.[12] They are rhetorical flourishes, not harbingers of any change in basic outlook; above all, they are not to be confused with the substantive and political considerations that determine Soviet foreign policy in the Third World. With each passing year, economic assistance becomes a less and less important component of the overall Soviet transfer of resources to developing countries (excepting, of course, the special cases of Cuba and Vietnam).

Third World elites, too, proclaim their commitment to economic development, but, while pronouncements abound, actions tell a different story. Some leaders are sincere; most are unwilling to make mobilization of internal resources and modernization the primary objective. They may want to modernize, but they covet power more. To paraphrase what Harold Begbie said about Christianity, it is not that development was tried and found difficult, but that it was found difficult and not tried. On occasion, a political zealot will, for a time, impose on a hapless people a model of socialism reminiscent of Stalin's policy in the 1929–1938 period. Pol Pot in Kampuchea in the mid-1970s and Mengistu Haile Mariam in Ethiopia in the 1980s are tragic examples. According to Paul Henze, "a self-serving 'Russian memorandum' " critical of the Derg "for 'leftist deviations' in economic policy" was circulated in Addis Ababa in the summer of 1986.[13] The Soviets were evidently trying to distance themselves from Mengistu's fanciful and costly approach to managing the economy.[14] They may also have been putting Mengistu on notice not to expect significant economic assistance from the Soviet Union.

---

[12] In October 1965, one month after the adoption of extensive economic reforms, *Pravda* editorialized, "In building socialism and communism, the socialist countries make the most important and decisive contribution to the world revolutionary movement. This is what determines their vanguard role in the contemporary revolutionary struggle." *Pravda*, October 27, 1965. In 1986, at the CPSU's twenty-seventh congress, Gorbachev argued along the same lines.

[13] Paul Henze, "Behind the Ethiopian Famine (III)," *Encounter* 67, no. 3 (September–October 1986), 25.

[14] Mengistu nationalized all farmland in 1975, but instead of carrying out a clearcut policy toward the peasant he left in abeyance the question of the peasant's stake in his allotted plot. Forced requisitions by the government and uncertainty over ownership have kept productivity low. Clifford D. May, *New York Times*, May 23, 1985. According to Ethiopian defectors, the catastrophic Ethiopian famine in 1984 and 1985 was caused as much by Ethiopian government policy as by the drought—in particular, by the government's collectivization policy. *New York Times*, May 21, 1986.

The diminished interest in the Soviet model of socialism has not, however, affected the desire of Third World leaders for closer ties with the Soviet Union. On the contrary, since it is weapons, not economic aid, that Moscow can supply in abundance, they shift their priorities or are subtly induced to seek fulfillment abroad rather than at home. Among Soviet clients or those who look to the Soviet Union for support in pursuing their regional ambitions, military considerations become ever more prominent, and with this comes a heightened interest in taking what Moscow is best equipped to provide—namely, the wherewithal for a potent military structure and police-state apparatus. By contrast, governments that do not look to the Soviet Union for a larger military instrument (in the late 1980s these would include Brazil, Argentina, Mexico, Malaysia, Indonesia, Singapore, and the Ivory Coast) are those who believe that development is important and recognize that economic progress is essential for their own security and retention of power.

THE MILITARY FACTOR IN REGIONAL PATTERNS OF CONFLICT AND COOPERATION

The long-term impact of Soviet military assistance has been the militarization of politics in the Third World. There is no evidence that this was Moscow's aim in the mid-1950s when Khrushchev sold arms to Egypt and Afghanistan, but in a variety of unanticipated ways this development has become integral to the overall advance of Soviet foreign policy objectives. It is not limited to affecting the outcomes of particular crises or conflicts; systemically, its even greater significance lies in the corruption of democratic values, in the encouragement of coups and conflict, and in the misdirection of resources. The net effect is to lead regimes nurtured by Soviet infusions of arms to focus their attention on the institutionalization of personal power rather than on the construction of economically viable political systems.

The impact of Moscow's policy on galloping militarization is evident in the ever-increasing percentage of the gross national product devoured by defense expenditures and in the soaring imports of weapons. Given the fragility of post-colonial civilian regimes, the narrowness of the democratic base on which most of them rested, and the ease with which the military could mount coups, the proliferation of military regimes may not have been avoidable; but Moscow's arms policy made it inevitable.

First, Moscow's infusion of arms exceeded the bounds of legitimate security needs, undermining civilian rule or the paramountcy that domestic transformation had for many of the early post-independence leaders. It was Khrushchev who pioneered the policy of acceding to the requests of courted regimes regardless of the effect of the arms buildup on the government's domestic or regional policy. The open arms tap, whose responsiveness to demand corrupted Mohammed Daoud Khan, Gamal Abdel Nasser, Sukarno, Mohammed Siad Barre, and others, was to have doleful consequences for their countries. Moscow knew from the beginning that the arms they sought were intended for offensive purposes, not for defense. Its availability as an uncritical and accommodating supplier fostered a major redirection of priorities and scarce resources, away from internal development and toward high-risk foreign policies. In a number of instances it not only led to the weakening of traditional and civilian elites and authority, but also to the ascendancy of military groups for whom Soviet weapons were the bricks and mortar that buttressed their position.

Second, Moscow has no qualms about supporting any regime that is anti-imperialist, meaning anti-American; if privileged access is provided, so much the better. It is indifferent to a regime's human-rights abuses or venality. The only ideological outlook that really matters is the intensity of the anti-Americanism. Moscow may well prefer to deal with military elites than with civilian leaderships who have strong commitments to internal development and the struggle against blighted socio-economic conditions that have been described as "a Malthusian nightmare."[15] It understands that in such circumstances the West's resources have far more to offer. A Mengistu is easier to cosset than a Mugabe; an Assad and a Qaddafi easier than a Corazon Aquino or a Chadli Benjadid. For example, in Ethiopia between 1977 and 1985, the Soviets provided about $4 billion in weaponry, "but all costs for operating this swollen military machine have had to be squeezed out of the country's own meager resources"—and this during a period of drought and famine.[16] This cornucopia of Soviet arms, which "brought neither internal security nor external peace," has enabled Mengistu to maintain an army of approximately 300,000, a force

---

[15] "According to a 1981 World Bank report, 'Accelerated Development in Sub-Saharan Africa,' the population of that region will almost double in the next 20 years, and growth far outstrips production. In the 10 years ending in 1979, per capita agricultural production in sub-Saharan Africa dropped by 1.3 percent a year as the population increased by an average of 2.7 percent annually. Overall growth, in terms of per capita gross national product, was recorded at only 0.8 percent. 'For most African countries,' says the World Bank, 'the record is grim, and it is no exaggeration to talk of crisis'!" Alan Cowell, "Africa's Angry Young Men," New York Times Magazine, December 19, 1982, 39.

[16] Paul B. Henze, "The Dilemma of the Horn," The National Interest, no. 2 (Winter 1986), 65.

structure more than six times the size of the one maintained by Haile Selassie.[17] It is the antithesis of economic development. Nowhere is this more evident than in the Horn of Africa:

> The Soviets have exacerbated all the region's political problems and inhibited economic development. The whole area bristles with arms—mostly Soviet-supplied. Everyone who lives in these countries, including the rulers, enjoys less physical security than he did 25 years ago. At least half a million people in the Horn have died as a result of violence during the past two decades; at least another half million have starved. Three or four million have been uprooted and live as refugees. The Russians lack both the means and the will to remedy or reverse this situation.[18]

In Africa, especially, Moscow's subsidies to leaders—more often than not military men playing a political role for which they are not suited—consist almost exclusively of military resources to help them retain control over a restive population. Realizing that military regimes seldom rest on a stable mass base, Moscow exploits their lack of legitimacy and consequent heightened sense of vulnerability and readiness to make concessions to the patron willing to underwrite their arrogation of power. This circumstance helps explain why the Soviet-Cuban military intervention on behalf of Ethiopia, for example, which upheld the existing territorial boundaries in the region, aroused so little criticism in Africa. The preoccupation "of most African states with domestic political stability" makes them tolerant of reliance on the USSR's weaponry and defensive shield, notwithstanding the accompanying spur to militarization.[19]

On occasion, Moscow may use arms to obtain hard currency or negotiate barter agreements for goods it needs—as in the early 1980s, when it exchanged arms for wheat with the Argentine military dictatorship;[20] but its supply of arms to military regimes is prompted primarily by political, not commercial, considerations. Its quest in the early 1970s for naval support facilities in Somalia offers a clear instance of a courtship and readiness to persist in funneling weapons to a military dictator in order to retain the privileges it had obtained, despite evidence that the arms were being primed for aggressive pur-

[17] Ibid.

[18] Ibid., 71–72.

[19] Olajide Aluko, "African Response to External Intervention in Africa since Angola," *African Affairs* 80, no. 319 (April 1981), 175.

[20] Robbin F. Laird, "The Latin American Arms Market: Soviet Perceptions and Arms Transfers, 1972–82," *Soviet Union* 12, no. 3 (1985), 297.

poses.[21] Whatever the mix of considerations that affect its policy in any given situation, Moscow is not put off by the military character of any regime.

A third way in which the Soviet arms policy has militarized Third World politics is by making war a feasible option for rulers whose bent is toward regional conflict rather than regional accommodation. In his maiden speech at the U.N. General Assembly on September 24, 1985, Soviet Foreign Minister Eduard A. Shevardnadze declared, "It is not the fault of the Soviet Union that local conflicts break out and are raging in various regions of the world."[22] Since the late 1960s, the record tells a very different story. A list of the major wars between Third World countries would show that most were made possible only because of the stockpiles and assured supplies of Soviet weapons: Egypt's war in Yemen (1962–1967), Arab-Israeli wars in 1967, 1969–1970, and 1973; Ethiopia and Somalia since 1977; Vietnam and Kampuchea since 1978; the Yemens in 1979; Iran and Iraq since 1980; Libya and Chad in the 1980s. With the exception of the Indo-Pakistani war in 1965 and 1971, every major local war between Third World protagonists was started by a Soviet-armed state.

The enhanced credibility of the USSR set in motion certain unanticipated developments: by arming the elites it was courting, Moscow reinforced small-power contentiousness and heightened the prospect of conflict. Soviet arms policy has been instrumental in the venting of traditional and ingrained antagonisms on the battlefield. Moreover, most of these wars "have become coalition wars":

> Not only do Third World states successfully exploit superpower rivalries in order to gain economic and military support from Washington or Moscow: they have also managed to induce (occasionally, coerce) the aid of other regional powers. The fighting in the Iran-Iraq War takes place between the armed forces of those two states, but the war in the broadest sense—the contest for power, influence, and prestige—takes place between an alliance of Iran, Syria, and Libya, on the one hand, and Iraq, the Gulf states, Egypt, and Jordan, on the other.[23]

Without "the involvement of the superpowers as bankers, arms suppliers, ultimate guarantors, or simply influential friends," this kind of

[21] Richard B. Remnek, "The Soviet-Somali 'Arms for Access' Relationship," *Soviet Union* 10, no. 1 (1983), 74–75.

[22] *New York Times*, September 25, 1985.

[23] Eliot A. Cohen, "Distant Battles: Modern War in the Third World," *International Security* 10, no. 4 (Spring 1986), 147.

freewheeling coalition formation, explainable more in terms of megalomania than of security, could not take place;[24] and more often than not the superpower responsible for the generation and continuation of these wars is the Soviet Union.

Moscow did not create regional rivalries and tensions, which are the legacies of history, but it is responsible for the frequency with which they erupt into local wars. According to Dmitri Volskiy, a leading Soviet journalist, "attempts to hinder the natural, law-governed course of events in the 'Third World' " are what "creates hotbeds of tension there fraught with dangers of not only a local but also a global nature."[25] How true. And it is the "unnatural" system-destabilizing intrusion of vast quantities of Soviet weaponry to clients whose purposes are clearly aggressive that is the single most salient catalyst of local wars in the Third World. But Soviet analysts never discuss the quantities or character of Soviet arms transfers or speculate on their consequences for domestic or regional developments in the Third World. They explain the perpetuation of regional conflicts and the aggravation of socio-economic problems within the framework of a modernized variant of Lenin's theory of imperialism—neo-imperialism and neocolonialism:

Having found it impossible to reshape the political map of the world as it did in the past, imperialism is striving to undermine the sovereignty of liberated states in roundabout ways, making particularly active use of economic levers. . . .

Imperialism's neocolonial policy is one of the main reasons for the emergence of so-called regional conflicts and the fact that they remain unresolved.[26]

---

[24] Ibid.

[25] D. Volskiy, "Local Conflicts and International Security," *New Times*, no. 5 (January 28, 1983), 5.

[26] For example K. Brutents, *Pravda*, January 10, 1986, as translated in FBIS/USSR International Affairs, January 14, 1986, CC5; and V. Goncharov, "Economic Problems of African Countries," *International Affairs*, no. 8 (August 1986), 51–52.
The Leninist perception of the roots of Western political behavior continues to find expression in statements of Soviet leaders. In a celebratory speech on the eve of the seventieth anniversary of the Bolshevik Revolution, General Secretary Mikhail Gorbachev noted that, despite the profound differences among states of the modern world, there has been an "internationalization of world economic links" and an all-encompassing "scientific and technical revolution" that affect everyone and that raise questions of whether "capitalism is able to free itself of militarism" and whether "the capitalist system" can do without neocolonialism, "one of the sources of its present life support? In other words, is that system able to function without its unequal exchange with the Third World, which is fraught with unpredictable consequences?" FBIS/SOV, November 3, 1987, 55–57.

Even the occasional, cursory references to arms transfers, appearing in the main in articles prepared for a Western publication, give no details. Witness the contribution of Dr. Yevgeny Primakov, the Director of the USSR's Institute of World Economy and International Relations, to a symposium on "The Superpowers in the Middle East" organized by the Washington-based American Enterprise Institute for Public Policy Research: all he did was mention that the Soviet Union sells arms to some of the countries of the Middle East to help them in "their struggle against the expansionism of Israel."[27] Not a hint, though, of the more than $30 billion in arms sold to Libya and Iraq, countries distant from Israel; or of the copious quantities of weaponry supplied a bellicose Syria.

In using arms to acquire influence and privileges, Soviet leaders try to avoid becoming involved in the local wars they make possible: their aim is "to profit from local conflicts without directly taking part in them."[28] They prefer to operate behind the scenes or through surrogates, but they are deeply involved. They may not want confrontation with the United States, but they readily accept the risks entailed in priming clients bent on besting a regional adversary or undermining U.S. policy. An active participant at every critical stage of the escalation to the brink of war—and beyond—Moscow does not jeopardize its standing with major clients by curbing arms transfers.

The USSR's arms-transfer policy has affected all four phases of regional conflict. At the first stage—conflict generation—the Soviet Union as an outside power supplies weapons far beyond its client's requirements for defense or credible deterrence. This makes a military option feasible and relegates internal development and consideration of a political solution to subordinate status. Flush with weapons, the client escalates tensions and gravitates toward the use of force. Afghanistan and Egypt in the mid-1950s, Egypt and Syria in the 1960s, Somalia and the PDRY in the 1970s, Iraq and Libya in the 1980s all attest to the disruptive effect of Soviet arms-transfer policy.

At the next stage, once war has broken out, the Soviet Union intervenes directly to prevent its client's defeat. Having developed a stake in the regime's survival, Moscow pours in arms, provides the shield needed to stave off defeat (which its original intrusion helped occasion), and insulates the client from the consequences of his actions through forceful conflict management. In the 1967 and 1973 Arab-

---

[27] Yevgeny M. Primakov, "The Soviet Union's Interests: Myths and Reality," *AEI Foreign and Defense Review* 6, no. 1 (1986), 31.

[28] D'Encausse, *Ni paix ni guerre*, 116.

Israeli wars, for example, which were very costly materially and in terms of lost opportunities to improve relations with the United States, Moscow's approach to conflict management suggested that it recognized the primary, not just secondary, responsibility that it had for the untoward sequence of events.[29] It undoubtedly moved to this stage of involvement out of fear that to do otherwise would result in a severe, perhaps crippling, setback to its forward policy in the Third World, and signal the end of the strategic line initiated by Khrushchev.

After surmounting a near defeat or crisis, the client must have his military capability upgraded. At the third stage, conflict maintenance aims to ensure the integrity of the client's home base, afford him a credible military option, and in this way dissuade him from changing policy in a way that might jeopardize Soviet standing or policy. It is also a time to reap some of the fruits of engagement, and many of the best military morsels have been obtained in the early post-crisis stage of a regional conflict.

Even when Moscow has been unhappy over the foreign policy a client is pursuing, it has provided the military wherewithal. It has persevered in this course, not allowing any client to falter for lack of weaponry or to be defeated or overthrown by U.S.-supported rivals, domestic or regional. Occasionally, however, even the open arms-tap policy is inadequate, but for reasons over which Moscow has no control, as when Sadat, wanting to regain Israeli-held Egyptian territory, switched from the military to the diplomatic option and plumped his political eggs in Washington's basket at the end of the 1973 October War. But more often than not the policy is successful. In the 1980s a liberally provisioned Assad surmounted the 1982 Israeli invasion of Lebanon and consolidated his claim to being the dominant foreign actor in that strife-ridden country; and the Sandinistas countered erratic

---

[29] Most studies of the events leading up to the 1967 June War, to take one well-mined crisis, ascribe secondary, but not primary, responsibility to the Soviet Union: "Even though the Soviet Union may not have been *directly* involved in Nasser's decision to have the U.N. Force leave Sinai and the Gaza Strip and to blockade the Straits of Tiran, it was nevertheless the Soviet Union that gave Nasser grounds and motivation for acting as he did on the strength of the (falsified) information it fabricated for him and on the strength of the political and propaganda support it afforded him by its campaign justifying the Egyptian stand against Israel." Joseph Govrin, *The Six-Day War in the Mirror of Soviet-Israeli Relations: April–June 1967*, Soviet and East European Research Centre, Research Paper no. 61 (Jerusalem: Hebrew University, December 1985), 16–17. What is absent in such authoritative assessments—and is perhaps unknowable—is the role that the antecedent massive Soviet military buildup played in Nasser's calculations and readiness to go to the brink of war.

and inept attempts by the Reagan administration to generate a credible insurgency against them.

Finally, there is the stage of conflict resolution. Moscow has never been prepared to pressure a prime client to make concessions in order to promote a compromise settlement that would end the danger of war but that might in the process also entail a loss of some privileges or trigger a change of orientation in a client. It is not Soviet policy to place at risk the gains it has acquired in the course of a regional conflict in the interests of fostering regional peace and stability. During the oft-cited Soviet role at Tashkent in January 1966 in helping to end the 1965 Indo-Pakistani war, Moscow acted as conciliator, bringing together the two parties who were looking for a way out. At no time was it jeopardizing its relationship with either India or Pakistan: first, it was not exerting pressure on either side to make concessions; second, it did not possess privileges in either country that might have been lost as a consequence of its diplomatic intercession; third, it agreed to help at the request of both sides. A successful conciliator usually needs a bit of luck, and this Moscow had in the death of Indian Prime Minister Lal Bahadur Shastri, a shock that probably disposed New Delhi to make a number of crucial concessions in order to get the crisis behind it and look to its internal problems. In the Horn of Africa, there was a brief period in the spring of 1977, when Moscow tried to bring about a reconciliation between Somalia and Ethiopia by persuading them to enter into a loose confederation of sorts. But at no time did it bring heavy pressure to bear on Somalia—its client in the region at the time—probably out of fear that Siad Barre might react by curtailing Soviet privileges. That he did in fact do just that six months later was due mostly to his misjudgment, not Moscow's bungling or pressure.

The record of the past few decades reveals that Soviet arms transfers contribute to the adoption of a high-cost military policy by assorted clients, whose one shared outlook is hostility to U.S. policy, usually as crystallized in U.S. support for their regional rivals. The process that encourages a Third World leadership to pursue a military line is insidious. Only a handful of countries have the potential to undertake large-scale military expenditures—the oil-rich Middle East countries, India, Egypt, Israel, Brazil and Argentina.[30] In most cases, arms production and arms expenditures drain their economies of scarce resources that could otherwise be utilized for modernization.[31]

---

[30] A recent study of arms production and procurement in the Third World, carried out by the Stockholm International Peace Research Institute, is Michael Brzosha and Thomas Ohlson, eds., *Arms Production in the Third World* (London: Taylor & Francis, 1986).

[31] In Peru, for example, Soviet sales of weapons to the military dictatorship that ruled

This process of militarization also tends to make countries unviable as stable political systems: it wastes resources, aggravates existing ethnic, religious, racial, and subregional cleavages, and perpetuates endemic backwardness. When Third World leaders play the power game, they are the most frequent losers, while the Soviet Union is the principal gainer.

THE EVOLUTION OF REGIONAL POLITICS

Soviet policies perpetuate regional animosities; their arms institutionalize hostility.[32] They act to create the illusion that victories can be achieved easily and without risk. Without the dangerous levels of arms that have inundated the Third World since the 1960s, local wars would be far less probable and local politics, shorn of a formidable military instrument, quite different.

Take the case of Syria. Hafez Assad's truculence—and the concomitant growing threat of another Arab-Israeli war—would lack all credibility without the surfeit of Soviet weapons at his disposal and the promise of more and of protection to boot. Restricted to levels of weaponry commensurate with Syrian resources and constrained by the absence of an undemanding patron, he would be a local irritant, not a regional threat. In sustaining Syria as part of its ongoing rivalry with the United States, Moscow demonstrates its ability to keep a regional conflict perennially on the threshold of conflagration.

Though the Soviet Union's role in aggravating regional tensions is evident in the Arab-Israeli sector, and elsewhere in the Middle East, Africa, Central America, and Southern Asia, there is no warrant for the brief that no comprehensive settlement of conflicts in these areas is possible without its participation. Moscow can be a "spoiler," can block a settlement, but only provided one of the regional antagonists is committed to continued conflict. Once regional adversaries opt for accommodation, they no longer have need of the Soviet Union. In the Arab-Israeli case, both Anwar Sadat and Menachem Begin were averse to a Soviet role. Having determined to make peace, they looked to Washington and not Moscow to broker the diplomatic process.

---

from 1968 to 1980 added significantly to the country's overall foreign debt. *New York Times*, July 24, 1983. The impact of military expenditures on economic development and modernization is still in its infancy. A recent study that grapples with the range of interrelated problems is Saadet Deger, *Military Expenditures in Third World Countries: The Economic Effects* (Boston: Routledge & Kegan Paul, 1986); see chapter 10.

[32] The same argument has been made about American arms transfers, though the examples (notably Pakistan's war with India in 1965 and Israel's invasion of Lebanon in 1982) are fewer.

The very limited Soviet experience with conflict resolution has made it aware of how quickly it can be rendered irrelevant by a client and how quickly its position can be adversely affected by a significant melioration in regional tensions, as in the case of the 1979 Egyptian-Israeli peace treaty. But, as long as there are key local actors wedded to the use of force to bring about political change, Moscow is assured of a regional role. As a supplier of arms, it has little incentive to work toward regional settlements, because the reality is that nowhere in the Third World has regional reconciliation served Soviet strategic interests.

Moreover, as an outsider, unemotionally attached by religion, culture, politics, or ethnic kinship to any of its clients (no more than they are to it), it sees no reason to believe that it might benefit equally with the United States (and the West) from an end to regional conflict. Thus, the presumption must be that the Kremlin will persist in the course that has brought it the leverage it has over developments in the Third World, especially as it relates to its rivalry with the United States.

Is Moscow a perpetual outsider? Though germane to any discussion of its policy in the Third World, most of the speculation on this question arises in discussions of the future of Arab-Israeli relations.[33] The argument goes as follows. If the USSR restored diplomatic relations with Israel, it should be included as a participant in any international effort to find a solution to the Palestinian issue and fashion a comprehensive settlement of the Arab-Israeli conflict. The uncertainty arises not over its inclusion, which doubtless would occur, but over its role. Would Moscow act as an "honest broker"? Would it, once it were part of the peace process on the basis of equality with Washington, pressure its own clients in the interests of an overall settlement, at the risk of alienating them and precipitating a turn to the West? Is not a bird in the hand worth more to the Kremlin than two in the bush?

Regional politics seem destined to remain fractious and dangerous, and, barring a reversal of Soviet policy, fueled by Soviet arms and the military ambitions that prompt their acquisition. In this anarchic environment, each ruler seeks security in more weapons and a superpower connection. Regional organizations are impotent. The League of Arab States, the Organization of African Unity, the Organization of American States, among others, are unable to mediate regional disputes or defend member states. Rivalry transcends reconciliation. Di-

---

[33] For example, see Alfred L. Atherton, Jr., "The Soviet Role in the Middle East: An American View," *Middle East Journal* 39, no. 4 (Autumn 1985), 708–15.

visiveness is pandemic, cutting across every ideological, religious, political, and ethnic line. The Nonaligned Movement's failure is especially noticeable.

When NAM was created at Belgrade in September 1961, it was with the foremost aim of developing an institution for dealing with the United States and the Soviet Union. NAM's early adherents believed they could ensure their national security better through nonalignment than through alignment. However, over time, NAM has become an integral part of the U.S.-Soviet Cold War, which many members exploit for their own ends. By the 1970s, it no longer had the relatively coherent and convergent world outlook combined with an essential complementarity of economic and political interests that had characterized the 1960s. With the passing of the charismatic Third World leaders (Nehru, Nasser, Nkrumah, Sukarno, U Nu, Boumédienne), the post-independence generation of leaders have turned out to be less international-minded, more preoccupied with narrow regional and national issues. Having for the most part come to power by bullets not ballots, they lack legitimacy and must concentrate on the task of retaining power. For this they have found the Soviet Union invaluable.

Moscow sees that well-armed client states do not seek fulfillment of national ambitions through bargaining and compromise; nor are they easy prey to U.S. pressure or blandishments. For example, during a visit to Syria in late 1985, Karen Brutents, deputy chief of the International Department of the CPSU's Central Committee and influential authority on Third World developments, lauded Arab opposition to Washington's "capitulationist solutions" to the Palestinian problem and, in particular, Syria's role "in confronting the imperialist plans aimed at imposing unilateral deals similar to the Camp David agreements" (that is, Syria's thwarting of the U.S. effort to bring about a peace treaty between Lebanon and Israel similar to the one signed by Egypt with Israel); he also emphasized that those Arabs who resist "imperialism" (the United States) "have the support of friends and allies. This will lead to the failure of the imperialist plans."[34] If there is Soviet uneasiness over Syria's policy, it has not led Moscow to reappraise the essential correctness of its support for "Arab opposition to imperialist plans in the Middle East."

The Third World has become the cockpit of competition, in important measure because of what the Soviet Union has done. Its environment of endemic conflict and instability is conducive to the advancement of a variety of Soviet objectives, and Moscow has adapted to it

[34] FBIS/USSR International Affairs, November 14, 1985, H4–H6.

quite adeptly and is most unlikely to expend much effort or resources in quixotic attempts to bring "progress" or foster "socialism."

THE OPERATING STYLE OF THE UNITED STATES

A key aim of Soviet policy is prevention of *Pax Americana* in the Third World. From any perspective, Moscow has reason for satisfaction. It can look back to the 1950s and 1960s with a sense of accomplishment, of having profoundly altered the regional environment in ways that have frustrated U.S. ambitions and jeopardized U.S. interests. With increasing regularity, the United States finds its diplomatic, political, military, economic, and cultural aims and policies thwarted as a consequence of Soviet probes and inputs. Indubitably, at the end of 1980s, the strategic position of the United States in all areas of the Third World (it will be recalled that this term does not include China) is worse than it was in the mid-1950s, when Khrushchev launched his forward policy.

Soviet involvement in the Third World has had a direct impact on U.S. foreign policy in three ways. It has limited U.S. options; raised the costs of safeguarding U.S. interests; and intensified anti-Americanism.

Time and again—in every Arab-Israeli war from 1967 on, and in Libya, the PDRY, Lebanon, and Nicaragua in the 1980s—Washington's military options have been limited by the presence of Soviet power. Of necessity, "vital interests" have had to be interpreted more restrictively, in a way that largely precludes the use of military means to help bring about a political change of alignment or an improvement in the political-military situation of a pro-U.S. client regime. This sharply narrowed strategic outlook is, of course, a consequence of the strong domestic pressures that arose out of the Vietnam experience. Each succeeding administration has attempted to come to grips with the constraints domestic politics imposes on the use of force.[35] The

---

[35] During the Reagan administration, Secretary of Defense Caspar Weinberger was in the forefront of those who warned of the limits of military power and the need for utilizing it only in certain, clearly defined circumstances. He suggested six criteria be applied before U.S. combat forces are used: (1) the particular situation must be "deemed vital to our national interest or that of our allies"; (2) once deployed, the forces committed should be sufficient "to achieve our objectives"; (3) the political and military objectives should be clearly defined; (4) "the relationship between our objectives and the forces we have committed—their size, composition, and disposition—must be continually reassessed and adjusted as necessary"; (5) before deploying forces abroad, "there must be some reasonable assurance we will have the support of the American people and their elected representatives in Congress"; and (6) the commitment of combat forces should

present fear of involvement in another Vietnam and the prevalence of countervailing Soviet power have changed the ability of the United States to act forcefully in ambiguous and complex political situations.

An illustrative case is that of Lebanon, a country that has never been viewed as a "vital national interest." In July 1958 the U.S. marines landed, unopposed, in response to a request from the Lebanese government for protection against pro-Nasserist groups bent on a seizure of power and in order to be positioned for a thrust into Iraq (or so it was conceived at the time) in the event that forces loyal to the just-deposed Hashemite monarch would coalesce to resist the putschists. The Lebanese part of the mission was a success. Khrushchev lacked the military power to do anything other than denounce the United States and threaten unspecified responses, and U.S. domestic opinion supported the President's use of military power.

However, in the summer of 1982, shortly after the Israeli invasion of Lebanon and the complex sequence of events that it triggered, the U.S. position and its available options were very different. In August and again in September, U.S. marines were despatched to Lebanon as part of a non-U.N. multinational peacekeeping effort—initially, to safeguard the evacuation of PLO forces from Beirut; then, to protect the Palestinians in the refugee camps and to prop up the beleaguered government of Amin Gemayel. This time, however, the United States was outmaneuvered by Soviet-backed Syrian power, bloodied, stymied, and forced to pull out of Lebanon in February 1984. Not even the deployment of four carrier task-force groups—a far larger force than the strictly local dimensions would normally have dictated—could compensate for the egregious misfit between objectives and constraints, the latter including the fractious situation in Lebanon, growing opposition at home, and a looming Soviet involvement should matters escalate to open conflict between Israel and Syria.

Looking only at the Soviet factor, it is clear that Moscow's military presence was enough to frustrate Washington's policy, which, admittedly, was poorly defined. The Soviets added only a few ships to their Mediterranean Fleet, which kept well clear of the U.S. Navy; the Soviet naval presence, though not a major inhibition on day-to-day operations of the U.S. fleet, had constantly to be factored into the calculations of the U.S. commander in the area. The most telling Soviet blows were struck through the Syrians. Hafez Assad, handsomely resupplied with arms and protected by a Soviet-manned thickened air

---

be a last resort. Speech to the National Press Club in Washington, D.C., on November 28, 1984.

defense system, unleashed his proxies and allies of convenience to dog Washington's ill-conceived involvement in Lebanon: the peacekeeping force that was to protect Gemayel's fledgling government and nudge him toward a formal reconciliation with Israel could not withstand the bitter communal violence triggered by Syria and had to be withdrawn in February 1984; the U.S.-engineered Israeli-Lebanese agreement of May 17, 1983, had to be scrapped by the Lebanese government a year later; and the effort to extend the Camp David peace process to include Lebanon and possibly Jordan was shelved indefinitely. Never has the ability of the Soviet Union to subvert a U.S. initiative in the Middle East through a strengthening of an anti-U.S. client been more dramatically displayed. Yuri Glukhov summed up Moscow's satisfaction at having stymied Washington's objectives:

> We are witnessing the collapse of Washington's Near East strategy elaborated at Camp David and later updated as the "Reagan Plan."
>
> The mirror of Lebanon's tragedy reflects particularly clearly the grave consequences which resulted from Washington's so-called "peace initiatives," the course of dealing with Arab countries "separately," in isolation. As a result, the complex problems, far from being unraveled, were drawn still tighter.[36]

Soviet intrusiveness raises the costs to the United States of maintaining extensive commitments and interests in the Third World and requires the development of forces that can cope with a wide range of contingencies.[37] Lebanon, a minor theater, has proved an expensive proposition. So has Nicaragua. Subsidized by the Soviet bloc, it drains U.S. political assets and resources in an area of intrinsic indifference to the Kremlin. Though not the bargain that Vietnam was, Nicaragua brings Moscow big political-military returns at the expense of the United States and is therefore a strategically sound long-term investment. It focuses attention on the seeming impotence of American power and exacerbates tension between Washington and the countries of Latin America and Western Europe. Considering Moscow's (and Havana's) modest expenditures (estimates vary, but $1 billion in aid between 1980 and 1985 is the generally cited figure), aid to Nicaragua has been extremely cost-effective.

As the Soviet Union keeps upping the ante of regional stakes, the

---

[36] FBIS/USSR International Affairs, February 23, 1984, H1.

[37] U.S. Secretary of Defense, *Annual Report to the Congress: Fiscal Year 1985* (Washington, D.C.: Superintendent of Documents, February 1, 1984), 36–37, 50–53, 173–84.

United States has followed suit, increasing defense spending on conventional forces and the aid packages given to prime clients. In the mid-1980s, Israel, Egypt, and Pakistan were the principal non-NATO recipients. El Salvador was fourth in importance, receiving more than $1 billion in economic assistance and upwards of $500 million in military assistance between 1983 and 1986. That a strategically and militarily minor country attracts such sizable outlays suggests that the "Great Game" the superpowers are engaged in will be a long and costly affair.

Moscow has used all available instruments of policy to force the United States into extensive outlays of resources in Third World areas. Its aim, primarily political, is to elicit a U.S. effort that is disproportionate to Soviet outlays and to the intrinsic strategic importance of the region, the crisis, or the protagonist(s). Unimaginative and indecisive American responses to problems such as Nicaragua increase anti-Americanism and must encourage Moscow. In Washington's growing frustration with developments in the Third World and regularly proclaimed intention to combat low intensity conflict and international terrorism, Moscow probably espies the seed of future opportunities.

Anti-Americanism is the outgrowth of decolonization, the pervasiveness of U.S. power and influence, and the rising centrality of mass media and mass politics in the domestic calculations of Third World rulers. It is a complex phenomenon the Kremlin exploits in its ongoing competition with the United States in the Third World.

The Soviet Union wages psychological war against the United States and spends lavishly on efforts to attract supporters and diminish U.S. positions and prestige. The Russian phrase *aktivniye meropriyatiya* (active measures) connotes a range of techniques and intrigues that includes disinformation, "media manipulations, forgeries, calculated rumors, falsely attributed radio broadcasts, and the activities of agents of influence."[38] The impact of these efforts is difficult to assess. One former U.S. official argues that it is considerable because governments in the Third World, "often unstable, economically stressed and lacking tested political institutions are more vulnerable to covert manipulation"; that the Soviet Union's "active measures" occasionally help bring to power a regime subject to its influence; and that they distract Third World leaders from "their primary task—development."[39]

[38] Lawrence S. Eagleburger, "Unacceptable Intervention: Soviet Active Measures," *NATO Review* 31, no. 1 (1983), 9.
[39] Ibid.

Indeed, as matters now stand, whereas in Western countries Soviet-sponsored communist front organizations can help mobilize public opinion against U.S. policy, in the Third World the situation differs significantly: most regimes, being dictatorships, do not permit private groups to demonstrate freely and all protest movements are subject to government control. Moreover, in such political systems, the communists are generally not trusted and are watched very closely, even though the government may have a pro-Soviet policy orientation.[40]

There is also a paradox operative: a dose of anti-Americanism may well be essential for the political well-being of pro-American regimes. It is useful in demonstrating independence, in pressing requests for increased U.S. commitments, and in undercutting the opposition's attempts to develop a mass base, in countries such as India and Egypt which permit open criticism of official policy.

For Moscow, two things are self-evident: anti-Americanism in the Third World is growing, and it complicates U.S. diplomacy and restrains pro-American clients from granting privileges. These are spurs enough for continued Soviet efforts to foster anti-Americanism.

Moscow's Policy

Khrushchev transformed the Cold War that followed the Second World War from a struggle to accommodate contrasting conceptions of security on the Eurasian land mass to a rivalry for position and influence in all regions of the world. In extending Soviet ambitions into the Third World, Khrushchev globalized Soviet-American relations—and the tensions that permeated their relationship. Whatever he may have intended, his policies, continued and broadened by his successors, doomed prospects for a long-term improvement in relations with the United States. Their continuation does not augur well for the future.

The USSR's overarching aim in the Third World is the weakening of American power. It acquires clients for reasons as varied as their chance availability, the access they give to strategic choke points, and the difficulties their pro-Soviet stance create for the United States. All are expendable, even Communist Afghanistan, whose contiguity brought into play traditional Russian ruthlessness toward weaker neighbors. Moscow invests for political and military payoffs. A patient, imperial-minded patron, it does not require immediate returns or in-

---

[40] Alvin Z. Rubinstein and Donald E. Smith, eds., *Anti-Americanism in the Third World* (New York: Praeger, 1985), 8–9.

sist on complete compliance to all Soviet preferences. As long as a relationship improves the strategic context within which Soviet diplomacy operates and keeps the United States off balance or at a disadvantage, it will be sustained.

Through involvement in the Third World, and with comparatively modest outlays, Moscow has wrought changes in the international environment in a number of ways that have strengthened the USSR's security and justified its strategic approach to coping with the United States. Aid to North Vietnam was a stunning success, draining American wealth and power, but so also was support for Cuba, Syria, India, Egypt (for almost twenty years), the PDRY, Angola, and Nicaragua, among others. It prompted a profligate squandering of resources. Of greater long-term consequence, it hobbled American power, and ultimately made it more manageable. Lenin's expectation that the Third World would undo "imperialism" is not so far off the mark in the 1980s as it seemed in the 1950s.

In the Third World, Soviet leaders have found an arena for engaging the United States in conditions that not only do not place any part of the Soviet imperial system in jeopardy but that permit setbacks to be absorbed without calling into question the wisdom of the policy itself. The same is not true for the United States, whose power, position, and prestige have steadily eroded. All of this must reinforce Moscow's conviction in the essential correctness of "peaceful coexistence" as a "form of class struggle between socialism and capitalism," as a suitable strategy for competing or cooperating with the United States, depending on circumstances.

Khrushchev's confidence in the inevitability of socialism in the Third World is not shared by his successors. The Third World is far more anarchic, polarized, and conflict-ridden than it was; its problems certainly seem insoluble. Soviet leaders see generally deteriorating economic conditions and intensifying political tensions, and what they now know about elites in the Third World reinforces their cynicism and their indifference to the plight of peoples in the regimes they support. None of this, however, vitiates the case for continued involvement.

In the course of searching for ways of countering American power, Moscow has learned to appreciate the utility of the Third World. Its wishes and inputs are important. Almost every issue of consequence—the main exception being regional and international issues with a strong economic dimension—has a Soviet component. The mesh between Soviet strengths and clients' needs makes for a durable political alignment. Having positioned itself on the Third World stage, the Soviet leadership is not about to tamper with the approach that has brought it a remarkable array of successes. In no other part of the world has Moscow so much to show for its efforts, since the mid-1950s. Khrushchev's policy has stood the test of time.

CHAPTER EIGHT

Prospects

The Chinese say it is very difficult to make predictions—especially about the future. The advent to power of Mikhail Gorbachev and a new generation of Soviet leaders—the class of the 1956 twentieth party congress—has occasioned a need for fresh assessments of Soviet policy and probable choices in the Third World in the years ahead. It goes without saying that the Kremlin will attend to its vital interests in Europe and the Far East and in negotiations with the United States in the broad field of arms control and disarmament. Beyond that, there are the questions of how Moscow will respond to opportunities in the Third World, the needs of prized clients, setbacks and pitfalls in different regions, and its perceptions of the benefits and costs attending alternative courses of action.

In assessing the whys and wherefores of Soviet policy, it is important to remember that successes (like setbacks) exist in the eye of the beholder. What Moscow considers an achievement may not be so viewed in Washington, and vice versa. I would suggest that since the mid-1950s Soviet leaders have regarded the following as criteria of "success" sufficient to warrant continuation of a line of policy:

1. diplomatic normalization;
2. establishment of an economic and/or military presence;
3. privileged military access;
4. opposition by a client/target to "imperialism" (the United States);
5. weakened U.S. influence;
6. consolidation of regimes with a Marxist-Leninist or pro-Soviet orientation;
7. greater reliance on the Soviet Union;
8. enhanced position of local communist parties;
9. creation of a Soviet-type vanguard party.

Of the nine criteria, only the first five are fundamentally significant, the others being welcomed gains but of lesser importance. What runs through them is a strategic-military dimension which turns out to be

259

crucial for the Kremlin. However, as one would expect, the mix of considerations influencing Soviet policy varies, depending on the re-gional environment, the state of Soviet-American relations, the oppor-tunities and probable costs, and the tension between short-term pros-pects and long-term objectives.

The notion of strategic context is a key to understanding what Mos-cow regards as success. Inherent in the policies that impel Soviet lead-ers and explain why they persist in believing that the game is worth the candle is their quest for local and regional advantages that make the general environment more conducive to the advancement of So-viet aims. Thus, in considering criteria for evaluating Soviet policy, I would suggest, in order of importance, (1) the changed configuration of regional alignments that emerge as a consequence of Soviet behav-ior; (2) the extent to which U.S. policy or interests are undermined; and (3) the increase in Soviet influence or privileges in specific coun-tries or movements.

Soviet strategy is not all of a piece but a quiltwork of adaptations. Nonetheless, there is an underlying conceptual and structural coher-ence, manifested in a restless probing for advantage, exacerbation of anti-Americanism, and instigation of the militarization of regional pol-itics that makes the USSR a sought-after patron. The opportune ac-commodation to changing conditions and alignments in the Third World is undertaken always with an eye toward these objectives.[1] A consistency over time in the pattern of reaction and response makes it likely that what is being observed is either a strategy or a shared stra-tegic outlook. All of this, it should be noted, is adduced from what the Soviets do, because there is no discussion of the assumptions or aims underlying their policies in the Third World to be found in Soviet writings. Western treatises on Soviet strategy must ultimately rely on inferences derived from a combination of, mainly, Soviet actions, and, marginally, putatively relevant official statements.

COMPARING ERAS

The youth of the Gorbachev era invites comparison with the Khru-shchev era of more than thirty years ago. Though no two situations or sets of circumstances are exactly alike, the task of locating Gorbachev's Third World policy somewhere along the spectrum of probable be-

[1] Russell L. Ackoff and Fred E. Emery, *On Purposeful Systems* (Chicago: Aldine-Ather-ton, 1972), 14, note that "an object behaves purposefully if it continues to pursue the same goal by changing its behavior as conditions change."

havior may be facilitated by examining essential similarities and differences between Gorbachev's approach and Khrushchev's.

The similarities are striking:

1. the struggle for power at a time of mounting economic and political dilemmas;

2. the quest for rationalization of Soviet–East European economic relationships, subject to Moscow's strategic-military control;

3. the need to improve relations with the United States and Western Europe;

4. the readiness to pursue objectives in the Third World though alert to their possibly adverse consequences for Soviet-American relations.

First, in the struggle for political ascendancy, each had to revamp the structure of power that he inherited. The key to Khrushchev's success was de-Stalinization; for Gorbachev it is de-Brezhnevization. Whereas de-Stalinization entailed the end of one-man rule that rested on the tyrannization of the party by the secret police and the restoration of the party as the preeminent political institution of Soviet society, de-Brezhnevization requires renewal of the middle-level bureaucracies that administer the country's economic, social, and political institutions. Gorbachev appears to have consolidated his position as the leading figure in the CPSU. Having staffed the Politburo, the Secretariat, and the Central Committee with likeminded contemporaries, he must now ensure that they impose his priorities and values on the various levels (national, republic, *obkom, raikom*) of the political system and implement his "new political thinking." De-Brezhnevization is essential for the success of his campaign to modernize the economy, weed out corruption, and foster the acceleration (*uskoreniye*) of economic development. Gorbachev's quest for *perestroika* (restructuring) entails more than just reform: it puts in jeopardy the Soviet people's long-held expectations of job security and risks unanticipated disruptive developments. Accordingly, he may be forced to a more modest setting of his sights by the obdurate resistance of the bureaucracies that flourished during the Brezhnev, Andropov, and Chernenko periods; for, as Khrushchev learned, wielding political power does not guarantee one the ability to transform the way in which the economy is operated.

Second, Eastern Europe is no less a problem for Gorbachev than it was for Khrushchev. In the past, when confronted with a choice between viability and cohesion, Moscow opted for the latter. Its absorption with security overshadowed its willingness to permit more rational, less exploitative economic relationships with its East European satellites. Khrushchev sought to decentralize the empire that Stalin had created from 1945 to 1953, to enhance its economic utility to the Soviet Union, but he was not prepared for the disruptive tidal consequences of de-Stalinization. As matters turned out, the effort at imperial decompression threatened the very foundations of Soviet rule. His successors groped unsuccessfully for a formula that would foster sustained economic growth and yet permit a considerable measure of autonomy within politically tolerable parameters. Brezhnev tried to loosen things up in Comecon, encouraging a degree of specialization and greater integration among the members, but Moscow's insistence on ultimate administrative and political control reinforced propensities toward bureaucratic inertia and innate conservatism in dealing with economic issues. Czechoslovakia in the late 1960s, Poland in the 1980s, and Romania throughout the Ceauşescu era attest to Moscow's continuing difficulties in extracting economic, political, cultural, or ideological benefit from its East European imperial system. Its experience bears out Winston Churchill's comment in 1944 that Russia "is a great beast . . . and it is not possible to keep her from eating, especially since she now lies in the middle of her victims," but she will not have an easy time digesting her prey.[2]

Gorbachev realizes the danger of economic and political reform in Eastern Europe. Soon after he came to power, Moscow expressed concern over the persistence with which the nationalism and national interests of individual East European countries complicated Soviet objectives in the socialist camp.[3] The call for bloc cohesion to counter "imperialism's anticommunist crusade" has not, however, been followed up by any specific or long-term initiatives. Gorbachev is undecided over what to do. Vladimir V. Kusin, Deputy Director of Research and Analysis for Radio Free Europe, nicely describes his behavior to date:

> He seems to have recognized that there are limits that he himself cannot overstep, as well as problems that his lesser allies have to cope with in their own way. He did not relax the Soviet grip on the area to the point where disintegration might, or almost certainly would, ensue. He has eschewed endorsing market-based reform for individual countries or as an underpinning of CMEA. He

[2] Quoted in John Lukacs, *A History of the Cold War*, 3d ed. (New York: Doubleday, 1966), 250.
[3] For example, *Pravda*, June 21, 1985.

has prodded all of the client states into domestic action designed to increase efficiency, discipline, and thrift, and he asked them to cut corruption and abuse of power. He affirmed Soviet primacy in coordinating the way the East-West relationship was to be shaped and conducted.

Nevertheless, Gorbachev has fine-tuned rather than bulldozed. . . . In other words, in not acting rashly either in tightening or in relaxing Soviet control over the area, Gorbachev has acted optimally. . . .

In at least one respect Gorbachev has so far failed to provide an adequate answer to the East European challenge. He has not charted a credible path toward making the region economically healthy. . . . From any perspective, Marxist or not, this shakiness of the economic base should be cause for considerable concern.[4]

A third similarity pertains to the problem of dealing with the West, particularly the United States. Khrushchev sought normalization of relations with the countries of Western Europe and the West's recognition of the territorial status quo in Europe, something that Brezhnev achieved at the Helsinki Conference in 1975; Gorbachev seems content to build on the status quo bequeathed to him. U.S.-Soviet relations in the late 1980s, as in the late 1950s, are in a state of flux in important measure because of the dynamics of rivalry in the Third World. Normalization is on the agenda but remains elusive: Khrushchev experienced crises over Berlin and Cuba; Gorbachev is faced by the Strategic Defense Initiative (SDI), Afghanistan, and Nicaragua; Khrushchev had knotty arms-control issues to tackle, and so has Gorbachev. Nonetheless, Gorbachev, like Khrushchev, was able to set in motion initiatives that conveyed a sense of the centrality that Moscow places on the U.S.-Soviet relationship. Developing better relations with the United States remains a pressing interest and for much the same reasons: the USSR's need for Western technology and credits; its quest for stability in Europe; concern over China; and interest in limiting or at least stabilizing the nuclear relationship.

Finally, Gorbachev seems determined to continue an ambitious, albeit less dangerous, course in the Third World. The essential continuity in the policy pioneered by Khrushchev, driven forward by Brezhnev and sustained by Gorbachev, suggests that it enjoys solid support among the key oligarchs in the party, military, and government, notwithstanding periodic setbacks and possible differences over

4 Vladimir V. Kusin, "Gorbachev and East Europe," *Problems of Communism* 35, no. 1 (January–February 1986), 53.

particular aspects of the overall policy. Nowhere in the Third World, other than in Afghanistan, is there yet any change in basic Soviet aims.

Before turning to the equally important differences between the two eras, let us note one change, minor in itself, that may, however, have long-term significance. Under Khrushchev, the slogan "peaceful competition" was emblazoned everywhere. He took it seriously and believed that the Soviet experience could serve as a model for the world, especially in the newly independent countries of Africa, Asia, and the Middle East. By the 1970s the slogan had been dropped, Brezhnev realizing that the Soviet Union was not going to catch up and surpass the U.S. economy and move into the communist stage of bountiful production and consumption by the next decade. Gorbachev, too, is realist enough to know that there is no possibility of the Soviet Union's competing economically with the United States in the foreseeable future. This modified expectation could entail a fundamental change of outlook and policy, in which his determination to ensure that the Soviet Union remains a world power will then, presumably, have to be based on military, not economic, strength.

There have been a number of changes in the international situation and in the Soviet-American relationship which must make Gorbachev's foreign policy outlook different from Khrushchev's and which must influence Soviet policy in the future:

1. Gorbachev's USSR is far stronger and is a credible nuclear power;
2. the Far East is a major foreign policy problem;
3. U.S. influence in the international system is less in the 1980s than it was in the 1950s;
4. Gorbachev has many more options in the Third World.

First, whereas in the 1950s the Soviet Union was a significantly weaker military power, with no credible nuclear force and no long-range bomber or SLBM capability, in the 1980s it enjoys essential equivalence or parity with the United States in the nuclear field. Khrushchev operated from military inferiority, but Gorbachev commands an imposing array of powerful forces. Whereas Khrushchev's reach was continental, Gorbachev's is global; and, whereas Khrushchev was driven by a need to catch up to the United States in strategic weapons or dramatically offset it with lesser systems, Gorbachev's problem is how to preserve the reliance on mutual assured destruction (MAD), confine SDI, and use political means to keep the arms race from draining away resources needed for domestic modernization.

Gorbachev's interest in stabilizing the nuclear arms relationship seems serious. In January 1986 he issued a major statement on arms control, which among other things called for deep cuts in offensive forces, an end to nuclear testing, and development of appropriate verification procedures. At the twenty-seventh congress of the CPSU, in February 1986, he discussed the problem at greater length and with considerable candor:

> The character of present-day weapons leaves a country no hope of safeguarding itself solely with military and technical means, for example, by building up a defense system, even the most powerful one. The task of ensuring security is increasingly seen as a political problem, and it can only be resolved by political means. ... Security cannot be built endlessly on fear of retaliation, in other words, on the doctrines of "containment" or "deterrence." Apart from the absurdity and amorality of a situation in which the whole world becomes a nuclear hostage, these doctrines encourage an arms race that may sooner or later go out of control.
>
> In the context of the relations between the USSR and the USA, security can only be mutual. ... The highest wisdom is not in caring exclusively for oneself, especially to the detriment of the other side. It is vital that all should feel equally secure, for the fears and anxieties of the nuclear age generate unpredictability in politics and concrete actions.

Though dismissing the policies that are pillars of Western security (containment and deterrence), Gorbachev's implicit call for strategic stability and renewed commitment to the SALT/START (Strategic Arms Reduction Talks) process elicited receptive reactions in the West and led to the first major arms-control agreement since the negotiation of the SALT I treaty in May 1972. The signing, on December 8, 1987, during the Gorbachev-Reagan summit in Washington, D.C., of a treaty eliminating shorter- and medium-range missiles (those with ranges between 300 and 3,400 miles) is a major development, not least because of the complex and extensive on-site verification procedures that are mandated.[5] However, it may be years before we are in a position to determine whether the INF (Intermediate Nuclear Force) treaty, as it is generally called, is a prelude to deeper arms reductions, not only of nuclear weapons but of conventional force levels as well; whether it is a turning point in U.S.-Soviet relations, or primarily a new plateau in the U.S.-Soviet nuclear relationship.

[5] *New York Times*, December 9, 1987.

Unlike Khrushchev, whose main problem in the nuclear field was to catch up to the United States, Gorbachev's is to keep abreast of qualitative advances. Concretely, he would like to contain the SDI genie in the laboratory in order to forestall a new escalation in defense expenditures and avoid straining the heavily burdened Soviet economy. He needs the respite to replace aging capital stock and physical plant and to train people to operate new capital equipment. Though better positioned militarily, he faces tougher obstacles in arms control: the issues are more complex, more interrelated, more momentous in their potential consequences than in Khrushchev's day.

Gorbachev is adept in projecting an image of reasonableness and pragmatism abroad, but he is far more respectful of the military than Khrushchev was, and far less likely to be high-handed with them in his efforts to trim defense expenditures. Today, the military may be even more influential in commanding scarce resources, partly because of the U.S. arms buildup under the Reagan administration and partly because of the mushrooming costs of defense modernization. The world is a more dangerous place for the Soviet Union than it was in the 1950s. Then, the only military threat was the American nuclear capability, which, while real enough, was sheathed for deterrent purposes. In present circumstances, however, besides the ever-present nuclear problem, NATO forces are stronger relative to Soviet-bloc forces than they were thirty years ago; China is an antagonist not an ally; the West and Japan are widening the gap in military-related technologies; and commitments in different parts of the Third World complicate the military's state of preparedness.

Second, the Far East is a more serious foreign policy problem for Gorbachev than it was for Khrushchev. Sino-Soviet relations turned sour under Khrushchev, though not until the late 1950s. The twin shocks of de-Stalinization and détente with the West rocked Mao Tse-tung's belief in a bipolar world that would keep the Soviet Union and the United States ideological-political antagonists. When Khrushchev's espousal of "peaceful coexistence" and doctrinal revision asserting that war was no longer "fatalistically inevitable"—the ideological rationale for Moscow's unwillingness to use its nuclear power on China's behalf to regain Taiwan—came into conflict with Mao's revolutionary line, then personal antipathies further worsened the deteriorating political relationship.

Khrushchev had no reason to fear China militarily; Gorbachev does have. Indeed, for the first time since the 1920s and 1930s, a Soviet leadership has cause for concern over the threat to its security from an Asian power. Khrushchev squandered Stalin's bequest of a military-political alliance with a dependent, ideologically congenial China. Gorbachev must find a way of restoring normality to a relationship that has profound implications for Moscow's future in the Far East and for U.S.-Soviet relations as well.

In a major speech delivered in Vladivostok on July 28, 1986, Gorbachev spoke of "the need for an urgent, radical break with many of the conventional approaches to foreign policy."[6] With the USSR's two-front problem in mind, he compared the situation in the Far East with that in Europe, noting that "the Pacific region as a whole is not yet militarized to the same extent as the European region," but the potential for this happening "is truly enormous and the consequences extremely dangerous." Declaring that the Soviet Union sought to improve bilateral relations with all the countries in the area, he addressed directly for the first time "the three obstacles" raised by the Chinese as preconditions for an improvement in Sino-Soviet relations: Mongolia, Afghanistan, and Kampuchea. He extended three conciliatory olive twigs, saying that "the question of withdrawing a considerable number of Soviet troops from Mongolia is being examined" by Moscow and Ulan Bator; that the Soviet government would withdraw six regiments from Afghanistan by the end of 1986; and that the Kampuchean issue "depends on the normalization of Chinese-Vietnamese relations." He also called for expanded economic cooperation, observing that "the mutually complementary nature of the Soviet and Chinese economies which has been historically established, offers big opportunities for the expansion of these ties, including in the border region." Gorbachev held out the prospect of concessions on long-festering border issues and joint cooperation on an Amur River basin waters project, a railroad linking the Xinjiang Uygur Autonomous Region and Soviet Kazakhstan. He is saying all the right things, but one swallow does not make a spring.

There have been a flurry of economic activity and a modest expansion of trade and cultural contacts between the Soviet Union and China, but to become significant they must be impelled by a political will to normalize all aspects of the relationship. This has so far been absent, because of China's insistence on progress in overcoming "the three obstacles." In the decade and more since Mao died, Moscow has waited, largely in vain, for the post-Mao leadership to reciprocate its interest in such a reconciliation. In the meantime, it has seen extraor-

[6] The quotes from Gorbachev's Vladivostok speech are taken from the translation in FBIS/USSR National Affairs, July 29, 1986, R11–R18.

dinary leaps forward in Sino-American and Sino-Japanese relations, and in China's pace of economic modernization.

A massive military deployment, of proportions unknown in most of the Khrushchev era, defines Gorbachev's Far East policy. Accordingly, his efforts to improve relations with China (and Japan) founder on an inherent "contradiction": Moscow professes goodwill but brandishes military power, including increase in the size of the Soviet Pacific Fleet and the acquisition of air and port facilities at Da Nang and Cam Ranh Bay in Vietnam and Wattay airport in Laos. To these must be added the continuously modernized conventional capabilities of the approximately 25–30 percent of its army and tactical aircraft positioned against China. Any meaningful improvement in Sino-Soviet economic and political relations would seem to be hostage to Moscow's penchant for relying on military power to foster diplomatic objectives. It will be interesting to see whether Gorbachev, in the interest of signalling peaceful intent to Beijing, thins out the approximately 75,000–100,000 Soviet troops stationed in Mongolia—an area that is stable, securely in the Soviet camp, and not susceptible to Chinese inroads, much less Chinese threats.

Japan also poses problems for Gorbachev. His intense interest in enlisting Japan's assistance for the economic development of Siberia and in exploiting Japanese-American trade tensions comes a cropper because of Japan's deep-rooted distrust of the Soviet Union. In particular, Japan fears the USSR's military threat to its sea lanes of communication and Soviet political intransigence on·the issue of the "northern territories" (the Soviet-occupied and militarized islands of Etorofu, Kunashiri, Shikotan and Habomai in the southern Kurils, off Hokkaido). The Japanese remember Khrushchev's quip that the Soviet Union will return the northern territories "when shrimps learn to whistle." Their reservations about closer ties with the USSR are not easily overcome by goodwill visits, such as the one by Eduard Shevardnadze in January 1986, the first by a Soviet foreign minister in ten years. Just as their suspicion of the Soviet Union is stronger than their desire for trade, so, too, is the USSR's belief in the efficacy of power and pressure stronger than its need for Japanese investment and technology. Moscow is patient: witness Gorbachev's cancellation of a planned visit in January 1987 when the Japanese refused to accept his condition that the issue of the northern territories should not be raised. Meanwhile, Soviet analysts have reason to feel vindicated by growing U.S.-Japanese economic tensions; they have long insisted that Japan will have serious economic troubles with the United States and that these will inevitably bring Japan to look to the Soviet Union for trade and raw materials—and on Soviet terms.

This outlook highlights the third difference between the Khrushchev and Gorbachev eras. The overall strategic environment within which the Soviet-American rivalry operates has become far less congenial to the United States than formerly and perhaps better suited to the advancement of Soviet than of American purposes. Relatively speaking, the Soviet Union's geostrategic, military, political, and even economic situation may be better than that of the United States. Gorbachev's Soviet Union has major problems, but so does the United States. The USSR is not a backward country. Indeed, in terms of resource potential, it may be far better positioned to expand its economic strength in the twenty-first century than any other country in the world. It alone is capable of pursuing a policy of autarky. True, the Soviet economy lags perennially behind countries of the West and Japan, but to lag behind is not to falter. The Soviet Union can absorb increased military spending by squeezing a nationalistic and politically compliant population. Lagging behind the United States by five or even ten years in some high-tech military fields does not mean that the USSR is becoming increasingly weaker militarily or unable to pursue the kinds of diverse policies that it has over the past thirty years— witness its commanding lead in the late 1980s in the number of space launches and experience in manning orbiting stations. Gorbachev is realist enough to appreciate that Soviet militarism drains men and resources and keeps the USSR from modernizing as extensively as he would like. But he is probably also ideologue enough to sense that the U.S. economy has profound problems (for example, the chronic U.S. balance-of-payments deficit, the Third World indebtedness, and the rising pressures for protectionism), any one of which could catapult the Western world into a depression having severe domestic social, economic, political, and military consequences. Though it is beyond the scope of this study to explore which of the two superpowers is likely to emerge in a stronger position at the end of the century or what are the implications of the various possibilities, such considerations must be part of Gorbachev's thinking about his foreign policy options.

Finally, Gorbachev's policy toward the Third World is significantly different from Khrushchev's in that it seeks not merely strategic denial, but strategic advantage: the weakening of U.S. influence regionally and globally, and the dissipation of its resources in areas of marginal utility to the Soviet Union. Judging by preliminary evidence, Gorbachev is prepared to exploit further the cost-effective indirect strategy of frustrating U.S. policy and aggravating discord in the Western alliance that his predecessors stumbled upon and gave their consensual support to over a period of three decades.

Khrushchev's ventures in the Third World were an understandable defensive counter to the U.S. policy of containment. They also mirrored the man's optimism and ideological conviction of the inevitability of socialism as a socio-political system that would attract newly independent countries in the era of decolonization and aversion to capitalism. The heavy economic component of early Soviet assistance to Third World countries (India, Afghanistan, Indonesia, Burma, Egypt) was desired by the recipients and was consonant with Khrushchev's belief in the relevance of the Soviet model of development for Third World countries. Military assistance was not unimportant, but it was only one component of an overall courtship that aimed at diplomatic normalization and a political presence.

Gorbachev's situation is quite different. Though prime clients such as Cuba and Vietnam receive economic assistance, Moscow's main contributions are military. Over the past twenty years, the Soviet Union has developed a power projection capability to safeguard clients and influence events in ways that were previously beyond its ken; and the Third World environment within which it operates has undergone a polarization and militarization that enhance the value of what Moscow is best equipped to provide: namely, protection and a method of institutionalizing power. The change in outlook in much of the Third World dovetails nicely with the strong military hand that Gorbachev has to play.

Gorbachev's Record: An Interim Assessment

Since coming to power in March 1985, General Secretary Gorbachev has inaugurated a policy best described as "activist." Given the enormity of the tasks entailed in consolidating power, mobilizing the country for internal restructuring, preparing for the party congress, normalizing relations with China, and dealing with the United States, he has moved on a far broader front than was generally expected. Yet, despite extensive personnel changes in the Ministry of Foreign Affairs and the International Department of the CPSU's Central Committee, adoption of a party program in October 1985 that downplayed the liberation struggle in the Third World, and Gorbachev's notable neglect of Third World issues in his report at the twenty-seventh party congress, on February 26, 1986, there has been essential continuity in Soviet policy, plus increments of intensity in a number of areas.

In his report, Gorbachev paid less attention to the Third World than to any other part of the world or to any other major foreign policy problem facing the Soviet leadership. Of the approximately 5,000 words that he devoted to "Basic Objectives and Directions of the Party's Foreign Policy Strategy," a mere 150 touched on Third World issues, and two-thirds of these spoke of Afghanistan. Toward the end of his comments on the difficulties experienced by the world communist movement and on the need to foster "class solidarity and the equal cooperation of all fraternal parties in the struggle for common goals," Gorbachev reaffirmed the CPSU's "invariable" solidarity with "the forces of national and social liberation" and close cooperation "with socialist-oriented countries, with revolutionary-democratic parties and with the Nonaligned Movement."[7] A few additional references of a general character marked the extent of his interest in Third World development.

Since Stalin's death and Moscow's surge of involvement in the Third World, no Soviet leader had, on such an occasion, spent so little time on the "zone of peace," the national liberation struggle, the various regional conflicts, and the prime targets of the USSR's commitment and concern. Except in referring to Afghanistan, Gorbachev gave no hint of difficulties, dilemmas, or new directions—and no intimations of any rethinking of Soviet priorities or of the problems that support for Third World countries and movements entails for Soviet foreign policy.

The distinctiveness of Gorbachev's treatment of the Third World quickly becomes evident when his report is compared with Brezhnev's presentation at the twenty-sixth congress, five years earlier.[8] First, about half of Brezhnev's report dealt with foreign policy, much of it with developments in the Third World, in contrast to Gorbachev's brief mention.

Second, Brezhnev exuded confidence over the course of events. He spoke at length of relations with liberated countries and of the "appreciable expansion of cooperation" with them. Of particular importance to him were the increased number of states with a "socialist orientation," and the revolutions that had triumphed in Ethiopia, Nicaragua, and Afghanistan. He noted that friendship treaties had been con-

---

[7] FBIS/Party Congress, February 26, 1986.

[8] For a thoughtful analysis of Leonid Brezhnev's reports to the twenty-fifth and twenty-sixth party congresses (1976 and 1981) and Yuri Andropov's speech to the Central Committee in June 1983, see Stephen Sestanovich, "Soviet Leadership Perspectives on the Third World: Brezhnev vs. Andropov" (unpublished paper presented at the annual meeting of the American Political Science Association in August 1985).

cluded with Angola, Ethiopia, Mozambique, Afghanistan, the PDRY, and Syria in the interregnum between party congresses. Gorbachev, on the other hand, completely ignored all these countries except Afghanistan, the treaties, and the ongoing revolutionary struggles.

Third, Brezhnev identified crises in different regions—the Iran-Iraq War and the continuing lack of progress toward a comprehensive settlement of the Arab-Israeli conflict, in particular. He said that the Soviet Union was prepared to work for a comprehensive settlement of the Arab-Israeli conflict involving all parties, including the PLO, and he deplored "the Camp David policy" of the United States as "anti-Arab" and as a step toward obtaining a "broader capitulatory-type agreement." Gorbachev's speech departed from this previous pattern of citing all major conflicts in the Third World as part of a general indictment of "imperialism."

Fourth, whereas Brezhnev commented on the economic aid rendered by the Soviet Union to developing countries and on its "help to strengthen the defense capability of liberated states," Gorbachev was silent on both points; perhaps this reflects his intention to avoid repeating the obvious, in favor of targeting priority considerations.

Finally, in their formulations of the Afghan situation, made after all, five years apart, several different emphases are worth noting. Gorbachev's use of the phrase "our vital national interest" in connection with Afghanistan and with the need for "good and peaceful relations with all states bordering on the Soviet Union" put Afghanistan in a radically different category from other Third World countries. It conveyed the view that no compromise with Soviet security could be contemplated and no challenge to the communist character of the Afghan regime permitted. In this sense, his line appeared unyielding.

At the same time, however, Gorbachev managed to suggest a flexible stance. He assumed the position of a reasonable man, announcing that a plan for a "step-by-step withdrawal" of Soviet forces "has been worked out with the Afghan" government, pending agreement on an overall political settlement with appropriate guarantees. He conveniently ignored the reality that was Afghanistan: namely, a government that was a captive creature of the Kremlin, that did not have, and could never have, a say in when and how a Soviet withdrawal was to be arranged.

In any event, the case of Afghanistan was too dramatic to be subsumed under the rubric of regional conflicts. When upwards of 120,000 Soviet troops were involved in a contiguous country ruled by a puppet communist regime in a war that was in its seventh year and that was a drain on Soviet resources, an international embarrassment, and a mote in the eye of the Soviet people, whose awareness of the struggle was increasingly heightened by the expanded coverage of the Soviet media, then the party leadership had to address the issue openly and reaffirm the offical position.

Elsewhere in the Third World there is no convincing evidence that Gorbachev intends to disengage from entrenched positions because of a desire to focus on domestic problems or out of pessimism over the prospects of countries with a "socialist orientation" or out of a desire to calm relations with the United States. If anything, he appears to be reaching out to moderate actors who are friendly to the United States, such as Mexico, Brazil, Indonesia, and Saudi Arabia, without neglecting established clients. Gorbachev's "benign neglect" of the Third World at the party congress did not signify impending retrenchment or curtailment of commitments or involvement. It meant merely that his priorities were exactly those that emerged from his report—domestic problems, U.S.-Soviet relations, and arms control.

Gorbachev may have a preferred agenda that he wants to tackle, but developments have a way of intruding and of forestalling departures from existing policies. His report gave one impression about his approach to the Third World, his actions quite another. Significantly, nowhere but in Afghanistan has the Soviet outreach been reined in. Until there is more evidence to the contrary, the assumption here is that he is streamlining Soviet strategy to make the USSR an even more formidable competitor.

To assess the accuracy of this basic hypothesis, it seems appropriate to examine the actions (or lack thereof) taken by Gorbachev, and not just the gossamer hints of new directions that individual Western scholars may sense from the internal "debates" at various Soviet institutes. In light of the limited evidence available, inferences about future behavior can more reliably be drawn from the record of what the Soviets have done and are actually doing.

Gorbachev's handling of his first Third World "crisis"—in the PDRY in January 1986—was far more suggestive of what we can expect than was his speech to the party congress a month later. A virtual Soviet preserve since the late 1960s, the PDRY has provided the Soviet Navy with access to the port of Aden "and has allowed the Soviets to build an airbase and other facilities near Aden, for use in support of the Soviet Navy's Indian Ocean activities, for maritime reconnaissance, and for staging flights to the Horn and beyond."[9] However, because

[9] Stephen Page, *The Soviet Union and the Yemens: Influence in Asymmetrical Relationships* (New York: Praeger, 1985), 209.

of the strong factional nature of South Yemeni politics, the Soviets "have been unable to manipulate the PDRY's political system sufficiently to ensure that their favorite stays in power."[10] On January 13, 1986, a shoot-out between rival party and tribal factions of the ruling Yemen Socialist Party (YSP) led to two weeks of bloody fighting and the flight of President Ali Nasser Mohammed al-Hassani. Moscow appears to have been caught by surprise.[11] After three days of silence, *Pravda* reported the arrival of the PDRY's Prime Minister Haider abu Bakr al-Attas from New Delhi, where he had been on an official visit.[12]

For about ten days the situation in Aden was confused, as the two sides hammered away at each other, and thousands of foreigners, including Soviet nationals, were evacuated by sea and air. On January 24, al-Attas returned to Aden to assume the post of President in the new government. By the end of the month, Soviet advisers were beginning to return and Moscow was airlifting relief aid. A Soviet military delegation visited Aden in March; and Ali Salem al-Bidh, the new General Secretary of the YSP, attended the CPSU's twenty-seventh congress and met with Gorbachev. In the year that followed there was a major inflow of Soviet economic and military assistance.

Faced with a potential threat to the USSR's political-military position in a key client state and embarrassment at the falling-out among the Soviet-subsidized Yemenis, Gorbachev showed a competent, adept hand at the helm. He proceeded cautiously, maintaining a prudent distance from the antagonists until the outcome was clear, after which he moved quickly to consolidate contact, having kept open lines to both sides. There was no hesitation over preserving the strong Soviet infrastructure: resources were provided, commensurate to the requirements of the moment. A commendable performance for an untested leader.

On a broader plane, Gorbachev's policy toward the different regions of the Third World has developed independently in response to a changing combination of concerns, opportunities, and calculations. A look at a few of the key regions should provide an adequate basis for an interim assessment of the man, the course he intends to follow, and the extent to which his policies suggest continuity or change in the years ahead.

The most important Third World issue that Gorbachev has tackled to date is Afghanistan, and in early 1988 he embarked on a course

---

[10] Ibid.

[11] For example, David Pollock, "Moscow and Aden: Coping with a Coup," *Problems of Communism* 35, no. 3 (May–June 1986), 56–58.

[12] *Pravda*, January 17, 1986.

intended to solve the problem he had inherited. On May 15, 1988, Soviet troops began their withdrawal from Afghanistan. After waging a relentless and cruel war for almost nine years, Moscow seems resigned to defeat at the hands of the anti-communist, anti-Russian Mujahideen. If all the provisions of the agreement, which was fashioned under the auspices of the United Nations and signed in Geneva on April 14, 1988, are implemented, the last Soviet contingents should be gone by February 15, 1989, and the Soviet Union's Afghan war will have ended.

The Soviet withdrawal is a momentous development. For Gorbachev it marks the apparent end of three years of searching for an alternative that would have permitted the Soviet Union to hold on, in the hope of consolidating the power of the pro-Soviet communist puppet regime in Kabul. Various considerations affected Gorbachev's decision: his desire to concentrate on the restructuring of Soviet society; the growing unpopularity of the war at home; the inability of the Soviet army and its Afghan client to destroy or divide the Mujahideen; the difficulties that Soviet involvement caused in relations with the United States, Western Europe, China, and some of the Muslim world (especially Pakistan, Iran, and Saudi Arabia); and the continued division within the People's Democratic Party of Afghanistan.

By the time Gorbachev came to power, the Soviet Union's war in Afghanistan had become Moscow's most pressing problem in the Third World. In his report to the CPSU's twenty-seventh congress, Gorbachev hinted at his determination to end Moscow's involvement. Afghanistan, he admitted, had turned into "a bleeding wound" and he wished "in the near future to bring the Soviet forces—situated in Afghanistan at the request of its government—back to their homeland."

Clearly dissatisfied, Gorbachev worked to find a solution that would allow the Soviet Union to retain a political presence. He proceeded on a number of fronts. First, he changed the leadership of the PDPA. On May 4, 1986, Najib (also known as Najibullah), the former head of the Afghan secret police, replaced Babrak Karmal as General-Secretary. A dedicated communist, with a record of loyalty to Moscow going back to his student days in the mid-1960s, Najib was given a mandate to end the factionalism in the PDPA and devise a more effective way of dealing with the Mujahideen.

Second, Gorbachev sought to convey that he was in earnest about bringing Soviet forces back "to their homeland." In his Vladivostok speech at the end of July 1986, he announced that six regiments (8,000 troops) would be withdrawn at the end of October, and they were. (However, Pakistani and Western intelligence reported that the total number of Soviet troops in the country remained fairly constant, and Gorbachev's use of invited Western journalists to put a political gloss on the pullback raised questions about the sincerity of the gesture.)

Third, Gorbachev stepped up his diplomatic efforts. During a state visit to India in late November 1986, he made new overtures to Pakistan, and a series of frequent top-level discussions started soon afterward between Moscow and Islamabad. He courted nonaligned leaders such as Robert Mugabe of Zimbabwe, Rajiv Gandhi of India, and Chadli Benjedid of Algeria, in the hope of allaying international opprobrium and the annual condemnation of the Soviet intervention by the UN General Assembly.

Fourth, he encouraged Najib to seek a political compromise with the Mujahideen. War-weariness was widespread, and Moscow may have reasoned that a combination of carrot and stick would make a settlement of sorts attractive enough to divide the resistance. Accordingly, on January 1, 1987, Najib called for "national reconciliation" and announced a six-month nationwide cease-fire effective January 15, subject to its acceptance by the Mujahideen. But the offer was an echo of earlier offers that had been made by Babrak Karmal in 1985 and was received with indifference.

Finally, the forces of the Soviet/Afghan regime intensified their military operations. Yet despite the Soviet High Command's increased use of mobile air and light troops and somewhat improved ability to interdict supplies and personnel coming across the borders, the overall military situation was no better for Moscow in 1987 than it had been in 1984.

This was due to the introduction of the Stinger. In late 1986, at a time when the Mujahideen were suffering very heavy losses and their morale was sagging, the United States supplied them with large numbers of Stingers, a thirty-five-pound, shoulder-fired surface-to-air missile that turned the tide in their favor. The achievements of this weapon, "once regarded as far too sophisticated technically for illiterate Afghan rebels to handle and too provocative politically to the Soviets to introduce in the Afghan war," convinced Gorbachev of the impossibility of a military solution.[13]

The Stingers changed the course of the war in a number of ways. First, their effectiveness "denied the Soviets uncontested domination of the air . . . and . . . dramatically enhanced the operational effective-

[13] David B. Ottaway, "U.S. Missiles Alter War in Afghanistan," *Washington Post*, July 19, 1987.

ness and survivability of resistance units, apart from providing a major boost" to their morale. Second, they enabled the Mujahideen to exact "a steep price from the Soviets both in terms of lost aircraft and casualties." Finally, they greatly strengthened the Mujahideen's combat capabilities and contributed to Moscow's realization that it could not "win the war by military means, an important psychological barrier" that had to be overcome before Moscow would seek a diplomatic way out.[14]

Gorbachev intensified his diplomatic efforts. In December 1987, at the Washington summit, he found Reagan willing to act as coguarantor of a settlement but insistent on an unequivocal Soviet withdrawal, with a definite timetable, that would be irreversible once it went into effect. On February 8, 1988, on the eve of a new round of UN-sponsored talks in Geneva between Pakistan and the Afghan regime, Gorbachev announced that the Soviet Union was prepared to begin the withdrawal of Soviet troops on May 15, 1988, "and to complete their withdrawal within 10 months," if a final settlement could be hammered out in Geneva.[15] Of equal significance was his comment that he would be only too happy to have as a neighbor "an independent, nonaligned, and neutral" Afghanistan. For the next two months in the Geneva talks, Moscow tried to get the best deal that it could for Najib. In particular, it insisted on the right to continue providing arms and assistance to its communist client.

The end of Moscow's bargaining game came suddenly. On April 6, 1988, Najib met Gorbachev in Tashkent. Two days later a joint Soviet-Afghan statement was issued, its eight points representing a virtual reaffirmation of the principles for a settlement set forth by Gorbachev in his statement of February 8.[16] After more than six years of intermittent but intensive negotiations under the skillful guidance of UN Under-Secretary of State for Political Affairs Diego Cordovez, a series of agreements were signed in Geneva on April 14, 1988, the most important of which calls for the withdrawal of Soviet troops from Afghanistan. The carefully crafted Geneva package of four separate but interrelated agreements reflected the desire of Moscow and Washington to defuse the Afghan issue before the Reagan visit to the Soviet Union from May 29 to June 1, 1988. It provides the Soviet Union with a face-saving formula for military withdrawal and the United States with an outcome that reverses Moscow's expansion in the area and

[14] Alex Alexiev, "U.S. Policy and the War in Afghanistan," *Global Affairs*, 3, no. 1 (Winter 1988): 90.

[15] FBIS/SOV, February 8, 1988, 34.

[16] FBIS/SOV, April 7, 1988, 10–11.

ends the specter of Soviet power entrenched at the Khyber Pass, the historic gateway to South Asia.

The agreements entered into force on May 15, 1988. They have serious shortcomings, and it remains doubtful that they can bring peace soon to Afghanistan. But the Soviet troops are withdrawing just about on schedule, and there is no reason to believe that Gorbachev will reverse his decision to withdraw. The Soviet Union has paid a stiff price in military personnel for its imperialist policy in Afghanistan. On May 25, 1988, the Soviet government ended its policy of secrecy about the exact number of Soviet casualties: at a press conference, General Alexei D. Lizichev of the Ministry of Defense disclosed that "13,310 soldiers had been killed, 35,478 wounded and 311 were missing."[17]

In acting to disengage and in affirming a readiness to work with a noncommunist and nonaligned Afghanistan, Gorbachev had to have surmounted a number of constraints: first, the risk of giving his opponents in the leadership a chance to label him "soft on imperialism," to raise questions about his fitness to defend Soviet strategic interests, especially along the periphery of the USSR; second, the undesirability of alienating the military establishment to whom withdrawal is, certainly psychologically, tantamount to defeat; and third, the reluctance to relinquish his own high hopes for cooptation, for in Najib, Gorbachev may have seen an Afghan counterpart, an able, forceful leader capable of mastering a difficult situation, with the support of thousands of Afghans, newly returned from the Soviet Union where they had been sent for training and indoctrination over the past eight years.

Finally, in weighing his options, Gorbachev must have considered the unpredictable consequences of withdrawal on the long term stability of Great Russian rule in Central Asia. Russian rulers are among the most successful colonizers in history. The cement that kept the czarist empire intact was Great Russian power. Under the Soviets, the Muslim peoples and regions of the USSR have benefited in many tangible ways. Still, there is nothing to suggest that *homo sovieticus* has evolved from the socialization and modernization of the past seven decades. As Alexandre Bennigsen observed, "If relations between Muslims and Russians remain more or less peaceful for the moment it is for no other reason than that the Russians are still overwhelmingly strong compared to their Muslim comrades."[18] Withdrawal under

[17] *New York Times*, May 26, 1988.

[18] Alexandre Bennigsen and Marie Broxup, *The Islamic Threat to the Soviet State* (New York: St. Martin's Press, 1983), 151.

pressure from Islamic fighters and leaving loyal satraps to an unpromising fate could well be perceived by millions of Turkic-speaking Uzbeks, Kirghiz, and Kazakhs in Soviet Central Asia as a sign of a weakening of Great Russian power. Without hypothesizing large-scale uprisings, one could yet conceive such a perception greatly heightening ethnic self-assertiveness and complicating Moscow's management of its Muslim nationality problem. The defeat of the Red Army by the Mujahideen could have an electrifying effect in Soviet Muslim Central Asia comparable to the rise of nationalism in the Far East after Japan's defeat of Russia in 1905. Already in Armenia, Azerbaijan, and Kazakhstan, there is evidence that one unanticipated and disruptive consequence of *glasnost* and *perestroika* is an exacerbation of ethnic tensions, which may well limit Gorbachev's freedom of action, at home and abroad.

We need to keep Gorbachev's decision to withdraw from Afghanistan clearly in mind when speculating about the future of the USSR's policy in the Third World, but we must not adduce too much from this one issue. Everywhere else in the Third World Gorbachev's activism belies impending retrenchment of interest or involvement. His approach to arms control may indicate a de-emphasis on military means to acquire influence in the Third World and the devotion of more attention to diplomatic means and to political and economic factors.

If the direction of Gorbachev's policy in Afghanistan has shifted, in India it shows remarkable continuity. The special place India holds in Gorbachev's thinking was evident at the twenty-seventh congress: it was the only other Third World country mentioned by name in his report. Gorbachev's state visit to India in November 1986 also highlighted the importance that the Soviet leadership attributes to its relationship with the world's most populous democracy. The trip, his first to a Third World country, was intended to convey a sense of India's importance internationally and to the Soviet Union.

For the last three decades, and especially since the signing of the Indo-Soviet friendship treaty in August 1971, India has been the centerpiece of Soviet strategy in the Third World. It has been protected from China by the Soviet Union's nuclear umbrella, armed with the most advanced aircraft and tanks in the Soviet arsenal, and supplied with oil and vital non-ferrous metal at bargain rates. Illustrative of its special treatment was the agreement to sell it the MiG-29, Moscow's most advanced aircraft. New Delhi had asked for this plane as far back as 1982, but then Defense Minister Dimitri Ustinov insisted that it did not exist. The first shipment began to arrive in late 1986 (probably in conjunction with Gorbachev's visit) and arrangements are under way for a co-production agreement.

Yet, for all of this, Moscow is without anything tangible to show for its enormous investment in India: no naval facilities for its Indian Ocean flotilla, no privileged access for repair and replenishment facilities, and no particular popularity in the country at large. Nor will the sale of advanced weaponry help Soviet hard currency-earnings, since rupee-ruble trade is bilateral and barter in character. In the area of trade, the best that Moscow can hope for is to pressure India into purchasing Soviet machinery and commodities to offset Soviet imports of manufactures produced in Indian factories and industries developed with Soviet assistance. One Indian journalist, with extensive experience in the Soviet Union, has written,

> The level of Indo-Soviet trade has been kept artificially high through the export of crude and other raw materials because, for the Soviets, trade is an important element in a political relationship. In India's case, trade has been reinforced by agreements for Moscow to buy products of Soviet-aided industries on production sharing, joint bids for contracts in third countries and the dovetailing of the two countries' plans. *The Soviets have already created vested interests among those who produce and market a whole range of goods from hosiery to tobacco, detergents to electric fans.* (Italics added).[19]

Although on completion of his visit Gorbachev had agreed to render assistance for a wide range of expensive, high-profile projects,[20] he left with an unallayed cause for concern—the mend in U.S.-Indian relations. Prime Minister Rajiv Gandhi's improving relationship with the Reagan administration was evident when, one month before Gorbachev's visit, Secretary of Defense Caspar Weinberger received a warm welcome, in part because of greater U.S. readiness to sell India various high-tech items and efforts to expand trade.

Ever since February 1955, successive Soviet leaderships have wooed India for a combination of long-term, strategically coherent reasons.

[19] S. Nihal Singh, *The Yogi and the Bear: Story of Indo-Soviet Relations* (New Delhi: Allied Publishers, 1986), 235. See also Dilip Mukerjee, "Indo-Soviet Economic Ties," *Problems of Communism* 36, no. 1 (January–February 1987), 13–24; and Jyotirmoy Banerjee, "Moscow's Indian Alliance," ibid., 7.

[20] The main projects are the construction of the Tehri hydropower complex; modernization of the Bokaro steel plant (which was originally constructed by the USSR); development of four underground coking mines in the Jharia coalfield; and offshore exploration for hydrocarbons in West Bengal.

For the Kremlin, Soviet-Indian friendship means many things: a link with the region's leading power and assurance against its alignment with any anti-Soviet military coalition; a showcase for Soviet assistance, demonstrating to Third World countries the tangible benefits to be derived from good relations with the Soviet Union; a guarantee that India will refrain from openly criticizing Soviet interventions in Eastern Europe and Afghanistan; an ally in containing China; and an association that enhances the USSR's position among the nonaligned countries.

On a formal level relations are good, but there are simmering strains that help explain Gorbachev's attention and his bringing to bear the full panoply of public diplomacy in order to strengthen private understandings. First, Moscow's incipient reconciliation with Beijing makes New Delhi nervous, for, at a time when there is little movement in its own quest for better relations with China, Sino-Soviet relations are proceeding steadily. The equanimity with which Gorbachev regards India's erratic courtship of China only heightens India's deep-seated anxiety over possible shifts in regional power alignments. Unlike his predecessors, Gorbachev seems to be more realistic and less ideological in his expectations for Indo-Soviet relations, and this puts pressure on New Delhi to play a complicated, uncertain, diplomatic game.

One of the issues Gorbachev must cope with is the imbalance in Indo-Soviet trade. India currently exports considerably more civilian goods than it imports. The balance-of-payments account is kept in approximate symmetry by the arms that India buys. If India were to turn to the West for the next generation of weapons (about 80 percent of its arms are currently bought from the Soviet Union), Moscow would lose much of its leverage in New Delhi and find itself unable to tap into India's sophisticated electronics and computer industry. Accordingly, it works to strengthen trade ties and make sure that it does not become irrelevant to India's developmental needs. Thus, for example, during a visit in November 1987, Soviet Prime Minister Nikolai Ryzhkov persuaded the Indian government to increase bilateral trade in 1988 by about 25 percent and accept an $800 million credit for the construction of an oil refinery and a 550 megawatt thermal power station. But the limits of his sales pitch were evident in New Delhi's unwillingness, during his visit to the industrial center of Bhilai, to announce its plans for the modernization of the Bhilai steel and metallurgical complex, which Moscow helped finance and build in the late 1950s and which it would, for prestige reasons alone, like to be asked to update. Nor is India looking to the Soviet Union for new civilian aircraft.[21]

Finally, Gorbachev must find a way to allay Indian suspicions of Soviet interference in its domestic politics. Moscow uses the rupees earned in trade to subsidize the activities of the pro-Soviet Communist Party of India and to persuade businesses having a stake in commercial contracts with the USSR to lobby their government in favor of closer Indo-Soviet ties. This old source of tension needs new handling.

Gorbachev's activist policy is notable not merely for the entrenched positions and established clients that it seeks to retain, but also for probes and risks in new areas of opportunity. This has been particularly noticeable in the Gulf, where he has shown considerable skill in maneuvering in a politically perilous situation. In the fall of 1985 he effected diplomatic normalization with Oman and the United Arab Emirates, and a year later introduced a naval presence in the Gulf, creating new uncertainties in the Soviet-Iranian and Soviet-American relationships. Concerned by the growing U.S. military involvement in the Persian Gulf, Gorbachev decided to undertake new commitments on behalf of Kuwait and risk alienating Iran. The incident that prompted the new policy occurred in September 1986, when Iran intercepted a Soviet ship bound for Kuwait and released it after several days, ostensibly on the ground that it had been found to be carrying "cement" (the cargo was weapons). Since then, Gorbachev has shown a readiness to use Soviet naval vessels to escort Soviet merchantmen bound for Kuwait. In this new flexing of Moscow's power projection capability, he has emulated Washington, which informally started escorting some of its ships in early 1986; he is determined not to be outbid or outmaneuvered by Washington in the high-stake great game in the Gulf. His greater assertiveness may also have been a reaction to the revelation in November 1986 that President Reagan had covertly sold high-tech arms to Iran in an effort to ransom American hostages held by pro-Iranian Shi'ite groups in Lebanon and open a political dialogue with Tehran. Moscow has cautiously increased its involvement in the area and, like Washington, taken to speaking out in defense of freedom of the seas—a signal to Iran that it implicitly shares with the United States the desire that Iran should not triumph over Iraq.

It raised its stakes by responding quickly and positively to the Ku-

[21] The state-owned Air India Corporation plans to spend more than $1 billion on new planes over the next three years in the United States and Western Europe, not the Soviet Union. *New York Times*, December 10, 1987.

waiti government's request, addressed to the Soviet Union and the United States in December 1986, for protection of its ships against Iranian attack. (Tehran's targeting of Kuwaiti ships is part of its tougher measures to prevent war matériel from reaching Iraq.) After several months, Kuwait decided to accept the U.S. offer to reflag eleven Kuwaiti tankers; but, to enlist the assistance of both superpowers, it also chartered three Soviet tankers. Though relegated to a lesser role, Gorbachev has seized the opportunity to engage the USSR more forcefully in the region. His aims are to ensure that the United States does not become the sole Arab protector in the Gulf and to prevent the United States from positioning itself as the only potential mediator of a settlement of the Iran-Iraq War; in addition, he seeks to demonstrate Moscow's reliability and interest in constructive measures to promote regional security and stability. Above all else, he is determined not to be outflanked in the Gulf.

For a man burdened with a full domestic and foreign policy agenda, Gorbachev has not been slow to set about "restructuring" Soviet policy in the Third World—not with the aim of pruning commitments and clients but, rather, of improving the Soviet Union's ability to consolidate existing stakes and make political and economic advances in new areas. While retaining Soviet links to Marxist-Leninist and militant regimes and perhaps dampening their regional perturbations, he has been unusually active in reaching out to leading moderate and conservative regimes. His aims are multiple and vary from region to region and problem to problem, but what all have at their core is the desire to broaden the base of Soviet–Third World linkages. They seek to convey a greater interest and readiness to cooperate in efforts to find solutions for the problems of regional actors; to bring to bear in more effective fashion the instruments of diplomacy in order to shore up and secure clients in trouble; and to expand Soviet political-commercial relationships, especially with Latin America and members of ASEAN (the Association of Southeast Asian Nations: Brunei, Indonesia, Malaysia, the Philippines, Singapore, and Thailand).

Symptomatic of Gorbachev's interest was the April 1987 visit of Deputy Foreign Minister Vladimir Petrovsky to Kuwait, Oman, and the United Arab Emirates. Part of the visit was intended to draw attention to Moscow's offer to provide protection for Kuwaiti tankers. However, Petrovsky was also interested in nurturing conditions that might lead to diplomatic contacts with the Saudis; and to drum up interest among the Arab moderates of the Gulf for an international conference to be held under the auspices of the U.N. Security Council, the aim of which would be to seek a comprehensive settlement of the Arab-Israeli conflict.

Gorbachev's handling of Israel has been a shrewd mix of openness and disinformation; so far, it has promised more than it has delivered, but there have been sufficient signs of flexibility to warrant a measure of guarded optimism.

The first indication that the Soviet government was rethinking its policy toward Israel came on May 12, 1985, when *Izvestiia* published a telegram from Israeli President Chaim Herzog on the occasion of the fortieth anniversary of the Allied victory in Europe. By printing the Israeli message in the commemorative celebration, Moscow gave rare diplomatic affirmation of Israel's right to exist. This hint of a thaw was followed up by a publicly acknowledged meeting in July between the Soviet and Israeli ambassadors in France. At the conclusion of the meeting, reports began to circulate of an early restoration of diplomatic relations. In Jerusalem, (then) Prime Minister Shimon Peres told a delegation from the World Jewish Congress that "once the Soviet Union reestablishes diplomatic ties and reopens its embassy . . . there is no reason why the USSR should not have a place in the Middle East peace process." A report by Israeli Radio of Moscow's willingness to renew diplomatic ties was, however, quickly denied by Soviet authorities. Nonetheless, the Western and Israeli media were optimistic, believing that the public nature of the contacts heralded a substantive change in policy. By the time that Prime Minister Peres met Soviet Foreign Minister Shevardnadze at the United Nations in New York on October 26, 1985, the Soviet-Israeli dialogue had become front-page news.

Indeed, in the period prior to the first summit meeting between Gorbachev and Reagan, in Geneva on November 19–20, 1985, and the CPSU congress in late February 1986, hints of an imminent Soviet restoration of diplomatic relations with Israel and an easing of restrictions on the emigration of Soviet Jews were heard with increasing frequency from Soviet sources and foreign dignitaries who visited Moscow or dealt with Soviet officials abroad. But both the summit and the party congress came and went with no change in Soviet policy. For several months, there was virtual silence. Then, in early August 1986, the Soviets proposed a meeting to discuss "consular affairs." On August 18, amidst high hopes abroad, Soviet and Israeli officials met in Helsinki for their first official contact since the rupture of relations at the end of the Six Day War in June 1967. The first meeting lasted only for ninety minutes; no second one was held. The following day Gennadi Gerasimov, the spokesman for the Soviet Foreign Ministry, denounced Israel's "very arrogant interference in the internal affairs of the Soviet Union"—meaning that Israel had raised the question of the emigration of Soviet Jews. Moscow wanted to discuss "consular matters"; Jerusalem, substantive political issues.

The underlying assumptions on which the expectations of a change in Soviet policy were predicated turned out to be less than compelling, but bear mentioning, in order to illustrate the pitfalls of projecting a change in the Kremlin's policy on the basis of ideas that seem reasonable to us.

There was the assumption that Gorbachev would quickly restore diplomatic relations with Israel so as to be included in an international conference convened to negotiate a comprehensive settlement of the Arab-Israeli conflict. However, conditions for such a conference were far from ripe, with the result that he did not have to extend himself to be acceptable to Israel. Nor was the assumption warranted that Gorbachev believed diplomatic normalization with Israel a necessary condition for improved relations with the United States. Moreover, the argument that Moscow recognizes Israel's right to exist does not mean it would, in the interests of a settlement, be prepared to use its leverage with Arab clients to fashion a compromise settlement that would be acceptable to Israel. At no time has Gorbachev been any more willing than his predecessors to risk jeopardizing good relations with prime Arab clients in order to advance the prospect of a peaceful settlement.

This is evident in Gorbachev's kid-gloves treatment of Syrian President Hafez Assad. In June 1985 Assad made an unscheduled visit to Moscow to meet Gorbachev, wanting, among other things, to coordinate their response to King Hussein's search for support for an international conference that would include a joint Jordanian-Palestinian delegation (an effort that collapsed in February 1986, when Hussein denounced Arafat's prevarication); to ease Soviet-Syrian tensions over Syria's support of Palestinian opposition to Arafat's leadership and over its policy in Lebanon; and to discuss increased arms deliveries.

Assad had reason to be satisfied. Since then, notwithstanding persisting policy differences, Gorbachev has kept the arms tap open; for example, in late December 1985, Moscow delivered an undisclosed number of fast-attack craft, equipped with surface-to-surface missiles; in early 1986, several hundred advanced T-80 tanks; and later in the year, SS-23 missiles, which have a range of 350 miles and could be used to neutralize or seriously affect the operational effectiveness of key Israeli airfields. By increasingly narrowing Israel's technological edge and changing the Syrian-Israeli military equation to a closer approximation of virtual equivalence, Gorbachev has given Assad a limited military option to exercise, if he so decides. Though this seems unlikely, given his domestic and regional problems, still, the possibility of Assad's unleashing a strictly limited war on the Golan Heights cannot be dismissed out of hand. His military position vis-à-vis Israel is as strong now as it is likely to be at any time in the foreseeable future; and, being a shrewd judge of Israeli domestic politics and mentality, he may calculate that Jerusalem would not react to a local thrust for symbolic territory with an escalation to full-scale war.

There are no signs that Gorbachev will distance himself from Assad, though in his dinner speech in honor of the Syrian President he said that the absence of diplomatic relations between the Soviet Union and Israel "cannot be considered normal";[22] and though the joint communiqué issued at the end of Assad's recent visit to Moscow in April 1987 prompted speculations of difficulties in the relationship. True, disagreements may be inferred from the calculated avoidance of Syria's policy in Lebanon, its role in trying to undermine Arafat's leadership, and its attitude toward Israel and the peace process; but there is nothing new in these Soviet-Syrian differences. More significant was the demonstration of a continuing closeness in the relationship, evident in Gorbachev's promise of additional weapons and acceptance of Assad's invitation to him to visit Syria; their mutual condemnation of Israel and call for an independent Palestinian state; their stated "nonacceptance of the Camp David policy and its consequences" (that is, opposition to the Egyptian-Israeli peace treaty); and their failure to mention U.N. Security Council Resolutions 242 and 338 as the basis for future negotiations to achieve a comprehensive settlement.

Still, Gorbachev has made clear his interest in an international conference on the Arab-Israeli conflict. Like other Soviet diplomatic activity, support for an international conference has multiple purposes: to demonstrate the USSR's ability to advance Arab political aims and reassure the moderate Arabs; to reverse the U.S.'s preeminence in the Arab-Israeli sector since the October War; and, of course, to enhance

[22] FBIS/International Affairs, April 28, 1987, H7. Gorbachev was not, however, as accommodating as these words imply. He went on to say that relations "were severed by Israel in the first place. It happened as a result of the aggression against the Arab countries. We recognize without any reservations—to the same extent as with all other states—the right of Israel to a peaceful and secure existence. At the same time, like in the past, the Soviet Union is categorically opposed to Tel Aviv's policy of strength and annexation. It should be plain—changes in relations with Israel are conceivable only in the mainstream of the process of settlement in the Middle East. This issue cannot be taken out of such a context."

Moscow's prestige by making it an integral part of the peace process. It is this search for a formula to bring the Soviet Union into the center of the Middle East peace process, coupled with halting moves toward improving relations with Israel and with moderate Arab states, that raises hopes of a major change in Gorbachev's policy. Whether Gorbachev wants a conference because he estimates that the costs of involvement along the lines of the past twenty years far exceeds the advantages is a matter of considerable debate in the West. Even if nothing substantive materializes, he stands to benefit from the favorable publicity surrounding espousal of such a conference.

Also illustrative of Gorbachev's interest in playing a prominent role in Arab-world affairs is his accommodative approach to Jordan, the Sudan, and especially Egypt (in April 1987, after more than a decade of wrangling, agreeing to reschedule Cairo's military debts on favorable terms). The visits of delegations and the signing of protocols suggest a deliberate effort to upgrade existing relationships.

Nor has Gorbachev been averse to exacerbating regional tensions. The flurry of missile exchanges at the end of March 1986 between Libyan missile sites and U.S. Navy aircraft might not have taken place had not the Soviet Union sold Libya surface-to-air missiles (SAM-5s) and installed them a few months earlier. Washington strongly protested at Moscow's sale of this new weapons system, which constituted a major upgrading of Libya's military potential to do serious harm to U.S. forces in the Central Mediterranean region. With prophetic accuracy, it made the point that, unlike the SAM-5s given to Syria in 1982–1983 for protection against possible attack by Israeli planes, the ones given to Libya were directed against the United States and added an element of risk to an already-explosive environment in which there could be unforeseen consequences for U.S.-Soviet relations. Moreover, in using Soviet naval vessels to provide Qaddafi with intelligence information about U.S. naval deployments, Moscow seemed to convey implicit assurances of its support in the event of a clash between U.S. and Libyan forces. In this sense, Gorbachev's unnecessary upgrading of Qaddafi's SAM-capability may have helped embolden the Libyan leader to fire off the six missiles on Monday, March 24, against U.S. aircraft on maneuvers in the Gulf of Sidra, which Qaddafi had stated was Libyan territorial waters and which the United States said was international waters. Gorbachev provided sophisticated weapons to a maverick leader whom Moscow has carefully kept at a political distance and whose frequent overtures for a friendship treaty it has repeatedly rebuffed.

More ominous has been Gorbachev's iron-fist approach to Angola, where he seems even more determined than his predecessors to solve the MPLA's UNITA problem by force. Far from lowering the threshold of violence or reducing Soviet commitments, he has poured enormous resources into major offensives for three consecutive years, in the summer and fall of 1987 provisioning the MPLA with about $1 billion worth of weaponry.[23] But, for all of that, its internal condition has grown progressively worse.

Generally, Gorbachev has maintained a high level of arms transfers, still the principal currency for securing political investments. Soviet-bloc military and economic assistance to Nicaragua reached $1 billion in 1986—the highest level since it started in 1980. Angola, Ethiopia, the Yemen Arab Republic—the list goes on. The apparent interest in widening the network of those with whom the USSR has a comprehensive relationship, combined with the usual heavy subsidies to stalwarts such as Cuba, Vietnam, Afghanistan, and Syria, attests to the Third World's continued importance in Kremlin calculations.

Gorbachev's "new political thinking" may have inspired the effort to guide beleaguered clients out of parlous situations through recourse to a modification of what in the 1920s and 1930s was known as the "United Front" strategy. But this is a different era, and, instead of calling on nonruling communists to enter into temporary coalitions with bourgeois-nationalist groups to defeat an immediate and more dangerous enemy, Gorbachev seems to be counselling ruling Marxist-Leninist elites beset by resilient insurgencies to permit noncommunists to participate in governmental coalitions of "national reconcilitation," a term Najibullah proposed in his January 1987 offer to the Mujahideen to come to a settlement with his Kabul regime. The differences in the epochs are, of course, significant: now it is the pro-Soviet Marxist-Leninists who hold power in, among other places, Afghanistan, Kampuchea, Angola, and Nicaragua; and the Soviet Union is not itself threatened, as it was in the earlier periods—only its expendable Third World clients are.

Gorbachev's suggestion is vintage Leninism. He encourages clients to explore compromises with their opponents, provided they do not threaten the existence of "socialism." In doing this, he has several possible payoffs in mind: dividing and eventually defeating the anticom-

---

[23] One contributing factor in the defeat of the Soviet-Cuban-directed MPLA offensive was the military intervention of South African forces on the side of Savimbi's UNITA insurgents. *New York Times*, November 16, 1987. Another was the U.S. government's delivery of Stinger (portable surface-to-air) missiles to Savimbi, enabling him to counter Angolan-Cuban-Soviet air supremacy. And the third, according to Fidel Castro, was the poor military tactics counseled by Moscow. *New York Times*, July 28, 1988.

munist insurgencies; reducing the need for Soviet subsidies; eliminating tension with the United States at a time when he seeks better relations; enlisting the support of socialistically inclined West European elites on behalf of pro-Soviet governments with a "socialist orientation"; and demonstrating that Moscow can contribute to the advancement of regional peace and security.

The obvious testing grounds for his late-1980s variant of the United Front strategy are Afghanistan, Kampuchea, and Central America, where, in the late summer of 1987, the leaders of Costa Rica, Honduras, El Salvador, Guatemala, and Nicaragua concluded an agreement (the Guatemala accords) calling for steps intended to find a solution to the U.S.-armed "Contra" resistance to the Sandinista regime.

OBSERVATIONS

The strategic rationale that guides Soviet policy relies heavily on military power and instruments. Gone is the belief in the suitability of the Soviet model of development; gone is the perceived need to extend economic assistance as a condition for long-term politically meaningful relationships; and gone, too, is the ideological optimism for socialism in our time. There is a cold-eyed realism about Soviet policy and the day-to-day political-military conduct of Soviet governmental relationships with key Third World leaderships that is antithetical to the ideologically pretentious writings of Soviet academics on "scientific socialism," "progressive forces" and the noncapitalist path of development, "revolutionary democracies," and the like. The way in which Soviet leaders have generally acted in the Third World—pragmatic and adaptive; forceful and forthcoming or equivocating and niggardly, as circumstances dictate; purposeful and sensitive to the limits of what is feasible—does not warrant the apocalyptic vision of Soviet aims and actions disseminated by ideologically conservative commentators in the West.[24]

Soviet policy is essentially intrusive, not expansionist: it seeks to in-

---

[24] François Revel and Michael Ledeen come to mind. When Michael Ledeen writes that "the underlying drive" for Soviet leaders "is the belief that theirs is a revolutionary society destined to provide the model for the future of the rest of mankind" and that the "intrinsic, structural expansionism of the Soviet Empire . . . is catalyzed and enhanced by the revolutionary dynamic of communism and given greater urgency by communism's mounting difficulties at home," he is oversimplifying complexity, distorting reality, and presenting dubious propositions as confirmed evidence. None of this is very useful for understanding Soviet–Third World policy or contributing to the policy debate in the United States on how best to cope with the Soviet challenge. Michael Ledeen, *Grave New World* (New York: Oxford University Press, 1985), 149, 152.

fluence developments that erode American power and prestige, not to absorb new territory. It will intrigue in a volatile environment for indeterminate morsels of advantage, for reasons that have little to do with concern for a client's condition, in the process pushing to the limit of its ability to affect the course of regional conflicts. Like a chessmaster playing simultaneously on several boards, Moscow recognizes that in Europe and the Far East nuclear deterrence has for the moment led to de facto equilibrium; but in the Third World there are still countless moves to weaken the opponent, to undermine his position, and, over time, to drain his resources in ways that enhance the security of the Soviet imperial order. Sir John Slessor, the British strategist, called the Soviet tactics of stirring up trouble wherever they could and corrupting and eating away at the stability of targeted adversaries "the tactics of the termite."[25]

Familiarity has long since disabused Soviet leaders of the fleeting illusions that may have possessed Khrushchev during the era of decolonization, when he presumed an ideological affinity between the Soviet Union and the elites in newly independent countries. Today, many Soviets realize that diverse national interests can cause serious clashes of policy. Setbacks are seen for what they are, unavoidable consequences of a disorderly environment. Underlying all of this is an inherently wary approach to any client or potential client; it is simply the way the Kremlin views the outside world. A young George Kennan wrote in 1935 that "the peculiarity of Soviet diplomacy, insofar as it affects all nations . . . is that it is openly regarded in Moscow as the intercourse between enemies."[26] In this respect, the Kremlin can be likened to the Mafia: its members inhabit a closed, tightly proscribed, organizational system, share basic values, and are intensely suspicious of outsiders, though they do recognize the need for temporary alignments with lesser adversaries in order to exploit the opportunities and weaknesses among major adversaries that can foster the preservation and strengthening of the Soviet system itself. This quintessential amorality makes it easy for Moscow to operate in the Third World— and for Third World leaders to deal with their Soviet counterparts. There is little reason to believe that Mikhail Gorbachev's arrival on the scene has significantly changed the distinctive way the Kremlin leaders view the non-Soviet world.

In view of the global rivalry with the United States, it takes a giant

---

[25] Sir John Slessor, *The Great Deterrent* (London: Cassell, 1957), 236.

[26] As quoted in Jiri Hochman, *The Soviet Union and the Failure of Collective Security, 1934–1938* (Ithaca, N.Y.: Cornell University Press, 1984), 176.

leap in faith to contemplate a major change in Soviet policy or outlook. This would require a revision of the cardinal assumptions on which Soviet policy in the Third World has been based: to wit, that regional conflicts are the main source of opportunity for Soviet intrusiveness; that these regional conflicts are extremely useful in weakening U.S. power and enhancing the USSR's advantages vis-à-vis the United States; and that the Soviet wares that are mainly in demand among Third World elites are increasingly arms to enable them to retain power and not plowshares to promote economic development.

A number of considerations might theoretically occasion a shift in Gorbachev's policy and orientation:

- a desire to shed burdens that drain Soviet resources and to re-trench (presumably) overextended military and economic assis-tance;
- a reordering of commitments and involvement in ways that would minimize the likelihood of becoming entangled in con-flicts and situations that are remote from Soviet security inter-ests;
- a belief that domestic reform, to the extent that it requires ex-panded intercourse with the West, would benefit from tension reduction in the Third World;
- a readiness to downgrade the rivalry with the United States in the Third World in order to ameliorate U.S.-Soviet bilateral re-lationships in fields that are far more significant for Soviet de-velopment and security and, at a minimum, to avoid a repeat of the precipitate deterioration of the mid-1970s;
- a readiness to place greater emphasis on economic instruments in the quest for influence: an export strategy that would make Soviet products competitive on world markets, especially in the Third World, where Moscow might find it easy to undersell Western firms;
- a willingness to reduce subsidies to clients, a move that would at one and the same time cut expenditures, require clients to reap-praise policies that demand high levels of Soviet support, and signal the United States of an intention to dampen regional ten-sions.

Yet in the past, in situations of promise or peril, when a fundamen-tal choice was required between commitment to a regional client and cooperation or accommodation with the United States, what was so striking about Moscow's policy was its readiness to jeopardize the prospects for obtaining the coveted Western technology, credits, and trade that would undoubtedly have been forthcoming had Soviet moves been less tension-generating and confrontional.

What makes this pattern of behavior all the more remarkable is the disparity between what the Soviet Union seems to obtain from the Third World and what it stands to gain from expanded connections with the United States and Western Europe. The hard currency that it earns from arms sales—the principal source of foreign trade earnings—is more than offset in stunted trade with the West and added defense burdens. But the temptation to create embarrassment for the United States remains. A case in point is Soviet policy toward Mozambique and Nicaragua. The regimes in both countries are Marxist-Leninist, seriously beset by externally supported opponents, in need of economic and military assistance to stay in power, and remote from the Soviet Union or any possible Soviet security concern. Though Mozambique signed a friendship treaty with the Soviet Union in 1977, it has attracted far less Soviet and Soviet-bloc help. Indeed Moscow has been sparing in its support of Mozambique in contrast to Nicaragua, where it ships significant amounts of advanced weaponry,[27] irrespective of the strains this creates in U.S.-Soviet relations. This selective generosity in subsidizing Nicaragua's Sandinista regime has little, if anything, to do with ideology, economics, or military prospects. It is explainable solely in terms of a desire to engage the United States at no risk and at minimal cost in a region that can drain U.S. resources, weaken its influence, and complicate its diplomacy at home and abroad.

If Gorbachev is serious about wanting better relations with the United States, the Third World would be the likely place to begin. It is there that the stakes are expendable, the effects on Soviet security negligible, and the moderation of policy apt to bring benefits in the form of Western investment and markets. The withdrawal from Afghanistan and the new stress on compromised political solutions to regional conflicts are promising steps. Noteworthy, too, is the first Soviet acknowledgment that Moscow's Third World policy was to blame for the collapse of détente in the 1970s and early 1980s. Written by Professor Vyacheslav Dashichev, head of the Foreign Policy Department of the USSR Academy of Sciences' Institute of Economics of the

---

[27] *Washington Times*, January 15 and May 22, 1987. However, after the December 1987 superpower summit, President Reagan told journalists at a White House picture-taking session that Gorbachev had told him that "he wanted to go forward with the [Guatemala accords] peace plans and he would withhold . . . all military aid . . . from the Sandinistas." *Washington Post*, December 16, 1987.

World Socialist System, the article appeared in the May 18, 1988 issue of *Literaturnaya gazeta*. It noted that,

> the United States, paralyzed by the Vietnam catastrophe, reacted sensitively to the expansion of Soviet influence in Africa, the Near East, and other regions . . .
>
> The expansion of the Soviet sphere of influence reached critical limits in the West's eyes with the introduction of Soviet troops in Afghanistan. . . . The spiritual and material resources of the capitalist world united against the Soviet Union . . .
>
> Could such a severe exacerbation of tension in Soviet-Western relations . . . have been avoided?
>
> Unquestionably so. It is our conviction that the crisis was caused chiefly by the miscalculations and incompetent approach of the Brezhnev leadership toward the resolution of foreign policy tasks.[28]

This assessment may well reflect Gorbachev's own thinking on the subject. If so, it would mean that he believes stabilization of relations with the United States is vital for creating the international environment that would allow him to concentrate on the task of internal transformation. Accordingly, he needs to ensure that the 1990s do not see a recurrence of the Soviet imperial covetousness that destroyed détente in the past. To this end, he could be planning extensive changes in Soviet policy and military strategy in the Third World. This does not mean, however, that the Third World is about to become a mere sideshow; on the contrary, Gorbachev shows signs of approaching it much as his predecessors did, as a strategic arena for fostering Soviet goals and diverting U.S. resources and interest away from Europe and the Far East. But he may intend to rely far more on diplomatic means, witness his attempt to develop "good ties to both sides of certain Third World regional conflicts"[29] (for example, the Arab-Israeli, Iran-Iraq, Indo-Pakistani, and Sino-Vietnamese), the settlement of which he identified as "one of the dictates of our time."

In setting himself the Herculean task of bringing Soviet society into the twenty-first century, it would make sense for Gorbachev to change the New Imperial Policy that was responsible for a great deal of the heightened tension of recent decades. But strategic advantage is not

---

[28] Vyacheslav Dashichev, "East-West: Quest for New Relations. On the Priorities of the Soviet State's Foreign Policy," *Literaturnaya gazeta* (May 18, 1988), as cited in FBIS/SOV, May 20, 1988, 7–8.

[29] Stephen Sestanovich, "Gorbachev's Foreign Policy: A Diplomacy of Decline," *Problems of Communism*, 37, no. 1 (January-February): 13.

something any leadership finds prudent to relinquish. In looking ahead it is important that we temper our expectations concerning Soviet-American relations with awareness of the underlying cause of the two sides' rivalry and of the strategic-military considerations that have acquired a central place in the Kremlin's thinking about how it can best advance its interests in a hostile world.

Epilogue

The past several years have seen a fundamental transformation in Moscow's approach to Eastern and Central Europe and a shift in its relations with the United States, China, and the United Nations. Gorbachev's "new thinking" has also introduced far-reaching changes in Soviet policy toward the Third World: in Afghanistan; in movement toward political solutions to regional conflicts; in hesitant but nonetheless detectable signaling to major clients that military instruments will not be uncritically provided for the pursuit of national ambitions (as in Moscow's recent dealings with Syria and the Palestine Liberation Organization); in the demonstrated readiness to work more closely with the United States to curb and even end long-festering regional conflicts, thus far, in Angola, Kampuchea, and the Persian Gulf; and in renewed interest in upgrading the peacekeeping functions of the United Nations. We are not sure of the reasons that prompted Gorbachev to make these policy changes and we may disagree on their significance, but they are too extensive and potentially important in what they portend for Soviet foreign policy and the future of U.S.-Soviet rivalry to be relegated reflexively to the realm of "tactics."

Much of Soviet policy is still in flux. The persistence of old patterns amidst new trends results in a kind of uncertainty as to the dominant direction of Gorbachev's Third World policy. In his record to date, there are emergent tendencies that merit comment and comparison with those of his predecessors. Evaluating them may help us assess the impact of his "new thinking" on the USSR's Third World policy and what this implies for the future of Soviet relations with the United States.

For analytical purposes, the distinguishing aspects of Gorbachev's policy may be categorized as follows:

- De-emphasis on the military instrument;
- Acceptance of linkage in U.S.-Soviet relations;
- Encouragement of negotiated solutions to regional conflicts;
- Movement toward reducing the costs of maintaining an imperial policy;
- Glasnost in foreign policy evaluations.

On the other hand, certain elements that have characterized Soviet foreign policy since the mid-1950s continue to be evident in Gorbachev's course:

- Regime maintenance;
- Comprehensive activism;
- Salience of arms transfers as an instrument of policy;
- Competitive rivalry;
- Limited insights provided for the basis of decisions.

Let us first turn to the differences under Gorbachev.

1. De-emphasis on the military instrument. The shift away from heavy reliance on fostering the military instrument as a means of achieving political goals is the most significant difference between Gorbachev's Third World policy and that of his predecessors. Afghanistan was undoubtedly the watershed. As he said on February 8, 1988, "any armed conflict, including an internal one, can poison the atmosphere in an entire region and create a situation of anxiety and alarm for a country's neighbors. . . . That is why we are against any armed conflicts." It was clear to him that Afghanistan could not be pacified short of massive new commitments, which were precluded by the need to concentrate on internal reforms and usher in an era of diminished international tensions. Moreover, the unending drain on resources in Angola, Ethiopia, Kampuchea, and Syria, to mention a few prominent cases, must also have forced Soviet leaders to face the unsustainability of seeking strategic advantage by essentially military means.

In Afghanistan, where Soviet forces were directly involved, Moscow manipulated the client regime at will, but still faced innumerable difficulties. Elsewhere in the Third World, where it exercised lesser degrees of control, the environment proved not only costly but intractable. As Melvin Goodman has observed, even when dependent on Soviet military aid, "Third World states have their own goals, capabilities, and independently determined priorities. When interests coincide, Moscow and a Third World leader cooperate; when interests differ frictions ensue. Continuing strains in Soviet relations with such close clients as Cuba, Syria, and Vietnam illustrate the perplexing difficulty of translating military power into political influence over clients."[1]

The downgrading of military means in the Third World is conso-

---

[1] Melvin A. Goodman, "The Soviet Union and the Third World: The Military Dimension," in Andrzej Korbonski and Francis Fukuyama (eds.), *The Soviet Union and the Third World: The Last Three Decades* (Ithaca: Cornell University Press, 1987), 56.

nant with Gorbachev's call for the "demilitarization of international relations," a theme he sounded in his speech before the United Nations General Assembly on December 8, 1988. That "force and the threat of force neither can nor should be instruments of foreign policy" was a principle that he held applicable not just to nuclear arsenals but to all aspects of international relations. This suggests Gorbachev's realization that the USSR's role in the militarization of regional politics in the Third World had not brought achievements commensurate with the costs, especially in light of tensions with the United States. Such being the case, we would expect to see some restraint in Moscow's policy of supplying arms to a regime merely because it is anti-imperialist, meaning anti-American. Its arms policy would manifest to clients that it was not about to make war a feasible option. This may be illustrated by the Soviet-Syrian relationship. While not distancing himself from Syrian President Hafez Assad, who is still Moscow's most important link to the Arab world, Gorbachev has put him on notice of changes in Soviet policy. During Assad's visit to Moscow in April 1987, Gorbachev said that the absence of diplomatic relations between the Soviet Union and Israel "cannot be considered normal."[2] Though Soviet arms continue to flow into Syria, and Moscow has upgraded Syria's "defense" capability, the message from Moscow is that Assad should not expect to be strengthened to the level of "strategic parity" with Israel; and disagreements with Damascus are permitted to become public in a way that marks a sharp departure from past Soviet practice.

One such expression of dissonance occurred on September 18, 1989. At a press briefing held in Moscow by the Ministry of Foreign Affairs, Alexander Zotov, the Soviet ambassador to Syria, said Soviet economic needs and reforms would inevitably affect relations with Syria. He suggested that in the future, Moscow might have to reconsider its level of economic and military assistance. Noting that Syria's requests for aid over the next five years were being reviewed, Zotov said, "I can tell you that they are being scrutinized critically and if there are any changes they will be in favor of reductions—all the more because the Syrian government's ability to pay is not unlimited."[3] If actually implemented, such relations would constitute a major shift in Moscow's attitude toward the arming of a prime client.

During Gorbachev's tenure, no opportunity in the Third World has yet appeared that might tempt him to undertake significant new mili-

[2] FBIS/International Affairs, April 28, 1987, H7.

[3] Reuter's, September 18, 1989. The TASS and Syrian versions of the press conference did not include Zotov's comments about aid possibly being reduced: see FBIS/SOV, September 21, 1989, p. 20, and FBIS/SOV, September 19, 1989, p. 25, respectively.

tary commitments, so the testing of the proposition that he is de-emphasizing the military instrument must await the future.

2. Acceptance of linkage in U.S.-Soviet relations. Unlike previous Soviet leaders, Gorbachev acknowledged that there is indeed a contradiction between the USSR's projection of military power in the Third World and its attempts to improve relations with the United States. Though Soviet writers were slow to face this dilemma directly, their allusions to it increasingly appeared in the months prior to Gorbachev's speech of February 8, 1988, announcing the withdrawal from Afghanistan and expressing the hope that this would serve as a model for solving other regional conflicts and removing them as barriers to better U.S.-Soviet relations.[4]

The most direct ascription of culpability to Moscow for the collapse of détente in the 1970s and early 1980s appeared in *Literaturnaya gazeta* in May 1988.[5] Dashichev's article was a landmark in *glasnost*. Relying on balance of power rather than "class analysis" as an analytical tool, Dashichev denounced Stalin for his "hegemonist, great-power ambitions" which "repeatedly jeopardized political equilibrium between states," and blamed him for the "conflicts and frictions [that] developed with other socialist countries." Without mincing words, he went on to say that the failure of detente to take hold in the 1970s and the resulting severe exacerbation of East-West tensions were "caused chiefly by the miscalculations and incompetent approach of the Brezhnev leadership" in its expansion of Soviet power in the Third World, the critical limits of which were reached "in the West's eyes with the introduction of Soviet troops into Afghanistan." His criticism of Moscow's mistakes went far beyond any previous public Soviet assessment of the issue:

> We were wrong in assessing the global situation in the world and the correlation of forces, and no serious efforts were made to settle the fundamental political contradictions with the West. *Though we were politically, militarily (via weapons, supplies and advisers) and diplomatically involved in regional conflicts, we disregarded their influence on the relaxation of tension between the USSR and the West and on their entire system of relationships.*
>
> There were no clear ideas of the Soviet Union's true national state interests. These interests lay by no means in chasing petty

---

[4] Viktor Yasmann, "The New Soviet Thinking in Regional Conflicts: Ideology and Politics," Radio Liberty Research, December 3, 1987, p. 3. *Moscow News*, November 8, 1987.
[5] As translated in FBIS/SOV, May 20, 1988, pp. 4–8.

and essentially formal gains associated with leadership coups in certain developing countries. . . . The uncreative nature of the decisions resulted in our foreign policy becoming exceptionally costly. (Italics added.)

Dashichev's explicit linking of the deterioration of détente in the past to Soviet behavior is still the exception in Soviet writings on the Third World. Since then, most analysts who discuss the problems in U.S.-Soviet relations arising out of their competing interests in the Third World may admit that the Soviet approach has some shortcomings, but their critiques are general, unfocused, and quick to attribute principal responsibility to the United States.[6] Linkages on this subject are more apt to be found in the periodic discussions published in Soviet journals and held on Moscow radio and television programs than in serious academic writings. Scholars such as Viktor Kremenyuk of the USSR Academy of Sciences' Institute of the USA and Canada, and Alexei Vasilyev of the USSR Academy of Sciences' Institute of Africa are of the few who have forthrightly admitted that problems with the United States developed because of Moscow's failure to take into consideration a "balance of interests" and because of an excessive funneling of arms to clients in the belief "that the more arms you pour into a country the greater the influence, including political influence, you win there."[7] The growing recognition of the importance of linkage may also be seen in Moscow's repeated calls for U.S.-Soviet cooperation to solve regional conflicts and problems and in the wide-ranging and continuous discussions taking place between American and Soviet officials. The implication is that if the superpowers cooperate in the Third World, not only will they be able to end or sharply limit the cycle of ever more costly and dangerous regional conflicts, but their own relationship will not suffer as it did in the past.

3. Encouragement of negotiated solutions to regional conflicts. Under Gorbachev the Soviet Union has, in the interest of fostering negotiated settlements, sought to establish contacts with all sides to regional disputes. The most striking example to date is the resumption of diplomatic contacts (though not formal ties) with Israel. Many Soviet scholars acknowledge that Moscow made a mistake in breaking off

[6] For example, Vsevolod Ovchinnikov, *Pravda*, August 23, 1988. A. Kolosovskii, "Regional'nye konflikti i global'naya bezopasnost," *Mirovaya ekonomiki i mezhdunarodnye otnosheniya*, No. 6 (June 1988), 32. A. Kislov, "Nove politicheskoe myshleniye i regionalnye konflikty," *ibid.*, No. 8 (August 1988), 40–42.

[7] See "The USSR and the Third World," *International Affairs*, No. 12 (December 1988), 137–41.

diplomatic ties with Israel in June 1967 at which time it saw a chance to heighten U.S. isolation from the Arab world by demonstrating its solidarity with the Arab cause in contrast to Washington's support for Israel's position. By 1989, Moscow had agreed to exchange de facto consular missions (though the Israeli mission in Moscow is still not authorized to issue visas); to permit a sharp increase in Soviet Jewish emigration; to meet frequently with Israeli officials to explore ways of generating movement on the Israeli-Palestinian issue; and to expand cultural and commercial contacts. Moreover, the decision of Hungary in September 1989 and Czechoslovakia and Poland in February 1990 to reestablish full diplomatic ties suggest that Moscow is prepared to follow suit, once it can do so without jeopardizing relations with the Arab states.

Wanting to be part of the Arab-Israeli peace process, Moscow advocates an international conference. However, it is demonstrating flexibility in giving guarded approval to Israeli Prime Minister Shamir's far more limited proposal that elections be held for Palestinians residing in the West Bank and Gaza strip. Its credibility was enhanced also by helping to persuade PLO Chairman Yasser Arafat to state publicly, as he did in Geneva in December 1988, his acknowledgment of Israel's right to exist, acceptance of UN Security Council Resolutions 242 and 338, and renunciation of terrorism. Gorbachev's policy has been to move this protracted conflict from armed struggle to political negotiation.

In southern Africa, Moscow played a constructive behind-the-scenes role in helping to fashion the Namibia-Angola settlement concluded at the end of 1988. Having recognized that "their Angolan stronghold, acquired on the cheap 14 years ago, ultimately proved to be a political and strategic quagmire, costing more to maintain than to acquire," the Soviets and Cubans accepted the need for a political settlement.[8] Moscow has also had contacts with the government of South Africa, thus hinting its desire to see diplomatic normalization pushed. According to Chester Crocker, "The Soviet Union and Cuba have given Pretoria a stake in regional peace-making by their decision to join with South Africa in the work of the Namibia-Angola Joint Commission, whose first challenge—getting SWAPO back under control after its April [1989] incursions into northern Namibia, in violation of the accords—was met."[9]

---

[8] Chester A. Crocker, "Southern Africa: Eight years Later," *Foreign Affairs*, vol 68, no. 4 (Fall 1989), 151. As Assistant Secretary of State for African Affairs in the Reagan administration, Mr. Crocker was instrumental in pursuing the patient, imaginative diplomacy that came to fruition in December 1988.

[9] *Ibid.*, 153. He notes also that Soviet officials speak of the African National Congress's

In the Gulf, Moscow joined with permanent members of the UN Security Council in passing Resolution 598, which served as the basis for the cease-fire that was eventually arranged in August 1988, ending the fighting between Iraq and Iran. In this instance, however, its policy was not as clear-cut as in Angola, possessing a competitive as well as a cooperative aspect: "Playing a complicated double game of trying to improve relations with both sides of the conflict, the Soviets sought to weaken American efforts to build a consensus against Iran, while positioning themselves to pose as mediators to end the war."[10]

Moscow tried its hand in Lebanon. In August 1989, it sent a special envoy, Gennadi P. Tarasov, to Beirut in an effort to arrange a cease-fire between the Christian commander, General Michel Aoun, and Syrian-backed Muslim forces. Lebanon, wracked by civil war since 1976, has become a surrogate battlefield for rival Baathist regimes in Syria and Iraq. Moscow's initiative may have been prompted by fear of a Syrian-Iraqi clash if the local balance of power were suddenly upset—if, for example, Syria's Hafez Assad were to overrun the Christian enclave of General Aoun, for whom Iraq has been the principal arms supplier. Iraq's Saddam Hussein, eager to avenge himself on Assad for siding with Iran in the Iran-Iraq War, has found in Lebanon's communal and ethnic feuds a cost-effective way of draining Syria's resources and undermining its pretensions and prestige. In this setting Moscow had little to lose in undertaking the series of diplomatic discussions with the various parties to the dispute, from which it hoped to gain prestige and leverage in being perceived as a concerned yet neutral outside mediator.

In Nicaragua, Gorbachev urged the Sandinista leadership to accept the Central American Peace Plan proposed in August 1987 by the region's five presidents and seek a political solution to the insurgency generated by the U.S.-backed "Contras." The implementation of the Arias Plan (named after Costa Rica's President Oscar Arias) resulted in the electoral defeat of the Sandinistas on February 25, 1990. Taking his cue from the kind of political pluralism that Gorbachev had introduced in Eastern Europe in 1989, Daniel Ortega agreed to the first orderly transfer of power in Nicaraguan history and, with it, the advent of an era of contested elections and competing political parties. A successful solution through elections and "national reconciliation"

---

need to move from armed struggle toward a political solution. Such a position is helping to transform the diplomatic environment and enhancing the prospects for political dialogue between "mainstream black opposition leaders" and the government of South Africa.

[10] Francis Fukuyama, *Gorbachev and the New Soviet Agenda in the Third World*, RAND Report R-3634-A (Santa Monica, Calif: The RAND Corporation, June 1989), 42–43.

in Nicaragua may lead Gorbachev to expect some kind of reciprocal moves by the United States to help bring an end to the Mujahideen insurgency in Afghanistan.

In at least two other areas, Moscow has been active in the search for a diminution of regional tensions. Its pressure was undoubtedly a key consideration behind Vietnam's decision to withdraw its forces from Kampuchea, effective September 30, 1989. And it has also apparently been trying to use its good offices to bring about the release of the kidnapped Americans held prisoner by terrorist groups in Lebanon.[11]

At a conference on foreign policy and diplomacy held for his staff on July 25, 1988, and devoted to examining key shortcomings and requirements of Soviet diplomacy in the era of *perestroika*, Soviet Foreign Minister Eduard Shevardnadze noted that given "the overriding task of diplomacy—to seek friends for the country or at least not acquire enemies" one priority was "to conduct energetic dialogue and talks *with all countries without exception* on the main areas of world politics." (Italics added.)[12] Moscow's continued emphasis on this principle, as in its talking to Israelis and South Africans, counselling moderation to the PLO, courting countries with which it had strained relations in the past (Iran, Egypt, Sudan), and stressing the inappropriateness of military means for the realization of diplomatic ends, is part of the Soviet policy to convey to client and competitor alike its serious interest in a peaceful resolution of regional conflicts. To the extent that future Soviet behavior bears out this assessment, Gorbachev will have significantly modified the policy of his predecessors.

4. Movement toward reducing the costs of maintaining an imperial policy. Underlying Gorbachev's policy of *perestroika* is the conviction that resources must be redirected from unproductive military-political purposes to the regenerative economic and social development of Soviet society. If he is to succeed, significant cuts must be made at home in the military sector and abroad in subsidies to prime clients like Cuba and Vietnam, which receive more than two-thirds of Moscow's outlay.

A recent study by the Congressional Research Service of the Library of Congress reported that "The Soviet Union registered a substantial decrease in its share of Third World arms transfer agreements, falling from 50.3% in 1987 to 33.4% in 1988. The total value of the Soviet

---

[11] According to a member of the Bush administration, "The Soviet response has been constructive, helpful and forthcoming. It's less than we would like them to do, but more than they would have done in the past." *The New York Times*, August 12, 1989.

[12] "The 19th All-Union CPSU Conference: Foreign Policy and Diplomacy," *International Affairs*, no. 10 (October 1988), 21.

Union's agreements also fell dramatically in 1988—from $19.4 billion in 1987 to $9.9 billion."[13] We cannot yet tell whether this represents the beginning of a redirection of Soviet resources away from arms production to civilian production or is merely a fluctuation in the highly variable cycle of arms sales and subsidies—the data are hard to measure on a year-by-year basis.

Gorbachev's "new thinking" seeks to reduce wasteful expenditures in the Third World, but thus far he has not made any drastic cutbacks in commitments, economic or military. Cuba, Vietnam, Afghanistan, Syria, and Ethiopia continue to draw the lion's share of the unproductive (and unremunerated) assistance that Moscow extends to client regimes. However, Mengistu's war against his Tigrean and Eritrean ethnic minorities has become an embarrassment, and there are reports that Soviet Deputy Foreign Minister Yuli Vorontsov told him in late October 1989 that Moscow did not intend to renew the Soviet-Ethiopian friendship treaty when it expires in 1991.[14] Elsewhere, though still limited in scope, the USSR's withdrawal of some air and naval units from Cam Ranh Bay,[15] and its repositioning of naval units from the South Indian Ocean (off Africa's southeast coast) to the North Indian Ocean, may be symptomatic of a broader initiative to curb military costs in Third World areas.

Gorbachev is groping for ways of retrenching militarily without jeopardizing political relationships or strategic advantages. Soviet diplomacy has been active in trying to drum up trade and investment, but there is little to show for the intensified round of visits to Latin America, Southeast Asia, and the Middle East. Moscow is short on the surplus needed to extend credits to attract new customers, and it lacks the goods and services that paying customers seek.

Meanwhile, though speaking as if he wants to make generous concessions, Gorbachev acts in a businesslike fashion. In the UN General Assembly on December 8, 1988, he spoke of the truly serious economic problems that faced Third World countries, particularly that of foreign debt. He said that the Soviet Union was ready "to establish a long-term—up to one hundred years—moratorium on the repayment of this debt by the least developed countries, and to write it off completely in a number of cases." However, during a visit to Cuba four months later, he showed no inclination to forgive or significantly re-

[13] Richard F. Grimmett, *Trends in Conventional Arms Transfers to the Third World by Major Supplier, 1981–1988* (Washington, D.C.: Congressional Research Service: The Library of Congress, July 31, 1989), 3.

[14] *The New York Times*, January 17, 1990.

[15] *Washington Post*, January 19, 1990.

schedule Cuba's debt, estimated at 10 to 15 billion dollars, or perhaps higher, even though this would have been "a relatively painless gesture since Cuba is too poor to pay back its loans in the foreseeable future."[16] According to Fidel Castro, the issue had been discussed but nothing was decided: "We are in favor of abolishing our debt to the Soviet Union. We have been wanting to abolish this debt for 30 years now. But during these 3 decades we have been continuing to receive credits from the USSR. For the time being, debates are taking place on problems of the foreign debt."[17] Gorbachev is using the carrot and stick with Castro. On the one hand, he did sign the treaty of friendship that Moscow had resisted for more than 20 years; on the other hand, he made no financial concessions, prompting Castro to state bitterly three months later that he could no longer expect "with certainty that supplies that have been coming to our country will continue to arrive with the usual clocklike punctuality and as previously guaranteed."[18] All of this may be part of Gorbachev's plan to use economic levers to extract political concessions from Castro regarding the withdrawal of Cuban forces from Angola and the diminution of Cuban arms to Nicaragua.[19]

On occasion, Shevardnadze has indicated that "only a certain portion" of Soviet economic activity in the Third World "will be, so to speak, 'subsidized.' "[20] But in the main it has been the leading Soviet economic reformers, like Oleg Bogomolov and Nikolai Shmelov, who have hammered at the necessity of bringing economic criteria to the forefront in aid-giving, of reducing uneconomic assistance and being more selective in the investments made and more businesslike in dealings with local elites. In his speech as an elected deputy to the first Congress of People's Deputies in June 1989, Shmelov proposed balancing the Soviet budget by, among other things, cutting aid to Cuba and Nicaragua: "Have you ever thought about how much our interest in Latin America costs? According to professional American calculations, it is around six billion to eight billion dollars a year. This source alone would suffice to maintain the balance of the consumer market for the years which we need to deal with our immediate problems, and step with both feet onto the road of reforms."[21] In late December, Yu-

[16] Bill Keller, *The New York Times*, April 4, 1989.

[17] FBIS/SOV, April 6, 1989, p. 26.

[18] Joseph B. Treaster, *The New York Times*, July 28, 1989.

[19] *The New York Times*, October 5, 1989.

[20] Quoted in Stephen Sestanovich, "Gorbachev's Foreign Policy: A Diplomacy of Decline," *Problems of Communism*, vol. 37, no. 1 (January–February 1988), 13.

[21] *The New York Times*, June 9, 1989. In the future, the debates in the Congress of People's Deputies, the new legislative structure created by Gorbachev, may be a source of criticism of official foreign policy positions.

rii Maslyukov, chairman of Gosplan (State Planning Committee), indicated that the government was considering a decrease in its aid to Third World countries, but he offered no specifics.[22]

Though his cost-reduction efforts have so far been suggestive rather than substantive, Gorbachev may be preparing to take some big steps in this direction, as regional conflicts increasingly wind down.

5. Glasnost in foreign policy evaluations. Gorbachev's decision to fill in the "blank areas" of Soviet history is slowly coming to terms with critical developments in past Soviet foreign policy. An official admission—long known in the West and among informed circles in the Soviet Union itself—was made on August 18, 1989, by Gorbachev's confidante, Politburo member Alexander N. Yakovlev, who acknowledged that Stalin had indeed signed a secret agreement with Hitler dividing Eastern Europe into spheres of influence on the eve of World War II. While there remains much to revise in the official account of Soviet-Polish relations since 1989, Moscow has given signs of accepting Stalin's responsibility for the massacre of thousands of Polish officers in the Katyn Forest in the fall of 1940. Khrushchev's Cuban policy in 1962 has been discussed critically by former officials. There has also been mention of Brezhnev's foreign policy mistakes— Afghanistan, the rupture of diplomatic relations with Israel, the invasion of Czechoslovakia in August 1968, and the deployment of intermediate-range missiles (SS-20s) in Europe in the late 1970s. The full story has yet to be told of any of these politically pivotal events. Official archives dealing with foreign policymaking during the Soviet period are still closed.

Still, these are signal steps. They may herald a process of providing authoritative information on how key decisions were made affecting Soviet foreign policy in general, and policy toward the Third World, in particular. Shevardnadze's call for "an influx of fresh ideas" and "a scientific analysis of past experience and a study of 'blank' and 'obscure' areas,"[23] differs significantly from the secretiveness of the Soviet foreign ministry under Andrei Gromyko.

Taken together, these tendencies in Gorbachev's policy denote an ongoing reassessment of Soviet behavior that could reduce the confrontational aspects of the superpower rivalry in the Third World. They are the logical expression of a policy in transition increasingly shaped by new thinking.

Concomitantly, there are certain characteristics of Soviet Third World policy that persist from the Khrushchev-Andropov-Chernenko

[22] Michael Dobbs, *Washington Post*, December 14, 1989.
[23] "The 19th All-Union cPSU Conference," *International Affairs*, 27.

periods. The following continuities sometimes reinforce, but also sometimes clash with, the direction of Gorbachev's changes.

1. Regime maintenance. Gorbachev is not abandoning the Third World. Thus far his expenditures on Third World clients have contravened Western anticipations of sharp reductions in order to redirect resources to internal transformation. Through a skillful mix of diplomacy and assistance, he seems as committed as his predecessors to keeping friendly regimes in power and helping them resist inroads by anti-Marxist or American-backed local/regional rivals. In Afghanistan, which was regarded as a barometer of his intentions, Gorbachev's withdrawal showed that he was no longer willing to commit Soviet ground forces to retain political control. However, his willingness to pour in enormous military and economic resources to back a beleaguered client at a time of deteriorating Soviet domestic conditions has been a surprise. Soviet arms shipments alone, at current estimates, will have exceeded $2 billion for the year 1989.[24] Gorbachev's determination to support the pro-Soviet communist PDPA regime as long as it is able to survive without Soviet troops perplexes U.S. officials and has somewhat dissipated the goodwill that accompanied his withdrawal of forces in February 1989, in accordance with the provisions of the UN-negotiated agreement of April-May 1988. Why is Moscow continuing to supply Najibullah's regime? According to one U.S. official, Soviet Foreign Minister Shevardnadze gave Secretary of State James Baker a direct answer, when they met in Paris in July 1989: "Because Afghanistan is next door."[25] Shevardnadze compared Moscow's concern to Washington's with Central America. If, in fact, he was implying that Afghanistan and Nicaragua are politically equivalent contexts, Gorbachev's intention to secure Afghanistan may be far more deep-rooted than a mere interest in a "decent interval" before finally disengaging. Najibullah's ability to maintain control in Kabul, the fratricidal fighting among the rival Mujahidin groups, Iran's interest in rapprochement with the USSR, and Pakistan's ambivalence about continuing the war lend support to the view that Gorbachev may see a chance for political advantage from the current situation—and with it some kind of justification for Soviet sacrifices and the Soviet army's having fulfilled its "international duty." Perhaps he hopes a show of resolve and toughness in Afghanistan will strengthen his bargaining position in negotiating other settlements with the United States.

[24] David B. Ottaway, *Washington Post*, September 10, 1989; *Washington Post*, September 2, 1989.
[25] Author's interview, September 1989.

In Central America (as in Kampuchea, Angola, and elsewhere), Moscow continues to provide the assistance necessary for the survival of key clients. At the Malta summit meeting between Presidents Bush and Gorbachev on December 2, 1989, Castro's Cuba and Ortega's Nicaragua were discussed, but apparently nothing was settled concerning the flow of Soviet aid: Cuba is to receive modern aircraft (the MiG-29); and Nicaragua, military and economic aid (about $500 million per year).[26] We must wait to see if the Sandinista defeat in the February 1990 elections will occasion a sharp cutback in Soviet military and economic assistance. Gorbachev has yet to disengage from costly undertakings. Strategic considerations continue to override economic constraints.

2. Comprehensive activism. Like his predecessors, Gorbachev is trying to develop comprehensive relations with virtually all Third World countries, irrespective of ideological or political differences. Careful not to arouse expectations, he keeps aid packages modest (like the credits extended to Egypt in May 1989 for power projects in Sinai) and counsels the need for a political approach to regional problems. He is working hard to repair Soviet fortunes in Egypt, Indonesia, and Iran; allay concerns about alleged Soviet subversion in the conservative regimes of the Gulf (in the process establishing diplomatic ties with Oman and the United Arab Emirates in 1985 and with Qatar in 1988) and Southeast Asia (Malaysia and Thailand); and deepen ties to Mexico, Brazil, and Argentina. As was true of previous Soviet leaders, his approach is essentially reactive and consists of being receptive to regimes who, for a variety of reasons, seek to improve relations with the Soviet Union.

The courtship of moderate states is not new;[27] but the opportunities for diplomatic normalization provided by regional actors, whose interests and outlooks have changed in response to altered circumstances both at home and abroad—these are new. Like the superpowers, whom they try to use for the advancement of their own national interests, these Third World regimes are manifesting their own brand of "new thinking": in a period of U.S.-Soviet accommodation, they see no reason for not improving relations with Moscow, in the hope that a Soviet connection will bring added leverage in dealing with the

---

[26] Soviet Foreign Ministry spokesman Gennadi Gerasimov said that the MiG-29s to be supplied to Cuba would be "used for air-defense purposes" and as such accorded with the 1962 Kennedy-Khrushchev understanding ending the Cuban missile crisis. FBIS/SOV, November 20, 1989, p. 3.

[27] For a contrary view, see for example Fukuyama, *Gorbachev and the New Soviet Agenda*, 21–22.

United States. As long as the Third World remains a competitive, albeit less conflictual, arena for the two superpowers, such an adaptation makes sense. It motivates Moscow to expand its diplomatic relationships, which are intended to improve the strategic context within which the USSR seeks the accretion of advantages and the curbing of U.S. influence.

Commitments in the form of credits and subsidies are being made by Gorbachev for the same mix of reasons that determined those of his predecessors. One does not detect in his behavior an avoidance of new outlays or a curbing of the costs of operating in the Third World. Though he would like the USSR to become an integral part of the international economic system dominated by the Western powers and Japan, attract foreign investment, and adopt more capitalistic criteria in dealing with clients and customers, his policies toward Cuba, Afghanistan, Kampuchea, Syria, and India do not indicate that economic considerations have yet taken command in the Soviet approach.

Recall that in the middle and late 1960s, as now, leading Soviet analysts were urging retrenchment, a rationalization of commitments, and a lower profile in the Third World, and there were Western counterparts who believed the Kremlin could not indefinitely afford "the costs of empire." These Soviet voices are more influential today, the position they argue is seemingly that of the Gorbachev leadership; and Western assumptions of inevitable cutbacks in commitments are even more convincing. Still, the lines of argument do not fully mirror what is actually happening. There has been no diminished commitment to the forward policy of Khrushchev and Brezhnev—only Gorbachev's search for a more effective, less militarily threatening, and hopefully more cost-efficient ways of sustaining pro-Soviet regimes in the Third World.

3. Salience of arms transfers as an instrument of policy. When a superpower is involved, arms transfers inevitably acquire a significance far beyond commerce alone. Ever since Khrushchev used them for quick entrée into Afghanistan, Egypt, and Indonesia, successive Soviet leaders have been interested in arms, primarily because they are the most reliable instrument for strengthening Soviet relations with key regional actors. Judging by the available data, no supplicant has been turned away. For example, in early 1989 advanced Sukhoi 24-D bombers were delivered to Libya, presumably for the hard currency that Moscow sorely needs. The case of Syria is more complex. Moscow knows that Assad has serious economic problems; that he is diplomatically isolated in the Arab world, his policy in Lebanon opposed by most Arab governments; that he is militarily dependent on the USSR for high-performance weapons, because he lacks the currency to contemplate an alternative supplier; and that he disapproves of the USSR's efforts to encourage the Israeli-Palestinian peace process and moderation of PLO policy toward Israel. To underscore his view that Soviet relations with Israel must be normalized, Gorbachev sent Alexander Zotov, the aide who is said to have drafted his admonition to Assad in April 1987, to serve as ambassador in Damascus. Yet, despite the difficult Soviet-Syrian relations, despite the outstanding $15 billion debt for arms purchases with no prospect of payment, Soviet weapons pour in, not as much as Assad would like, but in substantial numbers—MiG-29s, tanks, air defense systems, and so on. Thousands of Soviet military advisers are in influential positions at all levels of the Syrian army and in air command and control centers; combined Soviet-Syrian maneuvers do not, according to Israeli intelligence sources, reflect a merely defensive strategy and the number of Soviet naval port visits and their duration is on the rise.[28] Gorbachev's support for Assad continues mainly for the same geostrategic reasons that attracted Moscow to him in the past.

Arms transfers still maintain the security of prominent clients. They prevented Iraq from succumbing to Iranian offensives in the 1982–1987 period of the Iran-Iraq War; and they enable the communist PDPA regime to hang on in Afghanistan, and pro-Moscow Marxist-Leninist regimes in Angola and Ethiopia to survive.

As a major source of hard currency, arms sales have assumed even greater importance in Gorbachev's calculations. Libya, Iraq, Kuwait, Algeria, and Iran can pay for their weapons, and in the highly competitive international market, the Soviet Union wants to retain a significant share for itself against the United States, France, West Germany, and China.

Finally, Moscow continues to use arms in exchange for "overflight and landing rights, port facilities, bases, and prepositioning of equipment," in countries such as Somalia (until 1977), Ethiopia, the PDRY, Syria, and Benin.[29]

[28] For example, there has been an upgrading of the logistical and docking facilities available to the Soviet Navy at Tartus on the Syrian coast. Simon Elliott, "Syrian Base Boosts Soviet Power," *Jane's Defence Weekly* (July 29, 1989), 154.

[29] Mark N. Kramer, "Soviet Arms Transfers to the Third World," *Problems of Communism*, vol. 36, no. 5 (September–October 1987), 59. He mentions the rivalry with China and the opportunity for intelligence-gathering as other reasons for Moscow's arms transfers.

4. Competitive rivalry.

Like Khrushchev and Brezhnev before him, Gorbachev wants to deny strategic advantage to the United States, but without jeopardizing the improvement in Soviet-American relations of the past few years. After all, not even Brezhnev, whose actions went the farthest in exploiting Third World opportunities to undermine U.S. interests, willfully set out to destroy détente; what he did was misjudge the extent to which he could seek strategic advantage and still expect a passive Washington.

Gorbachev has been more prudent and averse to risk taking. But risk-avoidance does not mean that he intends to stop competing with the United States in the Third World or that superpower cooperation in regional conflict-containment will take hold. In the past, great powers have had interests in which were imbedded the seeds of future tensions. A period of testing is going on now, to see whether Gorbachev can calibrate Soviet ambitions in such a way as to avoid the missteps of the past. In Afghanistan, he withdrew Soviet troops, but continues to supply the Kabul regime; in the Gulf, Moscow played a wary hand, wanting to see the Iran-Iraq War end but not on terms that would benefit the United States or jeopardize the prospects for improved Soviet-Iranian ties; and in mid-May 1989, Gorbachev wrote Bush that no *Soviet* military assistance was any longer going to Nicaragua,[30] but U.S. intelligence sources reported a continued flow of military hardware and related goods from *Warsaw Pact countries and Cuba.*[31] Gorbachev's position may be technically correct, but if he quibbles over the source of weapons while upgrading the Sandinista capability, he will likely find the same kinds of barriers to long-term improvement in U.S.-Soviet relations that bedeviled his predecessors. Similarly, though denying any responsibility for the continued supply of Soviet weapons to the FMLN (Farabundo Marti' Front for National Liberation) insurgents in El Salvador, Moscow has been apprised of Washington's concern that the insurrection is being sustained by Soviet weapons.[32] Finally, in the fighting that has torn Lebanon apart, all the warring factions—political, communal, religious, ethnic—are armed with Soviet and Soviet-bloc weapons.[33]

In all, it is too early to know how seriously Gorbachev's speech to the UN General Assembly in December 1988 favoring expanded use of UN peacekeeping forces is meant to be taken.

[30] *The New York Times*, May 17, 1989.

[31] *Washington Times*, September 18, 1989; *Washington Post*, September 19, 1989.

[32] FBIS/SOV, November 28, 1989, p. 4; *The New York Times*, December 11, 1989.

[33] *The New York Times*, June 13, 1989.

5. Limited insights provided for the basis of decisions. Glasnost has given us glimpses behind the Kremlin curtain, but we still know little of how Soviet foreign policy decisions are made, how priorities are determined, and why commitments are sustained. The tidbits of information coming out, as on the Kremlin's decision to intervene in Afghanistan, are not terribly illuminating. The willingness of scholars such as Oleg Bogomolov (Director of the USSR Academy of Sciences' Institute of the Economy of the World Socialist System), Yuri Gangovsky (Head of the USSR Institute of Oriental Studies Department of Afghanistan, Pakistan, and India), and A. Prokhanov, a journalist, to criticize past policy is welcome; but they do not discuss the motives for the current policy of liberally sending arms to Afghanistan (in early October 1989, the Bush administration declared that Soviet military personnel are operating SCUD missiles for the Kabul regime). Not even Foreign Minister Shevardnadze's admission to the Supreme Soviet on October 23, 1989, that, in invading Afghanistan in 1979, "We had placed ourselves in opposition to the world community, had violated norms of behavior, and gone against common human interests," was accompanied by any new insights into Soviet decision making.[34]

Most Soviet writing on Soviet foreign policy until very recently was pap, and though Soviet publications no longer write about the "liberating mission" of the Soviet Union in the Third World, we have yet to see works that illumine current policy in the Middle East, Southern Asia, Africa, or Central America: there is no probing into objectives, no weighing of costs and benefits, no discussions of constraints on existing policy. The searching criticism of the 1939 Nazi-Soviet pact and Stalin's postwar policy, and the broad-brush swipes at Brezhnev's shortcomings in foreign affairs, may well foreshadow what is coming in the foreseeable future, but in the meantime we must continue to evaluate Soviet policy by its actions rather than by its words.

CONCLUDING OBSERVATIONS

Under Gorbachev the Soviet leadership has restructured its approach to the Third World. Implicit in the de-emphasis of the military instrument as a means of influence building, in the nurturing of solutions to regional conflicts, and in the consideration of normalizing diplomatic ties with all parties, irrespective of alignment or outlook, is the USSR's apparent realization that it must avoid again putting at risk its relations with the United States over their competition for influence

[34] FBIS/SOV, October 24, 1989, p. 45.

in the Third World. Frequent discussions between Moscow and Washington are designed to prevent threats to détente and to encourage regional antagonists away from the battlefield and toward the conference table. Soviet officials write, albeit in general terms, of the need for cooperation to reduce and eliminate the danger of proliferation of nuclear and chemical weapons, the dissemination of ballistic missile delivery systems, and the spread of terrorism.[35]

Gorbachev has begun the defusing of the Third World as a threat to the future of U.S.-Soviet relations. In our attempts to monitor the course of this policy, we might keep in mind several indicators of cooperation:

- Efforts to resolve existing regional conflicts;
- Restraint on arms transfers to clients perpetuating past policies;
- Retrenchment of commitments, especially to clients who cannot manage on their own;
- Avoidance of new commitments in areas peripheral to Soviet security;
- Manifestation of the "new political thinking" in concrete analysis of the USSR's policies in the Third World.

The full implications of these modifications will become clearer in the years ahead, but by changing the Soviet approach to the Third World, Gorbachev has opened the way for a new era in U.S.-Soviet relations.

[35] For example, Andrei Kolosovsky, "Risk Zones in the Third World," *International Affairs*, no. 8 (August 1989), 39–49. Mr. Kolosovsky is Assistant Deputy Minister of Foreign Affairs. Yevgeny Primakov, "USSR Policy on Regional Conflicts," *International Affairs*, no. 6 (June 1988), 3–9 declares that "war and the use of force in general should be ruled out from interstate relations"; however, he affirms that this does not imply "non-recognition of the possibilities of national and social liberation forces for making use of every means at their disposal to ensure their legitimate rights."

Selected Bibliography

ALBRIGHT, DAVID E. *Soviet Policy toward Africa Revisited.* Washington, D.C.: Center for Strategic and International Studies, 1987.
———, ed. *Communism in Africa.* Bloomington: Indiana University Press, 1980.
ARNOLD, ANTHONY. *Afghanistan: The Soviet Invasion in Perspective.* Stanford: Hoover Institution Press, 1981.
ASHBY, TIMOTHY. *The Bear in the Back Yard.* Lexington, Mass.: Lexington Books, 1987.
ASPATURIAN, VERNON V. "Nicaragua between East and West: The Soviet Perspective." In *Conflict in Nicaragua: A Multidimensional Perspective,* edited by Jiri Valenta and Esperanza Duran, 201–35. Boston: Allen & Unwin, 1987.
BACH, QUINTIN V. S. "A Note on Soviet Statistics on Their Economic Aid." *Soviet Studies* 37, no. 2 (April 1985): 269–75.
BANERJEE, JYOTIRMOY. "Moscow's Indian Alliance." *Problems of Communism* 36, no. 1 (January–February 1987): 1–12.
BECKER, ABRAHAM S. "Soviet Union and the Third World: The Economic Dimension." *Soviet Economy* 2, no. 3 (July–September 1986): 233–60.
BISSELL, RICHARD E. "Soviet Use of Proxies in the Third World: The Case of Yemen." *Soviet Studies* 30, no. 1 (January 1978): 87–106.
BLASIER, COLE. *The Giant's Rival: The USSR and Latin America.* Pittsburgh: University of Pittsburgh Press, 1983.
BRADSHER, HENRY S. *Afghanistan and the Soviet Union.* New and expanded ed. Durham, N.C.: Duke University Press, 1985.
BRUTENTS, KAREN N. *The Liberation Struggle of the Asian and African Peoples at the Present Stage and Revolutionary Democracy.* Moscow: Novosti, 1977.
———. *National Liberation Revolutions Today,* vol. 1. Moscow: Progress Publishers, 1977.
———. *The Newly Free Countries in the Seventies.* Moscow: Progress Publishers, 1979.
BUSZYNSKI, LESZEK. *Soviet Foreign Policy and Southeast Asia.* New York: St. Martin's Press, 1986.
CAMPBELL, KURT W. *Soviet Policy towards South Africa.* New York: St. Martin's Press, 1986.
CARRÈRE D'ENCAUSSE, HÉLÈNE. *Ni paix ni guerre: le nouvel empire soviétique ou du bon usage de la détente.* Paris: Flammarion, 1986.
CENTRAL INTELLIGENCE AGENCY, NATIONAL FOREIGN ASSESSMENT

CENTER. *Communist Aid Activities to Non-Communist Less Developed Countries.* Washington, D.C., various years.

CHUBIN, SHAHRAM. "Gains for Soviet Policy in the Middle East," *International Security* 6, no. 4 (Spring 1982): 122–52.

CIGAR, NORMAN. "South Yemen and the USSR: Prospects for the Relationship." *Middle East Journal* 39, no. 4 (Autumn 1985): 775–95.

CLARKSON, STEPHEN. *The Soviet Theory of Development: India and the Third World in Marxist-Leninist Scholarship.* Toronto: University of Toronto Press, 1978.

CLEMENT, PETER. "Moscow and Southern Africa." *Problems of Communism* 34, no. 2 (March–April 1985): 29–50.

COLLINS, JOSEPH J. *The Soviet Invasion of Afghanistan.* Lexington, Mass.: Lexington Books, 1986.

CONFINO, MICHAEL, and SHIMON SHAMIR, eds. *The USSR and the Middle East.* New York: Wiley, 1973.

COPPER, JOHN F., and DANIEL S. PAPP, eds. *Communist Nations' Military Assistance.* Boulder, Colo.: Westview, 1983.

CROZIER, BRIAN. *The Surrogate Forces of the Soviet Union,* no. 92. London: Institute for the Study of Conflict, February 1978.

DAWISHA, KAREN. *Soviet Policy toward Egypt.* London: Macmillan, 1979.

————. "The USSR in the Middle East: Superpower in Eclipse." *Foreign Affairs* 61, no. 2 (Winter 1982–83): 438–52.

DINERSTEIN, HERBERT S. *The Making of a Missile Crisis: October 1962.* Baltimore: Johns Hopkins University Press, 1976.

DISMUKES, BRADFORD, and JAMES M. MCCONNELL, eds. *Soviet Naval Diplomacy.* New York: Pergamon Press, 1979.

DONALDSON, ROBERT H. *Soviet Policy towards India: Ideology and Strategy.* Cambridge, Mass.: Harvard University Press, 1974.

————, ed. *The Soviet Union in the Third World: Successes and Failures.* Boulder, Colo.: Westview, 1981.

DUNCAN, W. RAYMOND, ed. *Soviet Policy in Developing Countries.* Waltham, Mass: Ginn-Blaisdell, 1970.

————. *The Soviet Union and Cuba: Interests and Influence.* New York: Praeger, 1985.

DURCH, WILLIAM J. "The Cuban Military in Africa and Middle East: From Algeria to Angola." *Studies in Comparative Communism* 11, nos. 1–2 (Spring–Summer 1978): 34–74.

EFRAT, MOSHE. "The Economics of Soviet Arms Transfers to the Third World—A Case Study: Egypt." *Soviet Studies* 35, no. 4 (October 1983): 437–56.

ERISMAN, H. MICHAEL. *Cuba's International Relations: The Anatomy of a Nationalistic Foreign Policy.* Boulder, Colo.: Westview, 1985.

ERLICH, HAGGAI. *The Struggle over Eritrea, 1962–1978: War and Revolution in the Horn of Africa.* Stanford: Hoover Institution Press, 1983.

FAHMY, ISMAIL. *Negotiating for Peace in the Middle East: An Arab View*. Balti-more: Johns Hopkins University Press, 1983.

FRANQUI, CARLOS. *Family Portrait with Fidel: A Memoir*. New York: Random House, 1984.

FREEDMAN, ROBERT O. *Soviet Policy in the Middle East since 1970*, 3d ed. New York: Praeger, 1985.

FUKUYAMA, FRANCIS. "Nuclear Shadowboxing: Soviet Intervention Threats in the Middle East." *Orbis* 25, no. 3 (Fall 1981): 579–605.

———. *Moscow's Post-Brezhnev Reassessment of the Third World*, R-3337-USDP. Santa Monica, Calif.: Rand Corporation, 1986.

GLASSMAN, JON D. *Arms for the Arabs: The Soviet Union and War in the Middle East*. Baltimore: Johns Hopkins University Press, 1975.

GOLAN, GALIA. *Yom Kippur and After*. New York: Cambridge University Press, 1977.

———. *The Soviet Union and the Palestine Liberation Organization: An Uneasy Alliance*. New York: Praeger, 1980.

———. "Gorbachev's Middle East Strategy," *Foreign Affairs*, 66, no. 1 (Fall 1987): 41–57.

———. "Moscow and Third World Liberation Movements: The Soviet Role." *Journal of International Affairs* 40, no. 2 (Winter 1987): 303–24.

GORSHKOV, S. G. *The Sea Power of the State*, translated from Russian. Annapolis: Naval Institute Press, 1979.

GU GUAN-FU. "Soviet Aid to the Third World: An Analysis of Its Strategy." *Soviet Studies* 35, no. 1 (January 1983): 71–89.

GUPTA, BHABANI SEN. *The Fulcrum of Asia: Relations among China, India, Pakistan, and the USSR*. New York: Pegasus, 1970.

HALPERIN, MAURICE. *The Taming of Fidel Castro*. Berkeley: University of California Press, 1981.

HAMMOND, THOMAS T. *Red Flag over Afghanistan*. Boulder, Colo.: Westview, 1984.

HARVEY, MOSE L. *Soviet Combat Troops in Cuba*. Coral Gables, Fla.: Advanced International Studies Institute, 1979.

HEIKAL, MOHAMED. *Nasser: The Cairo Documents*. London: New English Library, 1972.

———. *The Road to Ramadan*. London: Collins, 1975.

HENZE, PAUL B. "Communism in Ethiopia." *Problems of Communism* 30, no. 3 (May–June 1981): 66–74.

HORELICK, ARNOLD, and MYRON RUSH. *Strategic Power and Soviet Foreign Policy*. Chicago: University of Chicago Press, 1965.

HORN, ROBERT C. *Soviet-Indian Relations: Issues and Influence*. New York: Praeger, 1982.

HORVATH, JANOS. "Economic Aid Flow from the USSR: A Recount of the First Fifteen Years." *Slavic Review* 29, no. 4 (December 1970): 613–32.

HOSMER, STEPHEN T., and THOMAS W. WOLFE. *Soviet Policy and Practice toward Third World Conflicts*. Lexington, Mass.: Lexington Books, 1983.

HOUGH, JERRY F. *The Struggle for the Third World: Soviet Debates and American Options.* Washington, D.C.: Brookings Institution, 1986.

IMAM, ZAFAR. "Soviet Treaties with Third World Countries." *Soviet Studies* 35 no. 1 (January 1983): 53–61.

KANET, ROGER, ed. *The Soviet Union and the Developing Nations.* Baltimore: Johns Hopkins University Press, 1974.

KAPLAN, STEPHEN S., ed. *Diplomacy of Power: Soviet Armed Forces as a Political Instrument.* Washington, D.C.: Brookings Institution, 1981.

KAPUR, HARISH. *The Embattled Triangle: Moscow, Peking, New Delhi.* New Delhi: Abhinav Publications, 1973.

KARSH, EFRAIM. *The Cautious Bear: Soviet Military Engagement in Middle East Wars in the Post-1967 Era.* Boulder, Colo.: Westview, 1985.

KATZ, MARK N. *The Third World in Soviet Military Thought.* Baltimore: Johns Hopkins University Press, 1982.

———. "The Soviet-Cuban Connection." *International Security* 8, no. 1 (Summer 1983): 88–112.

———. *Russia and Arabia: Soviet Foreign Policy toward the Arabian Peninsula.* Baltimore: Johns Hopkins University Press, 1986.

KAUPPI, MARK, and R. CRAIG NATION, eds. *The Soviet Union and the Middle East in the 1980s.* Lexington, Mass.: Lexington Books, 1983.

KAZEMZADEH, FIRUZ. *Russia and Britain in Persia, 1864–1914.* New Haven, Conn.: Yale University Press, 1968.

KHRUSHCHEV, N. S. *On Peaceful Coexistence.* Moscow: Foreign Languages Publishing House, 1961.

———. *The Last Testament,* translated and edited by Strobe Talbott. New York: Bantam Books, 1976.

KIM, G. "Sovetskii Soyuz v natsionalno-osvoboditelnoe dvizheniye" [The Soviet Union in the National Liberation Movement]. *Mirovaia ekonomika i mezhdunarodnye otnosheniye,* no. 9 (1982): 25–28.

KLINGHOFFER, ARTHUR J. *The Angolan War: A Study in Soviet Policy in the Third World.* Boulder, Colo.: Westview, 1980.

KORBONSKI, ANDRZEJ, and FRANCIS FUKUYAMA, eds. *The Soviet Union and Third World: The Last Three Decades.* Ithaca, N.Y.: Cornell University Press, 1987.

KREMENYUK, V. A., V. P. LUKIN, and V. S. RUDNEV. *S.Sh.A. i razvivayushchiesya strany 70-gody* [The USA and the Developing Countries in the 1970s]. Moscow: Nauka, 1981.

KULISH, V. M., ed. *Voennaya sila i mezhdunarodnye otnosheniya* [Military Force and International Relations]. Moscow: International Relations Publishing House, 1972.

LAIRD, ROBBIN F. *Soviet Arms Trade with Non-Communist Third World in the 1970s and 1980s.* Washington, D.C.: Wharton Econometric Forecasting Associates, 1983.

LEGUM, COLIN. "The USSR and Africa: The African Environment." *Problems of Communism* 27, no. 1 (January–February 1978): 1–19.

LEGVOLD, ROBERT. *Soviet Policy in West Africa*. Cambridge, Mass.: Harvard University Press, 1970.

LEOGRANDE, WILLIAM M. *Cuba's Policy in Africa, 1959–1980*. Berkeley: Institute of International Studies, University of California, 1980.

LEWIS, WILLIAM H. "Emerging Choices for the Soviets in Third World Arms Transfer Policy." In *World Military Expenditures and Arms Transfers 1985*. Washington, D.C.: U.S. Government Printing Office, August 1985.

LEWIS, WILLIAM H., and STEPHEN C. MOSS. "The Soviet Arms Transfer Program." *Journal of Northeast Asian Studies* 3 no. 3 (Fall 1984): 3–15.

LITWAK, ROBERT S., and S. NEIL MACFARLANE. "Soviet Activism in the Third World." *Survival* 29, no. 1 (January–February 1987): 21–39.

MCCONNELL, JAMES M., and BRADFORD DISMUKES. "Soviet Diplomacy of Force in the Third World." *Problems of Communism*, 28 no. 1 (January–February 1979): 14–27.

MACFARLANE, S. NEIL. "Africa's Decaying Security System and the Rise of Intervention." *International Security* 8, no. 4 (Spring 1984): 127–49.

―――. "The Soviet Conception of Regional Security." *World Politics* 37, no. 3 (April 1985): 295–316.

MCCGWIRE, MICHAEL, KEN BOOTH, and JOHN MCDONNELL, eds. *Soviet Naval Policy: Objectives and Constraints*. New York: Praeger, 1975.

MALIK, HAFEEZ, ed. *Soviet-American Relations with Pakistan, Iran and Afghanistan*. New York: St. Martin's Press, 1987.

MENON, RAJAN. "The Soviet Union, the Arms Trade and the Third World." *Soviet Studies* 34, no. 3 (July 1982): 377–96.

―――. *Soviet Power and the Third World*. New Haven, Conn.: Yale University Press, 1986.

―――. "Soviet Arms Transfers in the Third World." *Journal of International Affairs* 40, no. 1 (Summer 1986): 59–76.

MIRSKII, G. I. *Armiya i politika v stranakh Azii i Afriki* [Army and Politics in the Countries of Asia and Africa]. Moscow: Nauka, 1970.

―――. *"Tretii mir": obshchestvo, vlast', armiia* ["The Third World": Society, Power, Army]. Moscow: Nauka, 1976.

MOSKALENKO, V. N. *Vneshnyaya politika Pakistana* [The Foreign Policy of Pakistan]. Moscow: Nau .a, 1984.

NATION, R. CRAIG, and MARK V. KAUPPI, eds. *The Soviet Impact in Africa*. Lexington, Mass.: Lexington Books, 1984.

NAYYAR, DEEPAK. *Economic Relations between Socialist Countries and the Third World*. London: Macmillan, 1977.

NIELSEN, WALDEMAR A. *The Great Powers and Africa*. New York: Praeger, 1969.

NOLUTSHUNGU, SAM C. "African Interests and Soviet Power: The Local Context of Soviet Policy." *Soviet Studies* 34, no. 3 (July 1982): 397–417.

OGUNBADEJO, OYE. "The Soviet Union and Africa: Andropov's African Policy." In *Africa Contemporary Record: Annual Survey and Documents*

1984–1985, edited by Colin Legum, 261–85. New York: Africana, 1986.

OTTAWAY, MARINA. *Soviet and American Influence in the Horn of Africa*. New York: Praeger, 1982.

OTTAWAY, MARINA and DAVID. *Ethiopia: Empire in Revolution*. New York: Holmes & Meier, 1978.

————. *Afrocommunism*. New York: Holmes & Meier, 1981.

PAGE, STEPHEN. *The Soviet Union and the Yemens: Influence in Asymmetrical Relationships*. New York: Praeger, 1985.

————. "Patterns of Soviet Activity in Southwest Asia." *International Journal* 41, no. 1 (Spring 1986): 300–23.

PAJAK, ROGER F. "Soviet Arms and Egypt." *Survival* 17 (July–August 1975): 165–73.

————. "Soviet Arms Transfers as an Instrument of Influence." *Survival* 23, no. 4 (July–August 1981): 165–73.

PAPP, DANIEL S. *Soviet Policies toward the Developing World during the 1980s*. Maxwell Air Force Base, Ala.: Air University Press, 1986.

PENNAR, J. *The USSR and the Arabs: The Ideological Dimension*. London: Hurst, 1973.

POLLOCK, DAVID. "Moscow and Aden: Coping with a Coup." *Problems of Communism* 35, no. 3 (May–June 1986): 50–70.

PORTER, BRUCE D. *The USSR in Third World Conflicts: Soviet Arms and Diplomacy in Local Wars, 1945–1980*. Cambridge: Cambridge University Press, 1984.

PRIMAKOV, Ye. M. *Anatomiya blizhnevostochnogo konflikta* [Anatomy of the Middle East Conflict]. Moscow: Mysl, 1978.

QUANDT, WILLIAM B. "Soviet Policy in the October Middle East War: II." *International Affairs* 53, no. 4 (October 1977): 590–601.

RADU, MICHAEL, ed. *Eastern Europe and the Third World: East vs. South*. New York: Praeger, 1981.

REMNECK, RICHARD. "Soviet Military Interests in Africa." *Orbis* 28, no. 1 (Spring 1984): 123–43.

RO'I, YAACOV. *From Encroachment to Involvement: A Documentary Study of Soviet Policy in the Middle East, 1945–1973*. New York, Wiley, 1974.

————, ed. *The Limits to Power: Soviet Policy in the Middle East*. New York: St. Martin's Press, 1977.

————, ed. *The USSR and the Muslim World*. London: Allen & Unwin, 1984.

ROTHENBERG, MORRIS. *The USSR and Africa: New Dimensions of Soviet Global Power*. Coral Gables, Fla.: Advanced International Studies Center, 1980.

RUBINSTEIN, ALVIN Z. *Red Star on the Nile: The Soviet-Egyptian Influence Relationship since the June War*. Princeton: Princeton University Press, 1977.

————. *Soviet Policy toward Turkey, Iran, and Afghanistan*. New York: Praeger, 1982.

RUBINSTEIN, ALVIN Z., ed. *Soviet and Chinese Influence in the Third World.* New York: Praeger, 1975.

SADAT ANWAR EL-. *In Search of Identity: An Autobiography.* New York: Harper & Row, 1977.

SANDFORD, GREGORY. *The New Jewel Movement: Grenada's Revolution 1979–1983.* Washington, D.C.: Foreign Service Institute, 1985.

SHAVROV, I. E., ed. *Lokal'nye voiny: istoriia i sovremennost'* [Local Wars: History and Contemporaneity]. Moscow: Voenizdat, 1981.

SINGH, S. NIHAL. *The Yogi and the Bear: Story of Indo-Soviet Relations.* New Delhi: Allied Publishers, 1986.

SMOLANSKY, OLES M. *The Soviet Union and the Arab East under Khrushchev.* Lewisburg, Pa.: Bucknell University Press, 1974.

SOROKINA, A. I., ed. *Sovetskiye vooruzhennye sily v usloviyakh razvitogo sotsializma.* Moscow: Nauka, 1985.

STARR, RICHARD F., ed. *Yearbook on International Communist Affairs.* Stanford: Hoover Institution Press, various years since 1972.

STARRELS, JOHN M. *East Germany: Marxist Mission in Africa.* Washington, D.C.: Heritage Foundation, 1981.

STEVENS, CHRISTOPHER. *The Soviet Union and Black Africa.* New York: Holmes & Meier, 1976.

STOOKEY, ROBERT W. *Yemen: The Politics of the Yemen Arab Republic.* Boulder, Colo.: Westview, 1978.

TOKO, COLONEL GAD W. *Intervention in Uganda: The Power Struggle and Soviet Involvement.* UCIS Occasional Working Paper Series, no. 1. Pittsburgh: University of Pittsburgh Press, 1979.

TROFIMENKO, HENRY A. "The Third World and U.S.-Soviet Competition: A Soviet View." *Foreign Affairs* 59, no. 5 (Summer 1981): 1021–40.

ULIANOVSKII, R. A. *Socialism and the Newly Independent Nations.* Moscow: Progress Publishers, 1974.

———. *Present-Day Problems in Asia and Africa: Theory, Politics, and Personalities.* Moscow: Progress Publishers, 1981.

VALENTA, JIRI, and DAVID E. ALBRIGHT, eds. *The Communist States and Africa.* Bloomington: Indiana University Press, 1984.

VALENTA, JIRI, and HERBERT J. ELLISON, eds. *Grenada and Soviet/Cuban Policy: Internal Crisis and U.S./OECS Intervention.* Boulder, Colo.: Westview, 1986.

VALKENIER, ELIZABETH KRIDL. "New Trends in Soviet Economic Relations with the Third World." *World Politics* 22, no. 3 (April 1970): 415–32.

———. "New Soviet Views on Economic Aid." *Survey,* no. 76 (Summer 1970): 17–29.

———. *The Soviet Union and the Third World: An Economic Bind.* New York: Praeger, 1983.

———. "Revolutionary Change in the Third World: Recent Soviet Assessments." *World Politics* 38, no. 3 (April 1986): 415–34.

VARAS, AUGUSTO, ed. *Soviet–Latin American Relations in the 1980s.* Boulder, Colo.: Westview, 1987.

WEINLAND, ROBERT G. "Land Support for Naval Forces: Egypt and the Soviet Escadra 1962–1976." *Survival* 20, no. 2 (March–April 1978): 73–79.

WHELAN, JOSEPH G., and MICHAEL J. DIXON. *The Soviet Union in the Third World: Threat to World Peace?* Elmsford, N.Y.: Pergamon-Brassey's, 1986.

WILES, PETER, ed. *The New Communist Third World.* New York: St. Martin's Press, 1982.

WILLERTON, JOHN P. "Soviet Perspective on Afghanistan: The Making of an Ally." *Jerusalem Journal of International Affairs* 9, no. 1 (March 1986): 114–44.

WOLF, CHARLES, JR., K. C. YEH, EDMUND BRUNNER, AARON GURWITZ, and MARILEE LAWRENCE. *The Costs of the Soviet Empire.* Santa Monica, Calif.: Rand Corporation, September 1983.

YODFAT, ARYEH. *The Soviet Union and Revolutionary Iran.* London: Croom Helm, 1984.

ZAMOSTNY, THOMAS J. "Moscow and the Third World: Recent Trends in Soviet Thinking." *Soviet Studies* 36, no. 2 (April 1984): 223–35.

Index

Abbas, Ferhat, 93–94
Afghanistan: 10, 13–14, 20, 24, 32–33; friendship treaty with, 59, 235–36; Gorbachev's policy in, 263, 272–73, 275–78; intervention in, 151–52, 227; Soviet withdrawal from, 275–78; post-Stalin Soviet relations with, 41–42, 52, 160, 209, 256, 264; Sino-Soviet relations and, 267
Africa: anticolonialism in, 104; East Germany's role in, 184; economic impact of surrogates on, 200–201. *See also specific African countries*
African National Congress (ANC), 117
Algeria, 66–67, 86, 210; Khrushchev's comments on, 89–90; Morocco and, 116; national liberation movement in, 92–95; Soviet military assistance to, 210
Ali Salem al-Bidh, 274
Alianza Revolucionaria Democrática (ARDE), 217
Ali Nasser Muhammed al-Hassani, 274
Alves, Nito, 194–95
Amin, Hafizullah, 151–52, 160, 219
Amin, Idi, 56, 210
Andrianov, V., 103
Andropov, Yuri, 180, 261
Anglo-Russian agreement of 1907, 14
Angola: Castro's involvement in, 188–89; Cuban support of, 104, 121, 175–76, 191; East Germany and, 185; Soviet-Cuban collaboration, 187–89, 194–95; Soviet support of, 104–5, 148–49; surrogates in, 173–74, 202
anti-Americanism: advantages to pro-American regimes, 256; of Castro, 186–88; intervention to foster, 161, 164; as a mobilizing force, 203, 219, 233; as an outgrowth of decolonization, 255–56; Third World politics and, 97, 242–43
Anyanya, 143–44

Aquino, Corazon, 118–19, 242
Arab-Israeli conflict: Soviet policy and, 103, 139–40, 142–43, 244, 250
Arafat, Yasser, 108, 237
ARDE. *See* Alianza Revolucionaria Democrática
Argentina, 56, 241, 243
Aristov, Boris, 54
Armed Forces Coordinating Committee (DERG), 112–13, 149–50, 189, 196
Arms-control negotiations: limited linkage and, 37n. 64; Strategic Arms Limitation Talks (SALT), 33, 38; Strategic Arms Reduction Talks (SALT/START), 265. *See also* nuclear weapons
Assad, Hafez, 152, 214, 237, 242, 247, 249; Gorbachev and, 285–86; Soviet economic assistance to, 50; U.S. military presence in Lebanon and, 253
Association of Southeast Asian Nations (ASEAN), 284
Azerbaijani Republic, 83–84, 166

Ba'athist party, 110–11, 147, 236
Babrak Karmal, 151–52, 275
Baghdad Pact, 24–25, 41, 43, 45. *See also* CENTO
Balabushevich, V., 44
Bandung Conference, 45
Barre, Mohammed Siad, 150, 163, 191, 197; Soviet military assistance and, 208–9, 242
Barzani, Mulla Mustafa, 83, 110
Bay of Pigs, 137–38
Becker, Seymour, 12
Begin, Menachem, 152; reconciliation with Sadat, 249–50
Ben Bella, Ahmed, 66, 94
Benin, revolution in, 180n. 17
Benjadid, Chadli, 242
Bhilai steel complex (India), 44, 281